Take
My Word
For It

Also by William Safire

NONFICTION

I Stand Corrected (1984)

Good Advice (1982)
with Leonard Safir

What's the Good Word? (1982)

On Language (1980)

Safire's Washington (1980)

Before the Fall (1974)

Safire's Political Dictionary (1968, 1979)

Plunging Into Politics (1964)

The Relations Explosion (1963)

FICTION

Full Disclosure (1977)

More **On Language** from
William Safire

Take
My Word
For It

𝕮𝖎𝖒𝖊𝖘
BOOKS

All rights reserved under International and Pan-American Copyright
Conventions. Published in the United States by Times Books, a division
of Random House, Inc., New York, and simultaneously in Canada by
Random House of Canada Limited, Toronto.

The "On Language" columns by William Safire were originally published
in *The New York Times*. Copyright © 1982, 1983, 1984 by The New
York Times Company. Reprinted by permission. All rights reserved.

Library of Congress Cataloging-in-Publication Data

Safire, William, 1929–
Take my word for it.

Includes index.
1. English language—Usage—Addresses, essays, lectures.
I. Title.
PE1421.S235 1986 428'.00973 86–1260
ISBN 0–8129–1323–X

Manufactured in the United States of America

9 8 7 6 5 4 3 2

First Edition

To A. M. ROSENTHAL,

who came up with the idea for this enterprise. One day,
he said to his *New York Times* colleagues, "Eureka! We'll
have Safire do a language column in the Magazine." He
added, " 'Eureka' is the Greek word for 'I found it.' "

Introduction

A couple of heavyweight professors were sparring recently on the *CBS Morning News* about the wisdom of the nuclear shield called "Star Wars." I was in bed in a hotel room, getting a second reprieve from a snooze alarm, when I heard the voice of Arthur M. Schlesinger Jr., a Distinguished Professor of the City University of New York (who happens also to be a distinguished professor, uncapitalized, in real life). He was knocking the President's plan, which did not interrupt my reverie, but then he said something about "not helping the *sclerotic economy.*"

Moments later, Professor Richard E. Pipes of Harvard, a Star Wars enthusiast, picked up the word, perhaps ironically, and talked of "the *sclerotic economy* of the Soviet Union." I sat up, smacked the snooze alarm again (*snooze* strikes me as a marriage of *snore* and *doze,* but the word has been drifting off since 1788), and waited for the interviewer to ask, "Wait a minute—what does *sclerotic* mean?"

She did not. Maria Shriver, an intelligent reporter, is not yet secure enough to admit ignorance of a word. Come to think of it, I have never heard any commentator or reporter say, "That's an interesting word—what does it mean?" The interviewer is either ashamed at appearing ignorant or worried that the guest will not know the answer and come apart in chagrin on the air.

In any event, the two professors went on with their verbal auto-scleroticism and I did not know the meaning of their favorite word, and in a hotel room the Gideons do not provide a dictionary. (Why doesn't some hotel chain lay in a stock of dictionaries, placed lovingly on the pillow, instead of a fattening chocolate? I would gladly forgo a bottle of fabric rinse, whatever that is, for a vest-pocket dictionary in the bathroom.)

Noodling it around, I asked myself, "What is *arteriosclerosis?*" and answered, "It's a high-priced specialist's way of saying 'hardening of the arteries.'" From that, I puzzled out that the adjective *sclerotic* had been formed from the noun *sclerosis,* which meant that the professors were talking about a hardening, or stiffening, or dangerous aging of an economy in stagnation. *Sclerotic,* then, means "inelastic, brittle."

Satisfied, I grabbed ten more minutes from the snooze alarm, which vies with the rye bagel as a major technological contribution to people's mornings. But dozing was denied: why did Arthur, eager to make a serious point with a wide audience, use a word that most viewers did not know? Why did Dick Pipes repeat it? I know both those guys, and neither has need to show off his erudition. Either they could not think of a simple word like *aging,* or they were willing to sacrifice immediate understanding by asking their audience to reach up for an unfamiliar word.

That poses a big question: Should you use a ring-a-ding word, smack on the button of your meaning, when your listener or reader is not likely to understand? Dilemma: Do you settle for a more generally understood term, thereby pandering to your audience's ignorance—or do you use the unfamiliar word, thereby failing to communicate and appearing to be a show-off? Is your job to communicate or to educate?

Another example: Peregrine Worsthorne, the tower of Kiplingesque conservatism at *The Sunday Telegraph,* in London, has taken to zapping his American neo-conservative cousins on the subject of hawkishness in foreign policy. Stung, our neo-cons have responded: in *Contentions,* a sprightly eight-page viewsletter published monthly by the Committee for the Free World (sent to contributors to the committee, at 211 East 51st Street, New York 10022), Neal Kozodoy described Perry's occasional Diary in London's *Spectator* accurately as "divagating with clubby ease and amiability on political events, on the virtues of the marmalade to be had in Vence . . . and 'Why do I find almost all women journalists who write about public affairs so tiresome?' "

Neo-con Kozodoy quotes tradi-con Worsthorne on terrorism in this way: "What is 'remarkable,' Mr. Worsthorne apodictically confides, 'is not that Westerners are terrorized so much as that they are terrorized so little.' "

Quick, now: Do you ever find yourself *divagating* with ease, clubby or otherwise, or confiding *apodictically*? I took Casey Stengel's best advice ("You could look it up") and discovered that *to divagate* is "to wander from a course or stray from a subject," a synonym for "to digress." *Divagate* is a dangerous verb to use, because listeners may assume you mean *divaricate,* "to diverge," similar but not the same.

Apodictically, with a Greek root meaning "demonstrate," means "with absolute certainty." I can say *apodictically* that you will get blank looks when you accuse somebody of *divagating.*

Back to the question: Should you ever use a word that you know most of your audience will not know?

My answer: Fly over everybody's head only when your purpose is to teach or to tease. In a political column, I wrote that Vice President Bush was "the Gus Lesnevich of American politics." I knew that few readers would readily recall Mr. Lesnevich, but enough would ask around to find out, and the allusion would gain impact in that way for really devoted readers who had a slow day. I also was quite apodictic that Mr. Bush would call up Richard Moore, his canny old adviser, to find out what the hell I meant, and that Mr. Moore would surely remember that Gus Lesnevich was the light-heavyweight champion of the world, virtually unbeatable in his class, but in the era of Joe Louis never able to win the heavyweight crown.

Admittedly, this was an inside derogation, a kind of infra dig: I was soon scratching my head from a message left by William F. Gavin, in the House minority leader's office, asking, "Does this mean that Jack Kemp is the Chuck Davey of American politics?" Thumbing through yellowed clips, I found that Chuck Davey was a well-educated welterweight of great promise who was stopped just as he entered the big time.

These are rifle shots in the shotgun blasts of mass communication, playful and permissible if done rarely; the reader is told, "If you want to know, go look it up."

Overhead flying is also allowed, in my view, when the writer or speaker is dealing with an elite audience that will appreciate arcana and consider unfamiliar words and obscure allusions to be delicious inside stuff, caviar for the general. Thus, in *Contentions*, where such writers as Mr. Kozodoy and Dorothy Rabinowitz sparkle, big words find a congenial home. Too few readers take the trouble to look them up, but more should, and more will as soon as we get dictionaries in hotel rooms, instead of packages of needle and thread that are sealed too tightly to open. But I divagate.

I would not, however, use big words to a mass audience when my primary aim is to persuade rather than to educate. Lay off *sclerotic*, fellas, lest frustrated viewers become choleric.

The best system, for those who want to educate while persuading, is to do vocabulary tricks in a context that makes meanings plain. For example, a few paragraphs up, I slipped in "caviar for the general," predefining it as "delicious inside stuff."

Most people don't know that allusion; most who do think it means "that expensive food appreciated by big shots," but they are wrong. The phrase was coined in *Hamlet*, as he told the players that "the play . . . pleas'd not the million, 'twas caviary to the general." The "general" was not some gourmet leader of troops, but the general public, which thought caviar was a mess of foul-smelling fish eggs and did not appreciate the delicacy. The phrase has been twisted into meaning "a delicacy appreciated by the General."

In using it above, I adopted the current meaning, and defined it in passing, so that you couldn't taste the medicine going down. That is fairer to the reader, even the highly educated readership that tends to forget, and is equivalent to a few rounds with Gus Lesnevich.

In this book, the guiding philosophy is to treat the reader with respect (O.K., let's get personal—to treat you smarter than either of us is). I agree with nonsclerotic Arthur Schlesinger Jr., who tells me, "I vote for aiming slightly over the head of the audience in the hope of awakening sleepy heads."

Accordingly, I now revise my citation of "You could look it up"; I once attributed it to Casey Stengel, as everyone does, and was informed by Professor Arthur Hoffman of Syracuse University that the original source was James Thurber in 1941, writing about a baseball manager, Squawks Magrew, who put a midget in as a pinch hitter, and his pal Doc.

Be a linguist elitist: say, "As Doc used to say, 'You could look it up.' "

Take
My Word
For It

Annul That Order

Airline lingo is easy to denounce; when Eastern Airlines calls its baggage sorting *sortation,* or when Pan Am tells passengers to *maintain* their seats, or when the Federal Aviation Administration describes one of its own regulations as *relaxatory in nature,* we can all hoot in delighted derision. But be careful when you knock railroad language.

"When the Federal Government in Washington closed one day last winter for the snowstorm," writes Richard Dine of Philadelphia, "my fiancée went to Union Station to take a train to visit me. While waiting at the station, she heard Amtrak announce that Metroliner service had been *annulled.* "

Mr. Dine thinks this word is divorced from reality. He notes accurately that the Latin *annullare* means "to make into nothing," and concludes: "Assuming the Metroliners did not collapse under the weight of the snow, *cancel* would seem to be the better choice."

But Amtrak is not backing up. *"Annulled* has been part of the railroad lexicon from time immemorial," says Clifford Black, the line's spokesman. *"Cancel* could be interpreted to mean that the train made some movement from the originating station. *Annulled* means that it is null and void, that there was no version of that train that day, that the train never left the starting block, that it is a profound nonentity. All our workers are corrected when they wrongly use *cancel*; in the railroad business, the verb is *annulled.* "

Fortunately, Mr. Dine is not one to take offense. "Though Washington was shut down, Amtrak brought my fiancée to me only one and a half hours late and returned her safely the next day. As Milton writes in 'Paradise Lost': 'This God-like Act . . . Annuls thy doom.' " He adds this impediment to the marriage of true minds: "My fiancée travels *somewheres else,* whereas I would go *somewhere else.* Where would you go?"

That's something else.

It is perhaps much easier to denounce Eastern Airlines for calling its baggage sorting sortation *than it is to condemn Pan Am for advising passengers to* maintain *their seats. The use of* maintain *to mean to continue in a specified state or position is legitimate. The passengers are initially* seated; *therefore, they are requested to maintain that position. Purists might contend that* seated positions *would be more appropriate; but, are we not allowed to use* seats *metaphorically in lieu of* seated positions?

Should you hoot in delighted derision at the Federal Aviation Administration's description of one of its own regulations as relaxatory *in nature? The Unabridged*

Edition of The Random House Dictionary of the English Language *lists* relaxatory *as a proper adjective form of* relax, *a transitive verb meaning (in this instance) to make less strict or severe certain rules, regulations et cetera. Moreover, if one chooses, one could consider the FAA as a* relaxer *which* relaxedly *issued a* relaxative *regulation which induced a state of* relaxedness *in the regulated group to which the regulation applied!*

> *Cassius M. Plair*
> *St. Albans, New York*

Several years ago, I departed from Grand Central Station aboard the 8:10 p.m. local train, which should have deposited me in Stamford some 62 tedious minutes later. By 9:15, we had proceeded, fitfully, only to the vicinity of Larchmont. After a further delay, it was announced that the train had been "annulled," and that we would be inched forward to the Larchmont station, there to be rescued by a following train.

I would have characterized the train, in the words of Amtrak's Mr. Black, as a "profound nonentity." Nonetheless, it did leave the starting block, and made some movement from the originating station, although not nearly so steady or rapid as might have been wished.

Delay may not have been part of the railroad lexicon from time immemorial, but it has been much discussed recently. Daily usage has now generated new meanings for the vocabulary of delay.

> *Andrew A. Glickson*
> *Norwalk, Connecticut*

Arguendo

William Zinsser has written a book, *Writing with a Word Processor*, which arguably gives the most helpful and humane treatment of the subject and is surely the most stylish book produced so far on that intimidating machine. I put it that way because, in recent correspondence, he added a postscript: "By the way, what the hell does *arguably* mean?"

He is not the first to inquire. "Have you missed the *arguably* craze?" asks Andrew Viglucci, editor of *The San Juan Star*. He blames sportswriters who use the word as a substitute for *perhaps*; unhappy with "He is, perhaps, the greatest right-hander since the Big Train," sportswriters have taken to "He is, arguably, the undisputed champ of all time." (Pound for pound, sportswriters are more suscepti-ble to cliché than most.) "I like sportswriters," avers Mr. Viglucci. "They

are, inarguably, essential to a daily publication. But they should not be permitted to hide behind such semantic copouts. . . . Do something, please."

Paula Diamond of New York smacks her hand against a Peugeot advertisement, which reads: "Arguably the most comfortable car in existence today." She says, "My dictionary defines *arguable* as 'open to doubt or dispute, not certain.' Is Peugeot's use of *arguable* arguable?"

Ordinarily, I would let out a whoop and a holler and proceed to savage the philistines of cliché for taking a perfectly good adverb like *arguably,* which used to carry the negative connotation of *debatably*—"unproven, suspect"—and twisting its meaning into a positive like *conceivably*—"it could be argued successfully."

But that would be wrong. (Why does that phrase keep coming back to me?) As an adjective, *arguable* means *debatable,* and has long carried a negative connotation; when you say, "That's arguable," you mean: "I'm not buying that line of guff." However, as an adverb, *arguably* has had a long line of positive precedents. When we say, "Arguably the sexiest legs," we mean: "Reasonable people could persuasively put forward the proposition that those legs are capable of driving most men wild."

That's strange; I don't know of any other adjective-to-adverb switch of meaning. Jacques Barzun, the great usagist, disapproves of the use of *arguably* in a positive sense, and suggests that advertisers only add an element of disbelief when using it in their copy, but I think we have tripped over a quirk in the language. (That should elicit a letter from Randolph Quirk, whose stimulating book *Style and Communication in the English Language* I have been trying to figure a way to plug for months.)

Instead of wrangling, let us study the adverb's development. The first use in the supplement to the *Oxford English Dictionary* is from an 1890 *Saturday Review*: "His policy, if sometimes arguably mistaken. . . ." A 1920 citation is about how a zeal for moral righteousness "is arguably more purely Jewish in its origin," and in 1959 *The Times* of London was describing Mozart's sinfonia *concertante* for violin and viola as "arguably the greatest of his concertos." In the Barnhart files, a 1960 *Harper's* use is "Since the world is absolutely stiff with arguably uglier objects. . . ."

In all these cases, the adverb is certainly not saying "not bloody likely"; on the contrary, the meaning is the positive "a good case can be made for." The Oxford people straddle the issue by defining the word with both positive and negative elements: "As may be shown by argument [that's positive—the connotation is *persuasive*] or made a matter of argument [that's negative—the connotation is *debatable*]." Lexicographer Bob Burchfield was playing it safe; he should put more trust in his citations.

My hunch is that the adverb *arguably*, while obviously sired by the adjective *arguable*, was crossed in its etymology with some legal usage, perhaps derived from the Latin *arguendo*, which means "in the course of the argument." There is no blinking away the fact that the positive way the sportswriters and copywriters are today using *arguably* is the way the word has been used from the start.

So to hell with consistency, brother Zinsser. Put this in your composition-cruncher and follow the bouncing cursor: The adjective *arguable* is negative ("I told Orville, I told Wilbur, and I'm telling you—it's arguable whether that thing will ever get off the ground"). The adverb *arguably* is positive ("The smile on that flight attendant is arguably the only reason people will take the middle seat between two fatties on the shuttle").

The first letter that comes in will begin, "Disputatiously. . . ."

Dear Bill:
    That is arguably the best lead I ever saw on a column of yours, and I am expectably appreciative.

                      Bill [Zinsser]
                      New York, New York

Dear Bill:
    Arguably, do you really "aver" or possibly even "opine," "assert," "remark," "declare," "state," "avouch" when you mean "say"? "Aver" and all the other affectations force me to express my irk.

                      Clinically,
                      Milton [Lewis]
                      Quondam, New York

Your comments on the arguable-arguably pair reminded me of another such oddity: constant-constantly. In mathematics, a constant is a non-varying quantity. It may be a number (4.36) or a string of characters (Danbury, Connecticut). A variable may be set equal to a constant (e.g. x = 7, or Address = "Danbury, Connecticut"). Of course, functions don't have to be constant. $y = \frac{gt^2}{2}$ describes the position of a freely falling body. What I have been seeing lately is the designation of a "constantly varying function" in place of "always varying" or "never staying the same."

So, here we have an adverb "constantly" really meaning "not constant." As the old Yankee announcer Mel Allen would have said: "How about that!"

Josef N. Friedman
Professor of Mathematics
Western Connecticut State
University
Danbury, Connecticut

The Latin arguendo does not mean "in the course of the argument," but "by means of the argument," since it is the ablative singular neuter of the gerund.

José M. de Vinck
Allendale, New Jersey

You might be interested to know that at the recent annual meeting of the American Dialect Society a small usage controversy was stirred up over the appropriate word to be used for usage critic, or usage commentator. The three forms introduced in the discussion were usagist, usageaster, and shaman. I myself tried to use usagist in print, but was brought to my senses by a vigilant editor. I wondered whether a usage commentator like yourself might care to exhibit a preference?

Dennis Baron
Urbana, Illinois

NOTE FROM W.S.: I like *usagist.* (But watch out for *usagizers.*)

Dear Bill:

I enjoyed your piece as I always do, but particularly (of course) your kind allusion to Style & Language. It's the nicest thing that's happened since a Japanese scholar listed me at the end of his prefatory credits with the words: "Not in the least am I indebted to Randolph Quirk."

Randolph Quirk
London, England

The Awful Pravda

To people with a good ear for language, the almost-right word makes a clanking sound. Mark Twain once clobbered James Fenimore Cooper's prose by showing how the formerly revered author didn't quite get his clichés right. When Russian propagandists work in English, they attempt to assume a breezy journalese familiar to Americans, and do not always bring it off.

In a news release from the Soviet Embassy, translating an explanation in the Soviet daily *Pravda* of the true history of Afghanistan, four clichés go clank-clank-clank-clank. "The people strove to break away from the medieval dark," it begins, breaking the reader's stride immediately. You don't break *away* from the dark, you break *out* of the dark. It continues: ". . . and to doff the shackles of feudalism." You don't *doff* shackles, you doff a hat; you *cast off* shackles.

"When the Shah's throne . . . began to wobble," the Soviet writer goes on, missing the cliché again. Native cliché speakers know that heads *wobble*; slowing tops *wobble*; but a throne *totters*. Similarly, "Blatantly trampling underfoot the universally recognized international norms . . ." is a few degrees off. *Blatant* means "glaringly conspicuous," and would be acceptable if the translator were not trying to write journalese; however, the standard hackneyed adverbs for the cliché "trampling underfoot" are *arrogantly* and *ruthlessly*. What is acceptably *blatant* is a *falsehood*.

"There's just a complete lack of the necessary sense of doom in *wobble* and release from imperialist oppression in *doff*," observes Don Shannon of *The Los Angeles Times*. He's right; let us hope that our own attempts to use journalistic clichés in Russian show an instinct for the jargon.

Your article reminded me of the amusing expression "meadows of force," a result, this time, of the translation into English of a physics paper in Russian.

Jacques Destry
Professor of Physics
Université de Montréal

The Awful Tooth

When Eileen Ford, the modeling mogul, selected a young Danish woman with a wide, bright smile to be this year's most promising mannequin, *Newsweek* wrote that the model agency "came up with blond and toothsome Renee Simonsen. . . ." Those who decide what shall be the most desirable face of the eighties lay stress on the mouth and teeth, which replaces the emphasis in the seventies on the button nose. "If you aren't toothsome—and don't even have a button nose," wrote reporter Cathleen McGuigan, "take heart: The 90's will get here eventually."

And none too soon for the word *toothsome.* Since the sixteenth century, *toothsome* has meant "palatable, pleasing to the taste"; a hundred years after its coinage, a historian wrote, "Your only News is not very Toothsom but it may prove wholesom." The meaning has never been "toothy" or "characterized by showing prominent teeth."

But wait: Here is a letter to *Time* magazine from novelist Norman Mailer, complaining that reviewer Stefan Kanfer, in writing about Mailer's *Pieces and Pontifications,* had quoted him out of context and thereby distorted his meaning. Mailer uses a masticating metaphor: "I hope the next reviewer *Time* picks for me doesn't bite the tip off my intent like toothsome Stevie Kanfer."

Is Mailer, one of our foremost wordsmen, using *toothsome* when he means *toothy*? Or does he find something curiously delicious about his tormentor's prose? Or has the meaning of *toothsome* changed to mean both "toothy" and "tasty"?

Let us bite down hard on this one. *Newsweek*'s writer was playing on words with her description of the tall, ravishing model with the wide smile as *toothsome*: She has a smile that flashes a set of the finest choppers around, and she is undoubtedly a tasty morsel. Such wordplay is fun, so long as we do not let the play confuse us about the meanings. Maybe my friend Norman intended the same play, but we must draw the line somewhere: *Toothsome* does not mean "toothy," any more than *fulsome* means "full," or *noisome* means "noisy." Fight cavities; stop the decay of a good word.

May I quote that literary composer Thomas Morley (1557–1603), who wrote around the turn of his century: "Whose malice (being as toothsome as an adder's sting) . . ."
   The O.E.D. says: obsolete, but what a toothsome use of toothsome.

                                                    Norman Mailer
                                                    Brooklyn, New York

Ay, There's the Rub

"I have come across a contemporary custom," writes Christian Rendeiro of Hamden, Connecticut, "particularly among the younger successful executive class. . . . For greeting, at one time, there was the bow. Then the embrace. Then kissing. Recently I have come to see more and more of that age group 'shouldering.'"

Mr. Rendeiro, like Adam on Naming Day in the Garden of Eden, has coined a word to describe a phenomenon that has gone unreported partly because it is unnamed.

At cocktail parties, or soirees after football games—usually when people have food in one hand and a drink in the other—a new and curious form of physical contact is made. It has nothing to do with sex, and is engaged in by men with men, men with women, and women with women. The greeter rubs his or her shoulder, gently but briskly, against the shoulder of the greeted, who smiles and either accepts the rub demurely or enthusiastically rubs back.

Before addressing the linguistic side of this, let us get an expert opinion on the social side from Judith Martin, the United Feature Syndicate's "Miss Manners," and author of the novel *Gilbert: A Comedy of Manners,* published by Atheneum.

"I have noticed the new social practice, too," says Miss Martin-Manners, "and would be delighted to have it given a name, although not 'shouldering.' In man-

ners, we may, within the outer limits of politeness, give someone the cold shoulder (an abrupt turn of the body, shoulder first, at the approach of someone one wishes to snub), but not a warm shoulder."

Is the new greeting correct, or at least acceptable? "The new gesture seems an excellent response to the current anarchy in social greetings," replies the arbiter and novelist. "With some people shaking hands, some kissing one cheek, some the air next to one or two cheeks, some hugging, there are a great many mishaps. Rubbing shoulders, or just lifting shoulders (the right one only, so it does not resemble a shrug), seems within the tradition of vestigial gestures and very practical, as Mr. Rendeiro points out, for those who have their hands full, as so many people do these days."

Although she accepts the practice, a tiny frown appears on Miss Manners's ladylike brow at the word *shouldering.* I would smooth out that line because the participle form is hot these days. *Parenting* has joined *mothering* and *fathering,* soon to be followed by a coinage for dealing with one's parents such as *childrening. Shouldering* has a clear analogy in *elbowing,* which is not a greeting but an action taken in shopping for clothes in discount houses. Other coinages for contact while clutching canapés will be entertained, but the new greeting is *shouldering* until further notice.

Your search to replace shouldering *is over. At your next cocktail party begin deltoiding. Grab your nearest anat. & phys. text (as I just did). You will find that skin deep under that shoulder is the Deltoid muscle; a perfectly legitimate, socially acceptable muscle.*

Why not give the Deltoid its place in the sun?
This should satisfy Judith Martin too.

Peggy Lange
Westport, Connecticut

In ballet, "epaulement" is an accepted term with the literal meaning of "shoulder-ing." It refers to the way a dancer tilts her/his head and shoulders compared with the usual manner of holding the hips and shoulders square.

Donald J. Kahn
Metuchen, New Jersey

Bad Mistake

In excoriating and humiliating some errant correspondent, I wrote that he had made "a bad mistake." Malcolm Forbes, editor in chief of *Forbes* magazine and the last of the great balloon enthusiasts, writes: "I think I've caught the master making one of same. Recently [Safire] referred to something as 'a bad mistake.' There are good mistakes? As Gertrude Stein might have put it, 'A mistake is a mistake is a mistake.' Or, Bill, am I wrong?"

Malcolm, you have not been so wrong since your balloon ran out of air over Peking. First, your paraphrase of Gertrude Stein is inaccurate: She did not write, "A rose is a rose is a rose"; she wrote, "Rose is a rose is a rose is a rose," and the addition of the first article changes the meaninglessness. But that is neither here nor there (Miss Stein also derogated Oakland, California, with "There's no there there").

When I, the master, come under usage attack, I run sniveling to a grand master like Jacques Barzun, Everything Emeritus: " 'Bad mistake' is not redundant," he assures me. "All mistakes are not of one kind. There are unforgivable mistakes, very bad mistakes, slight mistakes, funny mistakes and even happy mistakes which turn out to be advantageous."

As I started to smile and blow my nose, Professor Barzun added, "You really ought to do something about the derivation you gave for 'economics.' It is not, as you wrote, 'based on the Greek word for *work,*' but for *house* (same as ecumenical). Economics is household management, improbable as the fact may sound."

I needed that, having been thrown off etymological stride by a "*see economics*" reference in the *O.E.D.* supplement's entry on *ergonomics*. A host of Greek scholars (what's the collective for "Greek scholar"?) has been hooting at me, led by José de Vinck of Allendale, New Jersey, who adds, "It is a good thing for you that Nemesis, the Greek goddess of vengeance, is long dead."

That, Malcolm, is the grammatical equivalent of sinking slowly into the arms of irate Communist Chinese: a bad mistake.

Robert C. Maynard, the editor of the Oakland Tribune *(and very competent), told this fascinating story, which he said he'd got from his equally competent music critic, Charles Shere, about Gertrude Stein and the "No there there" in Oakland.*

According to Shere via Maynard, Stein and Toklas had come back from Europe for a visit. Toklas, whose people and friends were thick in San Francisco, was wined, dined, and feted; Stein, whose home town was Oakland, came back to find few family and almost no friends. The contrast was too much for her: "There's no there there."

Frederic D. Lewis
Oakland, California

Bag Lady

The A.P. dispatch from Miami Beach began: "A frightened 'bag lady' who wandered city streets shoeless and hungry. . . ."

No. That should be a "shopping-bag lady." A *bag lady,* or *bagwoman,* is one who transmits illegal payoffs; when Harlem Congressman Adam Clayton Powell tied that tag on a constituent, she sued and was awarded damages. Nowadays, many women—well-shod and hungry only for bargains—live out of shopping bags, but let us maintain the distinction: A *shopping-bag lady* is a derelict, no matter if her shopping bag comes from Hermès and she sleeps in a chic doorway on the Rue du Faubourg St. Honoré.

The citation above was supplied by Paul Hoffman, author of *Lions of the*

Eighties, and a longtime phrase-watcher. He also reports that the term *rainmaker* —a lobbyist capable of causing money to flow from seemingly arid budgets—has been supplemented with *knifethrower,* a "lobbyist who knows who the decision maker is three or four rungs down the ladder and knows how to get to him." Thus, one who lobbies expertly for the rights of female derelicts might be called a shopping-bag-lady knifethrower.

Hold on: I just used the term *derelict,* which carries the connotation of "drunken bum" and is stumbling into disuse. A less pejorative word now used is *homeless;* another preferred term appeared in a more recent A.P. story from Miami: "An elderly man who roamed the streets with a shopping cart full of tin cans and bottles was beaten to death by another 'street person' as hundreds of vagrants waiting for a hot meal looked on."

Street person sounds bookish; another, more colorful term was used in a caption in this magazine in 1982, under a picture of a man sleeping in the subway: "While some New Yorkers seldom use the subway, others live there. The police call such people 'skells' and are seldom harsh with them."

Skell is a beaut of a bit of slang. It is a shortening of *skellum,* meaning a rascal or thief, and akin to *skelder,* "to beg on the streets," first used in print by Ben Jonson in 1599, just after that playwright got out of jail after killing a man in a duel; it is possible he picked up the word from a cellmate's argot.

"It shows the sheer persistence of words," says Stuart Berg Flexner, editor in chief of Random House dictionaries, when shown this citation. "Here an Elizabethan argot word with some old literary use pops up again in a shortened form in the mid-20th century (about 1935 in the short form *skell*), showing that *skellum* had some underground oral use for centuries. It's a long way from the Elizabethan underworld to *The New York Times,* but *skellum/skell* finally made it!"

Let us not forsake drifter.

Donald Marks
Long Island City, New York

We were disturbed by the indifference to human misery shown in your column. Words may be playthings for pundits, but they do have—at least some of the time —denotative value. They refer to things or events in the real world and deserve to be used accurately.

Derelict does not describe all homeless women; nor is homelessness simply a "less pejorative" term for people living on the streets.

The term homeless is a means of taking the measure of a kind of penury not seen on the scale it has reached today since the Depression. One of the difficulties in using any of the other terms you toy with is the fact that so often they serve as anodynes, muting an otherwise disquieting sense that something must be desperately wrong with a society that relegates people to scrounging on the streets in order to survive.

> *Robert M. Hayes*
> *Kim Hopper*
> *Coalition for the Homeless*
> *New York, New York*

The word skellum *is used in the John Buchan novel* Greenmantle. *Buchan, known as Lord Tweedsmuir, later Governor-General of Canada, also wrote* The Thirty-Nine Steps, *which everybody has seen as a movie.*

   Skellum *is used by a "reconstructed" Boer, Peter Pienaar, a friend of the hero Richard Hannay, so the word is probably Dutch, Afrikaans, or maybe Flemish which is closely related: "I am not a British soldier to think all men are gentlemen. I know that amongst men are desperate* skellums, *so I soon picked up the game" (*Adventures of Richard Hannay, *Houghton Mifflin, 1939, p. 144).*

> *Irwin A. Levy*
> *New York, New York*

In relation to skell, *at least in the mid-19th century, the (or a) common street term for a thief in London was* gonoph. *At least, Dickens puts the word into the mouth of a London policeman in* Bleak House, *with no indication either in the text (or in the scholarly notes in my edition) of the word's Yiddish origin. I wonder if he knew it!*

> *Aaron H. Esman, M.D.*
> *New York, New York*

You mentioned the word skellum *as having reappeared in modern speech. In fact it is a common Scots word that has been in common usage for many hundreds of years. The Dutch use a variation,* schelm *as do the Germans. In Afrikaans it has become* skelm. *Several years ago we had a Swedish exchange student living with us and when he got annoyed with his Canadian "brothers" often referred to them by the word* skälm *pronounced "skellum."*

   The origin of the word for "rogue" or "rascal" is interesting. The Swedish root skäll *implies yelling in a loud voice and* skällord *means the use of foul language. I think, however, that the ultimate origin is the Latin* scelus *meaning "wickedness" and* scelum *a villain. Plautus has referred to* scelus viri—*a rogue of a man. In all probability the word came with the Romans to Northern Europe and has remained in the Northern tongues ever since, virtually unchanged in spelling or pronunciation.*

> H.H. Macartney, M.D.,
> F.R.C.P.(C)
> Victoria, British Columbia

It may be of interest that there is a German word closely related to your skell. *It is* Schelm. *The closest meaning would be "prankster," although Langenscheidt's German-English dictionary gives it as "rogue," to which the Muret-Sanders adds "scoundrel, knave, villain." I seem to remember it also from the medieval Mittel-hochdeutsch but cannot check this. In modern German the word has fallen into disuse but remains as the adjective* schelmisch, *which would mean pleasantly roguish, with a twinkle in his/her eye. The word also exists in Afrikaans as* skelm, *with the same meaning and has probably been taken into that language from either German or Dutch.*

> Ruth Mainzer
> San Francisco, California

Bizbuzz

Nobody can apply for a job these days—or interface with a personnel recruiter in the hopes of impacting on his bottom line—without a degree in "bizbuzz," the jargon that prioritizes the career path of the rising young ballpark figurer.

I have already flunked. The figures of speech used in the preceding paragraph are already business archaisms that might as well have been the patois of Commodore Vanderbilt or Andrew Carnegie.

"The biggest 'bad' corporate word," opines Walter Kiechel 3d, associate editor of *Fortune* magazine, "is *impact* as a verb." The former noun has been used so often in its verb form in bored rooms that *impact on* has lost its punch, and rising executives are now testing the effect of *affect.*

"*Interface* is a dying word in management," adds John F. Lubin, professor of management at the University of Pennsylvania's Wharton School. "It was taken from systems engineering, where it meant the juncture between two pieces. For a while, *system* was taking over the language of management, but this, too, is dying."

Bottom line is still kicking around, but too many outsiders have been using it, and in jargon, freshness is all. "The *bottom line* originally referred to earnings figures," reports Timothy B. Blodgett of the *Harvard Business Review.* "Bottom-line responsibility is responsibility for the economic welfare of a division or subsidiary that is supposed to turn a profit. However, the phrase has expanded to include more than just earnings and profits; it can mean, 'The onus is on us' for just about anything." Mr. Blodgett is a senior editor; he has a *straight-line responsibility* to the editor in chief, and a *dotted-line responsibility* to a bunch of other editors. Life follows chart. While we're entangled in lines, Professor Michael Porter at the Harvard Business School defines *dotted-line responsibility* as "when two people consult with or interact with each other, but one does not report to the other." In olden times, the "dotted line" was where the customer signed; now it is where the responsibility is diffused, and even that expression is fading fast.

Ballpark figure is developing a paunch, too. This derivation of "in the ballpark," an indication of proximity (in contrast to a ball hit clear out of the stadium), is being replaced by one of the new triple hyphenations that make up adjectival phrases dear to bizbuzz: *back-of-the-envelope.* There is a quickly figured difference in meaning, however: "A *ballpark figure* is a rough estimate," explains lexicographer Sol Steinmetz, "while a *back-of-the-envelope sum* is one simply or easily arrived at without the need of a pocket calculator."

Another example of the triple hyphenator is *top-of-the-line,* a compound adjective launched in the late 1960's by auto manufacturers to describe their most expensive models. The British equivalent is *top-of-the-market,* and the phrase is not considered run-down or ramshackle by bizbuzz linguists on top of the state of the art, which is the bottom line on *top-of-the-line.*

Now that we know what is out, what is in?

If you are sad about the loss of *impact on,* try the new *abstract away.* "This means to dwindle into nothing," says the *H.B.R.*'s Blodgett. "If something *abstracts away,* it has ceased to be definable." Nice phrase; to move from the concrete to the abstract and then to vanish, like the Cheshire cat, leaving only the grin.

Hands-on, a compound adjective with one measly hyphen, has a stranglehold on the throats of businesspeople today. (I almost wrote "businessmen." Somebody must be getting to me.) The original meaning was "vocational," and the first citation in the Barnhart files is "hands-on instruction" for vocational schools, and was a play on "hands off," or so theoretical that it abstracted away. Now it means "practical"; nobody with hands-on experience, in a job interview, would claim anything as outdated as "practical experience." A synonym is *line* experience; this time, the metaphor is probably not from accounting, as in *bottom line,* but from the military, which contrasts *line* (from "front line") and *staff* (or headquarters) experience.

When in need of a modern mystifier, and tired of systems and the same old interfaces, reach for the favorite new management noun: *matrix.* "This came out of organizational behavior," says Professor Lubin, "and was used to describe orthogonal relationships." Asked to put that on a dotted-line basis, Professor Lubin explained: "That's when you have two bosses, or when responsibility is shared between divisions. Came from mathematics, and it's overused." He can hands-on that again. In the Wharton 1980 catalogue, a course in matrix management is advertised in this way: "The unique problem of changing, implementing and fine-tuning matrix forms will be highlighted." According to J. M. Rosenberg's *Dictionary of Business and Management*, "a matrix organization exists when organizational members have a dual allegiance—to a particular assignment or task and also to their department." O.K.: two bosses, a matrix and (soon to come) a patrix.

Students of bizbuzz (not to be confused with jargon scholars, who are in buzzbiz) search for topical combining forms. For a generation, combination-oriented linguists were studying the use of *-wise*, while formwise lexicographers were collecting the usages of *-oriented*. You could be *job-oriented, leisure-oriented,* or even *Occident-oriented*; similarly, languagewise, you could be *advertisingwise, careerwise,* or even *smartswise.*

Forget all that. The new combining forms are *-wide* and *-intensive.* According to Judy Uhl, senior editor of the division of research for the Harvard Business School, about whose dotted-line responsibilities I have not inquired: "A very common thing is to add *-wide* at the end of things to mean 'a totality,' such as *corporate-wide, industry-wide.* This can also be done without a hyphen, as in *personnelwide.*"

On the *-intensive* front, the earliest entries were *labor-intensive* and *capital-intensive,* but Steinmetz has pockets bulging with citations for *profit-intensive, energy-intensive, people-intensive, assets-intensive,* and *technology-intensive.* His work is neologism-intensive, and applies dictionarywide.

Vision is a hot word in executive aeries, usually defined as "the ability to see around corners," rather than off into the distance. *Style* is equally sought after, and what *manager style* a corporation prefers determines its character. *Fortune*'s Kiechel points to the popular *earthquake style,* "which is when a manager comes in and shakes everything up."

Bailout has replaced *rescue* in bizbuzz: A dispute is raging among etymologists about its derivation. One school holds that it is from the act of a pilot donning a parachute and leaping out of a falling airplane; another points to the frenzied activity of a fisherman bailing out a boat that is taking in water.

If a bailout fails, a company no longer goes bankrupt; it goes *belly up,* also a fishing metaphor, perhaps influenced by "belly up to the bar." At *Forbes* magazine, such a term is frowned upon. Geoffrey Smith, an assistant managing editor, who has a wavy-line responsibility to Malcolm Forbes, points to a memo directing writers to stay away from such bizbuzz as *clobber, plummet,* and *soar* (trite descriptions of earnings gains or losses), along with *on stream, game plan, shortfall,* and *upscale.*

My top-of-the-line model has just intersected with my bottom-line judgment, forming a dotted-line responsibility to all those who want to bellow at bizbuzz and outplace all its speakers. That's earthquake style.

Didn't you leave out wise-wise, *as in "wise-wise, how is he?," referring to savvy or street-smarts?*

Simon Nathan
New York, New York

It's not straight-line responsibility versus dotted-line responsibility, but solid-line responsibility versus dotted-line responsibility.

Timothy B. Blodgett
Senior Editor, Editorial
Operations
Harvard Business Review
Boston, Massachusetts

Hands-on experience is redundant since experience that is not hands-on is not experience at all; it is observation.

I would also like to suggest a more likely source for the term bailout *than the ones you proposed. When someone is arrested but is unable to put up the money needed to avoid spending time in jail he finds someone to bail him out. It is a small wonder that Chrysler and others prefer the more dramatic and respectable derivations of leaping out of an airplane and clearing water out of a boat to this one.*

Bruce E. Altschuler
Assistant Professor
Department of Political Science
State University of New York
Oswego, New York

Ballpark figure, back-of-the-envelope calculation, *and* order-of-magnitude estimate *refer to approximate calculations that are done instead of or prior to a more detailed analysis. The* ballpark *estimates allow the experienced engineer to decide which parameters (also adopted as* bizbuzz*) are the important ones and which are significant enough to be included in further analysis.* Rough estimate *is a good synonym but does not tell why the approximate estimate was made.*

Myron Kayton
Santa Monica, California

It seems fairly obvious to me that bailout *probably refers to "bail" in the legal sense, as "Dear Mother and Father, I am in trouble/jail/debt. Come and bail me out" —from Old French* baillier. *Since the pilot normally bails himself out, and the boatman bails out his own boat,* bailout *in those cases is hardly equivalent to rescue (unless one can rescue oneself which surely robs rescue of all glamour).*

Legal bailouts also seem more appropriate since those bailed out, mainly collapsing companies in my experience, continue to have obligation to those who bailed them out.

D. B. Jones
Nairobi, Kenya

I believe the term belly up *refers to the fact that dead fish and other animals float "belly up" in the water because an air pocket forms in their stomachs during the decomposition process.*

David B. Weber
Daytona Beach, Florida

In the early 1950s, I worked part-time as a salesperson in a Sears, Roebuck store in San Francisco. At that time (and I think it's still true), Sears routinely carried merchandise in almost every department at three levels of quality (cheerfully called good, better, best). Salespeople and management personnel routinely used the term top-of-the-line *to describe the "best" merchandise, and I'm pretty sure that it was used officially in nationwide memoranda.*

It's not too uncommon for "social scientists," possibly including Professor Lubin, to borrow terms such as matrix *from the physical and mathematical sciences, and having distorted them, then to forget where they came from lest the distortion in meaning become evident.*

The theory of matrices, including the first outline of the related algebra on which all of the above is based, was the invention of the great mathematician Arthur Cayley (1821–1895), and first appeared in a memoir in 1858. Organizational behavior, indeed!

Gene Marine
Berkeley, California

The Bloopie Awards

Every year about this time, Madison Avenue operatives start coating their digestive tracts with antacids—once anti-acids, but the *i* was dropped in 1753 to avoid the clash of vowels, such as still exists in *anti-intellectual*—in anticipation of the coveted, or dreaded, "Bloopies." Scantily clad models sidle up to the lectern to hand me the envelopes containing the names and offenses of this year's winners, or losers. *(Scantily* is to *clad* what *hastily* is to *called.)*

The Gold-Plated Chain for Most Stunning Use of Sadomasochism in Advertising to Arthur Treacher's fast-food restaurants, for their unforgettable headline: "One Dozen Battered Shrimp, $3.99."

The So-So Cup, for tagging the word *so* onto another word in guilty acknowledgment of the arch nature of the usage, shared between Saks Fifth Avenue, for "Calvin Klein creates clothing that works, but *more so,* that enthralls," and Plymouth!, the store with the stridency built into its name, for "the newest skirt . . . *ever so* rich." (Italics mine, effusiveness theirs.) Saks has another entry for its "dinner dressing . . . and the flavors run the gambit from dazzling to demure!" (In chess, that is redundantly called an opening gamut.)

The Two Apostrophes Medallion, for creating a tongue-twisting plural, to Bloomingdale's department store, for: "What Could Possibly Be Better Than One Bloomingdale's? Two Bloomingdale's!" The plural is probably pronounced "Bloomingdales-ziz."

The Financial Redundancy Silver Dollar, to *Forbes* magazine, for "Before you invest another dollar, mail the card below first." Before we give the editors the award, we will give it to them first.

The Mom-'n'-Pop Humanitarian Noncorporate Flesh-and-Blood Purple Heart, to those companies which present themselves as agglomerations of nice human beings, an award shared by Weyerhaeuser Lumber ("the tree-growing people"), Eastern Airlines ("the people of Eastern welcome you"), and General Motors ("People Building Transportation to Serve People"). This category was suggested by Washington attorney Jonathan Weisgall, who restrained himself from advising a company in the defense business to call itself "the people-killing people."

The On-Course Navigational Sextant, to the Sheaffer Eaton division of Textron, for its ad for At-A-Glance personal planners beginning with "Set sail for Jamaica," going on to "Maritime Office," and then reminding the sailor-planner to "Pick up Sexton." This might be an available clergyman, but is hardly a navigational device.

The "I Sometimes Wrong the Word Order Get" Mink-Lined Raincoat, to Moe Ginsburg Men's Better Clothing, for its closing line "All items not on sale." Writes Gene Shalit of NBC: "Do you think that Moe means 'Not every item is on sale'? Otherwise, nothing is on sale." Perhaps Moe is smarter than either of us thinks.

The Never-Sample-the-Product-While-You're-Writing-the-Copy Crystal Shot Glass, to Irish Mist liqueur, for "Give someone a bottle of Irish Mist and you give them hills that roll forever, lakes that radiate light. . . ." Someone is forgetting their antecedents. First runner-up in this category is Howard Johnson's restaurants, which ask patrons to fill out a card reading: "Did the server introduce themself by name?" Second runner-up is Chivas Regal Scotch, for its copy line: "Disappears rather quickly, doesn't it." Shouldn't that have a question mark.

The Two-Dollar Word Glittering Tiara, to Time Inc., for listing under "Present Imperative" such verbs as "background" and "source," now acceptable in journajargon, and adding the toney "asseverate." The nominator, Paul Janensch, executive editor of *The* (Louisville, Kentucky) *Courier-Journal* and *The Louisville Times,* says, "Asseverate means assert. I wonder why they didn't say assert instead of asseverate." (*Time* had another entry from its records division, advertising a Chopin recording that "would assure his immortality for all time.")

The Huge Octavo Statuette of Charles Darwin, to New American Library, for its advertisement of Irving Stone's *The Origin* as "a hardcover-size paperback." Darwin's *Origin of Species* was a paperback-size hardcover.

The Old Suffragette Button for Sexism That Sells, to Mercedes-Benz, for "Makes better drivers—of aficionados and housewives alike." Nominator Eleanor Rawson leans on her horn to suggest: "Before they lift pen again, the Mercedes-Benz people [see Mom-'n'-Pop Award, above] should get in their 300D Turbodiesel, with its six separate brakes, seven shock absorbers and rigid unit body, and purr silently off to the nearest dictionary for advice about how to conjure up that elusive word *neophyte.*"

The All-Too-Honest Typographer Laurel Wreath, to the Montvale, New Jersey, homeowner who advertised a "Specious Ranch on One Acre"; runner-up was the Szechuan Garden restaurant of Rockville, Maryland, for the shuddering impact of its "Authentic Human Cuisine."

The Chivas Regal copy line "Disappears rather quickly, doesn't it" should definitely NOT be followed by a question mark. It is a statement made in the form of a question, to be read with a downward inflection rather than an upward inflection on the last two words. Chivas Regal ain't askin', it's tellin'!

> Lois H. Prentice
> Nokomis, Florida

The unfortunate sailor-planners who needed a sextant and got a sexton would have found themselves not with a man in holy orders but with a janitor-type, whose functions are bell-ringing and grave-digging. The OED *defines a sexton as "a church officer having the care of the fabric of a church and its contents. . . ." I especially like the 1596 reference to "[the] continuall crashing of sextons spades against dead mens bones."*

> Thomas Furcron
> Brooklyn, New York

In your All-Too-Honest Typographer *. . . category, I'll never forget the letter of application from a woman (then a schoolteacher) who said she wanted to change to journalism to "earn a salary commiserate with my ability."*
*   She didn't get the job.*

> Carrick H. Patterson
> Little Rock, Arkansas

*   1. Your use of "those companies which present themselves" is incorrect. "Which" is used when the subject is not limited; "that" when the subject is limited. "Which" acts as an appositive, and the which clause is set off by commas. My father-in-law once explained the rule by using an illustration of a farm boy with a rifle and 10 squirrels. If all 10 squirrels were in the barn one would say, "The boy shot the squirrels, which were in the barn"—i.e., shot all of the squirrels. If 5 of the 10 were in the barn one would say, "The boy shot the squirrels that were in the barn"—i.e., shot some of the squirrels. Another way of saying it is "the . . ., which" and "those . . . that."*

2. The use of "someone . . . them" and "server . . . themself" is explained by (a) reluctance to be accused of male chauvinism by using the masculine singular and (b) aversion to the awkward "him or her" and "himself or herself." The usage is of course incorrect but explicable, and I see no solution except to use the masculine singular with the knowledge it is the generic term. This may be the wave of the future. My daughter calls herself a "Yale man" and in the movie Star Trek II *a woman cadet is referred to as "mister."*

3. The lack of a question mark in the Chivas ad emphasizes the declaratory nature of the rhetorical question.

> Thomas R. Moore
> New York, New York

When may we expect The Huge Octavo Statuette of Charles Darwin *in honor of our designation of the Plume edition of Irving Stone's* The Origin *as "a hardcover-size paperback" book?*

We believe that terminology within the publishing industry would be confusing to the average reader. Hardcover books are also called "trade books" and in the area of paperbacks there are "trade paperbacks," "quality paperbacks" and "mass market paperbacks." Members of the publishing industry are able to distinguish these terms but are our readers able to do so? I think not.

The Origin *was published in hardcover by Doubleday and Co. New American Library purchased trade paperback and mass market paperback reprint rights from Doubleday, and our initial reprint publication was in trade paperback format and one year later we published our Signet mass market paperback edition.*

The ad to which you refer presented the Plume trade paperback edition which we called "a hardcover size paperback." That certainly distinguishes the Plume edition from the Signet mass market paperback edition but if you have a more effective way of communicating that information to our readers in a print advertisement I would love to know it.

> Robert G. Diforio
> President and Publisher
> The New American Library,
> Inc.
> New York, New York

The name of the company is Weyerhaeuser Company, not Weyerhaeuser Lumber.

The identity of the company is "The Tree Growing Company," not the "Tree Growing People."

I agree with you. There is a great deal of advertising that presents a "mom-and-pop, humanitarian noncorporate flesh-and-blood purple heart" image. However, to get the words confused as you did with Weyerhaeuser only discounts the validity of the important message you were attempting to convey. Your critique was particularly irritating because we have honestly represented the Weyerhaeuser Company as a company *that manages trees, not noncorporate humanitarians.*

Too bad. Our business needs criticism from responsible reporters.

Hal Newsom
President
Cole & Weber
Seattle, Washington

Extant Sextant

When you're handing out Bloopie Awards, you have to watch your step. It was pointed out in this space that *sextant,* a navigational device, was a far cry from *sexton,* a clergyman.

Much irreverent mail has slammed me against the wall for that definition. A sexton is a custodial worker at a church, who may be anything from an administrative officer to a bellringer to a gravedigger, but is not ordinarily an ordained minister, and is thus not a member of the clergy.

"The office of sexton isn't much used anymore," writes James Nelson, minister of the North United Methodist Church in Minneapolis, "particularly in America, where most of these duties are the janitor's job, who is, I think in some denominations, actually called the sexton." He suggests *custodian,* and supplies us with Shakespeare's metaphoric description of the job: "Old Time the clock setter, that bald sexton Time."

Bloopie II

More envelopes, please.

The Teeny-Tiny Golden Toothpick for Meaning Mix-Up, to Brownstone Studio for "Heavy crepe de Chine in a dress that pampers and belittles every lovely inch of the way." *Belittle* was used by Thomas Jefferson to mean "make less of" in the sense of "to disparage, bemean," and cannot be reduced to a literal meaning of "to make seem smaller."

The Bronzed Broken Airline Seat for Subjunctive Abuse, to Eastern Airlines

for "If all we gave you was low fares, we'd be just an ordinary airline." If all we got *were* on-time departures, my aunt would be a flying teakettle.

The Dual Coffin, Excuse Me, Casket, for Double Meaning, to Chambers Undertakers for a headline listing its fourth parlor: "In case of death there are *four* places you can go." To most of us, that means Heaven, Hell, Purgatory, and Silver Spring.

The Lacy-Drawers Peekaboo Nightie for Creative Orthography, to B. Altman & Company for "Provincial mahogany chest with draw now 90.00 . . . or choose this zippered draw chest." This competes with Northern Telecom's comparison of its word-processing system with the eleventh-century Domesday Book, which, Northern Telecom wrote, "gave the Last Judgement." (On Judgment Day, the last word I would misspell would be *judgment.*) The judges decided to call this contest a drawer.

The Twisted Jump Rope for the Confusion of the Same Word as Noun and Verb, to *U.S. News & World Report* for "Many magazine readers are inclined to skim. They skim to the sports. Skim to the movies. Skim to the gossip. . . . We give you the cream. Not the skim." I think the verb the copywriter had in mind was *skip.* When you *skim,* you take off the cream. The skim *is* the cream, leaving behind skimmed milk or, if you like old-fashion endings, skim milk.

The Limp Leather Horsewhip for Tense Tension, to Loewe Madrid 1846 (which is either the company's name or address or history) for "I wouldn't own anything but a Loewe handbag even if I have nothing left to put in it." Put *had* in your handbag and clutch it.

The Highest-Falutin Platinum Option for Ill-Chosen Modifier, to J. & W. Seligman, the bankers, for "It is, in the rarefied world of money management, somewhat unique to become quite successful and at the same time remain somewhat unknown." It is, in the plebeian world of grammar, incorrect to knock down an absolute like *unique* without its becoming all too well known.

The Crème-Filled Cookie for Unnatural Acts in Advertising, to Lancôme, Paris, for "Protective day crème . . . in naturel and tints." For years, *plain* was the word to describe "unaltered, uncolored, or unflavored." That was euphemized by *natural,* which was too plain, and now we have *naturel.* In a related development, Chanel's crème makeup (nobody can spell it *cream* unless it contains cream) offers itself with "allows skin to breathe, naturally." That shows what a comma can do: As it stands, the phrase means "allows skin to breathe, of course, as any fool can plainly see." Without the comma, the phrase reads "allows skin to breathe naturally," or, as they say at Lancôme, naturelly.

The Silver Erratum for Trying Too Hard to Show Off in Latin, to *Town & Country* magazine for "For the names, addresses and *modus operandae* of these craftsmen. . . ." Never pluralize the genetive when a Latin lover is in the room. (That comes from Winston Churchill's advice about Count Ciano and Mussolini: "Never talk to the monkey when the organ grinder is in the room.") As Latin alumni tell me, the nominative *modus,* not the genetive *operandi,* gets the plural: Those are the *modi operandi* of the craftsmen I know.

The Bend-Over-Backward Antisexist Computerized Statuette, to I.B.M. for "Everyone compares the quality of their electronic typewriters to the I.B.M. Electronic 75." When a reader asked why they matched the singular *everyone* with the plural *their* and *typewriters,* a spokesperson replied, *"Their* is used to avoid the sexist *his* or the awkward *his/her* or *his and her.* Once *their* is chosen, then *typewriters* is correct, being closer to *their* in the sentence than to *everyone."* All these contortions could be avoided by changing *Everyone compares* to *People compare.* As the great producers say, when in doubt, recast.

The Tattered Fun Fur for the Misplaced Little Word, to Neiman-Marcus for "You can only find it in our Fur Salon." Runner-up is the National Cancer Institute for its pamphlet "Everything Doesn't Cause Cancer"; if only that were true. Not Everything Causes Solecisms.

The Truth-in-Advertising Cherry Tree for Honesty Beyond the Call, to a Lake George boating outfit, not intimidated by the teen-agers' vogue term *bo-ring!,* for its slogan "The longest one-hour cruise on Lake George."

The Red-Faced Pundit's Ceremonial Mask for Subject-Predicate Disagreement, to The New York Times News Service, below pictures of its six stalwart columnists: "The News Service's depth and scope represents the best in American journalism." Either represents; both represent. (If I had to choose, profundity would beckon: In this dodge, depth beats scope hands down.)

When you're in the holier-than-thou business, you must be prepared to say a mea culpa *now and then. For example:*
Judgment—judgement. *The O.E.D. lists both spellings, but appears to prefer*

"judgement." The revisionist American Heritage Dictionary *prefers "judgment" but accepts "judgement."*

Skim—skip. Skim *also means "to glance over, without reading closely"* (O.E.D.), *or "to read . . . quickly or superficially"* (Am. Her.). U.S. News*'s copywriter erred in using "to." There's nothing improper about "Skim the gossip," which would have set up the tag line ("We give you the cream . . .") nicely.*

Jeffrey Kassel
Madison, Wisconsin

Altar boys and other passing Latinists will never confuse the genitive singular feminine with the genitive plural neuter. You were correct to chastise Town & Country *for their incorrect* modus operandae, *but incorrect in diagnosing their mistake. They have not pluralized the genitive; they have feminized it—something I'm afraid* Town & Country *does with almost everything it gets its hands on these days. I suspect what we have here is a bad case of hypercorrection. No doubt the editors of* T&C *are used to hearing the second word of this expression pronounced "operand-eye." Assuming that the pronunciation was correct, they opted for the Latin spelling that would yield it. (*Operandi *is pronounced "operand-ee," except by people who associate with EYE-talians and EYE-ranians.) The genitive plural neuter would be* operandorum *which sounds like a magician's incantation.*

Timothy J. Kenslea
Boston, Massachusetts

You blew it! You had the chance to right a long-standing grammatical wrong. Instead of giving IBM a Bloopie Award, you should have given them an award for bravery and good sense and grammaticality. Everyone *is plural in meaning; it makes no sense to insist otherwise.*

Since everyone *and* each *are both indefinite pronouns, they keep getting treated alike. But they're not alike.* Everyone *is a collective pronoun, singular in form although plural in meaning. Compare* everyone *with* family:

> *The family sat down to dinner; they enjoyed every dish.*
> *Everyone sat down to dinner; they enjoyed every dish.*
> *Everyone enjoyed themselves, didn't they?*
> *When everyone was seated, the hostess asked them to join her in a toast.*

Do you see what's happened? We've made the rules for the possessive case different from those we apply in the subjective and objective. And that's not the way we do things!

You're right, of course, that there are ways around the awkwardness (if you want to call it that): We can say people *instead of* everyone. *But wouldn't it be better to spread the word that speakers and writers who use the plural pronoun in reference to* everyone *are not only logical; they're right—and, for the time being, brave to boot?*

Martha Kolln
Assistant Professor of English
Pennsylvania State University
College Park, Pennsylvania

If the Lake George boating outfit had the fastest boat on the lake, they could honestly offer the longest one-hour ride on the lake.

Thomas E. Louis
Dobbs Ferry, New York

A Bloopie Award may be in order for you for your award to I.B.M. I question I.B.M.'s use of "compares . . . to" instead of "compares . . . with."

Peter T. Shalvoy
Melville, New York

Bill,

As the son of a teacher of Laughing and Grief, I fear that the former has brought you to the latter in your Town & Country *item.*

Operandi *is the genitive (note spelling; even the* OED *lists "genetive" as an obsolete form) of the gerund of the verb* operare. *You can tell that it's a gerund and not a gerundive because it's active, not passive: "of operating," not "of being operated" or "to be operated."*

Operandae, *for its part, could be the genitive or dative singular or the nominative plural of the gerundive of* operare, *but as a verbal adjective it would have to agree with its noun in gender, case and number. So it could have no truck with* modus, *a masculine noun.*

I'm afraid that this may be more about penguins than you really care to know, and it seems like returning evil for good after your generous mentions of cursors!, *but this is a case, you might say, of the djins of the father being visited by the son.*

Dan [Griffin]
The Washington Post
Washington, D.C.

Your criticism of the word skim *instead of* skip to *may have been too harsh. I am naturally indolent and don't always want to read every word in every section of a magazine; however, I do want to know what gems of information are in any article, so I "skim" the sports and business sections. This way I get the cream, by reading only the headlines, the topic sentences, and the picture captions. When I reach the gossip column, the literature and arts section, sometimes current events, infrequently editorials, but all of the letters to the editor, then I really peruse, as they say in the crossword puzzles.*

Madeleine H. Warlow
Carlisle, Pennsylvania

Blowing My Whistle

Whistleblowers are often successful; by figuratively blowing the whistle on wrongdoing, they cause evil to be rooted out of corporate or governmental bureaucracies. But many are laden afterward with the baggage of suspicion; few whistleblowers are trusted by new bosses.

Same thing with the word *whistleblower.* When a compound noun *(whistle blower)* fights its way through the purgatory of years of hyphenation *(whistle-blower)* and finally—by common consent and frequency of use—starts making it to single-word status *(whistleblower),* you'd think it would be given space in our dictionaries. Not so; lexicographers are still looking askance at this word. They don't trust its permanence.

The word probably first saw print in a piece in *The New York Times* on March 23, 1970, when John A. Hamilton wrote about "how well the majority leader handled a whistle-blower" under the headline "Blowing the Whistle on 'The Bosses.'" This word picture of a policeman blowing his whistle at an escaping thief is rooted deep in the language, and both *blow* and *whistle* have separate slang roots in the spilling of the beans: "Did nobody blow ye?" asked an accomplice in 1575, and in Shakespeare's *The Winter's Tale,* the clown asks about "when you are going to . . . whistle off these secrets . . . ?"

On January 30, 1971, Ralph Nader (whose two first names, contrary to popular belief, are not "consumer" and "activist") pressed the new word into the popular discourse with what he called a "whistle blower's conference" in Washington. With due credit to A. Ernest Fitzgerald, who had discombobulated the defense establishment with his disclosures about cost overruns, the conference featured such papers as "The Whistle Blower as Civil Servant," by Senator William Proxmire, and "Whistle Blowing and the Law," by Professor Arthur S. Miller.

Nader's follow-up book was titled *Whistle Blowing,* two words, and the hyphenated construction was used in Alan Westin's 1981 book; most newspaper usage, however, had compressed the two words into a single word.

In his 1983 book *Do It My Way or You're Fired!*—a real grabber of a title to an excellent work about employee rights—David Ewing uses the word in a corporate rather than a governmental context. In politics, a *whistleblower* is a hero, and a leaker is a bum, although both do the same thing; in business, the word has a specialized meaning. Mr. Ewing, managing editor of the *Harvard Business Review,* tells me that "whistleblowing in business need not mean going to the press with evidence of wrongdoing. It can also mean going up through channels to get a fair hearing. In business, you leak only when you are not allowed to blow the whistle."

Boulevard of Broken Words

Charlton Heston, the only actor who turns when somebody yells, "Moses!" or, "El Cid!" called me one morning recently. His stentorian voice over the telephone was indistinct—he was calling from a car, or from the top of Mount Sinai—but it was clear he had a language problem.

"I'm concerned about what I think may be anachronisms," he shouted, "in a script we're shooting down here." It turned out he was filming a television miniseries called *Chiefs* (which is about police officers, and has nothing to do with Indians) set in a small Georgia town in the 1920's. "The scriptwriter is willing to accept your judgment on whether these expressions would have been in use down here in that era."

I whispered to myself the code word for the twenties—*shenanigans!*—and prepared to hear the phrases Heston thought might not fit the time. Nothing is more off-putting—or, as they used to say, nothing sounds a more sour note—than a word or phrase in a historical movie that is in current usage but was unused at the time. "Lay it on me," I said (a 1960's term).

"Wear it in good health! is one of the phrases," the actor said. "And the other one is *So I lied."*

Yiddishisms both. Harry Golden, who did not move South and become editor of *The Carolina Israelite* until the 1940's, used the expressions, but it is unlikely that many Southerners in the 1920's would have spoken that way. Today, sure: "Y'all weah it in good health, heah?" Not three generations ago, before television.

Unhesitatingly, I pronounced judgment (which I spell no other way): Those were anachronisms, mistakes writers have been making since Shakespeare had a character in *Julius Caesar* say he heard a clock strike. (The Romans had no clocks; they wore hourglasses around their wrists, or something.) If he wanted a second opinion, I told him to call Leo Rosten, author of *Hooray for Yiddish.*

He did. Later, I spoke to my friend Rosten to make certain the phalanx of experts was sticking together. Sure enough, *Wear it in good health* is the English translation of the Yiddish-German *Trug es gezunderheit* (though Leo's mother used to say, "Vear it in good helt"). *So I lied* is probably the punch line of a forgotten Jewish joke; it sets aside the most common meaning of *so*, which is the chronological "and then," preferring a meaning synonymous with one of the many meanings of *nu*: a sly or ironic way of saying, "And what are you going to do about

it?" To give the flavor of the intonation, the phrase would better be written: "So? I lied."

Rosten's point to Heston, who has a good ear, is: "Even if it's right, it's wrong" —that is, even if the expressions had been used in rural Georgia in the 1920's, their use in a movie would distract an audience: "In 1924? Absurd."

This episode led me to a file I have been building for months, with the help of Lexicographic Irregulars. The file is labeled "Chronisms," the opposite of anachronisms. These are words quivering in the aspic of time, perfect for use by dramatists who want to give historical scenes the flavor of authenticity, starring Vera Similitude, my 1940's *heartthrob*.

One class of chronisms deals with the names for objects no longer in use. Such rumble-seat chronisms include *milk bottle* in an age of containerization, *slide rule* on a platter of efficient chips, *watch fob* in a steady dose of digitalis, *scooters* for the skateboard generation, *Butterfield 8* in the all-digit era, *snood* in the Hairspray Age. It is not the word that has disappeared; the thing itself is gone or going, and the word reverberates like a shimmering old photo. If you want Vera to seem at home in a bygone era, have her tell her kid to pull up his *knickers* and crank up the *phonograph.*

More interesting to the linguist are the nonce-word chronisms, those words that zipped through a decade like naked *streakers* of the 1960's or the *twenty-three skiddoo* of the 1920's. *Uptown* meant "ritzy," before *ritzy* became *upscale. Peachy* and *keen* merged, to be replaced by *nifty* and now *cool.* "We were *pupils* at school," writes Steve Cartwright of *The Central Maine Morning Sentinel,* a child of the Fabulous Fifties, "a bunch of *bozos,* but we were *pals.* It was *swell.*" *Atomic* is a legitimate dictionary entry, but in its description of an age, it has been nonced out by *nuclear.*

The pre-euphemism chronism offers a scriptwriter a marvelous vehicle for Miss Similitude's scenes of, say, the 1920's. After a trip to the *dime store* or *five-and-dime* (not the "variety store"), she blanched at her lover's *false teeth* (nothing dentured, nothing gained) and wore her *corset* with no idea it would become a "foundation garment." Rosie O'Grady was the *floorwalker's girlfriend,* not the "assistant manager's lady." You would never refer to a *porno dealer* in those days; that is today's euphemism for *smut peddler.*

To stud her speech with the talk of the time, Vera Similitude's creator should also employ backdated-label chronisms: words no longer in use for things still in use. *Nightclub* is one, for what we now call a *club, disco,* or *bistro,* where she ordered a *highball* for what is now a *mixed drink,* served in a *tumbler* instead of a *tall glass,* and watched the *floor show,* now the *revue.* Getting out her *compact* to reach for a *powerpuff* (rather than a *brush* for her *blush*), she would meet her *beau* in a *luncheonette,* not her *live-in lover* in a *coffee shop,* and feared he would be *smitten* by *cheesecake* in the 1930's or a *pinup* in the 1940's, not *freaked out* by a *centerfold.* Certain words were *risqué* in the twenties and *off-color* in the forties, and are *talking dirty* today. She would warn him not to *get fresh,* rather than *come on* to her, lest she be considered his *doxy,* now *armpiece.* If she ran off with him, they would pack their *valises,* not their *carry-ons*—"carrying on" was what they were doing—and would promptly *come down with the grippe* rather than *contract the flu.*

The same backdated-label chronisms apply to activities still under way but under new names. Howard Singer of Marlboro, New Jersey, remembers the *exercise classes* of the 1950's, where one wore *sweat suits;* these are now *workouts* with *warm-ups.* Many Lex Irregs have noted that *fooling around* was relatively innocent; now it denotes the action of the sexually active, with its unprintable substitute paradoxically taking on the innocent meaning.

In a similar vein, chronistic expressions mark the time: *So's your old man* is a caricature of a 1920's term, but *It's your nickel* rings true for the 1930's. When was the last time you heard *It'll put hair on your chest*? Or *Much obliged*?

Those assigned to write in rotogravure must look at life through sepia cheaters. Generations from now, scriptwriters yet unborn will massage their scene-processors to write about our times. Let us hope that, for Vera Similitude's sake, they will often hit the chronism key. It is a long *shlep* from now to then, with plenty of *kvetching* from *kibitzers* in store, but *not to worry.* Like *El Cid,* those are Yiddishisms.

Hold on. *El Cid* is not a Yiddishism, you say, but is based on the Arabic word for "lord," and was the sobriquet of a medieval Spanish captain named Rodrigo Díaz de Vivar.

So I lied.

Having thanked you for your authoritative support of my convictions on Southern speech in the twenties, I must do so again for airing our exchange so prestigiously. We mountebanks seldom make the pages of The New York Times Magazine.

Of course I enjoyed your piece and have seized on your coinage, "chronism." You're quite right, it's as useful to search for one as it is to avoid the other. Such words are sure echoes of their time. Thus, in our piece (with some watchful prodding), we say "telephone" and "automobile," instead of "phone" and "car," in 1924, and "colored" in 1945, but "black" in 1963. While all these are chronisms of time rather than place, the gradual shift in the proper appellation for what used to be called the Negro race was more highly charged in the South than elsewhere, and serves our story usefully.

You're quite right about Shakespeare, too. In his eye, of course, the clock in Caesar *(and in* Romeo, *" . . . The bawdy hand of the dial is hard upon the prick of noon"), the cannon in* Henry V, *and Cleopatra's cry, "Cut my lace, Charmian," were none of them anachronisms. In his lifetime and for some generations thereafter, his plays were always staged in contemporary dress.*

To the alert ear, chronisms can be very revealing. I still often say "icebox," "fountain pen," and "wrist watch," so you know I was born before the thirties. What a fascinating thing the growth of English is. What fools the French are to try and freeze their language in amber.

Charlton Heston
Beverly Hills, California

P.S.: While a modern Southerner might well say "Weah it in good health," he would never add "Y'all," which always refers to more than one person, who could hardly jointly wear whatever "it" was. O.K.?

Pillbox	*Pills don't come in little round boxes. Gun emplacements gone too. Also hats.*
Trig	*Neat word. Where is it?*
Sneak	*As in preview. Meaning gone. Sneak previews advertised in* Times.
Dial	*Changing. Hardly a dial left on radios. Pointer traveling in straight line instead of around.*
Timepiece	*No longer "consulted."*
Electric	*Now "electronic."*
Self-starter	*In car. Now just "starter."*

Henry Morgan
New York, New York

I tried to think of words, such as nightclub, *that have fallen into disuse even though the entity still exists in essentially unchanged form.*

That led me to a double whammy *which remains the best a week's recollections produced. A "davenport with antimacassers" wins for me.*

> Robert J. Connor
> New City, New York

Further candidates for your "outdated" list:
1. *Afflicted (handicapped)*
2. *Backward (retarded)*
3. *Central (operator)*
4. *Car coat*
5. *Filling station*
6. *Greensward*
7. *Hi fi*
8. *Hickey (pimple)*
9. *Kiddie car*
10. *Leggings*

> Jane T. Larsen
> McLean, Virginia

Your article reminds me of the days when I used to put on my plus-fours and golf socks, take my golf sticks (mid-iron, mashie, mashie-niblick, driver, and brassie), strap them to the running board, and go off to the golf links.

> George D. Vaill
> Colebrook, Connecticut

Dear Bill:

Some words have fallen into desuetude, with no word taking their place. Desuetude, for one, maybe. For those of us who were in college before 1970, the word parietals *had a certain meaning: visiting hours or other restrictions on having a person of the opposite sex visiting you in your dorm. Nowadays, you never hear the word.*

> Gary [Muldoon]
> Rochester, New York

Oh, but you hit home today. My sons stare at me blankly when I suggest they get a beer from the ice box or check the turtle hull to see if the spare tire is inflated. These new young 'uns insist on refrigerator or auto trunk; lordy but they've never even thought about an ice card *(the square of cardboard that went into the window, with the desired poundage at either end: 12½, 25, 37½, or 50). These terms were intelligible in East Texas in 1934–48, and I cling to them.*

Joseph C. Goulden
Washington, D.C.

How about Turkish bath*? Are any of those still steaming along out there today? Or have they, as I suspect, all migrated north and west and exchanged their slightly faded oriental glamour for the newer European chic of* sauna *and* spa*?*

Arnold H. Weiss
Lawrence, Kansas

You use the pun "nothing dentured, nothing gained." Peter Wegner, professor of computer science at Brown University, turned this into a very entertaining double pun by substituting "stained" for "gained" when I jokingly refused an offer of blueberries during a dinner at his home in fear of staining my dentures.

Scott Smolka
Stony Brook, New York

Shakespeare's having Caesar's clock strike three turns out not to be an anachronism after all. . . . The Roman clock was a clepsydra, or water clock. This was basically a vessel into which water was made to trickle at an adjustable rate, a float that rose as the vessel filled, a pointer attached to the float, and a scale on which the pointer indicated the hours. (There were many variations and refinements.) In addition, many clocks had means for indicating hours by dropping metal balls into bronze plates or otherwise making a racket. The striking clock actually antedates the clock with a circular dial and rotating hands, which is late Roman, or post-Roman.

L. Sprague de Camp
Villanova, Pennsylvania

I just can't accept "not to worry" as a Yiddishism. I first heard that expression in England from sundry Brits a number of years ago, and since then I've been seeing it in English authored books and whatnot. We Yanks learned it from the BBC-as-

told-to-Channel 13. Whereas I know our co-religionists have lived in England for lo these many years, it seems to me that their major impact on the culture has not been along the lines of language.

Zorgzuch nisht *is not "not to worry"; it is "don't worry yourself," which is an unqualified Yiddishism . . . Yiddishism, not a Briddishism. Maybe you didn't listen so good.*

> Evelyn R. Fowler
> Stamford, Connecticut

HAH! I finally caught you with your pants down! The naked truth is that streaking *was not a 1960's pastime, as you suggested. Rather, it roughly coincided with the 1973–74 academic year.*

> Dr. Clifford B. Saper
> Cheve Coeur, Maryland

Chronisms: I pulled out my boiled shirt, *lost my* collar buttons *under the* chifferobe; *finally found 'em, tied my white pique* batwing; *and climbed into my* monkey suit. *Very formal affair or I'd have worn my* smoking jacket. *Collapsed my* topper *into my tail pocket, went to have a quick* snort *only to find that the* iceman *hadn't made his delivery that day. So I downed it* neat *and strolled downstairs to the waiting* IRT *(or was it* BMT?).

> John Hyman
> Palm Beach, Florida

Dear Bill:

As a wide-awake contemporary who read tons of books, I can assure you that "Twenty-three skiddoo" was no longer current in the 1920s. My impression is that it dates from the late 1890s and had fire in its vitals till about 1910. Was it a railroad telegrapher's phrase interpreting the number 23 as a signal to get going?

> Jacques [Barzun]
> Charles Scribner's Sons,
>   Publishers
> New York, New York

Spanish is El Cid; Yiddish is El Sid.

> Mauri Edwards
> Short Hills, New Jersey

Dear Bill,

There is no such language as "Yiddish-German." There is Modern German and there is Yiddish, just as there is Dutch and Danish and Norwegian. At one time Yiddish was improperly called "Judaeo-German" just as Old English was called "Anglo-Saxon." No distinct language—and Yiddish is indeed that—needs hyphenation with some other related language of parallel derivation. Also, I would suggest that in Romanizing Yiddish items, you use the transcription of Standard Yiddish, now universal among scholars. You can get the key from YIVO or find it in Weinreich's Modern English-Yiddish Dictionary. *But you are right in calling "wear it in good health" an anachronism for the 1920s. It didn't come into general use—and then only jocularly—until about 1950.*

> *David [B. Guralnik]*
> *Vice President and Dictionary*
> *Editor in Chief*
> *Simon & Schuster New World*
> *Dictionaries*
> *Cleveland, Ohio*

About your comments on "wearing things in health" in last Sunday's Times: The Greeks use that expression all the time, in demotic Greek—which indicates it's an old expression. I suspect it's a turn of phrase as old as history. The Greeks, as usual, had a word for it.

> *Leopold LeClair*
> *Peterborough, New Hampshire*

About outdated words:

How about verandah? *It's always a porch now.*
And tumbler? *Dumbest word I've ever heard for a glass.*

> *George A. Woods*
> *New York, New York*

Dear Bill:

Are you sure an American would ". . . pull up his knickers . . ." or, more likely, doesn't it derive from English women pulling up their knickers (which are panties or were bloomers)?

At age 8, I may have pulled up my "plus fours" or "knickerbockers" but I would wager it was used many years before by a lover to his mistress upon being surprised by an amazed husband.

> *Edward [Bleier]*
> *New York, New York*

Your column regarding chronisms reinforced my belief that English and American really are two different languages. Our milk comes in bottles, delivered to the doorstep by a roundsman driving a milk float. Milk in waxed cartons is regarded as a debased French product permitted by Eurocrats. It is homogenized and treated so that it can be stored for months.

Knickers are worn by women under their other garments. Plus-fours are worn by sporting country gentlemen. "Don't get your knickers in a twist" means don't be so impatient.

Some rather old-fashioned people still refer to the wireless and the gramophone. But then, they also drive motor cars. One occasionally hears reference to cranking up the old motor. When I purchased a Lada motor car (a Russian-built Fiat), I discovered that it had a hand crank for use if the massive battery ever failed. As hand cranks were common until the 1950s, perhaps this isn't so outmoded after all.

S. Jay Kleinberg
Surry, England

Hypotypo

The Nitpickers' League is an international organization of professional infuriaters whose purpose it is to blame innocent writers for the errors of sloppy typographers. Its members are growing more numerous as writers do their own typography on word processors and have nobody to whom to pass the buck.

Several letters have come in on the misspelling here of *powderpuff* as *power-puff.* No, I was not trying to create a new word in some linguistic powderplay. It was just a typo. Sorry. My copy editor is sorry. Her boss is sorry. These things happen.

"The Department of the Treasury should receive one of your awards," writes Nitpicker's League member Walter Robinson of Riverhead, New York. He enclosed an envelope from the Treasury's Division of Disbursement reading: "OFFICIAL BUSSINESS, Penalty for Private Use $300." Mr. Robinson comments: "The penalty for letting 'BUSSINESS' through should be even more."

Naturally, I called this to the attention of the Treasury Department and wondered how many such envelopes went out. Ann Dore McLaughlin, Assistant Secretary for Public Affairs, set her jaw firmly and replied: "About six million checks went out in 'Official Bussiness' envelopes before they caught the error."

Mrs. McLaughlin, a talented and busy public servant, must think of me as a nitpicker. I know how she feels.

It seems to me that one calls a person's attention to something but one brings a matter to his attention.

> *Margaret Knowles*
> *New York, New York*

I want to raise one point about the government envelopes with the misspelled word: Of the 6 million checks they contained, were any returned, or did anyone refuse to cash one, because of the typo?

> *Leonard Koppett*
> *Palo Alto, California*

Buckle Down, Windsock

This department is always on the lookout for vivid new metaphors. Carol Conkey of Victoria, Texas, sends along a clip from *The Victoria Advocate* of an interview with Donald Rumsfeld, the former Secretary of Defense, who now rolls pills for G. D. Searle, the pharmaceutical outfit.

"The key," Mr. Rumsfeld is quoted as saying, "is to hold one policy long enough and calibrate it, not to treat the American economy as if it were a *windsocket.*"

Reached in Skokie, Illinois, Mr. Rumsfeld was forced to say, "The newspaper made a mistake. It must be the very first time I have ever found that to be the case."

What word did he have in mind? "As a broken-down ex-naval aviator, I occasionally find myself using words and phrases connected with aviation. The word I used was *windsock,* which is the cloth sleeve on a pole that is located on air fields, indicating the direction and speed of the wind."

The metaphor most often used to deride relativism, or to poke fun at those who follow the polls rather than fixed principles, is *weather vane.* However, that has taken on an archaic quality; how many weather vanes do you see on top of houses these days, and of those, how many are not rusted into a fixed position?

Now we have a word for it: windsock morality, a man who has a windsock where his compass ought to be, etc. Watch: As soon as *windsock* gets into the language, they'll stop using them at airports.

Bull Market in Words

Bearish Joseph Granville, the stock-market guru, sent out a flash to his subscribers during some recent happy days on Wall Street. "Here we have stock market *tsunami*, the great Wall Street bet on economic recovery with 11 million people out of work. To escape *tsunami*, sell all stocks."

I buy all words like *tsunami* at their low. In *The Bermuda Triangle*, Charles Berlitz used this Japanese word for huge tidal waves, reaching up to 200 feet in height, usually caused by earthquakes. By applying the word to investment advice —using the metaphor as a warning against a tidal wave that would wipe out the investor in his tiny rowboat—Mr. Granville may have coined a winner.

Stock-market terminology continues to fluctuate, grabbing its figures of speech from all fields. *Blip* has good upside potential: "They're going to look beyond the blips," said Union Pacific chairman James Evans, approving the policy of Federal Reserve chairman Paul Volcker to place less reliance on temporary changes in one measurement of the money supply. At the White House, after a day of sinking prices on Wall Street, spokesman Peter Roussel said, "We had one bad blip today." Asked for his definition of *blip*, Mr. Roussel explains: "I view *blip* as a synonym for fluctuation. It could be used to describe changes in either direction."

Blip is of echoic origin, meaning "light blow," now described as "a pop," first used in print by Mark Twain in 1894: "We took him a blip in the back and knocked him off." In the 1920's, it was used to mean the switching on and off of an airplane's ignition, and after World War II it was taken up by electronics magazines to describe the little elongated marks that appear on a radar screen.

The word then split its pronunciation and meaning. A *bleep* became the term for a quick, sharp sound, such as those associated with oscilloscopes in radar sets, probably influenced by *beep*. When a short, high sound was substituted for a dirty word on the airwaves, the technique gave rise to a verb, *to bleep out*, meaning "to delete, to censor." Some of Johnny Carson's best lines were *bleeped*.

Meanwhile, *blip* enjoyed a run-up, starting in the early 1970's, in its meaning of "brief and meaningless change." *The Wall Street Journal*'s editorialists evidently consider a *blip* to mean a change that could be upward or downward, requiring one of those words as a modifier: "Economists are not likely to start jumping out of windows because of the downward blip in the leading indicators," *The Journal* opined recently, locking in the pejoration of inconsequence.

"Words similar to *blip* are *uptick* and *fillip*," says Todd May, chief economist for *Fortune* magazine. The original meaning of *uptick* was "the sale of a stock at a price higher than the immediately preceding sale," but in the past decade the word has come to mean a minor upward trend, well short of an *upswing*. The older word, *fillip*, meaning a snap of the fingers, has recently come to mean "small move" in the stock market.

"I don't like *blip*," says Seymour Zucker, senior editor at *Business Week*. "Not clear, no sense of magnitudes. To me, it just means 'aberration.'" What words are used in his shop to denote upward movements? "*Surge*, although we haven't had many lately, except in the stock market; *soar*, which is cliché now; *roar*, *vault*, *skyrocket*. For small upward movement, there's *uptick* or *minuscule uptick*. There's also *nudge upward*. I like the word *nudge*." Among the preferred downward words at that publication are *downtick*, *decline*, *plummet*, and, of course, *nudge downward*.

At *Financial World* magazine, preferred upward verbs are *bulge*, *spurt*, and *run-up*, and downward terms on the rise are *collapse* and *nosedive*. Stephen Quickel, editor, is one of those rare birds who know the difference between a *blip* and a *spike*: "A *spike* is a quick, exaggerated up-and-down movement," he says, "much more dramatic than a *blip*."

A stock is said to *break out* when it moves upward in a manner contrary to its previous undulations. An *explosion* is a big rally; its antonym is a *plunge*. A selling climax that sops up all remaining pessimism is a *blowoff*. A *bull trap* is a rally that is destined to fail, and is sometimes called a *sucker rally*. The favorite verb of stock-market newscasters in connection with losses is *to pare*, meaning "to shave, diminish," as in the action of cutting the peel off an apple: "The market pared its losses before the close," intones the announcer, who wishes he could break out into becoming an anchorman.

Of all the stock-market terms, which will cross into the general language? My money is on *blip*, because of its lengthy pedigree, its modern radar connotation, and its growth potential in fulfilling the desire to describe movement on charts (a desire that has not yet peaked). It is a much shorter term than *flash in the pan*, a military expression taken from the flash of the priming in the pan of a flintlock musket that fails to explode the charge, and now means a quickly dashed hope. Don't sell *flash in the pan* short, however; it may be that *blip* will be just a flash in the pan, but we can be sure that time-tested *flash in the pan* will be no *blip*.

Although tidal wave *is indeed popularly used to denote a seismic sea wave, it is a misnomer when so used. There is nothing "tidal" about the phenomenon. Tsunami, which is much more handy that "seismic sea wave," and, let's face it, exotic, fills a need. The word has been in use by scientists in this country for many years, and is not always italicized.*

> *Taliaferro Boatwright*
> *Stonington, Connecticut*

P.S. Blip *was in use* during *World War II to describe an indication on a radarscope that a return echo had been received. The Addenda section in* Webster II *says that* pip *was also used for this purpose, but I never heard it used.*

A tsunami *is not always big, bad, and dangerous. In the open sea, i.e. in deep water, a tsunami would be practically invisible to ship or rowboat, having a height of only a foot or so and a length measured in hundreds of miles. Only when entering shallows does it become wild and dangerous.*

> *Merit P. White*
> *Whately, Massachusetts*

You attributed the first use in print of blip, *meaning "hit," to a Mark Twain story published in 1894. When I read this, a blip crossed my memory scanner. I pulled down my copy of Joel Chandler Harris's* Uncle Remus *and, sure enough, there it was, in "The Wonderful Tar-Baby Story":*

> *Tar-Baby stay still, en Brer Fox, he lay low.*
> *Brer Rabbit keep on axin' 'im, en de Tar-Baby, she keep*
> *on sayin' nothin', twel present'y Brer Rabbit draw back wid*
> *his fis', he did, en blip he tuck 'er side er de head.*

The question is, when did Harris first publish "Tar-Baby"? The New Columbia Encyclopaedia *(Lippincott, 1975) says that "Tar-Baby" was published as a book in 1904. But the* New Encyclopaedia Britannica *(Micropaedia, 1981, Vol. IV, p. 922) says that "In 1879 the 'Tar Baby' story . . . appeared in the Atlanta Constitution."*

This seems to be borne out by Paul M. Cousins's biography of Harris (Louisiana State University Press, 1968, p. 105): "The story of Mr. Rabbit and Mr. Fox as told by Uncle Remus" began as a series in the Constitution *on July 20, 1879. Cousins goes on to say that Mark Twain "greatly admired Harris's 'Uncle Remus'" and then refers to correspondence between Harris and Twain.*

John M. Leddy
McLean, Virginia

Bumper Crop

Look at the bumper of the car in front of you: There may be a new language on the license plate.

State governments have capitalized on a good way to raise revenue: charge motorists for "vanity plates." For about $25 a year, you can get your initials on your plates, but many drivers are far more imaginative, preferring to put occupations or short messages.

"Individualized tags offer evidence of popular strategies for condensing language," writes Frank H. Nuessel Jr., of the University of Louisville, in the winter 1982 *American Speech* magazine, "thus providing peripheral psycholinguistic evidence for perceptual and processing techniques." Well! Dunno 'bout that, but the examples are fascinating:

Some like to delete vowels before those consonants—like *l, r,* and *n*—which can be a syllable in themselves. So, if you're a cheerleader, you may write CHRLEDR.

Others employ phonetic substitution, squeezing in a message by substituting a number for what would be several letters. A dentist may choose 2TH DR; a teacher, EDUC8R; a net-leaping athlete, 10SNE1.

Motor-vehicle bureaus are on the lookout for vanity-plate writers who try to get away with dirty words or ethnic slurs. That's out. But if you see a clergyman driving along with a plate that says OREMUS, he's suggesting, "Let us pray," in Latin, and that's fine. Other examples will be happily received and covered in this space. SAME 2U.

License plate lingo is as American as APL1416.

Andrew Mollison
Washington, D.C.

I have an acquaintance whose plate is DSFA. When asked what it stands for this wag retorts "doesn't stand for anything."

> *Peter J. Briggeman*
> *Duxbury, Massachusetts*

Among the license plates spotted by the Department of Anesthesiology at the University of Washington (a maximum of six letters or digits are allowed in the State of Washington) are GAS DOC and EPIDRL. There are at least two ingenious plays upon the owner's name. The car belonging to Dr. Raymond Fink bears the plate SPHINX, evoking the reply to the question as to whose car that is "Oh, that's Fink's."

My own license plate reads NA2SO4, the chemical formula (actually Na$_2$SO$_4$) for sodium sulfate, also known as Glauber Salts. While this has provoked queries for explanation from innumerable pedestrians and motorists including bus drivers and, on one occasion, from a police car, only a tiny minority of persons has ever heard of the substance. This is in contrast to the situation in Europe where Glauber Salts, while obsolete, is almost as familiar a name as that other product of similar actions, Epsom Salts (magnesium sulfate).

> *Dennis T. Glauber, M.D.*
> *Seattle, Washington*

Licenses to Steal

The language of automobile license plates was looked at in a recent piece, accompanied by a request for other examples of the ways that letters and numbers can be compressed to deliver messages.

Mary Ann Lauricella, associate commissioner for public affairs of the New York State Department of Motor Vehicles, has surveyed the 300,000 "special registration" plates issued to please motorists and raise money for state coffers. Among them:

The owner of a snazzy sports vehicle, evoking the green-eyed monster, asks: YRUNVS.

A man named Robert Vowell is driving around with AEIOU, which is consonant with his name.

In fond farewell, an old-song lover has registered OWLBCNU.

A man who drives a white Volkswagen Rabbit has HARVEY, and another owner with the same car has ML8ML8; a registrant with a blue Horizon has BEYOND.

In other areas of the country, plate watchers have spotted a polite XQZE ME; a truck labeled "McDonald's Farm" with a plate singing EIEIO; a borderline-licentious RU12; an optimist's IM42N8; a Mazda with a rotary engine plated HMMMMM; a speech teacher's LOQSHUN; a pastry chef's 3.1416; a family planner's 4ZNUFF; a flight attendant's T OR ME; a physician's SAY AH.

All is not vanity. The most apt spotting, passed along by Jonathan Weisgall of Washington, is not a compression but gives a lyrical quality to a license: POETIC.

My favorite license plate appears on a gorgeous, gleaming tan and brown Rolls-Royce which is parked in our building garage. It reads: 2ND CAR.

> Doris M. Weissler
> Floral Park, New York

Quiz your friends on this license plate I observed in Lotus Land: UP 7TH.
It took me forever until I realized which planet is seventh in line from the sun!

> Richard Kline
> Los Angeles, California

The best I have seen is C NMNE. I spotted it in Berkeley, on, as I remember, a VW bug.

> Nancy Schimmel
> Berkeley, California

Burnout

A snipe posted on a wood fence near my Washington office warns of "burnout," an occupational ailment complained about by frustrated or exhausted government employees.

A recent *New Yorker* cartoon by George Booth picks up this vogue locution, now being overused by white-collar workers who feel overused themselves. The

cartoon shows a frazzled and graying schoolteacher climbing out of a classroom window to end it all, with one pupil explaining to another: "Teacher burnout."

"To burn oneself out"—applied to people, in the manner of a fire dying for lack of fuel—entered the slang lexicon around the turn of the century; in 1917, poet T.S. Eliot bemoaned "the burnt-out ends of smoky days," followed two years later by Fanny Hurst's "a tired, a burned-out, an ashamed smile"; and in 1955, four-minute miler Roger Bannister was refusing to run long races because "I shall burn myself out."

British author Graham Greene, in his 1959 *Congo Journal*, wrote that a "burnt-out case" was a leprosy that had been cured only after the disease had run its destructive course; he turned that into a metaphor and popularized the term in the title of a 1961 novel about a man ravaged by his career.

In political hyperbole, the same image had been used earlier by Benjamin Disraeli to describe his rival, William Gladstone. "An exhausted volcano" was his term, picked up by Richard Nixon in 1972 as he swept from his administration the people he considered tired, lest "after a burst of creative activity, we become exhausted volcanoes."

In drug lingo, *burned out* is a sclerotic condition of the veins, reported the late David Maurer in his *Language of the Underworld,* present in longtime addicts who have been shooting "up and down the lines."

But when did this familiar word picture turn into a noun? Ralph De Sola's new *Crime Dictionary* lists "burnout" as the gutting of a house or apartment by fire, but that's not the metaphoric meaning we're talking about. In *Webster's Sports Dictionary*, published in 1976, a drag-racing definition appears for the word: "A brief spinning of the rear tires of a drag racer in a small puddle of water. . . . The friction created by the burnout heats up the tires and softens the rubber so that they will have increased traction during the race." That cannot be the source of the burnout we mean, either.

The use of the word to mean an affliction of the pooped, disgusted person loaded down with ennui and unable to function in his job was probably coined in 1974 by a New York psychiatrist, Dr. Herbert Freudenberger (good name for a psychiatrist). He is the co-author of a book, *Burn-Out: The High Cost of High Achievement,* and defined *burnout* as "the extinction of motivation or incentive, especially where one's devotion to a cause or relationship fails to produce the expected rewards."

In 1980 several other books pushed *burnout* in their titles, including *Teacher Burnout and What to Do About It* by Stephen Truch, which stimulated *Time* magazine into writing a sizable piece and caused Miss Thistlebottom to head out the window.

The locution is now undergoing linguistic burnout.

I read with interest and disbelief your article on "Burnout." I don't doubt that your citations are valid, but the use of the term is, I believe, strictly space-age.

When I read, many years ago, the English version of Willy Ley's Rockets, Missiles, and Space Travel *the term* Brennschluss *was untranslated. (It means "end of burn.") NASA, however, came somewhat after the domination of American rocketry by Germans, von Braun notwithstanding, and the common translation was "burnout." This usage was scientifically applied to the missile at the point where all of its fuel was burned up, and it would then complete its trajectory in a ballistic manner—i.e., in accordance with the laws of physics as applied to unpowered moving bodies in a gravitational field.*

I believe that you will find that the American usage of the term burnout *became common only after the American people fell in love with space and rocketry. This may have been before Sputnik—I read Ley's book in the early fifties—but certainly not before the last War, and not likely before the Eisenhower administration at the earliest. This is an instance in which the first citation is likely to be deceiving: just because one writer (or speaker) used the term once does not mean that he created a household expression. The common usage derives from NASA. I'd bet on it.*

Douglas McGarrett
Jamaica, New York

Butterfly Words

In a recent piece about Henry Kissinger's careful choice of the word *incautious*, I wrote: "I chastised the former Secretary. . . ."

Arthur Morgan, one of the more regular Lexicographic Irregulars, points out that in *The New York Times Everyday Reader's Dictionary of Misunderstood, Misused, Mispronounced Words* Laurence Urdang defines *chastise* as "to punish or discipline by beating."

"What you did to Mr. Kissinger," writes Mr. Morgan, "was to *rebuke* him; or, the choices are myriad, to *admonish, reprimand, correct, scold, rebuff, reprehend, remonstrate, condemn, reproach, castigate, censure, criticize,* or *chide* him. Or you gave him a good calling down. As I just gave you."

What I have really been given is an opportunity to stick my pin in a butterfly word, one that has left its caterpillar state to flutter its new wings in a changed meaning.

Yes, *chastise* has long meant "to punish, especially by beating." The verb comes from the Old French *chastier,* derived from the Latin *castigare,* which I break down to mean "to drive toward purity." (I'll get mail from Latin scholars on that, to which I reply, with Shakespeare in *Henry VI, Part Two,* "Away with him, away with him! He speaks Latin.") *Chastity,* a related word, is the state of being pure and virtuous, which as we all know sometimes comes from dire threats of punishment by doublestandardbearing fathers.

Castigare has given us the verbs *castigate,* "to criticize, harshly and publicly";

chasten, "to punish mildly, in order to improve" (as when David Stockman was "taken to the woodshed" by President Reagan); and the aforementioned *chastise,* which used to have as its primary meaning a kind of pistol-whipping from a stern Godfather.

Not anymore. Let's face it: The metaphoric, second meaning has taken over. Out of this nettle, "punishment," we pluck this flower, "chastisement." (I should stick with the butterfly from the caterpillar, lest I be admonished—reminded, by way of warning—that two metaphors confuse the reader, just as one swallow doesn't make a gulp.) In current use, the "beating" connotation has faded; when you are accusing a fellow of wife-beating, that's heavy stuff, and you don't use *chastise;* in the same way, *a rap on the knuckles* no longer means corporal punishment in the classroom, but has emerged as a general term for mild punishment, one step short of the too-mild *slap on the wrist.* The verb *rebuke* also is rooted in beating with a stick, but long ago changed to "scold sharply, reprimand."

Does all this mean that I was right to use *chastise* when I meant "C'mon, Henry, you stepped out of line there and you know it"?

Almost. *Chastise* has gained a gentle, jocular connotation that is more modern than *reprove,* less formal than *reprimand* or *censure,* not as severe as *condemn,* and not as stiff as *criticize.* But if I had the piece to do over, I would choose *chide,* a word from the Old English that now means "to scold with good humor, to teasingly correct." That's the meaning I had in mind.

Another butterfly word is scan. *The man in the street thinks that* scan *means to look at casually, to glance over. The dictionary says it means to study minutely.*

> Warren W. Smith, M.D.
> Columbus, Ohio

Surely, you knew these words would come to "chastise" you upon the wording of your second paragraph: "Arthur Morgan, one of the more *regular Lexicographic Irregulars, . . ."*

When did you join the maddening crowd that erases the superlative of the language to sacrifice trivial distinctions? Or, did you truly mean that Arthur Morgan is one of only two Lexicographic Irregulars?

People like you give English teachers like me a difficult oar to pull. The "rules" we must teach high school by cannot possibly keep up with The Times.

> Susan Kerr Weston
> Tampa, Florida

NOTE FROM W.S.: Thomas Hardy wrote about the *madding* crowd.

Calumniations

"Calumniate! Calumniate! Some of it will always stick," wrote Caron de Beaumarchais in 1775 in *The Barber of Seville*. In the vocabulary of calumny, where people are besmeared by the denunciations of their opponents, useful new adjectives are rare.

On a recent trip to London, I found that calumny is in fine form among the leaders of the Labor Party. Dennis Healey was using alliteration to calumniate Prime Minister Margaret Thatcher: "not just a female Franco but a Pétain in petticoats." Neil Kinnock used a heightened metaphor to describe the Employment Secretary as "a boil on top of a wart," and then went on to blast the government for *"stocking-footed* Fascism."

Stocking-footed is a vivid adjective. It means "sneaky"; in World War I, a noiseless projectile that hit without warning was called a stocking-footer. In America, President McKinley was known, among other things, as "the Stocking-Foot Orator," but I suspect this was because he was inclined to take his shoes off during long orations, and did not refer to sneakiness. The equivalent term to *stocking-footed* in the United States at the turn of the century was *pussyfooting,* after the sobriquet of revenue agent W. E. (Pussyfoot) Johnson, so named because of the stealthy, catlike way he approached revenue-evaders in the Indian Territory. (Imagine Pussyfoot Johnson telling his targets to *"x* box if refund.")

Barefaced is another lively adjective in active use in both the mother country and the United States, usually in modification—or intensification—of *liar.* Political calumniators on both sides of the ocean searching for a bombastic synonym for "shameless, brazen" have asked me: "Which is correct: *barefaced, baldfaced,* or *boldfaced* liar?"

All three have impeccable lineage and can be used interchangeably. *Barefaced* has been the most popular, with Joseph Addison in 1712 denouncing "bare-faced Irreligion" and Harriet Beecher Stowe in *Uncle Tom's Cabin* nailing "a barefaced lie." *Boldfaced* started out meaning "confident," with Shakespeare writing of "bold-fac't Victorie," but that adjective was used by printers to describe type like **this** and that form has been superseded by *baldfaced,* which began as "undisguised by a beard" and has since made it to "shameless."

My favorite calumniating adjective is *revolving,* a word with a spin on it. When asked why he called someone "a revolving S.O.B.," Harry Truman supposedly replied, "He's an S.O.B. any way you look at him."

Your focus on the phrase "barefaced liar" (my choice) puts me in mind of other words which, inevitably it seems, find each other.

a	precedent	is	always	dangerous
"	hoax	"	"	cruel
"	denial	"	"	flat
"	decision	"	"	momentous
an	apology	"	"	heartfelt
	magnetism	"	"	animal
and	speed	"	"	breakneck.

> *Seena Lowe*
> *Cos Cob, Connecticut*

Dear Bill:

Your reference to Beaumarchais and calumny is a common misconception. What he wrote in The Barber *(Act II Scene 8) was: "Calumny, my dear sir—you don't know what you're neglecting: I've seen the most worthy people nearly brought down by it." He then goes on for 10–12 lines to describe how a rumor once launched becomes "public knowledge."*

But the more famous remark that you quoted is a much older saying and anonymous. Bacon used it in one of his works, On the Dignity and Increase of Learning *(1623), book VIII, ch. II:* audaciter calumniare, semper aliquid haeret.

> *Jacques [Barzun]*
> *Charles Scribner's Sons,*
> *Publishers*
> *New York, New York*

Cap the Entitlement

As the debate on Social Security heats up, or hottens up, a shadowy cliché slouches toward Washington: He is Cap the Entitlement. No, this is not Caspar (Cap the Knife) Weinberger, whose recent travels changed his sobriquet to "Cap the Suitcase"; it is the amalgam of two opposing rallying words.

Cap began as a noun in the early 1970's, drawing on the image of "capping" an oil well. The earliest citation anybody I know can find is in the files of Merriam-Webster: "We have a somewhat ambiguous citation from *The Wall Street Journal* of May 22, 1972," reports Frederick Mish, editorial director, "applying the term to a 'rule' (perhaps a Federal regulation) which limited the extent to which certain companies could raise their prices at that time."

How well I remember those halcyon days at Camp David on the weekend of August 13–15, 1971, when a band of us gleefully solved the raging inflation rate (4.8 percent) by imposing wage and price controls and flummoxing the economy for nearly a decade. I vaguely recall economists Herbert Stein and Arnold Weber talking about "a cap on prices," which comes close to a citation, but close counts only in horseshoes: Merriam-Webster has the first, and the second and third:

"Our earliest clear-cut instance includes *cap* as a piece of jargon meaning the same thing as *ceiling*," writes Mr. Mish. It is from the July–August 1973 issue of The Mailhandler, a union publication; then comes Martin Mayer's use in his 1974 book *The Bankers*: "In 1972, when Chicago's Continental Illinois offered some big borrowers 'cap' loans (long-term credits with a fixed-interest ceiling). . . ."

As conservatism reared its cost-cutting head, *cap* turned into a verb: Politicians volunteered to cap everything from welfare to property taxes.

But then the capping ran into the other side's word: *entitlements*. Nobody, said the benefit-minded, was going to cap entitlements.

That word lay aborning in a law passed by the Congress in 1944: ". . . it should be clearly provided that entitlement to pay and allowances is not to be terminated on the actual date of death. . . ." For a couple of decades, the word lay low, like Br'er Rabbit.* In the late 1960's, as the Great Society came to an end, Congressional aides began using it to defend against attacks on "welfare cheats."

For many, the new word was a euphemism for *welfare*, which once was a euphemism for *relief*. Then, in the mid-1970's, it was adopted by middle-roaders who felt the pressure to do something about spending: "He indicated a belief that something had to be done to hold down the growth of programs," wrote *The New York Times* about Representative Brock Adams, "granting an automatic 'entitle-

*See pages 221–22.

ment' to eligible individuals. Among these are food stamps, welfare and health-care financing."

Cost cutters took up the cry of "doing something about entitlements." To this day, people who believe in the redistribution of wealth (or compassion for the truly needy) resist the notion that *entitlement* is merely a euphemism for *welfare*: "Entitlement includes both earned benefits and unearned benefits," says Ceil Frank at the Office of Family Assistance in Washington. "Social Security and veterans' benefits are earned benefits, and unearned benefits are what *welfare* refers to."

Liberals take care to divide funds transferred to people by the Government into *public assistance*—welfare—and *entitlements,* which carries the connotation "earned, deserved." Conservatives tend to lump the two together and demand that a *cap* be placed on it. Ross Baker, political-science professor at Rutgers, puckishly defined *entitlements* as "tenure for the underclass."

May I call your attention to the scholarly game played by British classicists of "capping" lines from ancient authors.

Old books by long-dead writers often referred to this academic exercise in erudite competition but I never heard such nor can I recall any specific reference. Doubtless you will soon hear from an ancient Englishman whose Dons so capped.

> Anita E. L. Seligson
> Great Neck, New York

Where I come from, the saying is: "Almost (or close) counts only in horseshoes and handgrenades."

> Kalman A. Staiman
> Brooklyn, New York

Carry Me Back

It began as a malapropism, but its vivid imagery is earning the phrase a place in bureaucratic lingo.

Hand-carry is a term anybody who was in the Army remembers; it meant "Don't let this get stuck in the interoffice mail." When I worked in the White House, a special category of high-speed interoffice communication was marked with a red patch on the envelope, insuring delays of up to two weeks, and causing me to hand-carry everything I hand-wrote.

A synonym for *hand-carry* was *walk it over* or *walk it through,* as if through a shellpitted no man's land of undelivered parcels. By a process of consistent malapropping, these synonyms were merged into *hand-walk*.

Gladwin Hill, of *The New York Times* in Los Angeles, has established a hand-walkers' club. "With my own ears," he writes, "I heard City Councilwoman Joy Picus today declaring that she was going to expedite a state subsidy application by 'handwalking' it through the bureaucratic maze."

What a well-exercised figure of speech: I can see myself hand-walking a message to Jane Fonda, the blood rushing to my head.

Hand-walking Upvalue

Would-be usage dictators must not pussyfoot; the people hunger for certainty. That is why you see few shades of gray in my harangues about neologisms (pronounced "knee-OL-o-gism"; if you pronounce it "neo-LOW-gism," get off this page). With satisfying certitude—which is the certainty derived from blind faith, not necessarily based on conclusive evidence—a new word is either blessed herein for filling a need or damned for befuzzing the lingo.

Hand-walk is an example. That seemingly silly combination of *hand-carry* and *walk through* was derided here with great glee a few weeks ago. Under such withering ridicule, how can such a nonce word make it through to dictionary status?

Unfortunately, I might have been premature in my condemnation of *hand-walk* as a malapropism. "The expression has been used for years in stables," writes Elaine Sedito of Brookfield Center, Connecticut. "When a horse must be exercised, but for some reason shouldn't be ridden, it is *hand-walked*, or led around at a walk."

Having pulled up lame at that one, and puzzled about why *handblown* is used to describe glass blown by mouth, I was more cautious on the next lap. The offensive neologism: up-value. In a *New York Times* editorial about the ruckus between France and Germany on exchange rates—with France willing only to devalue the franc a fraction—the writer observed that "Mr. Mitterrand wanted the Germans to up-value the mark."

William A. Donlon of New York came running to me to set up a nontariff barrier to this sort of word. "Are you kidding me, *'up-value'*! I have heard advertising types talk about *upscale*, and I know how one can *upgrade* a Chevrolet Citation by buying a new Mercedes diesel. But I don't know how to *up-value* a currency."

I was about to join in—why coin a new word when *revalue* is the widely accepted term?—but my experience with *hand-walk* stayed my hand. I wrote to the 10th floor of *The Times*, where faceless and nameless editorialists turn out the newspaper's opinions ("Dear 10th Floor"), and received this vigorous defense from

Richard E. Mooney, whose choice to draft the reply in no way may be taken to suggest that he was the one who wrote the editorial.

"When a country reduces the value of its currency," writes Mr. Mooney, "it's called a *devaluation*—perfectly clear. When it raises the value, the financial lingo is *revaluation*—not clear at all. To say that the deutsche mark was *revalued* is really only saying its value was changed, as *reorganized* means that the organization was changed. Was it up or down?

"To help the reader understand," says Mr. Mooney, dropping all pretense to anonymity, "I use *up-value*. Financial experts may be offended that I don't use their jargon, but at least they understand what I'm saying. The 99 percent of our readers who don't speak Financial might not know that *revalue* means 'up'; *up-value* makes it clear."

The defense not only rests, but stretches out and takes a long snooze. My verdict on this coinage: not fuzzy. Unlike *upcoming,* which could mean "forthcoming" or "up-and-coming" (and, as my dentist says, should be avoided like the plaque), *upvalue* contributes to clarity by providing a parallel construction. As you see, I have just removed its hyphen, a defloration that adds legitimacy.

One tip to neologues (new word for neologists), however: When coining a new word, throw a handful of quotation marks around it, or use italics, or make some proud remark about minting a term on purpose. Even an arch "as it were" helps the reader and saves usage dictators from looking foolish.

Enjoyed your valuable discussion of upvalue in a recent column, but wish you had mentioned that other uppity word used by economists and financial types these recession-rebounding days: uptick.

The advent of uptick in Financial speak ostensibly means we will be having some downticks ere long when the economy reverses direction. No doubt we are in for some sideticks, too, as our functioning mechanism eventually slows.

> *Jack Pope*
> *San Francisco, California*

Don't you think the German language should be given some credit (or blame) for the coining of upvalue, especially since the German currency was involved? Aufwerten *has long been the antonym of* abwerten.

> *Harry Zohn*
> *Professor of German*
> *Brandeis University*
> *Waltham, Massachusetts*

You do not upgrade a Chevrolet Citation by buying a Mercedes diesel. You've upgraded your choice of car, but the only way to upgrade a Citation is by buying the light-and-trim package, power door locks, sunroof, etc.

> *Guy Henle*
> *Scarsdale, New York*

Dear Bill,
    Did your mind skip, and did you mean upstage *rather than* upgrade*? You might upgrade the owner of the Chevrolet by having him buy the Mercedes, but hardly the Chevrolet itself. However, the Mercedes could then upstage the Chevrolet. One tried to do that to me once but the diesel is slow to start.*

> *F. G. Cassidy*
> *Director-Editor,* DARE
> *Madison, Wisconsin*

Caught Red-Handed

Tass, the Soviet news agency, is fast on accusations and slow on double meanings in English. When Moscow expelled an American diplomat recently, Tass announced that the embassy attaché had been "caught red-handed during a spy action in Moscow."

As is well known, Communists, not capitalists, are the ones to be caught *red-handed*; red has been the color of radicalism since a red flag was used in France's 1789 revolution. That flag-waving began the linkage of the political symbolism of the color red to the metaphor *red-handed*—caught in the act of committing a crime, with the blood still on the perpetrator's hands.

An even more direct tie between *red* (the color of radicalism) and *red-handed* (caught in the bloody act) was made in Paris during the fierce insurrection of 1848, when red-capped *républicains rouges* demonstrators waved hands freshly dipped in their victims' blood. Soon afterward, German revolutionaries called themselves *rote Republikaner*, and the pattern spread worldwide.

Be careful of that word *red*; when President Harry S Truman unsuspectingly adopted a reporter's use of the phrase *red herring* to denigrate an investigation, he was clobbered by the double meaning.

What phrase should Communists use to charge capitalists with being apprehended in the act—without stumbling into the double meaning of *red*, with its historic Communist connotations? To give Tass's Reds a hand, I venture this suggestion: *in flagrante delicto*, possibly based on the crime of arson, meaning "while the crime is blazing." Although it has become associated with adultery cases, the phrase has a nice, erudite ring and cannot backfire.

Although *red-handed* was a gaffe, Tass's selection of another word in another context was a triumph. In rejecting the reasoning behind President Reagan's latest arms-reduction proposal, the Soviet news agency reported that West German Chancellor Helmut Kohl had been warned that if the United States went ahead with its planned deployment of missiles, East and West Germany would be looking at each other through "a *palisade* of rockets."

That caused some head-scratching in New Jersey, where the Palisades are the cliffs on the west bank of the Hudson River, as well as in a community on the West Coast of the United States known to Ronald Reagan as Pacific Palisades. In my youth, "Wanna go tuduh Palisades?" was a query about a visit to the amusement park in Joisey.

In the plural, *palisades* does mean "a line of cliffs," especially along a river, looking unscalable and forbidding. In the singular, a *palisade* is a sharply pointed stake set in the ground with other palisades to form a mean-looking, spiky fence. It comes from the Latin *palus*, a stake, which is also the root of *impaled*, always an uncomfortable position. Before the happy invention of barbed wire, a line of palisades was the most fearsome fixed defense a force of infantry could face.

"A palisade of rockets" is a fresh use of the old word, bringing to mind a threatening line of sharp stakes, but in this case the stakes are rockets. A fusillade of applause to Tass; *palisade* makes up for *red-handed*.

In a related development (a television newscaster's phrase that has replaced "meanwhile," and is televese for "I might as well stick this in here; it's too weak to rate an item on its own"), Westerners have adopted a famous Soviet weasel phrase to use in the arms-control debate. Glance upward: The second paragraph of this article begins with *As is well known*; in Russian, it is *kak vsem izvestno*, and it does not really mean "as is well known" at all. Usually tossed in before some outrageous lie about "ruling circles," it means: "This is our position, and it's too bad if you don't agree because this is the way we see the truth." The phrase is useful to Soviet spokesmen in diplomatic discourse because it also says: "We are not saying anything new, so this is not to be disputed."

At the soporific summit called Williamsburg, the Western industrial nations (a grouping that includes Japan, which is of the West but not in the West; a better phrase for that group would be welcomed) issued a statement on arms control that employed that old Soviet trick. If an agreement could be reached with the Russians, went the seven-nation statement, missile deployment would depend on that agreement; "it is well known that should this not occur, the countries concerned will proceed with the planned deployment. . . ."

Why do you suppose the phrase *it is well known that* was inserted before the forthright "should this not occur"? One, for the same reason that a diplomat on a panel show says, "As I have said before": It is a way of insisting, "This is not to be taken as news. This is not provocative in any way. This is dull, dull, dull, strictly old stuff, boilerplate really; I don't even know why I mention it. Still. . . ."

The second meaning of *it is well known* is: "We didn't agree to anything special in this. Nobody caved in, nobody carried the day. President Mitterrand's arm always looks a little twisted."

And in a development related to *that,* the French President's spokesman complained to reporters on one day that certain American pundits had made Mr. Mitterrand's ideas on monetary alignments seem too rigid; on the next day of the Williamsburg conference, the same spokesman complained that Mr. Mitterrand's ideas were being interpreted as too conciliatory.

Confused journalists wondered if a culinary metaphor might be useful in portraying the French President's position: rare, medium, well-done? The spokesman rejected that and came up with the sort of French-English amalgam that the Socialist Culture Ministry has been inveighing against: *cool mais musclé.* "Cool but tough." (Caught him red-handed.)

You state that the red flag of revolution was first used by the French revolutionaries, but in fact it was the standard of Americans in the first year of the War of Independence, 1775.

As an author researching that time period for several novels, I came across this information in an original diary written by a participant in the campaign to conquer Canada in 1775–76. It was this red flag that led the troops into battle, and saw the early victories and defeats, including the first invasion of foreign territory by troops of the Army of the United Colonies.

Oliver Payne
Canaan, New York

While kak vsem izvestno *is grammatically correct, it is almost never used in that form; the proper phrase is simply* kak izvestno—*as is well known to any reader of* Pravda *and* Izvestia.

As for your political interpretation of the phrase's usage by Soviet writers, it is at least an exaggeration to say it is "usually tossed in before some outrageous lie." Although this idea would nicely fit in with your concept of Soviet disinformation, kak izvestno is usually reserved for the less debatable statements, although there are exceptions.

Finally, on your chiding Tass for inappropriate use of red-handed: in view of your lumping together Communists as radicals, perhaps you should re-examine the definition of radicalism. Lenin was a radical; Yuri Andropov is by no means a radical. If anyone is a radical in the Soviet Union today, it is the handful of dissidents who call for reform. The Politburo (and Tass, too), in its context, is as conservative as Ronald Reagan.

Steven Shabad
New York, New York

So many people use the phrase in flagrante delicto *I no longer get excited at their mistake; but they say it* en passant, *whereas you are actively encouraging others to say the wrong thing.*

There is no preposition: flagrante delicto *(Justinian's law code uses the form* flagranti*)* is an ablative absolute construction, so that the "while" of your correct translation "while the crime is blazing" is implicit in the participle flagrante.

Similarly, the phrase absent malice, *about which you wrote some time ago, quite clearly (to a classicist) derives from an original Latin ablative absolute,* absente malatiā, *the long a being marked to distinguish it from the short a of the nominative. (This last sentence contains what grammarians of English call a nominative absolute, on the analogy with the Latin ablative and the Greek genitive absolutes.)*

David Sider
Flushing, New York

You missed a nice opportunity to point out a double deception in the Tass report of the warning to Chancellor Kohl that if . . . East and West Germany would be looking at each other through "a palisade *of rockets."*

The first deception is connected with the imprecise meaning of the little word a. It doesn't really say how many such palisades there are. By focusing on "a palisade" that would exist if a hypothetical event occurred, Tass diverts attention from the fact that in that event there would then be two palisades, ours and theirs, because theirs is already there, in East Germany.

The second deception is connected with the word palisade. You're quite right, *they really are fresh to use this word, whose previous meanings have all related to stationary objects, to designate things that are designed to fly off, at the discretion of their owner, and cause death and destruction at a distance. Clearly, Tass has an undisputable claim to the inventorship of the first-strike picket-fence.*

Otto Kauder
New York, New York

In discussing a palisade, you state that being impaled is always an uncomfortable position. Permit me to assure you that the impaling of genitalia by genitalia is frequently more than comfortable—it's ecstatic.

Jan R. Harrington
New York, New York

C.C.

A young editorial writer came into the office of Mike Gordon, deputy editorial-page editor of *The Los Angeles Herald Examiner*. She had a memo in hand from another editor and wanted to know what the "cc" stood for at the bottom of the page.

"Carbon copy," replied Mr. Gordon matter-of-factly. Then he realized the import of the question. "It was, of course, a Xerox copy—or, more likely, a cheaper generic substitute. How *are* carbon-paper sales these days?"

When will initialese catch up with the phrase initialed? If you want to send a copy and let the person to whom you are writing know about the copy, drop "cc"; substitute "copy to"—unless you are still using carbon paper (which some people still do), or unless you are dealing in cubic centimeters. If you like, stick with the old cc—but recognize the fact that you are dealing with vestigial vocabulary.

Character Letters

Certain letters of the alphabet have been developing characters of their own.

K has a reputation for kookiness. As Neil Simon pointed out in *The Sunshine Boys*, *K* is a funny sound; *cookie* is a funny word. Although the Ku Klux Klan gave *K* a sinister connotation for a while, and the trade name "Kodak" may have been conceived with futurism in mind, in recent years the herky-jerky use of *K* pioneered by the many Kit Kat Klubs has burgeoned.

"Why have so many businesses in Florida," writes Claire Martin of *The St. Petersburg Times*, "chosen to eliminate the hard *C* and *Q* from the alphabet when spelling their names?" Examples: *Kash 'n' Karry* supermarket, *Krispy Kreme* doughnuts (I do not spell it "donuts"), *Koin Kleen* laundry, which washes clothes and not coins, and *Kwik Kopy* duplicating center. "Some of us theorize that businesses had some reason to believe that *K*'s could attract more customers than *C*'s could."

Does the zany kwality of *K* kollect kustomers? Or has the letter emerged as a coolly self-mocking alliteration that appeals to a new generation of Kit Kat Klubbers? A recent issue of the newsletter *The Underground Grammarian* draws attention to a release from the University of Arizona's College of Education offering a "Kollege Kredit Kourse . . . limited to those who have taken Personhood Development."

Meanwhile, the letter *M* is muscling its masculine way in the language of category-namers: the M-1 rifle and its successor the M-16; the M-60 tank; the brawny M.P.'s. Missile terminology is riddled with *M*'s: the Minuteman, Midgetman, and MX. In Britain, there's M.I.-5, the mountainous molehill that Ian Fleming had headed by a man coded "M." (The letter was the title of a scary movie of the 1930's starring Peter Lorre.)

"The Federal Reserve has an M-1, M-2 and M-3, and while these measurements of the money supply are not in themselves weapons," says one of my journalistic colleagues, "movements within them can provoke murderous responses on the part of the Fed."

Dear Bill:

Your piece on the kraze for k *seemed to suggest that this is a new vogue on the slang scene. I think that it is basically a nostalgic revival of an old American fad.*

The very first issue (October 1925) of American Speech *featured an article by Louise Pound titled "The Kraze for 'K,'" in which she described a widespread alliterative vogue in the use of* k, *especially in advertisements. "All in all," she wrote, "there is no mistaking the kall of 'k' over our kountry, our kurious kontemporary kraving for it, and its konspicuous [sic] use in the klever koinages of kommerce."*

However, lest you think that the graphomania for k *in the 1920's was due to the popularity of* Krazy Kat *and the notoriety of the Ku Klux Klan, in 1964 Allen Walker Read unearthed evidence showing that the kraze for* k *was already rife a hundred years earlier. In the presidential campaign of 1828 wags joked about spelling* Congress *with a* K, *a year later Andrew Jackson's intimate advisers were referred to as the "Kitchen Kabinet," and in 1839 Henry Clay was described in a newspaper as "Mr. Klay, member of Kongress from Kentucky." According to Professor Read, it was this particular kraze for* k *that set the stage for the ultimate popularization of O.K., which of course stood originally for "Oll Korrect."*

> *Sol [Steinmetz]*
> *Clarence L. Barnhart, Inc.*
> *Bronxville, New York*

The first supermarket in America was devised by Michael J. Cullen. And wouldn't you know it: he misspelled his own (proud?) family name in favor of a K.

> *Dick Baker*
> America Illustrated *(USIA)*
> *Washington, D.C.*

A practical reason for the use of k's *rather than* c's *or* q's *lies in the vagaries of the law of unfair competition. If you use the ordinary words "Quick Copy" for your copy center, rather than the non-words "Kwik Kopy," and some lout opens a "Quick Copy" around the corner, you can't sue him for unfair competition. The words, part of the common language, cannot be appropriated for your business use. However, if they are spelled with a* k *instead of a* c *or a* q, *they can be. Hence the "mushrooming" of* k *and* k.

> *George Nicolau*
> *New York, New York*

The overuse of the letter k *in those fatuous advertisements you cite, i.e., Kwik Kopy, occurs, in my view, because of the supposed novelty of the phrase, as you suggest,* but perhaps for other reasons too. One, I suspect, is the unambiguity of the letter. The letter c is often pronounced as an s, as in center, and the letter q insists upon being followed by the u in English. However, k is always pronounced the same way.

Possibly another reason is the very configuration of the letter, which is more eye-catching than the three-quarter circle described by the c. And in advertising, attention-getting is more important than proper spelling.

Owen McNamara
Associate Professor of English
Herkimer County Community
College
Herkimer, New York

I was once married to an M-man. M was the first letter of his last name, and although socially acceptable perhaps, his M-for-Macho behavior and attitude did influence our marriage.

I am now married to a W-man. His last name begins with a W, which is the reversal of M. His personality follows suit, as he is not warlike in personal relationships. So, you can understand why your article "spoke to me," perhaps on a deeper level.

Virginia Watson II
West Orange, Texas

Chickening In

"If you want a fresher chicken," goes an advertisement from Holly Farms, "you'll have to grow your own."

"If you grew chickens," counters Perdue Farms, "they'd be golden yellow, too."

What's this about *growing* chickens? I always thought you *raised* chickens, *bred* horses, and *cultured* bacteria, but reserved *growing* for vegetables.

"Our nutritionists and geneticists prefer *raise*," admits Chris Whaley, who scratches around for a living at Perdue, "but our housing people prefer *grow*. We contract people to raise our chickens for us after we have hatched the eggs and the chickens are a couple of days old; we ship them to these people, who own their own farms, and they are called *growers.*"

"In the chicken industry," peeps William Rusch, high in the Holly Farms pecking order, "we generally speak of *growing* chickens."

For an outside opinion, let us turn to the elder statesman of usage, Jacques Barzun: "To *grow* a chicken is out of the ordinary and not proper," he says, refusing to cluck sympathetically. "You grow trees and lima beans. *You let the chickens grow for themselves.*" He added the classic differentiation in the viability game: "You *raise* cattle, *rear* children and *grow* things in your garden. Let's keep them separate."

That's an admirably clear position, but I have long ago caved in on the *raise-rear* issue. *Raise,* in the sense of *bringing up* children, has a two-century lineage, and

was especially fostered in Canada: Thomas Haliburton, in *The Clockmaker* in 1837, had a Canadian character say, "I don't know as ever I felt so ugly afore since I was raised."

There is an essential insult, however, in applying *grow* to animals; it is as if to say they were no different from a crop of alfalfa. Certainly there is precedent in this use—cattle growers abound, and I'm sure many of them treat their herds with devotion and re-

spect—but the idea smacks of presumption. Usage is made by foils like me, but only God can grow a chicken.

It's got so you can't say anything without insulting someone or something. In your remarks on the use of grow, *you insult alfalfa. In spite of Mr. Barzun's comment about letting chickens grow, you don't let chickens grow. You have to feed them at least, and a chicken grower will tell you he has to do a lot more than that. But trees, lima beans, and alfalfa, to use your examples, make their own food and their own*

vitamins, and that's more than you or I or the chickens can do. Alfalfa, with its root nodules, even helps fertilize itself. As far as biochemical abilities go, any green plant is so far ahead of any animal that a comparison between alfalfa and a chicken is favorable to the chicken, not the other way around. I'll be willing to give myself equal status with an alfalfa crop when I can get a nourishing breakfast by taking a drink of water and lying in the sun. It's the plants, not the chickens, that grow themselves. As far as usage goes, it seems to me that the best expression is the one that most accurately carries a clearly understandable meaning. If I should ever be so unfortunate as to have to keep chickens, I shall grow them.

Donald D. Ritchie,
Professor Emeritus, Department
 of Biological Sciences
Barnard College
New York, New York

On your next occasion addressing growers *and* raisers, *I wish you would also discuss the expression* raisin-growers. *Admittedly,* raisin-grape-growers *is an awkward alternative.* Raisin producers *might be an acceptable compromise. But surely, children should not be raised to believe that raisins grow on vines.*

Sandy Small
Mountainside, New Jersey

You found the use of "to grow" replacing "to raise" bothersome. I find even more unpleasant the use of "to harvest" when referring to deer, cattle or fish, replacing "to slaughter" or "to kill."

   On at least four or five occasions in the recent past, I have seen or heard of the "harvesting" of living creatures. Is this a sop to our delicate sensibilities, or do "sportsmen" feel that nobody will really mind unsportsmanlike activities if they are thought of in terms of a harvest?

   It probably makes little difference to the creatures, but it sure irks me!

Doreen Valyear
Kenmore, New York

Cold War

As one often denounced as an "unreconstructed cold warrior," I enjoy reconstructing the origin of the most powerful diplomatic coinage of the past generation.

Herbert Bayard Swope coined the expression *cold war* in 1946, or so readers of my political dictionary were led to believe. Mr. Swope was a Pulitzer prize-winning reporter, editor, and publicist who late in life enjoyed drafting speeches for his friend Bernard Baruch.

"The first time I ever heard the expression 'cold war,' " Baruch wrote to Swope in 1949, undoubtedly at Swope's request, "was when you first said it some time about June 1946. We decided not to use it at that time. I first used the phrase in April 1947 . . . immediately afterward, it was very much commented on."

One of the commentators at the time was Walter Lippmann, and Swope worried that the pundit who popularized his phrase would be credited with the coinage. After Lippmann mentioned to Swope that he recalled a French phrase, *la guerre froide*, spoken in the 1930's, Swope wrote him sharply: "The first time the idea of the cold war came to me was probably in '39 or '40, when America was talking about a 'shooting war.' To me, 'shooting war' was like saying a death murder—rather tautologous, verbose and redundant. I thought the proper opposite of the so-called hot war was cold war, and I used that adjective in some letters I wrote, before our war. . . . I've always believed that I happened to be the first to use the phrase."

Thus, Swope arranged for credit from Baruch, who first spoke the phrase, and suppressed a claim for credit by Lippmann, who disseminated the phrase widely. That's how to lock your place in history.

Now comes Joseph Siracusa, a reader in American history at the University of Queensland in St. Lucia, Australia. "Greetings from the Antipodes," he writes, in the first greetings this department has ever received from that place. "I believe I have discovered the earliest known use of the phrase 'cold war.' "

His citation is from the German newspaper *Neue Zeit* in 1893. Social Democrat Eduard Bernstein, complaining about the arms race in Europe, wrote: "This continued arming, compelling the others to keep up with Germany, is itself a kind of warfare. I do not know whether this expression has been used previously, but one could say it is a cold war (*ein kalter Kreig*). There is no shooting, but there is bleeding."

"I should like to share this information with your readers," writes Dr. Siracusa, "and ask them if they can go one better." To date, we have Swope's first use in English in 1946, and Bernstein's first use in German in 1893. If any unreconstructed cold warrior can find an earlier use in any language, the discovery will stir phrase buffs from Times Square to Queensland.

Finally, the source of the adjective *unreconstructed.* In 1867, Congress passed the Reconstruction Acts, reorganizing the governments of states that had seceded from the Union. Those former rebels who refused to reconcile themselves to the federal victory were called "unreconstructed," and the word has retained that connotation of a refusal to recognize the outcome of a war. Hence, "unreconstructed cold warrior."

Bitte, *you should your Cherman dictionary get out before you spell* dot Wort. *You do very well on* kalt *but not so hot on* Krieg.

Arthur W. Hoffman
Syracuse, New York

It's not ein kalter Kreig, *but* ein kalter Krieg. *Unlike the notoriously erratic English orthography, German spelling is so phonetic and so logical that* ei *is always pronounced "eye" and* ie *invariably as in "eel." I was just about to suggest* Kliegkrieg *as a mnemonic device for remembering the correct spelling (my coinage for the jockeying for position, at newsworthy events, by people with movie cameras) when I discovered that some dictionaries sanction both* klieg *and* kleig. *Since klieg lights were named for the German-American inventors John and Anton Kliegl, this permissiveness only reflects American confusion about a very simple point.*

This confusion, of course, may well be exacerbated by the fact that many a Lied *(song) reflects* Leid *(sorrow) and that a* Liebeslied, *or love song, often is an expression of* Liebesleid. *(A* Leibeslied, *it may be argued, would be a Walt Whitman hymn to the "body electric," and* Leibesleid *could well refer to aches and pains.) But I won't give up on* Krieg, *and even though I generally bristle at missing or misplaced umlauts, I suggest that the present conflict between Burger King and McDonald's, though it has not yet precipitated a civil war, be termed a* Burgerkrieg.

Harry Zohn
Professor of German
Brandeis University
Waltham, Massachusetts

In regard to your interesting discourse on the notion and the phrase of cold war, *allow me to contribute the following, from my* Politics and Culture in International History *(Princeton Univ. Press, 1960), n. 69, p. 426:*

> *A Thirteenth century Spanish writer, Don Juan Manuel, applied the term* guerra fria *to the situation that prevailed in his native land during the coexistence of Islam and*

> *Christendom. See Luis Garcia Arias,* El concepto de
> guerra y la denominada "guerra fria," *(1956) reviewed in*
> Annuaire Français de Droit International, *1956, p. 925.*

I had discussed the cold war *in my book under the chapter heading "Mediterranean Elites," noting in particular that voluntary and involuntary intellectual encounters between Christians, Jews, and Muslims occurred during the Middle Ages in a world environment not unlike the present one. They took place then, as they do now, in an uneasy state of "no-peace, no-war": "Indeed, the very term 'cold war,' commonly applied today to the chronic tension between communists and liberals, was used first in medieval Spain in order to denote the conflict between Muslims and Christians." (p. 69)*

> *Adda B. Bozeman*
> *Bronxville, New York*

Kreig *has now joined the company of* Kleig, Neilsen, Zeigler, *Maya Angelou's* Freida, *the pseudo-learned* zweiback, *and* seige. *The last of these has, of course, nothing to do with the wished-for outcome of a hot war* (Sieg), *but is simply the French* siège *which must have been deemed handier for this sitdown operation than a potential Germanically based* beleaguerment. *("Lift the siege!" ought to be part of little boys' toilet training in modern France, who subsequently might have more fun with their history books than I did in Germany, where the corresponding term* entsetzen *has the nonmilitary meaning of "horrify" ["greatly upset," to make the semantic connection]). Those with French in their background are therefore not likely to misspell* siege. *But the old "i before e" rule can be made to fit all the items herein,* not, *however,* seize, *which, as the hoped-for outcome of a siege, might be responsible for its prevalent misspelling. Incidentally,* Webster 4 *will have to recognize the prevailing pronunciation with /žh/ instead of /j/, which* Webster 3 *does recognize as an alternative for* liege, *which may have influenced* siege.

> *Louis Marck*
> *New York, New York*

War on Kreig

I wrote that the first use of "cold war" may have been in German, *"ein kalter Kreig."* As the press secretaries say, I misspelled myself. *"Kreig,"* writes Louis Marck of New York City, deliberately spelling the word wrong, "has now joined the company of *Kleig, Neilsen, Zeigler,* Maya Angelou's *Freida,* the pseudo-learned *zweiback,* and *seige."* All wrong.

The spelling of German, unlike English, marches along with logic and consistency. *Ei* is always pronounced *eye,* and *ie* is always pronounced *ee,* as in *eek!* Harry Zohn, professor of German at Brandeis (*BRAND-eyes*) University, has coined a word —*Kliegkrieg*—to denote the jockeying for position by cameramen at news events. A good word, which can also be used as a mnemonic for the spelling and pronunciation of German words.

Professor Zohn was distressed to learn that some dictionaries tolerate the spelling of klieg lights as *kleig,* although the pronunciation is always *kleeg.* "Since klieg lights were named for the German-American inventors John and Anton Kliegl," he writes, "this permissiveness only reflects American confusion about a very simple point." The point is, in pronouncing German, it's *eye* before *ee* in pronouncing the sound of *ee,* and it's *ee* before *eye* in pronouncing *eye,* spelled *ei.*

Got that? *Ein halter Krieg* starts with *Eye-n* and ends with *eeg. Ja wohl.*

Please allow me to offer German Lesson #2: Ja—*and then again, maybe* wohl.

To begin, a simple "yes" in English is usually enough to convey assent. "Yes, yes" is already tinged with impatience, "yes, indeed" sounds almost too enthusiastic, and the more vernacular "yessir" often falls just short of obsequiousness.

By comparison, the plain German ja *tends to be somewhat less affirmative. Oh, it does mean "yes," or "I understand," in literal translation. Behind such a* ja, *however, there often lurks an unspoken "but." To be sure, these doubts can be banished through the addition of other affirmative words, such as the German equivalents of "naturally," "certainly," "clearly," etc., but these do rather lend an air of self-importance and officiousness to the initial* ja.

There remains only the unequivocal jawohl. *It is uncompromising, a rousing combination of assent, full understanding, and enthusiasm. It is so certain of its duty and impact that it is always written as one word.* Jawohl *leaves no doubts, brooks no arguments, defies all opposition. If* jawohl *is yin, it is, alas, yangless*—nein *always stands alone, no matter how irrevocably negative it may have to be. Perhaps Professor Zohn of "Brand-eyes" University can explain this discrepancy?*

> *Pamela Jones*
> *Philmont, New York*

E-i, e-i, *oh my!—what about Neiman-Marcus?*

> *Rosemarie Williamson*
> *Basking Ridge, New Jersey*

I do not know how the late Justice pronounced his family name, but as a recent graduate of Brandeis University, I can tell you that the current pronunciation is not "BRAND-eyes." It is "BRAN-dice."

James Marill
Glen Rock, New Jersey

Collective of Greeks

During an extended grovel after getting a Greek derivation wrong, I complained about hearing from a large group of Greek scholars, wondering in passing what the best collective noun for them would be.

A *host* of Greek scholars? No; that comes from the Latin, and if I were grouping Latin lovers, I would have a *forum* of them. Esther Lafair of Philadelphia suggests a *phalanx* of Greeks; J. V. Costa and Graeme McLean of New York prefer an *attic* of them; Saul Rosen of Bethesda, Maryland, likes *chorus* and Marvin Jaffe of Huntingdon Valley, Pennsylvania, *plethora.*

David Sider, of the Department of Classical Languages at Queens College in Flushing, New York, comes up with an unkind cut: He suggests a *sounder* of scholars. Since the origin of that seemed more Teutonic than Greek, it sent me to an unabridged dictionary. Obsolete, but perhaps pertinent: A *sounder* is a collection of boars.

Your column on collective nouns brings to mind the account of a group of professors of English emerging from a conference where the collective noun had been discussed. Just then a group of ladies-of-the-evening wiggled by.

"What noun would you ascribe to them?" asked one of the professors.

"A jam of tarts," suggested a colleague.

"How about a flourish of strumpets?" offered a second.

"You might call them an essay of trollops," contributed a third.

They seemed to have exhausted the possibilities when a fourth concluded with "an anthology of pros."

Edna Branower
New York, New York

I believe the term is singular of boars—and sounder of swine (when one hunts them —otherwise herd).

The reference is An Exaltation of Larks, *second edition, by James Lipton, Penguin Books. Lipton also gives a brow of scholars, a pallor of night students, and a fortitude of graduate students.*

John H. Monaghan
Hampden, Massachusetts

Any Greek scholar would know that a collective of Greek scholars is comprised of Hellenists. However, if a collective of Latin scholars is a forum, then a collective of Greek scholars is an agora.

Christos G. Tzelios
Long Island City, New York

Comma Killers

"*Red ripe tomatoes . . . ,*" reads the label on the ketchup bottle.

The comma is under attack. This most flexible of punctuation marks, rivaled only by the period in frequency of use, was invented to separate words or thoughts within a sentence that could not stand as sentences by themselves. (If you want to separate a dependent clause from the main part of the sentence, use a comma. Sometimes you have two connected thoughts that can stand by themselves; in that case, use a semicolon.)

We are into a run of deliberate runnings-on. The most obvious function of a comma (from the Latin "to cut off") is to separate items in a list: *Kilgour, French and Stanbury.* The use of a comma after the word *French* is optional. (I've been consulting too many grammar texts; change that last sentence to read, "You can use a comma after *French* if you like.") The purpose of the comma in that case is to say, "I mean that guy, and that guy, and that guy." Without a comma, *Kilgour French* could be one tailor.

"Where have all the commas gone?" writes Gilbert Cranberg, former editorial writer of *The Des Moines Register.* "Dow Jones, Merrill Lynch, Doyle Dane Bernbach. Commas are free. Why don't they use them?"

Charles Dow and Edward Jones were individual men. Their firm was founded in 1882 as "Dow, Jones & Company." About 1950, the comma disappeared. "The comma was dropped from *Dow, Jones,*" says Lloyd Wendt, who wrote *The Wall Street Journal: The Story of Dow Jones and the Nation's Business Newspaper,* "because it was felt that it detracted from the name and was unnecessary. *Dow Jones* has a one-name quality. . . ."

That response is strictly from Hog, Wash & Company. The truth, I suspect, is that the admen were disposed to dehumanize poor old Dow and Jones. (They went even further at Sears, Roebuck—they obliterated the memory of Alvah Roebuck, relegating his memory to the name for "Western wear.") The comma took up time, space, money. *Dow Jones* is snappier and more modern-looking than the old, plodding, accurate *Dow, Jones.*

Can you imagine how Charles Dow feels about being remembered in history as the first name of Edward Jones? That's what comes from playing the averages.

The late William Bernbach, one of the founders of Doyle Dane Bernbach, used to answer the comma question with a quip: "We didn't want anything, not even punctuation, to come between us."

Over at Merrill Lynch & Company Inc., holding company for the brokerage firm of Merrill Lynch, Pierce, Fenner and Smith, there is this explanation of why there is no comma between *Merrill* and *Lynch*: "In 1916 or 1917, on an early stationery order," says spokesman Henry Hecht, "a printer dropped the comma. Mr. Merrill and Mr. Lynch decided to keep the paper anyway. This is a true story. Then after the paper ran out, the comma was reinstated and kept until the company incorporated in 1938. Then it was 'Merrill Lynch' without the comma; why it was dropped, we don't know."

Thirty years ago, I interviewed Charles Merrill for the New York *Herald Tribune,* and wondered why there was no comma between *Merrill* and *Lynch*, when there were commas between those names and the rest of the "thundering herd," as the long list of names came to be called. "Merrill Lynch was my company," he replied, "and then we added the other guys."

Thus, there is often sinister purpose in the kamikaze comma-killing. Advertising men profess to see style in the absence of punctuation. Others see error and see red. In examining the label about "red ripe tomatoes," with nary a pause between the adjectives, I am reminded of the character of archy, the cockroach created by Don Marquis, who could not use the shift key for capitals and punctuation on his boss's typewriter. He wrote: "soon ripe soon rotten" (no period, of course).

I think you should join William Strunk and E. B. White in protecting the serial comma. You point out that omission of the comma in "Kilgour, French and Stanbury" could fuse Kilgour and French—in the (unwary) reader's mind—into one person. The omission of the serial comma in that example is not apt to confuse, but given common rather than proper nouns, that omission may cause misunderstanding. For example: "toast, butter, cinnamon, and sugar" is a mere list, but erase the serial comma and you've stirred cinnamon and sugar together and have all but the pleasant smell of cinnamon toast.

I should not give away commas as generously as Gilbert Cranberg does ("Commas are free. Why don't they use them?"). Commas after restrictive clauses are expensive. What is one to make of: "People, who live in glass houses, shouldn't throw stones"?

Elizabeth Chapman Hewitt
Lincoln, Massachusetts

I wrote the president of ABC, asking why ABC omitted the comma in the date shown at the beginning of each night's news broadcast. I received a printed postcard informing me that the network recognizes the "controversial nature" of some of the material in some of its broadcasts.

I replied, "What, sir, is controversial about the comma?"

To this question I received no reply, so I started writing inflammatory letters to the sponsors of ABC News, threatening to lead a boycott of Jell-O, Lysol, and assorted antacids. "If we let these guys disregard the comma today, what will they do tomorrow?" I asked the corporate giants.

The public relations personnel in most firms assured me they believe in the promotion of "outstanding television programming" and in their own ads share my concern that "both punctuation and grammar are correct." Someone from Kellogg's wrote he could understand how a teacher would notice such an error. Am I wrong in thinking he sees me as a little old crank who sleeps with the Harbrace Handbook *under her pillow?*

The president of the company that makes Lysol wrote that although ABC might have good reasons for not using the comma, he'd sure like to know why they didn't show the common courtesy of an explanation—and he was going to ask them.

I soon heard from ABC News. Their representative informed me they leave the comma out in other places besides the date—as "attention getting devices":

> *I hope you can understand our viewpoint and that you do*
> *not think we are eliminating the comma in the opening date*
> *of our news broadcast as an intentional grammar mistake.*
> *It is intentional, but only for visual impact.*

It's a little thing, I guess. What's a comma here or there? Maybe I am just a little, old fuddy-duddy teacher, but I sure wish those fellows at ABC would stick to the news and visually-impact-me not.

Susan Ohanian
Schenectady, New York

You still haven't learned how to read Mr. Guralnik's excellent dictionary: The English word comma *is not "from the Latin 'to cut off' "; it's from the Greek "to cut off"* (koptein). *The etymological entry "L. < Gr. komma . . . < koptein, to cut off" means that* comma *originated in Greek but was borrowed into Latin and* *then passed along to English. Greek words were normally mediated through Latin in this way before entering English and other modern languages, but that doesn't make them any less Greek.*

> Louis Jay Herman
> New York, New York

I have found the following to be useful in deciding on the proper use of a comma prior to the word and. *A comma should always be used before* and *in a list, unless the two last elements are commonly connected.*

As an example: The large department stores in New York City include Macy's, Bloomingdale's, and Abraham and Straus.

Alternately: The large department stores in New York City include Macy's, Abraham and Straus, and Bloomingdale's.

> George S. Schneider
> New Haven, Connecticut

Has the acknowledged guru of grammar become careless or have I forgotten the rules of usage on which Bro. Benedict, F.S.C. "wasted" so much of my valuable fifth grade day? Surely, he would not have accepted "You can use a comma . . ." and I suspect there would have been a lengthy discussion surrounding ". . . thoughts that can stand by themselves. . . ."

> Thomas P. Dougherty
> Roselle, New Jersey

NOTE FROM W.S.: You may not say "You can use a comma" when you mean "You may use a comma." *Can* denotes ability, *may* permission. That is a thought that can stand by itself.

Merrill Lynch and Dow Jones are not the problem. What needs whining about right now is the comatose overuse of the comma. Consider the widespread misapplication of the "commas in a series" rule—a misunderstanding, apparently shared by Safire, which regards all side-by-side modifiers as coordinate adjectives.

Mr. Safire, "red ripe tomatoes" are fine. They describe what the bottler meant to convey: that the bottle contains ripe tomatoes only, and that these ripe tomatoes are attractively red. In other words, "red" modifies "ripe tomatoes." I quote from my cozy old (not "cozy, old") Foerster and Steadman Writing and Thinking *(1931): "Do not use a comma between adjectives when the last adjective is so closely connected to the noun it modifies as to form with the noun a single unit of thought."*

Your call for "red, ripe tomatoes" will only inflame and exacerbate the existing plague, that "vast, unbottom'd, boundless pit" of flawed literacy where uncharted churning commas ceaselessly proliferate. (Note that I intend "uncharted" to modify "churning commas." By contrast, Burns's three adjectives each in turn modify "pit.") Are there many copy editors under thirty who still know enough to leave the comma out of "nice old lady" or "fine young fellow"? Mr. Safire, your superfluously comma'd tomatoes are leading us down what frequently enough nowadays appears —thanks to an overdose of misleading commas-in-a-series exhortations—as "the short, garden, path" [sic] of punctuation incompetence.

Cynthia Ozick
New Rochelle, New York

Funny thing about Kilgour French being one tailor. In a way he was. Mr. Stanbury used to tell my grandfather that there was no Mr. French. Apparently Kilgour's wife was French and the two partners thought a third name would give the company a better image. So Kilgour and Stanbury became Kilgour, French and Stanbury.

Francis McInerney
Toronto, Ontario

Concessionaires

On election night, losing candidates across the country will be faced with the grammatical conundrum: Shall I concede defeat, or would it be more proper to concede victory? Many will do the wrong thing.

As a political speechwriter in a previous incarnation, I specialized in concession speeches. Entranced by the gracious, sentimental, bite-the-lip, hold-back-the-tears art form, I prepared concessions even for candidates who were shoo-ins and who resented having the pessimistic draft submitted. Freighted with that expertise, I can offer this usage advice:

If you wish to emphasize your disappointment, if you feel self-flagellation is in order, and if you want to start a general blubbering among your supporters, *concede defeat.* This adopts the meaning of *concede* as "admit to be true."

If, on the other hand, you have a positive mental attitude, if you hope to fight again another day, and you want to give your victorious opponent (the miserable smear artist) a cheery send-off, you *concede victory.* That meaning of *concede* is "to acknowledge something to somebody."

The difference is subtle but important: To *concede defeat* is to say, "I lost"; to *concede victory* is to say, "You won." The latter has more class.

Controversial Computer

A few years ago, the off-putting vogue word was *abrasive*, used mainly by liberals to describe hard-hitting conservatives; that was quickly followed by *strident*, used by hardliners to rail at articulate softliners; more recently, the vague vogue adjective to cast aspersions in both directions is *controversial*. (And whatever happened to *off-putting?*)

Modern technology has provided us a way to prove the spread of a vogue word. *Winners & Sinners*, the bulletin of cheerful second-guessing issued from the news desk of *The New York Times*, reported recently on a project undertaken during a lull on night rewrite by Timesmen David Dunlap and Ed Gargan: They drew on the Information Bank computer to compile a list of the way the word *controversial* had been used in the newspaper during the preceding month.

The adjective had been used to look slightly askance at "Glenn Gould's recording techniques," "a no-first-use nuclear weapons policy," "Linda Ronstadt's 'new wave' album," and "a U.S. stamp honoring St. Francis of Assisi," among many other items.

The computer search showed that too many reporters and editors were leaning on the word as a crutch, unwilling to say *much-criticized* and unready to let the item stand by itself without some pejorative modifier. *Controversial* is a way of saying, "I'm out of this"; or, "Lookame, I'm being fair," or, "This one is hot and I'm not about to say why."

I can hear the newscaster saying: "The ultracontroversial U.S. stamp honoring the recording techniquies of Linda Ronstadt's no-first-use album." But the sound is not the simple "con-tro-VER-shul"; it is the controversial pronunciation of "con-tro-VER-see-ul" in the voice of Brent Musburger of *The N.F.L. Today* (welcome to the language dodge). By branding as controversial the pronunciation of *controvershul* as *controverseeul*, I stigmatize that sound from ambush—maybe I mean it is affected, or mistaken, or even forthright and courageous.

This was not the first use of a computer to examine the subtle bending of language. Tom Bethell, when at the American Enterprise Institute, applied the Nexis system (don't ask me to describe it, I have enough trouble with this green-eyed word processor) to adjectives like *provocative* and *bellicose*.

He discovered that Soviet media used the word *provocative* frequently to threaten retaliation in the *arms race*, another favored phrase; in the United States media, *provocative* is used almost exclusively in describing Western, not Soviet, actions. Similarly, *bellicose* was ferreted out of the Nexis system frequently next to the name of President Reagan, never next to Leonid Brezhnev. Mr. Bethell is now busily tracking the application of *intransigent* (to guess what country) to *unreconstructed* (to guess what kind of bird).

Fear not 1984, and the onset of computerese; a little computer will lead us away from the vagaries of voguery.

Countdown to Damage Control

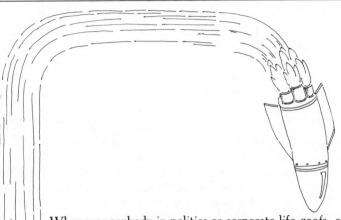

Whenever anybody in politics or corporate life *goofs*, commits a *gaffe*, or makes a *boo-boo* (all are current vogue terms for *blunder*, having replaced *foot-in-mouth disease*), the people who race to minimize the reaction or fix the *glitch* are said to be engaged in *damage control*, or if they want to make it even more dramatic, in *a damage-control operation.*

I used to think *damage control* was launched by space-program spokesmen, who have produced a fistful of terms for general usage. For example, *liftoff* is now any auspicious beginning, coming from a *launch pad*, which made all springboards obsolete. (Whatever happened to *blastoff*? Maybe it sounded too warlike, and the peaceniks at NASA chose to push a gentler term. I got more of a lift out of *blastoff*.) Similarly, *thrust* has moved from space lingo and passionate poetry to mean "main goal or purpose," and *re-entry* has replaced *comeback*. (Relax; *comeback* isn't through yet.)

"*Damage control* is not a NASA term," reports David Alter, a space-program spokesman. "It is a Navy term." Over at the Navy, Lieutenant Robert Schmermund agrees: "It's been around since at least the early 1930's." He whipped out a copy of the *Dictionary of Military and Associated Terms*, put out by the Department of Defense, which

defines the term as "measures necessary aboard ship to preserve and reestablish watertight integrity, stability, maneuverability and offensive power; to control list and trim. . . ." Any old salt knows that *list* means to tilt left or right on a fore-aft axis, and *trim* means to dip your nose or drag your tail.

If your interest in this subject is simultaneously listing and trimming, let me employ damage control by changing my thrust. In a piece on *flip-flop*, a couple of alternatives were mentioned: the neutral *U-turn*, and the more euphemistic, space-age *midcourse correction*. If you're against the change, call it a *flip-flop*; if you're for it, call it a *midcourse correction*.

A few eagle-eyed nitpickers have insisted on mid*flight* correction. In the term's original sense, both *flight* and *course* are used; NASA traces it back to the Apollo program, where we had to make nonalarming changes while shooting the moon. In its extended form, both are used as well: "It's entirely possible to make a midflight correction," said Senator Daniel P. Moynihan, campaigning in New York. "We obviously need midcourse corrections," said budgeteer David Stockman, arguing for a tax increase after the big flip-flop, or slight deviation from previous policy, or strategic withdrawal, or U-turn, or whatever term served best in that damage-control operation. If you've got that, we have liftoff.

I must quibble with your contention, serious or not, that NASA shies from using blastoff *for fear of sounding warlike. It is more likely that accuracy is the primary concern.*

While many of the definitions of blast *(a violent gust, a loud noise, an explosion, etc.) may be descriptive of a Saturn launch, none of them accurately defines what makes a rocket take* off. *I suggest you consult Newton's Laws of Motion.* Blastoff *apparently entered the language in the science fiction of the 40's and 50's. It was inaccurate even then.*

On the other hand, liftoff *has a very specific meaning. The firing of a large rocket occurs up to several seconds before it moves off the pad. Or, rather,* ignition *precedes* liftoff.

NASA has, however, at least once, replaced a warlike term for a gentler one: the Army's Redstone *missile became NASA's* Redstone *rocket.*

> *John T. Pieret*
> *Centereach, New York*

You discussed "midcourse corrections" and its variants. I thought you might enjoy a typo from India: "A problem with long term planning is that it does not allow for mid-course concoctions."

> *David Seckler*
> *New Delhi, India*

Curb the Halting

You think synonymy is a waste of time? You think all this fiddling with semantics is an arcane and abstract diversion, far from the applied science of life?

Tell that to members of the National Conference of Catholic Bishops. For months, they have been wrestling with one little noun, and their struggle to find just the right word has demonstrated the usefulness and topicality of the close study of English synonymy.

It all began with the movement for a nuclear *freeze*. That word immediately became controversial, taken by its proponents to mean an end to the arms race and by its opponents to mean the concession of permanent superiority to the Soviet Union.

Reluctant to associate themselves with one side in the current political debate, the bishops—in the first draft of a long pastoral letter that would become teaching doctrine for the Roman Catholic Church—eschewed *freeze* and chose the word *halt*. That is close in meaning to *freeze*; both words signify the *discontinuance* or *suspension* of an action, though with more of a temporary connotation than the noun *stop* or the most permanent *end*.

But many bishops believed that *halt* was too severe a word, too closely allied to the doves in the debate; in the second draft, *curb* was substituted. Rooted in

the Latin for "bent," *curb* means "restraint, restriction, limitation"—the action is to be guided or controlled, but not halted and far from ended.

In the third draft, the bishops swung back to *halt*. In the general retoughening, the verb *resist*, referring to the administration's military policies, was changed to *oppose*. Presumably, it was felt that *oppose* was stronger, and the choice was described in *The New York Times* as a "hardening," but I think that was a mistake: *Resist* implies the recognition of a threat and a positive effort to ward it off, while *oppose* is the more general term that covers anything from a shake of the head to demonstrations in the streets. (In politics, the *opposition* sits in the legislature; the fiercer *resistance* conspires underground or takes to the streets.)

When it came to *halt* versus *curb*, however, the bishops were clear about the differences in meaning and were determined to express a definite position; in this, their drafting contrasted with the fashioning of diplomatic communiqués, in which neutral or ambiguous words are chosen to conceal differences.

President Reagan was sensitive to the political significance of the bishops' choice of the key word, and sought to play it down by wondering why the press played it up. "I think that too much attention was being paid to the one word, *curb* or *halt*," he protested, "when you think there's 45,000 words in it."

True enough about the word count, but the word that counted most was the one that caused the struggle, and the decision to go with the stronger *halt* was the news in the bishops' letter.

We have been dealing here with nouns; those who want to examine varieties of stopping action by using verbs have an even wider choice: To hold something back, you can *arrest, restrain, curb, inhibit,* or *check*; to suspend more strongly, you can *stop, cease, desist, discontinue,* or *quit*; to conclude permanently, you can simply *end,* or more forcefully, *cut it the hell out once and for all.* Which is a good place to finish.

Dangling Man

Richard Nixon recently came to Washington to speak to a U.S.-China trade group and provided grammarians with a wrong way and a right way to use participial phrases.

Calling for a summit meeting with China before a summit with Russia, the former President said: "Speaking as an old friend, there has been a disturbing tendency in statements emanating from Peking to question the good faith of President Reagan on issues like Taiwan and the tennis star."

Nixon dangled his participial phrase. (Not a crime, but it would be wrong. When I worked in the Nixon White House, my job was to turn out the lights after a meeting ended and shout into the empty room: "But it would be wrong!") A participial phrase—like "speaking as an old friend"—is a group of words that begins with a participle, which in its present tense is a verb in its -*ing* form. That verb must be connected to a subject and must not be left twisting slowly, slowly at the start of a sentence.

George O. Curme's *A Grammar of the English Language* condemns the floating *-ing* phrase unequivocally: "Although occasionally found in good authors, it is felt as slovenly English in spite of its frequency in colloquial speech." He provides a suitably silly example: *"Being not yet fully grown,* his trousers were too long." In the more recent *The Writer's Hotline Handbook,* Michael Montgomery and John Stratton advise: "Such dangling modifiers can be corrected either by including a subject in the phrase or by making the phrase refer to the subject of the sentence."

Thus, Mr. Nixon should have said: "Speaking as an old friend, I want to say this about that. . . ." That would have attached the phrase to a subject. Or he could have included a subject in his opening phrase: "I speak as an old friend, as well as the one who built the bridge between our two nations during those ten days that changed the world, when I say. . . ." Either way, the dangling would have been avoided; a bridge must be built between the offshore phrase and the mainland of the sentence. (The reader will note a subtlety worthy of Zhou Enlai in the opening of the second paragraph of this piece: The participial phrase modifies the subject, "the former President." I was trying to inculcate good habits.)

As if in recognition of his error, Mr. Nixon said later in his speech: "Speaking candidly, I believe some of our Chinese friends have misunderstood and misjudged President Reagan's position on the Taiwan issue." That was grammatically perfect: The participial phrase properly modified "I." Had he left out the "I believe," and shortened his sentence to "Speaking candidly, some of our Chinese friends . . . ," he would have distorted his meaning: It is the speaker who is being candid, not necessarily the Chinese friends.

Therefore, let us reject excuses for slovenliness from pusillanimous permissivists who say, "In an abridged adverbial clause, the connection with the subject is understood." Let me say this about that: The dangling abridgment is most often misunderstood. A participial phrase without a subject is like a lover without an object or a prosecutor without a target. Make no mistake about it.

Thrice shame upon thee, Mr. Safire. You seriously misrepresented the problem of dangling participial phrases.

First, your definition of a participle is not precise. As you define it, the verbal could refer to a gerund. (Gerund: Skiing is fun. Participle: Skiing down the mountain, I fell down.)

Second, participles may incorrectly dangle whether in the present or the past. Present: Learning to drive, the car was smashed. Past: Learned in a week, I mastered the French verbs.

Third, any verbal may improperly dangle at the hands of a slovenly writer. (Incidentally, the sentence you quote from George O. Curme's A Grammar of the English Language *is so tortured in its syntax that I question his reliability. His use of* felt *is deplorable.) Verbals run the risk of dangling when they are used as modifiers. Participles only modify. Occasionally a gerund when used as the object of an introductory preposition may be a problem. Example: On reading the newspaper, an article by William Safire struck my attention.*

Another potential dangler is the elliptical clause. (An elliptical clause is an adverb clause with the subject and, often, part of the predicate omitted because it is repeated in the subject.) Example: When only five, Safire's grandfather took him to a baseball game.

Sometimes even infinitives can dangle if they are improperly used as modifiers. Example: To read Safire, a dictionary is necessary.

*Alan Shaler
Warrensburg, New York*

Dead Cat on a Line

A recent *Smithsonian* magazine piece by Fred Strebeigh followed up on a story that was begun here a couple of years ago: the Javertlike trackage of the mysterious phrase "dead cat on a line," undertaken by Professor Frederic Cassidy as part of his *Dictionary of American Regional English*, the first volume of which was published in the fall of 1985.

DARE's interviewers put this question to hundreds of Americans across the country: "When you suspect that somebody is trying to deceive you, or that something is going on behind your back, you say, 'There's . . .'?" Twenty-one respondents came up with "There's a dead cat on the line."

In speculative explanation, Lexicographic Irregulars told *DARE* that the phrase originated to describe (1) third-party eavesdropping on a party line, (2) a "line dance," when the movements of a stranger were "dead" because he did not know the local steps, and (3) an abandoned Caterpillar tractor that had been used to lay a gas pipeline.

Of these and other submissions, Professor Cassidy thinks the one closest to the mark is a submission by an old Louisiana fisherman: In fishing for catfish, a trotline is used that contains many hooks. Each day, the fisherman is supposed to check his trotline; if a neighbor comes by and finds a dead catfish on the line, that signals something suspicious; for some reason, the fisherman has not been checking his trotline.

I hope *DARE* has not closed the books on this one because I have a couple of new entries. Ronald Foreman Jr., director of the Afro-American Studies Program at the University of Florida, has unearthed a series of recorded sermons made between 1926 and 1942 by the Reverend J. M. Gates. A 1929 sermon has this to say:

> I want to preach from this subject: If a child is no way like his father, *there's a dead cat on the line.* They tell me that once upon a time, they had some trouble trying to get a message over the telegram wire. The company sent a man out to inspect the line. In making his report, he said that a cat had gone up the telegraph post and died on the line. That was the reason why they couldn't get the message over the line. Now, if a child doesn't favor his father in *no* way, *there's a dead cat on the line.*

Professor Foreman concludes that "in practice, the expression is extended to outcomes, behaviors, products, and so on which are not what they should be."

The old recording is not conclusive, since the preacher was also speculating about the origin. But there is other evidence that the "cat" may be an actual cat, and not a person, catfish or tractor.

Jody Powell, press secretary during the Carter administration, qualifies as a native speaker of the Southern dialect. (I used to refer to him as Joseph L. Powell Jr., to differentiate myself from those scribes currying favor by using intimate nicknames, and to needle the press secretary, but now that he is a fellow columnist, I call him "Jody.")

"It used to be common practice," he recalls, "for people who didn't want the responsibility for a new litter of kittens, and who couldn't give 'em away, to put 'em in a bag and drown 'em." His background as an official spokesman caused him to add hastily: "I never condoned this in any way, but it's what happened a lot. Now, if you were out there fishing in a creek, and you got something heavy on the line, you hoped you had a fish—but then you'd pull it up, and all you had was a bag with a dead cat on your line. It meant a disappointment, a letdown, something that wasn't what it was supposed to be."

To see if the metaphor of dismayed discovery applied to current affairs, I asked Jody if he recalled any dead cats on the line during his White House service. The reply: "Dead cat on a line? Happened almost every day."

Dear Sir: You Slur

"This malarkey about the 'gypped generation' has poisoned the atmosphere," said Lane Kirkland, president of the A.F.L.-C.I.O., referring to charges that the Social Security system was unfairly helping the old at the expense of the young. Mr. Kirkland, one of the last public figures to write his own speeches, is sensitive to zingy phrases—especially those alliterations that build resistance to causes supported by organized labor.

As the original malarkeyer (the phrase first appeared in a political harangue of mine), I should warn Mr. Kirkland not to let the verb *gypped* pass his lips, even in opposition to the term.

"Shame on you, Mr. Safire, for engaging in ethnic slurs," writes Rabbi Jonathan Miller of Los Angeles. "Once upon a time, I learned that 'gypped' was derived from the word 'gypsy.'" Professor William Lockwood of the University of Michigan adds, "I was shocked and dismayed to see this ethnic slur over your name. Gypsies seem to be the last minority in America whom people slur without second thought. Would you, for example, have used the term 'jewed' in a similar context?" From New York City, Cara De Silva, an official of the Gypsy Lore Society, adds her objection: "Because the etymology of words such as *welshed* and *gypped* are not as obvious as that of a word such as *jewed,* many of your readers will not feel the full weight of your use of a defamatory term, but there are many who will. Shame on you."

Does the verb *to gyp* come from *gypsy*—and if so, is its use proscribed because it derogates a race, nation, or group? Let's see: The first printed citation of *gyp* is as a noun in the 1889 *Century Dictionary,* defining the term as "a swindler, a swindling horse-dealer, a cheat." An earlier citation from a Philadelphia newspaper in 1880 was described but has never been found. Because of this evidence, the term is considered to be an Americanism.

Students of language from Eric Partridge to H. L. Mencken have assumed *gyp* to be a clip of *gypsy* (which comes from *Egyptian,* because the dark-skinned Hindu wanderers were mistakenly thought to have come to England from Egypt). In carnival talk, carny barkers used *gyp* without pejoration—some of their best friends were gyps. Both the *Merriam-Webster* and *American Heritage* dictionaries assert that *gyp* is "probably short for gypsy"—but no proof has yet been found. The word has a separate root as a male college attendant in the old English schools, and a third root as a name for a female dog, and another as a clip of *gypsum.*

Let's just say there is a likelihood that *gyp* comes from *gypsy,* and that Americans who thought that gypsies were born cheaters turned the first syllable into a verb for cheating. To the next question: Should we ban the word derived from the name of an ethnic group as an ethnic slur?

When *jew* or *jew down* is decapitalized and used as a verb meaning "haggle" the intent is usually bigoted, and Jews as well as others properly take offense. When *welsh* is used—"He said he'd pay off on the bet but he welshed"—the speaker's intent is rarely if ever to attach the people of Wales and their descendants to the practice of running out on creditors, and the term should not cause ethnic offense; however, since Welsh people wince at the verb form of their exact name, it's a good idea to avoid using it.

But *gyp* is just a piece of *gypsy*; it's not as bad as saying, "I was gypsied." And a language should not lightly be purged of any word: Are we to do away with *Indian summer* because the *Indian* means "false," or with *Dutch treat* because it is a sarcastic jab at Dutch cheapness? Lexicon-scrubbing, once made easy, would never end: If *swindle* and *cheat* were the officially approved forms of *gyp,* we would one day hear an outcry from the family of George P. Swindle and from the League of Concerned Adúlterers.

I will continue to use *gyp* as a verb, secure in the fact that I harbor no bias toward the entire clan, which suffered persecution in Hitler's Germany. Nor will I banish the word *Oriental* because somebody tells me I must always say *Asian*; such fiats are to be resisted. But after a few hard glares, I have learned to use it as an adjective, not a noun—"Oriental art," not "He's an Oriental." As that last concession indicates, careful users of language want to take people's feelings into account; now that I know that more than a few people consider it a slur, I'll think twice before warning a bona fide Gypsy that those three-card-monte experts operating on Times Square are likely to gyp him.

When I explained to my Dutch friend Jöep (who has never visited the U.S. but speaks excellent "American") what a Dutch treat meant, he laughed and informed me that a cheap B.Y.O.B.-type gathering in Holland is referred to as an "American party"!

> Lois McCoy
> Wood's Hole, Massachusetts

Having considered the relative pejority and ethnicity of to gyp, to jew, Indian summer, to welsh, and Dutch treat, why did you not consider also that classic example of the type—to wit, to pontificate?

When Pontiff is decapitalized and put to use as a verb indicating the pompous, ignorant, and arrogant proclamation of (presumptively) false ideas, is this too not an exercise in insensitivity?

And is the fact that those who wince at the offensive use of jew down rarely notice the religious pejority of pontificate not itself interesting?

> Patrick G. Derr
> Worcester, Massachusetts

Your item about being gypped brought back memories of the Slovak expression that my father used when he referred to any person (or action by someone) who was not telling the truth. The Slovak word for the British "Gypsie" is Ciganý. *(In Czech it is* Cikany.*) Whatever the origin of this word, there are the following similar sounding words:* Tsigani *(Bulgarian),* Tigani *(Romanian),* Zingari *(Italian), and* Zigeuner *(German). The similarity of the word may indicate the route of travel of these nomads.*

To be called Ty Cigāniš *is to be called a liar. There were other characteristics attributed to this group, similar to those attributed to any person or group who had no place to call home or evidence of legal occupation.*

In German, the American slang gyp *is translated to "swindle," and the Old German word for "Gypsie,"* Zigeuner, *was* Zieh-Gauner, *or "pickpocket."* Zieh *is to pull or draw, and* Gauner *is a swindler. I do not know whether this reference is still in use. Yet the acceptable word for pickpocket is* Taschendieb *(pocket thief). I would imagine that other languages have similar expressions and meanings.*

> *Henry J. Bartosik*
> *Greenville, New York*

Waverly Root and Richard de Rochemont, in their book Eating in America: A History *(The Ecco Press, New York, 1981), p. 79, offer this explanation of Indian summer:*

> *It was with relief that the settlers welcomed the arrival of winter, when they might normally expect a respite from the incessant [Indian] attacks, during which they could safely venture into the fields to prepare the soil for next spring's plantings; but they ran the risk of being caught outside their stockades, exposed in the open, if, after the first bit of frost, the weather turned temporarily mild again, as it so often did, and the Indians swooped down unexpectedly, out of their normal raiding season; it was for this reason that such weather was called Indian summer.*

> *Wendy J. Ehrlich*
> *Brooklyn, New York*

Domineer Theory

Margaret Thatcher is the first Conservative Prime Minister to be returned to office in this century; that says a lot about her personality. During the campaign, however, her supporters were worried about her way of conducting Cabinet press conferences. Image makers fretted about her schoolmistresslike way of telling her key aides to shut up when they strayed from her policy; she was accused of being *domineering.*

Since the English care about English, the Home Secretary at the time, William Whitelaw, issued a clarification: "She is a *dominating* person, as all Prime Ministers should be expected to be, but she is not *domineering.*"

What a smooth way of parrying an accusation. Both words are rooted in the Latin *dominari,* "to rule." *Dominate* means "to control by superior authority" or "to hold a pre-eminent position"; *domineer* means "to rule arrogantly, to tyrannize." In Harry Shaw's *Dictionary of Problem Words and Expressions,* both the similarities and differences in the words are drawn: "*Domineer* has more unpleasant and unfavorable connotations than *dominate,* but neither suggests a happy situation for those being regulated." (The *-eer* ending is often pejorative: No electioneering near the polls.)

The Tories won the battle of synonymy, and the sometimes-domineering Mrs. Thatcher will dominate British politics for years to come.

You left out the most important distinction between domineering *and* dominating *—that is, the sexual stereotyping implicit in the choice between the two: dominating men and domineering women.*

Although domineering men do pop up in our collective consciousness (Captain Bligh is an example), by and large our language, conversation, and humor are full of descriptions of domineering wives, mothers, and mothers-in-law, always abusing power and usually making the men under their thumbs miserable.

The pejorative intended by those who called Mrs. Thatcher "domineering" was surely more subtle than the simple suggestion that she's too aggressive. It serves to remind the electorate that a woman is in power, and that women with power are inappropriate and a cause for alarm.

I think that this is a case in which the uses to which words are put are at least as important as their dictionary definitions.

> *Carolyn Grillo*
> *New York, New York*

Don't Make a Move

"Clarity begins at home," adjures dermatologist Stanley Spatz of Hallandale, Florida. "I call to your attention a headline in *The New York Times*: 'A Famed Pastry Chef's Moveable Feast.' Are we to resign ourselves to these nouveau acceptable spellings (likeable, loveable, sizeable), or can someone somewhere insist that the editors and proofreaders demonstrate at least a fourth-grade level of spelling ability before entrusting to them the power to set linguistic standards?"

Sorry, Stanley, you're scratching the wrong itch: *Moveable* has been spelled with an *e* since the days of the writing of the Book of Common Prayer in 1549, in which appeared a "Table of Moveable Feasts." (The moveability referred to the dates.)

Ernest Hemingway picked up the phrase and used it as the title of a book about life in Paris in the good old days. "If you are lucky enough to have lived in Paris as a young man," he wrote, "then wherever you go for the rest of your life, it stays with you, for Paris is a moveable feast."

Unfortunately, when that quotation and the book title appeared in *Bartlett's Quotations*, it was spelled the way Dr. Spatz prefers: *movable*. Betsy Pitha, copy editor for that publication, says: "The spelling of *movable* in your edition was caused by an overscrupulous proofreader. Hemingway spelled it with an *e*. The error was caught and corrected in the second printing."

Does this mean that *moveable* is correct? Not necessarily; in Great Britain, the spelling with the *e* is preferred. In the United States, we go along with the rule that calls for the dropping of the *e* when the suffix is added. Go with *likable, provable*, and—unless you were intimidated by Hemingway at an early age—*movable*. (That rule does not apply to an ending with a double *e*; let's not get disagreeable.)

I spell *movable* without an *e* when writing about types of type, but defer to the Old English spelling when using the word as a modifier for "feast," because I like to preserve the phrase as originally used and because I am a generally lovable fellow.

I'm afraid that most people think of Franklin Roosevelt's unlamented experiments with setting a day for Thanksgiving when they think of movable *or* moveable *feasts.*

As you say, I think moveable *is the accepted British spelling. Samuel Johnson spells the word* moveable *in his Dictionary, at least in the edition I have. Also, Walker's Dictionary, another British dictionary, published in 1809, has it* moveable, *and has this note under the definition: "It may be observed that the mute e is preserved in this word and its relatives because the preceding* o *has not its general sound."*

Both Johnson *and* Walker *list* proveable, *and not* provable.

It would appear that the British in the 18th and early 19th centuries followed a different rule than that which you cited. Or maybe I'm just not knowledgeable enough about the rule.

Incidentally, neither Walker *nor* Johnson *lists* lovable *at all. Perhaps it wasn't a quality recognized by the Brits of that day.*

Taliaferro Boatwright
Stonington, Connecticut

Duke's Mixture

Be a linguistic hawkshaw; follow a strange phrase to its roots.

"For years I have used an expression," writes Nancy Montgomery of Washington, "to describe a strange combination of people, objects or events, calling it *a duke's mixture.* It never occurred to me that this was a phrase not in everyone's vocabulary until my new assistant asked me what it meant."

Where to begin? Start with *duke,* from the Latin *ducere,* "to lead," a quality expected of noblemen high in the aristocracy. One hypothesis would be that *a duke's mixture* is a blend of tea, similar to the *Foochow mixture* which first introduced the *-mixture* combining form in 1895.

Blind alley. Look at all the dictionaries, push all the buttons, and nothing comes up for nobility.

Second hypothesis: *Dukes* is a slang term for *hands,* as in the boxer's challenge to "put up your dukes." Eric Partridge speculated that this came from Cockney rhyming slang: *Duke of Yorks* stood for forks, which in turn were like fingers, parts of the hand. Maybe. Could not the *duke's mixture* be a tossing together from the dukes, or hands?

No. Try again.

Hypothesis No. 3: James Buchanan Duke, after whom Duke University is named (Trinity College was willing to change its name for $40 million), and who was million-heiress Doris Duke's father, made his fortune in tobacco. He and his American Tobacco Company acquired such firms as P. Lorillard and R. J. Reynolds to set up the "tobacco trust" until Teddy Roosevelt busted it into four companies in 1911. Did James Duke have a tobacco mixture that died long ago but whose ghost lingers in the language?

Jackpot. The Duke is James Duke, and Nancy Montgomery is not the only person to use the phrase. When the teams of researchers working for the *Dictionary of American Regional English* asked, "What do you call a dog of mixed breed?" two people in Oklahoma, one in California, one in Iowa, and one in Wisconsin replied: "A duke's mixture." (Others said *mutt, mongrel, pot-licker, pot-hound, mutton hound, soup hound, bone eater, biscuit eater, cur, Heinz,* and *suck-egg dog.* Dog lovers who take offense at the derogations are invited to send in suitable euphemisms.)

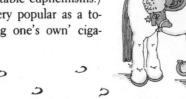

"*Duke's mixture* was once very popular as a tobacco mixture for use in 'rolling one's own' cigarettes," reports Fred Cassidy, director-editor of *DARE.* "It came in a small white cloth bag with a drawstring and was advertized with cowboys on horseback rolling cigarettes with one hand. This was part of a campaign to make cigarettes seem a masculine type of smoke. (At first, they had been thought sissy or less than he-man.) Also to add to the masculine idea, they were advertized with a huge black rampaging bull: *The duke* is a Western euphemism for a bull. This was a pun on *Duke,* the owner of the tobacco company."

That also explains John Wayne's nickname. (It does not explain why the world's leading dialect lexicographer spells *advertise* with a *z*, but I hesitate to correct him because I suspect a trap.)

"Used most generally, *a duke's mixture* can mean any sort of miscellany," concludes Professor Cassidy, "with somewhat unfavorable implications. I doubt that *Duke's mixture* is still made nowadays. The Marlboro he-man smokes a manufactured cigarette."

A check with the American Tobacco Company, which is bringing back Lucky

Strike, shows he is right: Duke's name is perpetuated only at the university, not at the company he founded.

Thus, fellow hawkshaws, do blind alleys and cockamamie hypotheses lead to the sources of our expressions. (O.K., to avoid hordes of lazy curiosity-seekers: *Hawkshaw* was the name of the detective in an 1863 play by the English dramatist Tom Taylor, and was popularized in the United States by cartoonist Gus Mager in the comic strip *Hawkshaw the Detective.*)

As a boy, circa 1912, working in my family's country store, I often sold the little cloth bags with the drawstring containing smoking tobacco, "Duke's Mixture." In the same kind of bag, we also sold "Bull Durham," the label and advertising of which showed a bull standing by a rail fence. The Durham in the brand no doubt came from Durham, N.C. I am not sure whether it was put out by Duke's company or a competitor. To further popularize cigarette smoking, and "roll your own," all stores also gave free packets of cigarette paper. At that time, however, chewing tobacco, "scrap," which cost only five cents a paper, was most popular with farmers; the dudes went for the cigarettes; pipe smokers bought "Edgeworth" in a blue tin, or "Prince Albert"! Real tough guys could choose "Army and Navy" plug cut, which came in a large piece and was cut with a knife.

> Milton W. Hamilton
> Glenmont, New York

James Buchanan Duke founded Duke University in 1924 as a memorial to his father, Washington Duke. *It is for* Washington Duke, *not* James B., *that the university is named. The Duke family had supported Trinity College, which was founded in 1859 as a Methodist institution, and moved from Randolph County, North Carolina, to Durham (Bull Durham Tobacco) in 1892. When the $40-million Duke Endowment was established in 1924, Trinity College became Duke University (as you told).*

A seated statue of Washington Duke graces the entrance to the university's east campus. According to campus legend, when certain requirements are met, the old gentleman will stand up.

> Betty Taylor
> Vero Beach, Florida

"Duke's Mixture" is commonly used in the livestock industry (especially sheep) to describe crossbred, or "commercial," animals whose breeding is pretty random—i.e.,

without scheme: "What kind of sheep you raise?" — "Oh, Duke's Mixture, I guess."

Tom Bryan
Erieville, New York

The phrase duke's mixture *was not the basis for John Wayne's nickname, Duke. His famous nickname came instead from his dog, Duke! As John Wayne related the tale on the Johnny Carson show in the early 1970's, he received the soubriquet even before he changed his name from Marion Michael Morrison to John Wayne. As a lad growing up in Winterset, Iowa, he would often walk his dog, Duke, past the local firehouse. The firemen did not know the lad's name but did know the dog's name. They therefore called him "Duke." The nickname held throughout the years. After Duke Wayne completed the story, Johnny Carson breathed a sign of relief and commented that America could be grateful that the dog's name was not "Spot." For how could the penultimate American hero inspire Americans if he were named "Spot" Wayne?*

Albert J. Golly, Jr.
New York, New York

Several years ago I worked with a Dane who had spent quite a bit of time in England. In one of our discussions, he used the English expression "That's a real dog's breakfast." Asked for an explanation, he told me that a dog's breakfast in England usually contains leftovers from the previous day's meals—thus an olio of many questionable items. Since then, I have found this term to be helpful in describing certain situations.

Robert I. Stevens
Wantagh, New York

I should like to add a slight footnote to your column on Duke's Mixture. *As you may know, I am a friendly rival of Fred Cassidy, involved in three of the regional linguistic atlases but freely offering him whatever incidental information that comes up. But this involves not so much my role as a scholar as the fact that I have been associated with Duke University since 1931, having earned my M.A. in 1933 and my Ph.D. in 1935, and having been honored with a Litt.D. in 1972 and membership in Phi Beta Kappa in 1975.*

Probably such a well-known name must have been registered sometime as a trade

name (like the successor Bull Durham*), but the story told on campus, and probably
appearing in some of the official records of the university (I think I recall seeing it
there), is worth repeating.*

*In 1865, central North Carolina like the rest of the late Confederacy was
bankrupt, and the only currency was that of the occupying troops. Washington
Duke, of the Durham area, and his sons packaged home-grown tobacco and sold
it; it was so popular (as you know, one of the few things lacking the northern army
was tobacco) that they went into the manufacturing, with considerable success.
Later, the business was expanded by two of the sons, James B. ("Buck") and
Benjamin, who diversified the family investments into hydroelectric power, textiles,
aluminum, and the other interests specified in the Indenture by which Duke University was established in the 1920s, and of which every Duke graduate received a copy
along with his diploma. Buck, as you know, established the original American
Tobacco Company, which—like Rockefeller's Standard Oil—was broken up by
Teddy Roosevelt's trust-busters. By that time, however, Duke's Mixture and other
types of jawbone (as we used to call home-rolled cigarettes and the tobacco used for
making them) constituted a small part of the tobacco business, for the family had
converted to machine-made cigarettes as the greatest part of its business.*

*The involvement of the family in education came, according to legend, when
Washington Duke was approached by prominent North Carolina Methodists seeking to save Trinity College, which (like many small denominational colleges) had
wandered from one place to another without secure financial backing. At this time,
supposedly, Washington Duke was having bad luck with his stable of horses; so he
gave the track and adjacent land and a considerable endowment to the Methodists.
The campus of Trinity College, now the East Campus of Duke, was built on the
site. Connoisseurs of aerial photography are fond of pointing out the outline of the
old track.*

*It is not surprising that the first two classroom buildings on the campus at
Durham were* East Duke *and* West Duke*. Nor that the most prominent Methodist
church in Durham is the* Duke Memorial*, situated near the old Duke Mansion.*

*As you know, the Duke Indenture offered the major share in Buck's estate to
the North Carolina Methodist Conference, provided they would change the name
from* Trinity *to* Duke*. But the older name survives in various ways, including the
distinguished* Trinity College *Historical Society, whose publications were widely
recognized even before World War I.*

I hope this helps clarify the situation a little. Duke's Mixture *clearly antedates*
Buck*. And it appears in various other contexts; I know it is used here and there for
a dog of indeterminate ancestry—I have recorded it thus myself in some of the 550
interviews I made—but I don't have all of the evidence immediately to hand.*

As a nonce-name for the dog of uncertain pedigree, Duke's Mixture *appears in
one of the Upper Midwest records from SW Nebraska; one of Cassidy's from
Appleton, Wisconsin; one from Stark Co., Ill.; and one from Gibson Co., Ind. Were
the records from the Middle and South Atlantic States to hand, I suspect more would
occur.*

If there's anything I can do to help keep a lively column lively, say so. Right now my files are in a chaotic state; but there's no trouble running things to earth if there's no emergency. I will be updating an observation or two of Fred's along with his copy of this letter—or perhaps updating *isn't quite the right word, since the* Atlas *files represent investigations before* DARE *went into the field; even the Oklahoma tapes, which I am now transcribing in what is humorously referred to as spare time, were all made 1959–63. But they do provide further evidence on the complexity of American English, and its richness as a field for future investigations.*

Raven I. McDavid, Jr.
Linguistic Atlas Project
University of Chicago
Chicago, Illinois

NOTE FROM W.S.: Professor McDavid, one of the giants in the field of linguistics, died in 1984. As this letter demonstrates, he was an enthusiastic helper to just about everyone in the field.

Your column reminded me of something that has puzzled me for some time—the use of "curiosity-seekers." It seems to me that curiosity is not being sought; it is in place. What is sought is the satisfaction or gratification of that curiosity. Should not the term be simply "the curious" or, if the adjective is not acceptable, "curious persons"?

Ruth H. Donoghue
Rochester, New York

Dum Dum-De-Dum-Dum, Dum Dum!

In a recent *New Yorker* cartoon about the ravages of inflation, Roz Chast drew a barbershop window with this sign in it: "Shave and a haircut, 200 bits."

For many years, I have been tracking the source of that phrase. Whenever I knock on a door, I beat that tattoo: *dum dum-de-dum-dum, dum dum!* That is how people know it is me. (No, not "it is I." Harvard student: "Who's knocking at the door?" "It is me." "You can't be anybody I know.") I suspect that others use the same secret signal.

Which came first, the rhythmic tap or the phrase?

Ruth Marks, librarian at the Society for the Preservation and Encouragement of Barber Shop Quartet Singing in America (SPEBSQSA), reports that a 1933 song

by Abner Silver and Eddie Maxwell was entitled "Shave and a Haircut," with the first five notes as we know them, but without the *dum dum!* or *two bits!* She suspected it came from advertising. A quick check with the Doyle Dane Bernbach library of advertising slogans unearthed nothing except a good steer to *The Book of World-Famous Music*, a 1966 work by James J. Fuld, which reveals a 1939 ditty, "Shave and a Haircut—Shampoo," by Dan Shapiro, Lester Lee and Milton Berle, and a similar number in the same year, "Shave and a Haircut, Bay Rum," recorded as a folk melody by Rosalind Rosenthal and Herbert Halpert.

But wait—Mr. Fuld found evidence that the sound antedated the phrase. In 1914 a song was published with music by Jimmie Monaco and words by Joe McCarthy: "Bum Diddle-de-um Bum, That's It!" And the musicologist thinks the origin was "probably considerably older."

At that point, the trail vanishes into the mist. A vital piece of Americana remains a mystery. If a Lexicographic Irregular has a clue to previous usage, send it around. I'll recognize the knock.

In Dorothy Sayers' Gaudy Night (c. 1936) there is this sentence (Avon Ed., Ch. 18, p. 301): "Lord Saint-George, finding his elders dilatory, blew a cheerful 'hi-tiddley-hi-ti, pom, pom' on the horn."

That even has the "two bits" tag!

Lisa Terry
New York, New York

Dum Dum-De-Dum-Dum, Dum Dum!
Shave and a haircut, two bits.
Who is the barber? Tom Mix.

Who did he marry? Pearl White.
When did they marry? Last night.
How is the baby? All right!

Circa 1938, upstate New York.
For your use when friends don't answer the first tattoo.

> Harold Pohl
> Rochester, New York

Dear Bill:

I've been hearing the musical phrase "Shave and a haircut, two bits" for as long as I can remember, and my memory in such matters goes back to about 1918. Your examination of the origins of the phrase did not go into the meaning of the words "two bits," which is simply a quarter, or 25¢. That is about what a shave and a haircut used to cost in my childhood in Zebulon, N.C.

I seem to recall that shoeshine boys in barbershops used the rhythm of the phrase in making their cloth-snapping final flourish when polishing a customer's shoes. In any case, the phrase was certainly tacked onto the end of popular musical numbers, usually by instrumentalists, as I recall. It is still used by orchestras in a humorous way to conclude a golden oldie, as the musical notes of "Good evening, friends" are also used.

> Clifton [Daniel]
> New York, New York

Since junior high school I have known how to write "It is I." In the past year or so I have managed to train myself to say "It is I." Now comes your article.

At the risk of sounding paranoid—Why me?

> Ed Sedarbaum
> Jackson Heights, New York

NOTE FROM W.S.: When *me* sounds like the object, use *me*. If anybody asks who told you this—say it was me.

I remember the old joke about someone knocking at St. Peter's gate and he says, "Who is it?" A voice answers, "It is I." St. Peter: "Heavens, another damned schoolteacher!"

> Rachel T. Bastian
> Ayer, Massachusetts

Economic Writer

In error is the gentlest way of saying somebody is wrong. *Mistaken* or *incorrect* is the next nicest way; a bit of a zinger appears in *inaccurate,* which implies sloppiness, and a sly accusation of stupidity is embedded, like a rock in a snowball, in *misinformed.* The most red-faced way is *wrong wrong wrong!* and then you're into *that bald-faced prevarication is the effulgence of a disingenuator out of his cotton-pickin' mind!*

A generation ago, I reported that F.D.R. aide Samuel Rosenman told me he had written F.D.R.'s acceptance speech, in which "New Deal" was popularized; Raymond Moley, another close Roosevelt aide who had a hand in that speech, sent me this note: "When Rosenman says that he wrote it, he is in error." That word implies a state of incorrectness, like a state of nongrace; it says that the other fellow is saying something that is not true, but imputes no venality or lack of integrity.

All of which is a windup for saying I am in error about "an economic writer" and need to get out of error fast.

In a recent obiter dictum, I parenthesized: "An 'economic writer' is a writer who uses as few words as possible." Boing! Fillet of solecism.

"Didn't you really mean 'economical writer'?" comments George Kelley of *The Youngstown* (Ohio) *Vindicator.*

"And a 'criminal lawyer' is a lawyer who is a criminal," jeers law professor Ralph Slovenko of Wayne State University in Michigan.

A couple of satiric couplets came in from Edward Ruff of Weston, Connecticut:

> *A mystery writer must sign "Anon."*
> *A Presidential writer's first name is Ron.*
> *A religious writer must be a priest,*
> *A wildlife writer a sort of beast.*

What pushed me out on that pedantic limb was a reference to my colleague Craig Claiborne as "food editor." He and I think he should be a "food-news editor," because he edits news about food, not food itself. Food is what he cooks, not edits. And so I tried to apply that fine distinction to financial-news writers, but it doesn't fly.

Economic is an adjective from the Greek word for management of a household, and has several meanings: (1) pertaining to the creation or distribution of wealth, (2) having to do with the science of economics, as in "the economic debacle is really a blessing in disguise," and (3) thrifty.

Economical is also an adjective, but its meaning is limited to one of the meanings of *economic*: thrifty, frugal. A person who is economical is on the lookout for a bargain, and an economical writer does not waste words, or better, wastes no words.

Economics is a plural noun always construed as singular: Economics *is* a dismal science. Anybody who says, "Economics are" is the sort of outlander who would ask, "Where *are* the Bronx?" One meaning is "the consideration of cost and profit," as in "What are the economics of writing columns that can be parlayed into books?" (Well, I guess a native speaker can construe "economics" as plural once in a while.) Another meaning is the science of producing, distributing, and consuming goods and services, or the art of inducing a recession to stop inflation while denying it all the while.

So how do you describe somebody who writes about economics without confusing him with somebody who wastes no words? *Economic writer* could mean either, so that's no good; *economical writer* is limited to thrifty, but that could mean his prose is spare or his life style is cheap, so I would skip that locution.

The answer comes from Owen Ullman and Sally Jacobsen of the Associated Press, who wrote to record-straighten an entirely different matter. (I had credited *The Wall Street Journal* rather than the A.P. with a quotation about the possibility of a depression, which some academic economists refer to in scholarly terms as "an economic no-no.") They signed their letter "A.P. economics writers."

By Keynes, they've got it! A writer on economics is not *an economic writer* but *an economics writer,* using the noun rather than the adjective as modifier. Let the readjustment roll: We are no longer in error.

An Egoistic Diktat in Fortuity

Shortly before he died, Leonid Brezhnev assembled his nation's military leaders to read them the riot act for producing the sort of equipment that was clobbered by the Israelis in Lebanon. (The Riot Act was passed in England in 1715 to enable mayors to issue pronouncements banning the assembly of twelve or more persons; it exists now in vestigial form only as something that is "read," meaning "the administration of a bawling-out." But I digress.)

The text of his speech was distributed by Tass, the Soviet press agency, and its translation contained three interesting words.

First, the speech denounced "attempts to impose American *diktat. . . .*" A spokesman for Tass in Washington, asked about that word, replied: *"Diktat* is a Russian word for an order or decree, and appears in both the original Russian text and the translation unchanged."

In current political parlance, accusations abound for "being domineering" or "acting arbitrarily." No superpower likes to be accused of throwing its weight around; that is why a word like *hegemony* stings, and the verb *impose* elicits red-faced denials from diplomats. *Diktat* is a German word, based on the Latin

dictare, and has been adopted by Russian speakers to derogate actions taken by the Soviet Union's adversaries.

One word deliberately avoided by Soviet speakers is *ukase,* a Russian word rooted in czarist edicts that carried the force of law. Some American speakers like to characterize readings of the riot act by Soviet leaders as ukases (pronounced as in "get off my ukases").

What can third-world leaders who wish to avoid taking linguistic sides do to describe pushing-around by great powers? A neutral term is *fiat,* Latin for "let it be done"; it is more pejorative than the meek *decree,* less literary than *edict,* not limited to ecclesiastical use as is *bull.*

My favorite derogation of any government announcement is from the Spanish: *pronunciamento,* meaning a proclamation or pronouncement, especially related to a change in government. In English, it conveys a nice overtone of pomposity— an iron fist in a bemedaled glove.

In his remarks about Washington's global strategy, Mr. Brezhnev assailed "the adventurism, rudeness, and undisguised *egoism* of this policy. . . ."

"*Egoism* is the translation of the Russian word *egoizm,*" reports the Tass spokesman, "and means the same in both languages." Was he certain that the word intended was not *egotism?* "No; *egoizm* means 'self-interest.'"

True; the English and Russian words, taken from the French *égoïsme,* mean "interest in self," a policy based on concentrating on one's own needs, the opposite of *altruism.* When you stick the *t* into the word, changing *egoism* to *egotism,* you mean "a tendency to attract attention to one's self." The egoist looks to himself; the egotist demands that others look at him. I am indebted to Comrade Brezhnev for this chance to remark the difference.

Finally, he was reported to have said, "No *fortunity* will take us unawares."

No such word. "That should be *fortuity,*" says the Tass man. "You printed it wrong. The Russian word was *sluchainosti,* meaning 'chance, opportunity.'" Evidently, Mr. Brezhnev's *fortuity* was a translator's back-formation from *fortuitous,* meaning "accidental" (and not "fortunate"). The noun form does not appear in all dictionaries, and I doff my rabbit-fur cap to the Russians for making this fortuitous addition to the English vocabulary.

Dear Bill,

If I read your statement correctly, you are refusing to yield to folk usage in re: fortuitous. *Our mutual friend David Guralnik now allows "fortunate" as a second meaning.* Also, W-3 cites "lucky" as one of the definitions.*

The abandonment of the old restriction seems logical, in a way. Fortuitous and fortunate *have the same Latin root.*

Gene [Eugene T. Maleska]
New York, New York

*See Webster's New World Dictionary, *Second College Edition.*

Et Tu, Brutalize?

On the subject of international denunciations, let us try to retire a confusing verb from the field.

"Nor can we simply turn our heads and look the other way as Soviet divisions brutalize an entire population in Afghanistan," Secretary of State George Shultz told the United Nations. Jimmy Carter, in his memoirs, uses *brutalize* in the same way: to treat brutally.

Until recently, this *-ize* verb usually meant "to make brutal." When critics of our policy toward Cambodia in the early 1970's discovered that the gentle Cambodians included some fairly bloodthirsty Khmer Rouge fighters, the critics charged that our bombing had "brutalized" the Cambodians—that is, had turned them warlike. The verb was akin to, but not the same as, "dehumanize," and served a purpose in the lexicon.

A second meaning, "to treat brutally," long lurking in the background, has now befogged the picture. When we use the word, we no longer know what it means, because it has two entirely different meanings. Let's get tough. Throw it out of your speeches, George.

Exit Haigspeak

Al Haig, the former Secretary of State whose vocabulary was so often skewered in this space, will no longer be using Foggy Bottom as his forum. Policy differences aside, his departure is saddening: Al was just getting the hang of the language.

For a time, at the Versailles summit, it appeared that he would suffer a reversal. He began a briefing using the French word *potpourri* in its correct meaning—a mélange, or hodgepodge—but pronounced it "pot-POUR-y." That wasn't wrong, but the preferred pronunciation is "po-poo-REE," especially if you're in France.

He then recouped by using a Kissingerism correctly, which many of the press corps found confusing. "I think both leaders are extremely sensitive," said Haig, speaking no ill of Presidents Reagan and Mitterrand, "not to look like we're developing a condominium between Paris and Washington." (Read that "like" for "as if" and let it go.)

Condominium? "If they did develop one," commented ABC correspondent Bill Stoller, "it would have to be advertised as 'six million rms, ocn vw.' " In this case, the current meaning of condominium—shared ownership of an apartment house—is antedated by the diplomatic meaning: "joint rule or sovereignty." Today, a diplomatic condominium is a sort of highhanded divvying up of power to the sound of resentful hollering from alliance partners.

When a lack of direct communication between Haig and Jeane Kirkpatrick, our chief delegate to the United Nations, led to a certain embarrassment, he used a good word to dismiss the shortcomings of diplomats, calling them "personal peccadilloes which tantalize you gentlemen so much."

A peccadillo is a minor fault or petty sin, from the Latin *peccare*, to sin. Its use by a secretary of state recalls one of the great diplomatic code messages based on a pun, from Sir Charles Napier, who had been sent to gain control of the Indian province of Sind in the 1840's. After the battle of Hyderabad, the British general sent back his report in a single word: *Peccavi.* At the Foreign Office, his Latin-speaking colleagues immediately knew its import: "I have Sind."

But Haig's linguistic triumph, really, was not in what he said but in what he caused to be written. In a story in *The New York Times,* this phrase appeared: "The pro-Government press, whose support is more nuanced than that of the conserva-tive papers' opposition. . . ." *Nuance* as a verb, and *nuanced* as an adjective, is pure Haigspeak; a nuanced approach has so many shades of gray that the nuancee cannot tell black from white.

Thanks to my old comrade in arms, that obvious word *subtle* has had it; *nuanced* is the new calibration of sophistication.

On the hunch that he was on the ropes and down in the mouth (shouldn't mix metaphors), I had a one-on-one lunch with the originator of Haigspeak the day before he resigned. His private speech, I can report, is direct and often pungent, especially concerning White House aides; none of the press conference look-ma-I'm-nuancing locutions.

To cheer him up, which I obviously did not, I passed along the observation of comedian Mark Russell: "Who would have thought, between Secretaries of State Henry Kissinger and Alexander Haig, the one with the accent would be the one we can understand?"

You referred to potpourri. *In French, it is hyphenated and no syllable is accentuated.*

J. Vuillequez
New York, New York

Expansive Feeling

"This morning, Mr. George Herman was questioning our F.B.I. director on *Meet the Press,*" writes Dr. Abraham Nathan of Brooklyn. "A statement was made and Mr. Herman requested him to *dilate* upon that statement. He obviously meant *expand*—or is this a new meaning for *dilate?*"

"Don't tell me I heard George Herman on *Face the Nation* say, 'Would you dilate on that?'" adds Marianne Roberts of Farmington, Connecticut. "That F.B.I. Director William Webster could respond without a twitch says something about his self-control—or is this now a new use of the word?"

On behalf of my eye-widened pupils (and not *in* their behalf, as I am acting as their agent and not as their benefactor), I slammed CBS correspondent Herman up against the wall and demanded his response, à la Larry Spivak in the days when panel shows were inquisitions.

"Clearly I used *dilate* intransitively, and not insensitively," replied Mr. Herman, attaching a copy of the definition offered by the *Random House Dictionary,* which includes "to speak at length, expatiate (often followed by *on* or *upon*)."

Why, then, if he meant *expatiate,* did he not say *expatiate?* "It is not a word I care for in oral English," writes my old friend George, thereby hinting that he uses it in written English all the time.

A new use of the word *dilate?* "I point to the second meaning," says Mr. Herman, fending off the relentless panel of questioners, "'archaic, to describe or develop at length.' Lacking an *O.E.D.,* I cannot cite early uses but am sure they are given. The smaller Latin dictionary I keep on my desk here gives me '*dilato,* 1st conj., to spread out, to pronounce broadly.'" (I keep all thirteen volumes of the *Oxford English Dictionary* in my lap at all times; the earliest use of *dilate,* meaning "delay," was in 1399; it was not until 1489 that the meaning of "prolong" entered the language, and in the sixteenth century the meaning of "amplify" was added.)

Comfortable in the hot seat, Mr. Herman adds, "No need to expatiate endlessly"—he does use that word in every letter—"it is clear I defend this as a good and worthy word, of clear [George also leans heavily on *clarity* in its many forms] and obvious meaning to both Mr. Webster and to the audience; a word deserving of being *clarior e tenebris.*" Put a Latin dictionary on a man's desk, and he'll drive his colleagues crazy; the phrase means "more brightly from out of the darkness."

The phenomenon we are witnessing in this case is Unfamiliar Correctness, or Solecism Entrapment. Mr. Herman's defense is unassailable; the verb *dilate* has a meaning of "expand," which can legitimately be extended to "comment further"; yet that is not the meaning with which most people are familiar. *Dilate* is a word most often associated with the pupils of eyes; it jars some ears to hear that word used otherwise. The adjective, *dilatory*, has a pejorative connotation. A congressional aide denounced two nuclear-freeze amendments as "meaningless, dilatory" (and for that clipping I am indebted to Clarior E. Tenebris of Black Rock, New York). With that meaning of "wandering aimlessly" in mind, listeners wonder why any questioner would ask a panelist to *dilate* on any subject.

The decision that each speaker must make is this: When you know a word has an unfamiliar meaning, is it your duty to use it and stretch the range of meanings, thereby educating your audience—or should you limit your usage to the ready grasp of your listeners, thereby pandering to their ignorance?

As any practitioner of the art of the slanted question knows, the answer I am setting up is: "Go ahead and use the Unfamiliar Correct, and when you entrap your target, zap 'em with The Word on the word."

For a printed copy of this discussion, as the panel shows used to say, send 10 cents in coin—I think that meant a dime—to the program of which George Herman is moderator, which close-listening sticklers for accuracy think is either *Meet the Press* or *Face the Nation.* Do not address him at *This Week with David Brinkley.*

Farewell, My Lovely

As the collect telephone call comes to an end, the kid in college says, "Lay-tuh!" The parental voice replies, "Buh-bye."

The rich and varied language of farewells is thus advanced. In olden times, a few years ago, the collegiate call would be "See you later, alligator." From this neo-Cockney rhyming source, by the natural process of shortening, *seeya* became popular; recently, the end of that first phrase, *later,* has come into its own. With

the emphasis on the final syllable, the favored farewell is
"lay-TUH."

Meanwhile, *goodbye* has
been changing. For generations, an erosion of the *d*
changed that word to *g'bye*
or *guh-bye*; then the baby-
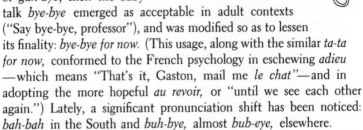
talk *bye-bye* emerged as acceptable in adult contexts
("Say bye-bye, professor"), and was modified so as to lessen
its finality: *bye-bye for now*. (This usage, along with the similar *ta-ta
for now*, conformed to the French psychology in eschewing *adieu*
—which means "That's it, Gaston, mail me *le chat*"—and in
adopting the more hopeful *au revoir*, or "until we see each other
again.") Lately, a significant pronunciation shift has been noticed:
bah-bah in the South and *buh-bye*, almost *bub-eye*, elsewhere.

That has to do with the speed with which we now get rid of each
other. *So long* is no longer so long, having been clipped to a slangy *s'long*.
The new, rapid-fire telephone closing, which is not really part of a dialogue,
is "O.K. fine thanks you too bub-eye," fired staccato at the person on the
other end, who is simultaneously saying, "Havva good one take care bub-
eye." In such a simultaneous barrage, a full-length *bye-bye*, with its two long
vowel sounds, would seem to drag on and on.

This rise of what cryptographers would call "the leave-taking burst" does
not necessarily mean that Americans are becoming less gracious. The Southern style offered by the person who is being left can still be heard: "Y'all come
see us again, heah?" and its shortened form, "Y'all come," are in use, as is
"Hurry back." In New England, the same gentility can be found in "Don't be a
stranger, now."

Grace in exiting can also be seen in the informal blessings uttered by the person
doing the leaving: By snipping the *you* off *God bless you*, the speaker changes the
meaning of the phrase from "I notice you sneezed" to "Goodbye." Although the
leave-taker's Spanish *adios* ("to God") and the leave-taken's *vaya con dios* ("go
with God") continue to show strength, the *have-* construction is more prevalent:
Have a good day and its derivative, *Have a good one*, are forms of benediction,
although the most recent *Have a special life* is an example of farewellian overkill.
Peace is acquiring political overtones.

The leave-taking warning is strong: *Take care* is as warm as *Take off* is cold,
and *Take it easy* along with *Take it slow* is in heavy use. The last of those has been
updated with a rhyme: *Take it slow, bro*, which is heard more among the brothers
than the sisters. *Behave yourself* is an affectionate admonition, which has appeared
recently as *Stay clean*, *Be good* has its users, and occasionally one hears the more
resigned *If you can't be good, be careful.*

The sympathetic farewell is undiminished: *Hang in there* vies with *Hang tough* and *Hang loose,* and *Walk light* may cheer up the overweight, but the imperative goodbye is now considered insulting: *Call me, Drop me a line,* and *Keep in touch* are put-downs, and *Stay cool* is as ill-received as the old *Don't take any wooden nickels* or the military *As you were.* The ultimate insult in farewells is the airy *Let's have lunch.*

The reminiscent goodbye should not be forgotten: *It's been a gas* is out of style, but *It's been real* remains a reality, a shortening of *It's been really (whatever).* Variant forms include *This is a memory* and the more time-consuming but lilting *It's been nice, it's been sweet, but now it's time to hit the street.* (Not exactly *Parting is such sweet sorrow,* but at least it shows effort.)

Foreign borrowings by Americans are led by the British *cheers,* which has been moving from a toast to a farewell, and the Italian *ciao,* modified to the rhyming hybrid *ciao now,* a favorite of brown cows. In Spanish-Slavic neighborhoods, *adioski* has been heard, as has *hasta-pasta.*

The hipster lingo that once featured *Plant you now, dig you later* has degenerated into a brief *Digya,* but was reborn under *See you later when your hair gets straighter,* an obvious updating of *See you later, alligator* and its ritual response, *In a while, crocodile.*

Why have large reptiles clamped their long jaws on the business of leave-taking? Answer: the power of rhyme. Long before Lacoste and Gatorade, the alligator was the symbol of farewell, and remains in short form as *Later, gator.* Some sarcastic types drop the *gator* to say, "Later . . . much."

Among the young, who are always leaving and who constantly need new-phrase fixes, there seems to be a growing desire to blame any leave-taking on external forces. *Gotta go* is the most frequent form of denying any desire to leave, but more imaginative examples are *Gotta bail,* presumably from "Must bail out of the aircraft," *Gotta cruise* and *Gotta blaze* (auto usage), *Gotta split* and *Gotta jam,* which may be rooted in *jam session* or a desire for a peanut-butter lubricant. *Catch you on the flip side* is an updating of *Catch you on the rebound,* but the most uncertain farewell is a hazy *Whenever. . . .*

The most interesting new expressions among departing youth can be grouped under "the declaratory future": While still present in body but mentally long gone, the youth frantically grabbing a glass of juice and digging under

cushions for a misplaced book cries, "I'm outta here!" This may stem from "I've got to get out of here" (external-force leave-taking) or a science-fiction afterimage, "You think I'm still here, but I have already gone," or a response to an irate parent's "Get outta here!" A variant of this creative farewell is *I'm there* or *I'm gone,* or in slightly more restrained form, *I'm booking,* rooted in the British "I'm booking (making a reservation) a flight for. . . ."

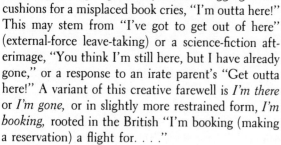

Many Lexicographic Irregulars, whose contributions give this piece its scholarly authority, included the word *toodles,* a shortening of *toodle-oo,* which can now be heard in American business circles. Sandi Beare of Atlanta writes: "I have heard that *toodle-oo* comes from the French *à tout à l'heure,* meaning 'in a little while.' Is this true?"

Big controversy about that. Most dictionaries consider the origin to be imitative of an old-fashioned automobile horn. However, Monique Benesvy, professor of French at Harvard, says, "The consensus here is that *toodle-oo* comes from *à tout à l'heure,* though we can find no written documentation. Consider the consonants: *t-d-l* for the first, *t-t-l* for the latter."

Without tooting my own horn, I lean toward the French-derivation theory. That is because I do not want to play favorites in ending this column, and Rue Witten Sandler of Cedar Grove, New Jersey, has provided a way out: She reports that her brother, who has spent much time in France, often waves goodbye with *Tout à l'heure, alligateur.*

I was surprised to note that you did not include the British admonition that I have heard in London frequently: "Mind how you go."

I take it to be a kindly, pleasant warning, meaning a big concern, such as "look out," "be careful," "watch out," or "I am concerned that you will get safely on the right path to your destination."

(A New York City friend suggests that it means avoid dog-leavings on the sidewalk.)

The Southern pronunciation of bah bah *is sometimes shortened here by my Texas friends to one very firm "bah." It's hard to translate, but it is friendly, a cutoff, and not meant meanly; it has a very full "ah" sound, but with an added vowel that is kin to "eye" (or naturally "bye"), and, as I say, done only once. It is a definite ring off.*

When I was younger and telephones were new, a farewell that made clear sense and was not intended to be rude, but a simple declaration of what was going to happen: "I'm going to hang up my end now . . ." and that's what people did.

> *Paul A. Milikin*
> *New York, New York*

There is a new riposte here to the distasteful, baby-talk farewell "bye-bye." It is "good-good."

> *Graham Wilde*
> *Hong Kong*

Although I have yet to have anyone hope (out loud, anyway) that I will "Have a special life," the number of "Have a good day(s)" increases with every phone call.

There is, however, a form of disentanglement that I and many of my friends and business associates use which I find satisfactorily polite, though transparent. It is, "I'll let you go now," bracketed of course by a variety of words of phrases that reinforce the leaver's intentions. It lets the listener at least feel active in the wake of someone who, for the moment, has something more important to do than to talk to them (a boon in these days of Super Achievers).

Barbara Tober
New York, New York

Aha! Caught you at last. You give credit to the English for booking. The verb to book is cop talk. When a felon flees, he "books." The police officer then reports, "He booked on me."

Jeanne Walsh
Providence, Rhode Island

I understand the phrase I'm booking to mean "to run or perform another action very quickly." This comes from running (in my case) or doing something fast enough to set a record and therefore, put your name in the "book" of records for your sport. Thus, when my cross-country teammates or I say "I'm booking" or "I'm going to book" we mean "I am going to run as fast as I possibly can."

Most of us who run for Beekmartown Central School use this expression quite frequently, and we don't take flights too often.

Susan Klein
Plattsburg, New York

In response to "Later, 'gator," don't omit "While, 'dile."

John Foster
Oxford, New York

Possibly my training as a gastroenterologist leads me to offer another origin to the expression toodle-oo. My understanding is that when taking one's leave for excretory purposes one said "To the loo." In Britain at least this became "Toodle-oo" and became an all-purpose expression of leave-taking. Much like "I've got to see a man about a horse," an old euphemism for a forced exit for an unforced (hopefully) function.

Steven Kussin, M.D.
New Hartford, New York

It is common knowledge that toodle loo *had its origins in Blandings Castle, where it was preceded by "pip pip," the sound developed by the British Ministry of Posts and Telegraphs to solicit an additional farthing or thruppence for public telephone usage.*

"To the 'Loo'" was frequently used by young men departing from Waterloo Station to those horrible public schools, University or War. "Loo" then later deteriorated into an euphemism for water closet.

> *Deirdre McNamara*
> *New York, New York*

The case for the French origin is very strong. To the British Tommies in World War I à tout à l'heure *sounded like* toodle-oo. *They picked it up and brought it home, where it became popular. A wartime song of the period contained:*

> *Don't cry-ee,*
> *Don't sigh-ee,*
> *There's a silver lining*
> *In the sky-ee.*
>
> *Bonswor, old thing,*
> *Cheerio, chin chin,*
> *Napoo, toodle-oo,*
> *Goodbye-ee.*

> *Alicen White*
> *Rumson, New Jersey*

I was surprised to see no mention of the phrase "Let's blow this pop stand." Surely, this is a shortened version of the longer farewell "Let's blow this popsicle stand."

> *Andrew J. Friedland*
> *Philadelphia, Pennsylvania*

My husband and I were visiting relatives in the village of Gulacs, Szabolcs Szatar County, in northeastern Hungary. In response to our Viszont làtàsra *(Until we see you again), we were taken aback by* Seeyàztok, *or the pluralization of "See ya," adopted, no doubt, from those American films and television shows permitted in Hungary.* Kojak *was a big hit there that summer, as was the Woody Allen movie* Jàdzd El Megint, Sam.

> *Elizabeth Agoston*
> *Montville, New Jersey*

Here's a farewell I picked up on my last TV commercial shoot in L.A. which is gaining wide usage in Adspeak circles: "I'm history."

It's also an effective meeting-ender as in "Are we history? Terrific."

If you wish to imply that someone is of so little importance as to barely exist, it's "I'm telling you, the guy is history."

> Theodore Bell
> Chicago, Illinois

"Let's make this history," or "I'm history" should have been included in your column on farewells.

> Vicky Oliver
> New York, New York

Feinschmecker Productions Presents:

"If it is laudatory for black voters to vote as a bloc" was the beginning of a sentence in one of my political harangues. *The Los Angeles Herald Examiner* disagreed with my politics and my choice of word in a single phrase: "defensible, if not 'laudatory.'"

Laudatory means "expressing praise"; *laudable* means "praiseworthy." I should be *laudatory* about what is *laudable,* just as I am hortatory about constructive corrections.

For example, in a recent language piece, I wrinkled my nose at "pecksniffian purists." David Chasman of Culver City, California, evidently saw the movie of Dickens's *Martin Chuzzlewit,* in which the character of Seth Pecksniff embodies hypocrisy and selfishness.

The term *pecksniffian* became a synonym for hypocrisy. "Surely, you don't mean to imply that language purists are hypocritical about it? The idea suggests that, in public, they praise grammatical speech, but in private lapse into all manner of solecisms." (Yes, that is what we do, but no, I did not mean to imply that.)

It occurs to Mr. Chasman that I used the word *pecksniffian* for its onomatopoeia: "It *sounds* as though it means 'finical' or 'overly fastidious'—but it doesn't. There *is* a word in German," adds the movie executive, *"Feinschmecker,* which means 'gourmet' or 'epicure,' and which, by extension, has come to mean 'an overly fussy person.'"

It was the *sniff* that got me; I was obtuse.

Female Avuncular

We all know that the adjective based on "uncle" is *avuncular*, and all of us who are uncles can inscribe letters to nephews and nieces "with avuncular affection." But what of aunts? A query to Lexicographic Irregulars for a word to fill this black hole in our vocabulary produced a variety of suggestions.

Punsters who did not see this as serious scholarly inquiry came up with *auntique* and *auntiquated*, assuming such women to be in their auntidotage. These I have rejected out of hand (a locution of obscure origin), along with noun forms like *auntler* and *detante*.

The *tant-* prefix offered more hope, and suggestions ranged from the spidery *tantular* to the futuristic *tantoid*, with a light stop at *tantative* from a Floral Park, New York, reader.

Classicists across the nation went to town on this. Bruce Macbain, who teaches classical studies (Why "classical studies"? Why not just "the classics"?) at Boston University, points out that Latin offers two sets of words for uncle and aunt. "On the father's side, they are *patruus* and *amita*, respectively; on the mother's side, they are *avunculus* (literally meaning 'little grandfather'; don't ask me why) and *matertera*. If you don't care for *materteral*, I suppose you could use *amital*, but that sounds to me like a barbiturate."

Arianna Stassinopoulos of New York, biographer of Maria Callas, now writing the life of Picasso, reviews the same four-way split and comes up with *patruitous* for your father's brother, to go with *avuncular* for your mother's brother, and then: "As for the aunts, there is already an English adjective (first recorded in 1823), so that one's auntie on the mother's side should end her letters 'Yours materterally.'

"The Latin for a father's sister is *amita*," Miss Stassinopoulos reminds us, "but so far no English word derived from it exists. There is, however, no reason why we cannot here and now invent it and proclaim that all aunts on the father's side must from now on end their letters 'Yours amitally,' or, if they want to exercise some freedom of choice, 'Yours amitously.'"

To my ear, there's an echo of incest to *amitous*—sounds too much like that old standby *amorous*—but *amitally* is a fine adverb. Its adjective form is the happily drugged *amital*.

Solved! The void is filled, and that auntsy feeling is gone.

It was with some interest and a considerable amount of chagrin that I read in your column what was claimed to be the coinage of an adjective for aunt. You were more than a year late. I coined such an adjective and it appeared in a column in the

Chicago Sun-Times *on 4 June 1981. The* Sun-Times *subsequently syndicated the column and it appeared in newspapers elsewhere in the country.*

Charles-Gene McDaniel
Chicago, Illinois

If your rank as a Lexicographic Regular has been earned, it is dismaying that a battle-tried soldier can't use the Webster's New Collegiate Dictionary *(1977 edition) to discover that your avuncular relative female could have signed those letters ". . . with auntly affection."*

Clayton Braddock
Memphis, Tennessee

You note that the "locution" out of hand *has obscure origins. I'm going out on a limb by offering the Hebrew expression* miyad, *which is used as "immediately," but means "from the hand."*

William Cutter
Hebrew Union College
Jewish Institute of Religion
Los Angeles, California

Lots of folks in patriarchal clan societies call their mother's brother "Little grandfather" (avunculus). *They call all their mother's brother's male descendants in the male line the same thing. If I call you* avunculus, *you call me* nepos; *hence* nepotism, *literally "looking after your sister's child as any decent man would." The relationship is indulgent, as between grandparents and grandchildren most places; not tinged with patriarchal discipline, hence "Little grandfather." This sort of usage is called "Omaha-type" terminology, since the Omaha Indians used it too.*

There is a term for amita, *"amitilocal," referring to sending a child to live with her father's sister. It needs some necessarily tedious explaining. Many horticultural societies are organized around matriclans, local groups made up of women related to each other solely through women, plus their in-marrying husbands and unmarried kids. If something makes it advantageous to have groups of related men living together, these societies reorganize as patriclans (local groups of men related to each other solely through men, plus their wives and unmarried children). Sending boys to live with their mother's brother before or at marriage is a compromise, creating a local group of men related to each other solely through women, plus their wives and unmarried children. This sort of postmarital residence is "avunculocal." An-*

thropology's problem is why the only possible pattern remaining does not occur. There are a lot of guesses, which I'll spare you, but talking about them necessitated coining words like "amitilocal" and "amiticlan."

> *Robert K. Dentan*
> *Professor of Anthropology &*
> *Chair of American Studies*
> *State University of New York*
> *Buffalo, New York*

Fence

The hot new verb on Capitol Hill is *fence.*

Most Americans know that *to fence* means "to sell stolen goods." A few old-timers can recall the original, nonmetaphoric meaning of the word, "to build a fence around." Occasionally, they can be heard singing, "Gimme land, lotsa land . . . don't fence me in."

When President Reagan was struggling to find a compromise for the basing of the MX missile, he brought Senator John Tower of Texas before the cameras in the press room. The senator announced that "funding for production of the MX missile would be retained in the bill but would be fenced."

The cognoscenti knew what he meant, of course, because the President has used *fence* that way. Bill Kovach, the Washington editor of *The Times,* recalls an early usage by Democratic Representative Sam Stratton of New York.

"In Senator Tower's statement," explains Linda Hill, who explains these things on his behalf, "the word *fence* was used to mean 'restrict.' The money for the MX was to be approved, but before it could be used, certain requirements had to be met—that was the restriction, or the fence."

Therefore, if you want to put a limit on something's use, *fence* it. But what is this going to do to Washington's hottest word of 1982, *cap?* In political parlance, *to cap*—to place a cap upon, as oil workers cap a gusher—became the preferred term for "ceiling." Does the onset of *fence* blow the lid off *cap?*

Not necessarily. Here is the synonymy: *To cap* means "to restrict in height," and is most often applied to sums of money; *to fence* means "to restrict in width," and is most often applied to conditions laid down or requirements to be met. Thus, to limit the size of the defense budget would be to cap Cap, while to place conditions on the way the F.B.I. conducts its sting operations would be to fence fences.

Dear Bill:

Now that you've lunged *into a sin of omission, it's only a simple* parry *and* riposte *to note that* to fence *is to engage in controlled combat under a strict set of rules as in the sport of* fencing.

I both parry *and* riposte *because while you can* parry *without* riposting *as a rather aimless exercise, to* riposte *without* parrying *is to not* riposte *at all. Joe Kraft does that a lot (using* riposte *without* parry*).*

I await your discussion of to box *which I presume provides the dimensions to both* cap *and* fence.

> Bernie [McGovern]
> Tampa, Florida

P.S.: My other interest is the United States Fencing Association.

You state "Most Americans know that to fence *means 'to sell stolen goods.' With all due respect to your expertise I don't believe that you're totally right. According to my* American Heritage Dictionary, *a fence is "one who receives and sells stolen goods."*

From my experience as a kid who grew up on the N.Y.C. streets most folk would consider a "fence" to be a "receiver" or "purchaser" of stolen goods—if one were to leave one half of the definition unstated—rather than a "seller" of that stuff.

There appears to be a much closer and urgent relationship between "a burglar," for instance, and "a fence," who takes the hot goods off his hands, than between a purchaser of stolen goods and a fence. The urgency is missing in the latter instance.

> Marc Valdez
> Riverdale, New York

What's in a Nom?

The word *synonymy* was misspelled here as "synonomy." The first bale of corrections has come in; that's only the beginning.

I have always wanted to run a correction like the one Bernard Levin, the brilliant iconoclast at *The Times* of London, ran at the bottom of a 1982 column: "I wish to express my warmest gratitude to the only three people in the British Isles who have not written to point out that my reference to the Doppler shift two weeks ago was, however politically apposite, scientifically inaccurate. To the other 55 million I offer gratitude only slightly less heartfelt."

You use synonomy *when the correct word is* synonymy. *This is a word familiar to biologists who classify plants or animals (taxonomists, studying taxonomy), as it should be to linguists (how I abhor "language experts"). So, although it is taxonomy and economy, please do not perpetuate* synonomy—*one sees it far too frequently in scientific papers by sloppy scientists.*

You also bemoaned "Classical studies" instead of "Classics." I am happy to report that our Department of Biology has not (yet?) succumbed to changing its name to Department of Biological Sciences. Our university's Department of Geology, however, recently renamed itself Department of Earth Sciences, after having absorbed part of the Department of Physics (Geophysics section). Among the subjects absorbed by the new Department of Earth Sciences was Astronomy!

Guy R. Brassard
Professor of Biology
Memorial University of
Newfoundland
St. John's, Newfoundland

Fire in the Belly

"We're going through the motions," said a disconsolate White House aide to a *Washington Post* reporter on a background, or half-whistleblowing, basis. "I don't sense fire in anyone's belly, including the President."

That is a phrase we will be hearing more as the hats start being tossed into the ring. Four years ago, I asked Senator Howard Baker, who was beginning an easygoing campaign for the Republican nomination, if he had the requisite lust and blind ambition to attract support. "I have the fire," he said mildly, patting his stomach, "in the belly." He had evidently been asked that question before; in light of his new, self-chosen lame-duckiness, it will be asked again.

The phrase means more than mere ambition; it means a hungering and a yearning, a willingness to inflame the innards with the drive to achieve your goal. *Fire in the belly* is not biblical: "The belly was not considered the repository of emotions long ago," says David Guralnik, boss of *Webster's New World Dictionary.* "Passion was in the heart; it is therefore unlikely that this metaphor is that old."

The earliest citation is 1951 in the *Supplement to the Oxford English Dictionary* (Burchfield strikes again) by N. Annan: "There is no fire in the belly, no sense of urgency." The first few uses were British, and evidently Americans hankering for a metaphor for ambition adopted it quickly. Where did it come from? We can speculate: perhaps an allusion to stoking a potbellied stove for heat, or perhaps from a form of heartburn—that fiery sensation, felt by upwardly mobile executives, sometimes developing into ulcers.

And so the question will come: Does Fritz Mondale have the fire in the belly needed to become President? The follow-ups: What happens to the fire when the campaign goes belly-up? Should a President be afflicted with fire in the belly? Is it an insult to say of a calm candidate that he has a "fire extinguisher in the belly"? As we ask these questions, we should thank our fire-eating British cousins for their contribution to American political metaphors.

Flip-Flop

When a reporter asked President Reagan if his reversal of past form—to support a tax increase—could enable critics to say that he had "flip-flopped on the tax issue," the President replied: "There is not any flip-flop on this at all."

The President's ready acceptance of this reduplication proves that *flip-flop*— both verb and noun—has a firm place in the language, especially in political parlance. It is used as frequently as *helter-skelter* and far more often than *higgledy-piggledy.*

The hyphenated word first appeared in English three centuries ago to describe large ears, and reappeared briefly to imitate the sound of slippered feet on a wooden floor. These nonce meanings soon died, replaced by the meaning of somersault— not the gentle, rounded-back type, but the somersault in which the performer holds his body stiff and throws himself over, first on his hands and then on his feet.

This tumbling feat—not to be confused with a handspring—gained metaphoric use in the 1940's, when fickleness was described as "heart flip-flops."

Political orators, ever on the lookout for colorful ways to accuse opponents of opportunism, quickly seized upon it: Richard Nixon's decision to impose wage and price controls in 1971, after reviling them for many years, was denounced—accurately—as a flip-flop, which he countered with a bland observation that "circumstances change."

However, most political figures shy away from charges of flip-floppery; sudden shifts of opinion, or reversals of previous positions, are considered admissions of previous error. Hence Mr. Reagan's insistence that his new position did not constitute a flip-flop. His most ardent supply-side critic, Representative Jack Kemp, showed a certain subtlety in his choice of words: Rather than offend his longtime leader with the harsh *flip-flop*, Congressman Kemp preferred *U-turn*, which means the same (a 180-degree change in direction), but carries no acrobatic connotation.

Diplomatists making the same charge of turnaround often select the French term *volte-face*, akin to the military order *about-face*. (In diplomacy, the charge is not as stinging: The response is a cool "I would rather be flexible than rigid.") In German, a word for turnabout is *Kehrtwendung*, but politicians in West Germany have also sensed the need for a lively word to accuse opponents of sudden reversals. "The German equivalent of the English *flip-flop,*" advises Karl Prince, of the Federal Republic's embassy in Washington, "would be *umfallen* for the verb and *Umfall* for the noun. When the Liberal Party switched from one side to the other on October 3, 1969, it was called 'the Umfall Party'—the Flip-Flop Party. The charge hurt."

Each side of *flip-flop* is doing remarkably well in English. The *flip* side (or reverse side of a disk) has slang meanings that range from "irreverent, cocky" ("That's a flip attitude, young man"—from *flippant*) to a verb meaning "to get excited about" ("That flips me to the point of doing acrobatics") and, finally, "to go completely bonkers" ("I just flipped out").

Flop is making a big hit, too. In computerese, a *floppy disk* stores information: "It is called *floppy* because it is flexible," explains Jim McCartney of Shugart Associates, manufacturers of the gizmos that drive the disks. "The floppy disk is like an LP record, only not rigid, and the disk drive is like a stereo. Smaller storage systems are called *minifloppies.*" (Nobody knows who first used *floppy* to describe a flexible disk; claimants for this honor may submit their names with early citations.)

So you think *flip-flop*, complete with its three centuries of etymology, is mere slang, to be sneered at and not welcomed into dictionaries? Consider a radical change of position, no matter what they call it.

From at least the mid-1950s, the term flip-flop *has been used for one of the elementary logical circuits used by all digital computers (as well as pocket calculators and other digital devices). There's an explanation of the flip-flop circuit and its function on page 399 of the third edition (1958) of* Van Nostrand's Scientific Encyclopedia.

The flip-flop circuit is like a coin that can be either heads or tails up. Within a computer the flip-flop circuit represents "yes or no," or 1 or 0, enabling the machine to do the binary arithmetic that is the basis of electronic digital computation.

The "yes or no" quality of the flip-flop circuit makes it an apt metaphor for a sudden change of human mind. Until I read your column I had no idea the present general popularity of flip-flop *could have originated anywhere other than the flip-flop circuit.*

> G.J.A. O'Toole
> Mt. Vernon, New York

Flip-flop *is the name of the key electronic circuit, duplicated in the giga-millions, in electronic calculators and computers. This basic circuit was designed in the early days of radio and consists of a pair of two electronic gates connected together so that if either gate is turned "ON," the other gate of the pair is turned "OFF."*

An incoming pulse of electricity is always directed through the "ON" gate to the "OFF" gate, causing the "OFF" gate to flip to the "ON" mode and resulting in the previously "ON" gate flopping to the "OFF" mode, and so on and so off.

Today, endless arrays of flip-flop circuits form the basis for all counting circuits in electronic calculators and computers. The "ON" or "OFF" condition of each microscopic gate corresponds to the "1" or "0" of the binary code utilized by these electronic marvels to record numerals and letters in their memory banks.

More to the point, the "ON" or "OFF" condition of each electronic gate corresponds to "Yes" or "No" in the logic circuitry of the computer. Here we find the true meaning of the critical use of the word, as applied to present or past Presidents.

In the early days of science, names were picked from dull Latin derivatives, as in the field of medicine. Our electronic geniuses prefer a touch of humor in naming their brain-children.

> Howard I. Podell
> New Rochelle, New York

In order for an acrobatic performer to hold his body stiff and throw himself over, first on his hands and then on his feet, he must have started out by standing on his feet. Hence, a 360-degree turn has occurred, of which U-turn ("a 180-degree change in direction") is only half. Merely a flip?

Perhaps the wisdom of diplomatists (diplomats?) in choosing volte-face *lies in their suspicion that we voting plebeians are less sure of our expertise in French than in our native American English, thus less likely to scent fickle opportunism. Could this be what separates them from politicians and extends their viability?*

> Mary Jo Groppe
> Shaker Heights, Ohio

The Former Ex

How do you explain the way the dictionaries are describing the pronunciation of *explain?*

Go look it up: Most dictionaries say *ik-SPLANE,* not *ek-SPLANE.* Why the *ik?* Why not *ek?*

"In an unstressed syllable in English," iksplains David Guralnik of *Webster's New World Dictionary,* "there is a tendency for all vowels to be reduced to a neutral sound. With some words, like *ex-* words, tertiary stress reduction goes all the way to the schwa. Rather than use that upside-down 'e' symbol, which confuses some readers, we use the *ik* to make it clearer that the syllable has a neutral quality, and that you do not say *eks-*plain."

Over at American Heritage Dictionary, editor Dolores Harris agrees: "When the vowel is not stressed, it becomes reduced—in the case of *explain,* it is reduced past the *eh* sound to the *ih* sound in most dialects. There are exceptions," she added, pronouncing it *ik-*ceptions.

There are all too many exceptions, complains Karen Hageman at Yale University's School of Medicine, a leading *iks-* exorcist. "Even if the pronunciation key in my *Random House Dictionary* were consistent," she writes, "I am sure that the members of the laboratory where I work would steadfastly refuse to perform ixperiments, ixtrapolate data, or ixplicate the causes of disease."

I stand shoulder to shoulder with the irate Karen Hageman, and wish lexicographers would think over their conclusion that the *ex* is no longer pronounced that way in unstressed syllables. At least give the reader a choice; the *ex* is not so unused as to deserve total banishment from our dictionaries.

"My tone may be ixtreme," adds the Yale pharmacologist, "but I wish to be ixplicit: No one in his/her right mind pronounces *ex* as *iks.* I have ixtended myself as far as possible, and I wish to ixpose these linguistic offenders and force them to ixpurgate their next idition (yes, it happens with *ed* as well)."

The woman ikcells at satire.

Dear Ms. Hageman:
Thank you for your very perceptive letter to William Safire and Jess Stein

concerning the pronunciation of words beginning with ex- in the Random House Dictionary.

You are, of course, absolutely right in deriving our general rule for handling the pronunciation of ex- words: if the first syllable shows stress, we pronounce it as (eks) or (egz), as in excavate and exaltation, while unstressed ex- is usually shown as (iks) or (igz), as in explore and exact.

It is this second part of the rule that you question—and the unstressed ex- does indeed lead to further details or niceties of our system. Basically, there is general agreement among phoneticians that this unstressed ex-, when uttered as part of normal speech flow, is pronounced differently from, and not accurately rendered by, the (eks) pronunciation used when ex- is a stressed syllable. An unstressed vowel can be shown as either (ə) or (i), and the sound of the vowel in this unstressed ex- is, in most situations, considered to be closer to the quality of the "short i." There is a real consensus among phoneticians and Lexicographic Regulars that this short (i) symbol is the proper choice.

Although dictionaries list entries word-by-word, we feel it is important to record the pronunciation of each word as it would be said in a stream of continuous speech (not as it would be enunciated if said slowly and in isolation). Thus, since the ex- in words like exactly and example is, in the flow of normal, relaxed speech, pronounced as something like a short i, we represent it as an (i).

Words such as expeditate and exfoliate are a separate case. The problem is that some syllables that do not actually show a stress mark do have a kind of "understood stress." This usually occurs in technical terms that might be difficult to understand without a relatively, but not fully, emphatic pronunciation of the ex- prefix. We have used the "short e" to indicate the pronunciation of such words. Thus the apparent inconsistency in our system is actually a deliberate, logical, and consistent subrule or detail of it. It is a nicety of our system of which only a few alert readers become aware (though we trust it also helps the others in the proper pronunciation of the words they look up). Besides this there are, of course, other niceties that are part of our system and that cover other situations that you may come across.

Stuart B. Flexner
Editor in Chief
Reference Department
Random House, Inc.
New York, New York

cc: William Safire

Dear Bill:

Let me expand a little on my reply to the query about the pronunciation of words beginning ex-. The sounds and spellings of words often have only a historical connection. Many people, including apparently Karen Hageman, allow their eyes *rather than their ears to determine what they think they hear. Cultivated native speakers of English in their relaxed, unstudied speech (when they are more concerned with what they are saying than with how they are saying it) reduce the vowels in unstressed syllables either to /ə/, or in some environments to /i/. Even platform speech, thanks to electronic amplification which obviates the need for unnatural enunciation to make the speaker understandable to the guy in the last row, is today characterized by the same vocalic reduction.*

The prevailing pronunciation, in virtually every variety of American and British speech, of ex- *in an* unstressed *syllable—Hageman in her sportive catalog includes* explicate *and* expurgate, *which are regularly pronounced with the full vowel sound —is with either /i/ or in very rapid speech with /ə/. There are a few people, retired elocutionists among them, who use /e/. They probably also say (tə wôrd′) for toward and (ôf′ten) for often. All speakers on occasion, in emphasizing a word to make a point, will use the /e/. "I'm trying to* explain *it to you!" You will note that at the entry for the prefix* ex- *in our WNWD, we make allowance for that pronunciation; it has not been "banished" from the dictionary, but there is no room to repeat the information at the hundreds of entries beginning with* ex-.

While I'm at it, let me add that environment (the surrounding sounds of a phoneme in a word) as well as stress affects pronunciation. When ex- *is followed by an unvoiced consonant (actually, in English, it is never followed by a voiced consonant) it is pronounced (eks) in a stressed syllable and (iks) in an unstressed one. When it is followed by a vowel, which is always voiced, its consonantal sounds are usually voiced to (egz) for a stressed syllable (eg′zit), or to (igz) for an unstressed one (ig zist′).*

To conclude with a quotation from Good Advice *(p. 321): "Consult a dictionary for proper meanings and pronunciations. Your audience won't know if you're a bad speller, but they will know if you use or pronounce a word improperly." —George Plimpton.*

David [B. Guralnik]
Vice President and Dictionary
Editor in Chief
Simon & Schuster New World
Dictionaries
Cleveland, Ohio

*As a pronunciation editor of long standing (*American Heritage Dictionary, *Funk & Wagnalls* Standard College Dictionary, *among others), I should like to defend current lexicographical practice in the matter of* ik-SPLANE *and similar words. Your comments applied primarily to words beginning with unstressed* ex-, *but it is necessary to take the broader view and consider this class of words in the context of all unstressed vowels in English, be they in initial (*explain, observe), *medial (*amplify, singular), *or final syllables (*honest, senate).

Although entry words in dictionaries are presented in isolation, the modern pronunciation editor attempts to record them as they would sound in the normal flow of speech, avoiding the artificiality of "spelling pronunciations." Do you, for example, actually say ek-SPLANE or ob-ZURV in ordinary discourse, or do you just think you do—because of the spelling? Listen with your ears, not with your eyes, and you will be amazed at the extent to which the unstressed vowels in English are reduced, most of them to that catchall we call the schwa.

As for Karen Hageman's "ixplicate" and "ixpurgate," these pronunciations would never occur either in speech or in any dictionary as the initial vowel here is in a stressed, not an unstressed, syllable.

> *Ramona R. Michaelis*
> *Supervising Editor*
> *Funk & Wagnalls Standard*
> *College Dictionary*
> *Piedmont, California*

Freeze Is Hot

"Freeze!" barks the F.B.I., kicking in the door and catching the lawbreakers red-handed. This is a crisper command than "Don't move" and is less ambiguous than "You're covered," which can be an incentive to continue gambling.

"Nuclear freeze" is a direct metaphoric derivative of that adjuration not to move. Whether or not that arms-control movement leaves you cold, it has had both diplomatic and linguistic results: "Heat from the Freeze" was the headline chosen by columnist Tom Wicker over an Op-Ed article, and an automotive product was evoked by strategist William G. Hyland in his own Op-Edder, "Freeze and Anti-Freeze."

The most recent use of this stop-'em-in-their-tracks verb-turned-noun is "the COLA freeze," which is not a way to serve a soft drink on a summer's day, but is a suggestion to halt the cost-of-living adjustment in Social Security benefits. All such economic uses of "freeze" stem from the "price freeze" of October 1942, the usage popularized by the magazine *Business Week.* In its verb form, this meaning was a product of the Roosevelt Brain Trust, first recorded by Harold Ickes, then Secretary of the Interior, in a diary entry in 1933: "This contemplates the freezing of prices at their present level."

Although "chilling effect" and "cold war" have pejorative connotations, *freeze* stimulates thoughts of resolute action in a crisis. The verb putting the noun into action is "impose" or "institute." A problem arises when a freeze has been in effect

for some time: The cry then is usually to "lift" the freeze, or to "unfreeze" whatever has been suspended, or to seek a "thaw."

The excessive use of *freeze* has led to a virtual ice age in political labeling. An alternative is to be desired, though I am loath to call for a "freeze" freeze. *Halt* is a good word, though it is less permanent than *stop.* (A wage-price halt? A nuclear stop?) Another untried word with a similar meaning is *fix,* which I commend to phrase makers. Breathes there a politician without a hidden desire to put in a fix?

Your contention that the verb form of "price freeze" was a product of the Roosevelt Brain Trust left me cold. On 6 March 1931, Bernard Baruch appeared before the War Policies Commission, a special body composed of senators, representatives, and cabinet officers that was charged, inter alia, with studying ways of preventing wartime profiteering. Drawing on his experience in World War I as head of the War Industries Board, Baruch proposed to the commission a program of price control that went beyond the piecemeal fixing that had characterized the Great War. He recommended "freezing the whole price structure" at the beginning of any major conflict in the future. (War Policies Commission, Hearings, 71st Cong., 2d sess., 1931, p. 34.)

But if the Sage of Wall Street's ghost sues you (everybody sues today) for misattribution of coinage paternity, you may employ the following defense. Baruch most likely did not write the prepared statement from which the quotation above is taken. The author probably was Hugh Johnson, who performed many such services for Baruch and who sat at Baruch's side during the hearing on 6 March 1931.

Terrence J. Gough
Arlington, Virginia

Full Figuring

The story has long been told among public-relations professionals of the railroad president who received an irate letter from a passenger-stockholder who had found a bedbug in his roomette. The executive sent back a letter thanking the stockholder for bringing this outrage to his personal attention, and assured him that the car had been removed from service, taken to the maintenance yard and fumigated; he added that only through the vigilance of management and stockholders could passenger service be maintained, etc., etc.

Unfortunately, a secretarial slip-up took the steam out of his engine: Attached to the letter, and mistakenly mailed to the stockholder, was a scrawled memo: "Send this joker the bug letter."

Along similar lines, in 1981 Leonard Zoph of San Francisco became incensed at a television commercial for a brassiere showing Jane Russell saying, "For we full-figured gals. . . ." He wrote Miss Russell in care of the sponsor, International Playtex Inc.: "I propose that you change your TV commercial from 'for *we* full-figured gals' to 'for *us* full-figured gals.' "

Back came the response from Leonard Berger, who then bore the title of Director of Consumer Affairs. (Letters that I send to magazines with changes of address are answered by a person with the most satisfying title in all corporate affairs: "Fulfillment Manager." What greater role in life than to manage fulfillment? But I digress.) "You are correct," wrote Mr. Berger, starting off on the right foot, "in citing the fact that standard English usage would require the objective-case pronoun 'us' to follow the preposition 'for.' "

He then gallantly absolved Miss Russell: "Please be assured that Miss Russell was in no way responsible for this grammatical license. International Playtex and our advertising agency, Grey Advertising, are mass communicators and believe we must be prepared to adapt as American English evolves into commonly spoken and accepted language usage."

Having set up this excuse for permissiveness, the executive had the temerity to invoke my name: "William Safire addressed this subject recently. One example of required adjustment cited in his column was the commonly used 'It's me,' which has replaced the grammatically preferred 'It's I.' Just as awkward and unnatural as 'It's I' would sound today, so in our opinion would 'for *us* full-figured gals' sound."

He then gushed through a final paragraph—"We do endorse your interest in maintaining standards of grammatically correct English usage. We shall, in future advertising, be most alert," etc., etc. (I can hear it now: "Send that joker the bra letter.")

Two years later, I heard from Gracy Banks, a teacher of English in Chicago. She, too, had objected to Jane Russell's "for we full-figured gals," and received the

same old letter, this time signed by Dawn Moretta, Supervisor, Consumer Affairs. The time has come to strike back.

We are dealing here with the case of pronouns. In the nominative (sometimes called the subjective) case, pronouns look like this: *I, we, you, he, she, it, they.* In the objective case, those pronouns look like this: *me, us, you, him, her, it, them.* I will now get off your case and get down to cases.

Long ago, not realizing how it would be misconstrued at the brassiere factory, I pointed out why "It is me" is acceptable: When a word sounds as if it is the object, use the objective form. "It is me" looks and sounds correct, even though the linking verb, *is,* should not be followed by the objective case. Although "It is I" is grammatically pure, it is idiomatically out of whack—to most normal human beings. (If anybody demands to know who told you "It's me" is O.K., tell them it was me.) When established idiom clashes with grammar, correctness is on the side of the idiom. Put another way, if sticking grimly to rules of grammar makes you *sound* like a pompous pedant, you *are* a pompous pedant.

Now here is why poor Jane Russell is being made to appear a linguistic outlaw on television: *We* is a pronoun in the nominative (subjective, if you like) case. That means it substitutes for the name of the subject. We grammarians agree on that. (We idiom-respecters agree, too. The advertising slogan "Us Tareyton smokers would rather fight than switch" was not idiomatic; it was wrong. If the plural pronoun is the subject, it's *we* or *they,* not *us* or *them.* Them Tareyton copywriters delivered a blow for bad grammar.)

If Miss Russell had said, "We full-figured gals need this," she would have been absolutely, cross-your-heart right: *We* is the subject of that sentence. If she had said, "Us full-figured gals need this," she would have been wrong: *Us* is an objective-case pronoun and should not be used as the subject.

What she did say was, "for we full-figured gals." That is wrong because *for* is a preposition; the pronoun that follows *for* is the object of that preposition. What case must an object be in? You got it (actually, *you've* got it): the objective case —namely, *us*. Not *we*. *I* and *we* cannot be properly used as the object: To say "for we" is as incorrect as saying "between you and I." It's always "for us" and "between you and me." Take that not merely as a rule of grammar, but as a guide to living a rewarding and law-abiding life.

I will not belabor the people at International Playtex or my old friends at Grey Advertising for using *gals* in an era that prefers *women* or even *guys,* or for using *full-figured* as a euphemism for *well-developed,* which is a euphemism for *buxom,* which doesn't need a euphemism at all. We language-lovers and Russell-remember-ers want our gal done right by; that's the least you guys can do for us sagging, rubber-tired types.

So you think "It is I" sounds "idiomatic" and "only pompous pedants use the term." There goes the neighborhood!

> *Shame on you,*
> *Rachel Kerby*
> *Lenexa, Kansas*

"It is me" does not look correct or sound correct and is not correct. To contend that "when established idiom (read ignorance) clashes with grammar, correctness is on the side of the idiom" is ridiculous.

This is the first step on the primrose path taken by Dr. Gove, that harmful drudge, who believed that a dictionary "should have no traffic with . . . artificial notions of correctness or superiority."

This brought a proper rebuke from E. B. White, who said, "This approach struck many people as chaotic and degenerative, and that's the way it strikes me."

> *Richard E. Griffin*
> *Richmond, Virginia*

I say "It is I," and I resent being called a pompous pedant! Where a sufficient number of people make a grammatical error, does that error then become an idiom?

In correct usage the word is *takes the nominative case, not the objective case. Yes, I am a teacher, as you may have guessed.*

> Sadie Buchferer
> Bayside, New York

"If anybody demands to know who told you 'It's me' is O.K., tell them [sic] it was me." This is gymnastically cute but grammatically wrong. Since when does a singular pronoun (read "anybody") become complemented by a plural pronoun (read "them")?

> Richard J. Ruh
> Amherst, Massachusetts

I begin with two premises:

1. Natural, correct English requires us to say things like "It's me" or "Is that us (in the photograph)?" The alternatives "It's I" or "Is that we?" at best sound stilted, and at worst are just plain wrong.

2. On the other hand, the word is *is surely a* linking verb *so it would seem that we use a predicate nominative, not an accusative case.*

It would seem reasonable to take a look at other languages and see how the problem is resolved there. Das bin ich, *where* ich *is in the predicate nominative. Not only is* Das bin mich *grammatically incorrect, but no native German speaker, no matter how illiterate, would even be tempted to say it. So, in German, one simply follows the grammatical rule, and there is no problem.*

In French, on the other hand, one would say, C'est moi *(cf.* L'état c'est moi*). One certainly would never say* C'est je, *where* je *is the nominative form of the pronoun. But, no grammarian of French would argue that the* moi *in this expression is accusative. Indeed, it is not, since the accusative form is "me." French grammars will tell you that the pronoun* je *has two nominative forms,* je *and* moi, *where the* moi *form is often called the emphatic (as in expressions like* Moi, je ne suis pas fatigué *("Me, I'm not tired"). So there is no problem in French either:* moi *is an alternative nominative form of* je. *Why can't we adopt the same incredibly simple point of view in English? The pronoun "I" has two nominative forms, "I" and "me," the latter being an emphatic form or a predicate form. It is just an accident that "me" is also the accusative form of the pronoun.*

I wonder if this analysis couldn't be justified on historical grounds, if it isn't possible that during the several centuries when French was spoken in English that English speakers didn't pick up expressions like C'est moi *and adapt them to "It's me"—because we are* not *using an illogical accusative as the "purists" tell us, but simply using an Anglicized version of a French alternate nominative.*

Peter Braunfeld
Department of Mathematics
University of Illinois at
Urbana-Champaign
Urbana, Illinois

When an ad agency chooses to say ". . . for we full-figured gals" or "Us Tareyton smokers would rather fight than switch," I believe they are deliberately trying to project a desired image: in the bra case, the incorrect we *sounds more ladylike; in the Tareyton case, the incorrect* us *more macho—to change the public's perception of filtered Tareytons as an "effeminate" cigarette. Some years ago when I was teaching in Baltimore, I used the Tareyton example to try to wake up a class of bored middle-class high schoolers to whom I was trying to explain the uses of the subjective and objective cases. As I recall, they all thought "Us" in the Tareyton ad was correct usage, and that "We Tareyton smokers . . ." sounded "wrong" and prissy.*

Thus, an incorrect pronoun can indeed be le mot juste *to convey a subtle advertising message.*

Henrietta Wexler
Washington, D.C.

I think us *was ruined forever by "us chickens" of the "nobody here but etc."*

Saul Steinberg
New York, New York

Fulsome Complaining

"A writer whose first novel is fulsomely praised must pay forever after an excruciating tax," began a *Newsweek* review.

"I wrote a letter to *Newsweek*," writes Max Garber of Flushing, New York, "pointing out the erroneous use of the word *fulsome* in a Peter Prescott review of a new William Wharton novel. I am not satisfied with the reply."

The newsmagazine's Priscilla Baker, writing for the editors, took this position:

"Peter Prescott was using (not misusing) the word *fulsome* according to the first definition in *Webster's Third New International Dictionary* of *fulsome*, which is *copious, abundant*. Therefore he was saying that William Wharton's first novel was abundantly (or copiously) praised."

The first definition in some dictionaries is not the word's most common meaning, and the permissiveness of the *Merriam-Webster Third* is legendary. To most lexicographers, and to most careful users of the language, the word *fulsome* means "disgusting, offensive because excessive and insincere." Its etymology takes the "full" that began in "abundant" and crosses it with "foul," to give us a useful slam at phoniness: *Fulsome* praise is the gushing of a toady, not to be confused with *lavish* praise, which is evidently what Mr. Prescott had in mind.

Is the distinction worth preserving? Or had the mistake been made so often that it is no longer a mistake? *Newsweek*'s editors have decided to cave in, and that decision will be embraced by permissivists everywhere. But I stand shoulder to shoulder with Mr. Garber of Flushing for using *fulsome* only to mean "excessive and insincere," since we already have a copious supply of words for "abundant."

We have few enough words in the language to impute baseness of motive. Novelist Wharton has been unintentionally maligned. People who misuse *fulsome* to mean "full" are the sort who use *noisome* when they mean "noisy."

That first definition in Webster III *is clearly labeled* obs! *If the skill of reading dictionaries were not such a sadly neglected area in our educational establishment, the noisome and noisy permissiveness legend anent* Webster III *might never have arisen.*

Webster III *also provides a listing for* skellum *as a "chiefly Scottish" word, tracing it to the Dutch-German* schelm *of similar meaning. It also appears in* Johnson's Dictionary, *with [Stephen] Skinner (1623–67) cited as the authority. The connection with* skelder *sounds plausible but is unacknowledged by* Webster III *which has [origin unknown].*

Louis Marck
New York, New York

NOTE FROM W. S.: No, the first definition of *fulsome* in Webster's Third is "1.a. copious, abundant" and is followed by "1.b. *obs* plump, fat." The skill of reading dictionaries is indeed sadly neglected.

Fulsome's Last Word

Newsweek's editors were castigated in this space for defending the use of *fulsome* to mean "full." The word's primary current meaning is "offensive because excessive and insincere"—*fulsome* praise is to be avoided, while *lavish* praise is something to be desired.

That thrust at solecism has drawn a response from Jim Quinn of Philadelphia, the Prince of Permissivists. His book, *American Tongue and Cheek,* made him a Professor Moriarty to all Lexicographic Irregulars. All of us—language shamans, pecksniffian purists, and defenders of the prescriptivist faith—recognize Quinn as The Archenemy, articulate spokesman for the hosts of tongue-tied Language Slobs.

"People who use *fulsome* to mean full are using it as it was used when it originally appeared—way back circa 1250," he writes in his devilishly logical way, using good scholarship to corrupt good English, "formed from *full,* meaning full or copious, and *some,* an adjective-forming suffix (as in *gladsome, winsome,* etc.). Possibly because the words *full* and *foul* were pronounced alike at one time, the word began to pick up other meanings. I am tempted to say the word was corrupted. But words don't corrupt, they simply change."

Seeking to show that the current mistake is no mistake at all—thereby undermining the cause of preserving clarity in meaning—Quinn traipses through the *Oxford English Dictionary*: "The original meaning lasted several centuries (last *O.E.D.* cite 1583), but in the meantime *fulsome* also meant 'fat, overgrown' (1340–1678); 'overfed' (1642–1805); 'gross and satiating' (1410–1770) . . . 'morally foul, obscene' (1604–1726); and finally 'gross or excessive, offensive to good taste' (1663 to the present). What a spectacular career! What a wonderful word! How it should please all our many purists to see this much abused and much misunderstood word finally, after centuries of wayward use, returning to its etymologically correct meaning!"

Pretty tricky. The philosopher of anything goes, with his damnable erudition, argues that today's mistake was yesterday's correctness, and therefore we "purists" who like to keep a word's meaning from fraying at the edges are playing a mug's game.

The "correct" answer: Words work best when they convey specific meanings, and work worst when they are laden with ambiguities and confusions. Words mean what they mean *now,* which may not be what they meant when they were first issued; meaning is a snapshot of today, not a film of the history of the word. Therefore, let us not festoon our words with archaic meanings that rob us of clarity in communication. Let us go with today's meaning, and resist the intrusion and confusion of yesterday's and tomorrow's meanings.

Certainly the meaning of a word changes, and yes, it is silly to try to freeze a living, growing language. But it is useful to defend today's meaning from the encroachment of fuzziness, even when that confusion bears the most impeccable etymological credentials, because clarity is a worthwhile goal. In a thousand years, change will win, but if we do not fight change, there will not be much left to be changed.

Coming back to earth, it turns out that *Newsweek*'s editors were vigorously defending a mistake their writer did not make. "I'm amused (and distressed)," writes Peter Prescott of the newsmagazine, "that somebody is defending me without consulting me, and going to great lengths to defend me wrongly. . . . When I used the word *fulsomely* in the context you mentioned, I meant 'fulsomely': praise that was, as in the *American Heritage* definition, 'offensively excessive.' " He adds a shot with a good word in it: "I shouldn't have used a word that is so often misused that its correct use will set the grammaticasters (*O.E.D.*, IV: 346) to fluttering."

You wrote, "Words work best when they convey specific meanings, and work worst when they are laden with ambiguities and confusions." Your remarks about fulsome *were a fitting illustration of the confusions that regularly arise.*

A recent headline in The New York Post *read, "Boris Sports His Chauvinism." Because* Boris *referred to Russia, I concluded that* chauvinism *referred to Russia's attitude toward the United States. Since* chauvinism, *in strict usage, means overzealous nationalism, my assumption seemed reasonable. Only by reading the article itself did I realize that* chauvinism *was being used as a synonym for* sexism.

There is no need for this loose usage. If someone feels that women belong only in the kitchen, we can call him a sexist, not a chauvinist. The misuse of words such as chauvinism *and* fulsome *not only causes ambiguity and confusion, but also threatens to rob us of words for which we have no exact alternative. By observing the distinction between* chauvinism *and* sexism, *we are preserving the meaning of a word that is badly needed in our vocabulary. In a recent article on microphysics in* The New York Times, *the writer described the competition of the nations that try to be the first to make an important scientific discovery. He compared this competition to the chauvinism of the Olympics.*

If language must change, then let it change not through ignorance or carelessness, but through enrichment. An example of what I think is linguistic enrichment is a word coined by one of my high school Latin teachers to describe the people who condone ignorance, and sometimes even cultivate it, by debasing our language. My teacher said, "These people are linguicides."

George Patrick Whalen
Dover Plains, New York

Gender Offender

"Republicans Worry About 'Gender Gap,'" frowned a recent headline. The ostensible problem is the disparity of support for Mr. Reagan between men and women: A far greater percentage of men than women approve of the way he's doing his job. The difference is "the gender gap."

The real problem is the misuse of the word *gender*. Although that word was used in the eighteenth century to mean *sex*, it has lost that meaning: Usage has worn *gender* down to a description of the categories of words, such as masculine and feminine; such classifications are not a big deal in English. But since *masculine* and *feminine* are adjectives reeking of sex, therein lies the confusion.

Gender applies to grammar and *sex* applies to people. As they say over at the rifle association, words aren't sexy, people are. If you have a friend of the *female sex*, you are a red-blooded American boy; if you have a friend of the *feminine gender*, you have an unnatural attachment to a word.

"In the text of the equal rights amendment," reports Kathy Bonk of the National Organization for Women, "we had a big problem over the wording of the phrase 'on account of sex.' Some people believed that *sex* could be construed to mean 'the act of sex,' and that the use of 'gender' would have avoided that. But we stayed with 'sex' because E.R.A. parallels the Nineteenth Amendment and we wanted the language to be parallel."

But since NOW officials know the right and wrong use of *sex* and *gender*, how could the organization issue press releases pointing to "the gender gap," an obvious solecism?

Kathy Bonk made it clear that a mistake in usage is not as bad as a double entendre: "Because 'gender gap' did not have the unseemly connotations that 'sex gap' would have had."

While you are doubtless right about the proper usage of sex *and* gender *and the distinction between them in general language,* gender *does have a sexual meaning in medical terminology. When a child has congenitally defective sexual organs and is of ambiguous sex as a result, one of the main considerations in making a decision whether to convert it surgically to a clear-cut male or a clear-cut female is its "gender identity," that is, whether it thinks of itself as a male or a female. Here* gender *is used exactly in a sexual sense, just as you say it was in general usage in the eighteenth century.*

I don't think this is a survival of old terminology in an isolated subculture (i.e., the medical community); rather, it seems to be a deliberate resuscitation of an obsolete usage to provide a precise meaning for which no other word was available.

Thus your calling the use of gender *to mean* sex *an obvious solecism was slightly off the mark.*

Barnett Zumoff, M.D.
Chief, Division of
    Endocrinology and
    Metabolism
Beth Israel Medical Center
New York, New York

Getting "Obtain"

"On the international front," wrote my colleague in columny Joseph Kraft, "the same benign political results obtain."

This is an example of literary language. Most people use *obtain* in its transitive form—*to obtain something*—meaning "to get, to procure." In its intransitive form, *obtain* has a different meaning: "to prevail," stemming from its Latin root, *obtinere,* "to have, hold, possess."

Mr. Kraft's usage is solidly grounded in English, from 1618 ("Their opinions have now obtained for a hundred years") to Gore Vidal's 1963 use: "All the arguments used against his candidacy in 1960 will still obtain." But that meaning has a bookish quality: *Krapp's Guide to Good English* in 1927 called it "literary," and Nicholson's *A Dictionary of American-English Usage* in 1957 called it "right —but for learned contexts only—*prevailed* will usually do."

Why, then, did Mr. Kraft use the almost archaic construction in a newspaper column? One reason may be that *prevail* has been seized by the Reaganauts (a Richard Allen coinage, along with *Reagoons,* the storm troops of Reaganism, and *Reaganinnies,* the more timid among them). Evidently the word *win* is taken to be simplistic in current White House use (Gerald Ford's WIN button, for "Whip Inflation Now," also casts a shadow on *win*), and the word *prevail* is used to describe what we shall do vis-à-vis Communism. It has a Churchillian sound with Faulknerian overtones, and is less stentorian than old-time prizefight announcer Harry Balogh's "emerge victorious."

A second reason for the Kraftian *obtain* may be that some writers like literary style. Sol Steinmetz at Clarence Barnhart Books notes that several words usually confined to literary contexts surface in contemporary journalism: "The question *abides*" is one, using that word to mean "remains," as in "Abide With Me," rather than the more common "to tolerate," as in "I can't abide him."

Another literary usage is "He is jealous of his honor," rather than "He is jealous of his boss." Yet another is the use of *awful* as "awe-inspiring," as in "the awful power of nature," rather than in the more common "what an awful dress." Or *save*, meaning "except," as in "all save one."

Though it may be jarring, the occasional use of literary language in a nonliterary context strikes me as refreshing—not in the least elitist. As Steinmetz puts it: "If the right conditions obtain, Mr. Kraft's usage will prevail."

Your comments on the word obtain *to mean "prevail" instead of "get" remind me, tangentially, of something that happened in a class I was teaching in a junior high school. The student, having used the word* get *several times in an essay he was assigned to write, referred to the thesaurus. He then wrote, "How do you obtain from here to Brooklyn?" Something bothered him about this, so he crossed it out and corrected it: "How do you receive from here to Brooklyn?"*

Still uneasy, he tried once more: "How do you procure . . . ?"

Rena Garter Kunis
Bellerose, New York

I like your expression, "colleague in columny." I can't find that word in my dictionary, but its meaning seems obvious. Did you also mean to hint at calumny?

George M. Grasty
Whittier, California

NOTE FROM W. S.: Yes, *columny* is a play on *calumny*.

Glacis

The award for the best new politico-diplomatic usage of 1982 goes to Sahabzada Yaqub-Khan, foreign minister of Pakistan, who used a word I never heard before to describe the country that lies between the Soviet Union and the gateway to the Persian Gulf: "Afghanistan might one day be intended by the Soviets to be a glacis."

"A what?" asked a press corps eager to advance its erudition. Mr. Yaqub-Khan, who converses easily in Romance languages as well as Russian and Urdu, was puzzled at the lack of understanding by the American press: *Glacis* is an old, established English word with a modern figurative meaning. From the sentence context, I offered *buffer* as a synonym, which the foreign minister accepted.

But *glacis,* pronounced "GLAY-sis," is metaphorically much richer. Derived from the Old French *glacier,* "to slip, slide," a *glacis* began in English more than three centuries ago, meaning a fortification that sloped gradually to ground level, permitting an unrestricted field of fire. Later, *glacis plates* were sloping armor plates on ships. Finally, the figurative use took over: East Germany was seen by *The Times* of London in 1955 "as part of Russia's defensive glacis," and *The Observer* five years later agreed that the countries of Eastern Europe "form the glacis between the Soviet Union and the West."

A *glacis state,* then, is one that forms a defensive barrier between one power and its potential enemies. Because Canada is located between the United States and possible across-the-pole missile attack, it is a glacis state, much as Canadians would resent that role. How accurate a definition of Afghanistan, if the Soviets agree to withdraw and insist on leaving behind a Soviet-influenced government.

The phrase, with its defensive connotation, is much better than the in-between *buffer state* (from *buff,* or blow, meaning now a padding to absorb shocks), which means "a state between two powers whose position lessens the chance of conflict." A *buffer* separates both; a *glacis* does that, too, but especially forms part of the defense of one.

Glacis! Just when I needed it most. Thank you, Mr. Safire. I've finally put your column to good use. I was writing a paper on the British occupation of Egypt in 1882, and I would have described an old Palmerstonian policy as "using the Ottoman Empire as a buffer against Russia," had it not been for you, sir.

Jack Kaufman
New York, New York

Good as a Mile

In a piece about "terrific honorifics," I came down on the side of *Ms.* as a useful way of addressing a woman without poking into her marital status. Most of the mail ran the other way: "A woman who wants to be addressed as 'Ms.,'" wrote Mrs. Havens Grant of Greenwich, Connecticut, "is either ashamed of not being married or ashamed of being married."

However, support for *Ms.* comes from a woman who does not have a shame problem at all. She is Ellen Goodman, *The Boston Globe* columnist, whose observations enliven Op-Ed pages across the country, and she offers her own case as an example of the confusion that results from a newspaper's insistence on the old Miss-or-Mrs. style.

"Consider my own cameo appearances in *The New York Times*'s pages," Ellen Goodman writes. "They have referred to me each time as Miss Goodman. Actually, my Miss name was Holtz. My Mrs. name was Goodman. But I am in fact no longer married to Goodman, or Dr. Goodman as *The Times* would put it. Now Miss Holtz isn't exactly right. Nor is Miss Goodman. Nor is Mrs. Goodman.

"To compound the problem," writes Miss Goodman (I must use *Times* style), "I will be marrying a perfectly delightful person with a single flaw. His name is neither Goodman nor Holtz but Levey. I will not become Mrs. Levey, needless to say. Nor will I go back to Holtz. Due to bylines and children, I shall forever remain Goodman, unless I change my name this time to Goodperson. Or simply Good.

"*The Times*, however," continues this good woman, "in its tenacity will go on referring to me as Miss Goodman. (Maybe what I need is a Ph.D.) This seems to be one area in which *The Times* is far more invested in tradition than accuracy." She signs herself "Ellen May Holtz Goodperson."

At *The Philadelphia Bulletin*, before that newspaper became defunct, editors also held the line against *Ms.* until Marci Shatzman dumped 300 letters addressed to Ms.'s on an editor's desk: He conceded the term was in widespread use and put the concession in the stylebook. Miss (or Mrs., or Dr.) Shatzman, now an editor for Time Video Information Services, recalls a line spoken by a friend who would once have been called a spinster: "Don't call me Miss, call me Ms.—because I haven't missed as much as you think I have."

Dear Bill,

I never could understand how The Times, *which reacted with horror to the cost of printing a single unnecessary period in every copy of the paper, could for so long remain indifferent to the cost of hour-upon-expensive-hour of research into the marital status of women—not only in news stories but also in its business correspondence—when, in most instances, that status has nothing whatsoever to do with the price of broccoli. Economic considerations alone provide a strong argument for your position.*

Betty [Pomerantz]
Canandaigua, New York

What is the plural of Ms.?

Judith A. Sokoloff
New York, New York

NOTE FROM W. S.: Good question. Ask Gloria Steinem.

Regarding your column on the use of "Ms." and Miss or Mrs. Ellen Goodman, I would say that the usage is pretty definite. When she is using a name gained by marriage, she is Mrs.; otherwise, she is Miss. Whether or not she is actually married need not enter the picture.

A woman who is widowed or divorced would still be Mrs. when using her married name; she would be Miss, even if still married, when using a different name. The onetime Miss Holtz (she still is Miss when using that name) would be Mrs. Goodman, even though divorced from Dr. Goodman, or Mrs. Levey, if she elects to use his name. If she should call herself Goodperson I imagine it should be considered an obvious variant of Goodman, varied according to feminist ideology, and hence Mrs.

If she should call herself Miss Goodman, I might go along with her simply to avoid an argument; but it would be wrong to give her credit for correct usage. (Or, for that matter, to give such credit to The Times.) Still, the use of Ms. isn't bad.

You will recall that it is in pronunciation and usage pretty much the same as the old Southern Miss/Mrs. ambiguous title Mizz—only the spelling is new, and in fact it is an improvement. "Ms." has a formality, a pertness, a neatness about it—it is appropriate. "Mizz," never really a formally correct word before, is dowdy, slovenly. So, for once I have to say we have an improvement in the language.

Other feminist usages are worse than bad. They are clumsy, and impress me as a kind of thought control. Did my generation fight mightily against censors of the old style only to fall prey to the new prudery, which aims towards castrated speech, emasculated men, and unfeminine women? And a crude and clumsy variation of thought control? I say resist; the use of -person endings in particular strikes me as a passing fad, because no matter how many times I hear it, it still sounds wrong. The feminists would have done much better to inveigh against the usage of man *as meaning "male," if they had to pick this fight. I predict in maybe five or ten years anybody using the ending -person will be thought of in the same way we think of a liberal who allowed himself to complain of "reactionaries"—as someone who exposed himself as something of a jerk.*

> *Michael N. Tierstein*
> *Brooklyn, New York*

Have the Usual

"Keep an eye on *traditional*," said a *Times* colleague, Peter Kilborn. He collects and—whenever possible—kills that word in copy when it is an affected form of *usual* or *customary*.

In most synonymy studies, *usual* (common or frequent occurrence) is compared to *customary* (conventional, or conforming to previous practice), *habitual* (unfailing repetition), and *typical* (following a pattern). Similar meanings, but not the same.

Along has come *traditional*, which used to mean "time-honored," as befits a word with a Latin root of "to hand down." These days, *traditional* is undergoing a vogue use to mean just about everything in the paragraph above.

A *Times* article about black colleges reports on tests that "present a misleading view of the mission that such institutions have traditionally undertaken. . . ." *Customarily* would have been a better choice.

The abuse of *tradition* in its adjectival form is making history: That is, a word was needed to take the place abandoned by *traditional.* We can find it in the same piece, identifying the United Negro College Fund as "an organization of forty-two historically black colleges." *Historical* means "what existed in the past" (as differentiated from *historic,* "what is important in history"); in that sense, *historically* is not wrong, but I would choose *traditionally,* or the more specific *formerly all-black.*

When in doubt, remember Claude Rains in *Casablanca*: He did not say, "Round up the traditional suspects."

As a historian, I applaud your clarifying for your readers the distinction between historical *and* historic. *Now, why not note the common mistake of using* an *as the article before these adjectives, as well as before* history *and* historian? *The rule is clear, requiring* a *if the consonant* h *is pronounced, as in these cases, and* an *if it is silent. Fowler calls the use of* an *here "nostalgic or pedantic."*

Milton W. Hamilton
Formerly New York State
Historian
Glenmont, New York

Not really related to, but brought to mind by your piece on traditional, *is the increasingly cloying use of the word* legendary—*particularly by purveyors of "Greatest Hits" albums on late-night TV (UHF channels)—to refer to any person, however undistinguished, who is now simply "dead"; e.g., the legendary Buddy Holly, the legendary Janis Joplin, the legendary Karen Carpenter, and (I heard advertised for an appearance in Philadelphia this week, though still alive) the legendary Sammy Davis Junior.*

Michael J. Sullivan III
Associate Professor of Politics
Drexel University
Philadelphia, Pennsylvania

Pointing to the misuse of traditional *brought to mind a similar misuse of the adjective* classic. *My own preference is for its use in describing standards established by the Greeks or Romans.*

Nowadays that classic (if I may) usage has been obscured by attempts to make it synonymous with such adjectives as ground-breaking, innovative, *or* pioneering. *While I can accept that the word may be used to imply that a film is a model of its kind—taking* Webster's New World, *first meaning, as definitive—its overuse in those terms has diminished the word's true meaning as an adjective. For some strange reason, my dander is less aroused when I read* Citizen Kane *described as a film classic than when I read it described as a classic film.*

Richard W. Charteris
Toronto, Ontario

Hearts and Minds

During the Vietnam War much was made of winning "the hearts and minds" of the people; a colleague of mine at the time, Charles Colson, had a framed motto about applying pressure to another part of the anatomy: "and their hearts and minds will follow." In a blurb for *A Killing Pace*, an engrossing novel by Les Whitten, a private eye says with un-Hammettlike fervor, "No writer in America has ever looked so deeply into the heart, soul and mind of a big-league investigator. . . ."

"Now that the controversy about what to do in El Salvador is heating up," writes Ruth Murray Brown of Norman, Oklahoma, "we are beginning to hear again about winning the 'hearts and minds' of the people." She has tracked the phrase to John Adams in 1818—"The Revolution was in the hearts and minds of the people"—and to the Bible's Philippians 4:7—"And the peace of God, which passeth all understanding, shall keep your hearts and minds. . . ." She asks: "How did the phrase in the Bible, which is merely part of simple benediction, come to mean the goal of a revolutionary or counterrevolutionary effort?"

Timely question; if you see light at the end of that tunnel, send it in.

He Kept Us Out of War

As United States Marines are deployed in the Middle East, some political figures are recalling the highly effective, if ultimately misleading, slogan of Woodrow Wilson in the campaign of 1916: "He Kept Us Out of War."

Joseph Goulden, author of a forthcoming dictionary of spookspeak, provides us with the hard-to-find citation that locks in the coinage. Albert S. Burleson, of Austin, Texas, who had been President Wilson's Postmaster General, wrote to biographer Ray Stannard Baker on July 14, 1928: "I beg leave to state that the phrase 'He kept us out of war' originated with the Hon. Martin F. Glynn of New York, but its use as a slogan during the campaign was suggested by me. Ex-Governor Glynn used this expression in a speech he made before the [Houston] Convention."

President Wilson—reserved, aloof, professorial, and not much of a stump speaker—invited attack as an elitist, but was surely no wimp. His best campaign advice has been taken by some of today's candidates who allow opponents to blaze away at their own feet with denials of wimpiness: "Never murder a man who is committing suicide."

Henry the Impetuous

Once in a while, you can tell when a word is selected with care. In the Eisenhower era, when Sherman Adams wanted to describe his exchange of gifts with an industrialist—admitting error but not wrongdoing—he chose the Yankee fiduciary's word *imprudent.*

In the same way, when Henry Kissinger returned from Vietnam negotiations in 1972, he needed a phrase that said peace was soon to come: *Nigh* was too old-fashioned; *around the corner,* too Hooverian; *soon* would accentuate the time rather than the peace. Hence, "Peace is *at hand.*"

Recently, Dr. Kissinger was attending a conference in Morocco. A friend asked him if the agreement he drew up while Secretary of State—that the Israelis would withdraw from strategic passes in Sinai in return for an American pledge not to deal with the P.L.O.—precluded any meeting between a private American citizen and a Palestinian Arab. Henry Kissinger said he was willing to talk to the man, and the two met in a hotel lobby for thirty or forty minutes.

Later, it was revealed that the Palestinian was a top negotiator for Yasir Arafat, and King Hussein leaped on that meeting as evidence that the Americans were secretly undermining his dealings with the P.L.O. In a political column written by the Mr. Hyde in me, I chastised the former secretary for his back-channel machinations; when we next spoke, and he lugubriously remonstrated with me, I put it plainly: "Henry, you were being either dopey or devious. Which was it?"

If faced with the stark choice between those two words, Henry would probably have reversed earlier form and preferred *dopey,* since his position is that he was unaware of the Palestinian's official position. However, experienced statesmen do not accept word choices that damn them either way. Henry thought it over and put forward a word with which he felt more comfortable: "I was *incautious.*"

He That Filches from Me . . .

The word in Laurence Barrett's book, *Gambling With History,* that started all the commotion was in this line: "Apparently a Reagan mole in the Carter camp had filched papers. . . ."

Filch is a bit of sixteenth-century slang, origin unknown, that began as a word for stealing small things like poultry. Shakespeare put the word in Iago's mouth to give a contrast of slyness to the forthright *steal:* "Who steals my purse steals trash . . . But he that filches from me my good name. . . ." The connotation of pettiness was changed to cunning: *filch* meant to Shakespeare, and means to us, "slyly stealing." (Had I been Shakespeare's copy editor, I would have changed "he that filches" to "he who filches," but the poet might have wanted to minimize the accent on the syllable between "he" and "filches.")

A spokesman for David Stockman, the director of the Office of Management and Budget who was the source of Mr. Barrett's explosive anecdote, then quoted the great debate-briefer as having admitted to knowledge that the material from the Carter camp had been "pilfered."

Pilfer accentuates the pettiness of a theft, although it is rooted in the French *pelfre,* "booty," and made its name in a line of poetry by Sir Walter Scott: "Despite those titles, power, and pelf." Stores consider *pilferage* infuriating but routine, and allow for it in profit projections.

Some journalists used the verb *purloin,* derived from the French *pur* (for) and *loin* (distant), to set far aside, or to remove to another place far away. It is a bookish verb, recalling Edgar Allan Poe's story of "The Purloined Letter," which was hidden by being placed in plain sight. *Purloin* is a word typed with lifted pinkie, and could not last long in the developing story's terminology. (In the sweepstakes for slugline, "Debategate" was first used in my hearing by Gerald Rafshoon, a former Carter aide; I preferred "Briefingate"; Ned Burks, night editor at *The*

Times's Washington bureau, picked up on the frequent use of *purloin* to suggest
—his friends hope, facetiously—"Purlygate.")

Steal is the verb that most clearly implies "serious crime." People who steal
go to jail, at least sometimes, and when that verb is sounded, all other synonyms
pale. *Stealing* is to *filching* what a *crime* is to a *caper.*

At a presidential press conference, ABC's Sam Donaldson countered Mr.
Reagan's dismissal of the importance of the episode by asking, "Does it matter,
if it was stolen, whether it was sensitive or not?" (*Was,* not *were,* is correct
following that "if," because the speaker did not mean the clause to be contrary
to fact. Mr. Donaldson is very good on the subjunctive.)

"Is it stolen if someone hands it to you?" responded the President, elevating
the study of semantics to prime-time television. That disquisition on the meaning
of *steal* sent the matter to the F.B.I., which knows that the word *steal* comes from
Old English and is more earthy than *purloin,* more serious than *pilfer,* and more
straightforward than *filch.*

As of this writing, nobody has used *rip-off, pinch, cop, snatch, swipe,* or the
British *snaffle.* Another favorite synonym is *"borrowed,"* always in quotes to give
an arch, we-know-it-isn't-so connotation, and the favorite from World War II is
liberated, with its good-guy-taking-the-wine-the-Nazis-left-behind connotation. I
would give more examples, but my thesaurus was snatched.

If Shakespeare had had a copy editor, our language and its poetry would no doubt be immeasurably the poorer. Had you been the editor in question, you would have introduced a solecism by converting Shakespeare's "that" to "who" in the passage you quote from Iago's speech. As Fowler points out in his article on "Which, that, who," a generic person may properly govern "that" in defining clauses. He goes on to observe that a peculiar sort of politeness might restrain some writers from using "that" for persons, but this consideration could hardly have stayed Shakespeare's pen as he contemplated the sort of wretch that would deem Iago's good name worth the effort of removal.

William Bennett, M.D.
Cambridge, Massachusetts

You produced a picayune piffle of piddle with your description of "pilferage" as an allowance in profit projection. Go to the bottom of the accounting class! Pilferage is a purloiner of profit. It is a hidden cost that must be added to price to maintain profit.

Herbert Jaffe
Freeport, New York

Your thesaurus was snitched, not snatched. The implication is that it was pulled out of your hand and you no longer had possession of it. If I know you, the snatcher would have had the impact of onomatopoetic words hurled at him/her to say the least.

You don't have to be present to have something snitched from you. It can be done behind your back or while you are at your typewriter punching away at the keys. You have no hand (snatch) in the process. It is a small thing, snitching is, whether of a word or an object or, as now, snitching a bit of time from one's labors to bring it to your attention.

Louis I. Grossman
Newtown, Pennsylvania

P.S. Snitch is just as eligible as swipe for mention in your columns because both are slang words, and have a better right to be used than pilfer and purloin.

It seems to me that Alexander Pope (1688–1744) might deserve a prior credit line for this reference in An Essay on Man:

What e'er the Passion, knowledge, fame or pelf,
Not one will change his neighbor with himself.

There appears to be, incidentally, a haunting similarity between Scott's couplet and Pope's earlier one. Do you suppose Scott, ah, say, slyly filched or, with lifted pinkie, deftly purloined, something from his predecessor?

Francis G. Weller
New Orleans, Louisiana

If, as copy editor, you had changed Shakespeare's "he that filches" to "he who filches" you would have demonstrated that you have a tin ear—itself an interesting expression.

E. F. Bleiler
Ridgewood, New Jersey

Is it "was" . . .
Or was it "were"?
If I was he?
Or I were her?
As I read
My mind's a blur
Of conjugated English, sir.

On top of that my trials semantic
Have got me positively frantic.
All of my time, it seems, is spent
On what the writer really meant.

And, as I analyze each phrase,
Parsing each one willy-nilly,
The purist soul within me prays,
"Is it acceptable to Willie?"

I read now only to detect
The structure . . . Is it quite correct?
And when I turn the final page
I tear each book up in a rage.
Alas, my syntax sullied head
Cannot remember what it read.

The cause of all my mental anguish?
The column, sir, you call "ON LANGUAGE."
(Excuse me if I raise a doubt . . .
Mayhap that "ON" should be "ABOUT"?)

Now, take this verse so full of error;
(Your criticism holds no terror)
Although it really doesn't scan
I pose this question man to man

"In the course of your employment
Do you ever read for pure enjoyment?"

> Robert E. Stout
> River Vale, New Jersey

I believe that in England the word nick *is much more commonly used as a synonym for stealing than is* snaffle.

> Gerald Shirley
> Tuckahoe, New York

Horde

In a piece about the way the French were slowly squeezing Japanese imports through a small town near Tours, thereby protecting French markets from the influx of videotape recorders, I drew a parallel to the battle of Poitiers in 732, where Charles the Hammer protected Europe by "driving back the Moslem hordes."

In the *Columbia Encyclopedia* (which treads on the no-longer-preferred spelling of "encyclopaedia") that moment of defeat for the Saracens is described as "turned the Moslem tide." I wish I had used *tide* because *horde* is surely pejorative and should not be used to describe a religion even when its members are assembled in large crowds.

"Perhaps you were merely making use of an archaic phrase to conjure up a feeling for the period of the eighth century," writes James Zogby of the American-Arab Anti-Discrimination Committee, giving me the benefit of the doubt, then adding the zinger: "Would you be inclined to use the phrase 'Jewish hordes' in reference to the invaders of Lebanon? Or the 'Christian hordes' which stormed the beaches of Normandy?"

He's right: *Hordes* is a word with a history of treating opposing armies with contempt. It is rooted in the Turkish *ordu,* meaning "camp," and picked up an *h* in Polish before entering English. Originally, *horde* was applied to nomadic tribes of Tatars or other Asiatics and has retained that uncivilized connotation: Benjamin Disraeli wrote in the novel *Tancred* that "I am sprung from a horde of Baltic pirates."

By the seventeenth century, the word was being used to sneer at any great company of savages: Whites wrote of "the Mongol hordes" and non-Moslems of "the Moslem hordes." But these were armies—often well disciplined and brave— and would better be described with the neutral *forces.*

I will now drop *hordes* from my military vocabulary, using the word in its current "great assembly" sense, as in "hordes of shoppers returning Christmas presents" and "hordes of irate pupils demanding an end to the teaching of grammar."

If I Was King . . .

When I thrilled to the timbre of Ronald Colman's voice, or somebody imitating that voice, saying, "Ah, if I were king . . . ," little did I realize that this was an example of the subjunctive mood. Speaking subjectively, I admit the subjunctive is not a mood I like; it reminds me of fusty French lessons from Miss Moore at Joan of Arc Junior High. The French are very big on the subjunctive. (I used to think the Chinese were, too, but Chinese menu writers have dropped the "subgum" from "subgum chow mein.")

We are now going to tackle this subject because I am tired of guessing about when to pick *if I were* instead of *if I was.*

"If the fellow was an A student in English," writes Jack Smith in his lively column in the *Los Angeles Times,* "he would not misplace an *only.* . . ." You're not all right, Jack: If the main verb in a sentence is conditional—*would*—then the *if*-clause verb should be subjunctive—*were.* (If I were sure of this, I would write it with greater authority.) The rule of thumb is to use *were* with *would.*

For example, "If wishes were horses, beggars would ride." That's right, not only because the *were* hitches up with the *would,* but because the *if* clause makes a statement contrary to fact, or at least expresses an unlikely condition. That's the essence of the subjunctive—use it when it ain't necessarily so. Writing about a film by Constantin Costa-Gavras, a *New Yorker* reviewer observed: "Its techniques of excitation could as easily be used by a smart Fascist film maker, if there were one. Luckily, there isn't." *Were* is right because it refers to a situation the writer thinks does not exist. *Were* is also used after hypothetical indicators like *as if* and *as though.*

So, the lazy reader is thinking, whenever I see an *if,* I'll use a *were.* That's a mistake, if there ever was one.

When you're calling up a possible fact in your *if* clause, scorn the subjunctive. "If Reagan runs again, he will win in a walk." (I have been saving that for a mixed-metaphor item, but it fits here.) Similarly, "If Kennedy waits to run until he is Reagan's age, it will be the year 2000." (Not *were to wait . . . would be.*)

The point is that you should use *was* after *if* when you are talking about a fair possibility of fact. Let's say you just shot your spouse for the insurance money, you are about to enter a grand-jury room, and you know the foreman is an English teacher. The phrase to keep in mind is: "If I *was* at the scene of the murder, I do not remember it."

If I were you, I'd use the subjunctive only to call attention to phoniness. (I'm not you, which is why *were* is right.) Making understandable the impenetrable subjunctive is a far, far better thing I do than I have ever done before, as Ronald Colman used to say, but if I miss the deadline on this column, it will not run. (There is a good chance that I will miss the deadline, which is why it would be wrong to write "If I were to miss.")

I was pleased to find myself in your column, if only as a bad example.

Actually the sentence you quoted ("If the fellow was an A student in English he would not misplace an only*") was first written by a reader—an English teacher —and was the subject of a subsequent column in which I defended it against numerous critics on grounds that were concerned as much with conjectures about the woman's sexual inclinations as with her grammar.*

Anyway, I'm happy to have been the springboard on which you leaped into the subjunctive bog, even though I don't believe the were-would *rule always works. (By the way, that was a sly example you chose—"If wishes were horses, beggars would ride"—since the* were *is demanded by the plural* wishes, *and couldn't possibly be* was.*)*

Ironically, I've been thinking for a long time of asking you to get into the subjunctive were, *because I believe its misuse is the most common solecism among good writers today, and you can probably do more about it than anyone else.*

As you say, the root of the trouble is the notion that were *automatically follows* if. *However, the singular* were *may also be wrong in a* were-would *sentence in the past tense. "If he was hungry, he would eat at the diner" is not a subjunctive, but a statement of fact. It might also be written as "When he was hungry he would eat at the diner." He would* means *it was his habit to.*

If you wanted to put this into the subjunctive mood, indicating what our hero would have done had he been hungry (which he wasn't), you would use the past subjunctive. "If he had been hungry, he would have eaten at the diner." (But he wasn't hungry.)

If this were a rare exception to the rule, the rule might still work as a general guideline; but this particular form of the false subjunctive occurs today in almost every newspaper, and in most novels I read.

I have an idea that were *is used instead of* was *for the same reason that* I *is used for* me, *or* he *for* him. *("There's nobody between he and the goal line," or "I'd like you to have dinner with my wife and I," because of a vague notion that* were, he, *and* I *are more elegant than* was, him, *and* me. *(Because you and Ed Newman have pointed this out, people who still don't know whether to say* me *or* I *are saying* myself.*) Like the objective* I *and* he, *the false subjunctive* were *seems to be a contemporary phenomenon. I don't find it in books written by Evelyn Waugh, for example, or in* Madame Bovary *or* Alice in Wonderland. *(Actually, I haven't looked lately.)*

What is happening, I think, is that were *after* if *is becoming idiomatic, and before long it will be right because everybody does it. Of course it is only the more literate people who make this mistake. The unlettered still say "If he was hungry he ate at the diner," just as they say "between you and me," and they may save us from ourselves yet.*

Meanwhile, thanks for "If I Were King." I think you were right on the mark, and certainly have helped to clarify this murky question for me. (I have read Fowler and all the others on it, but didn't have any better a grip on it when I came out than when I went in.) But I do think your rule overlooks that one pervasive exception.

Jack Smith
Los Angeles, California

Although your discussion of the subjunctive is basically correct, you have made things seem somewhat simpler than they really are. Your rule, "Use were *with* would," *of course applies only to the verb* to be, *and even then it is only part of the story.* To be *makes a four-way distinction in* if *clauses:*

> *If that is Jack, tell him to come in.   (real, present)*
> *If that were Jack, I would tell him to come in.   (unreal, present)*
> *If that was Jack, I hope you told him to come in.   (real, past)*
> *If that had been Jack, I would have told him to come in.   (unreal, past)*

For all other verbs, this four-way contrast gets blurred to three; to use your example:

> *If Reagan runs again, he will win in a walk.   (real, present/future)*
> *If Reagan ran again, he would win in a walk.   (unreal, present/future)*
> *If Reagan ran in '76, I don't remember it.   (real, past)*
> *If Reagan had run in '76, he would have lost.   (unreal, past)*

What may have been puzzling to some readers is that the two rules you give for was *and* were *have nothing at all to do with your example with* run.

John Underwood
Assistant Professor
Hispanic Studies and
    Linguistics
Mills College
Oakland, California

Impropaganda

"I know I may be used for propaganda," said the Reverend Billy Graham on his return from a controversial trip to Moscow, "but I believe my propaganda—the Gospel of Christ—is stronger."

Can the word *propaganda*—which has come to mean "lies used to persuade" —be applied to the preaching of an evangelist, even to the words attributed to God?

You bet it can; religion is where it came from. Pope Gregory XIII commissioned his cardinals in the sixteenth century *de propaganda fide,* and Pope Urban VIII set up an organization of missionaries to propagate the faith called the *collegium de propaganda* in 1627.

But in the middle of the nineteenth century, the word began picking up a bad name. In 1843, lexicographer W. T. Brande wrote: *"Propaganda* is applied in modern political language as a term of reproach to secret associations for the spread of opinions and principles which are viewed by most governments with horror and aversion." After World War I, the word was thoroughly associated with organized efforts to mislead. Some World War II propagandists on the Allied side tried to differentiate "white" from "black" propaganda, but the idea never took hold.

That's why it is nice to see Dr. Graham use the much-abused term in its original sense. It may help explain the word to visitors to Rome, who stroll toward St. Peter's along the Via Propaganda.

Ing-ing It

I picked up a bottle of Del Monte ketchup (they spell it *catsup,* but most others spell the Chinese-derived word *ketchup*) and read the label: "Made from red ripe tomatoes, natural sweeteners, distilled vinegar, salt, and natural flavorings."

Why does the label read *flavorings* instead of *flavors*? The gerund form is in most dictionaries, of course—"an essence or extract added to a food to give it a certain taste"—but that is also one of the meanings of the base word, *flavor.* So who needs *flavorings*?

Randall Rothenberg, formerly senior editor of *New Jersey Monthly,* has been crusading against what he calls "the nominative gerund," a label he says describes "the addition of *-ing* to a noun, to create another noun that seems to have more

class." He sends this example, or exampling: "*Shirtings* by Kilgour, French and Stanbury."

A quick check with James McCawley, professor of linguistics at the University of Chicago and author of *Thirty Million Theories of Grammar*, straightens Mr. Rothenberg out on his label: "not *nominative* (which is a case, contrasting with *accusative, genitive*, etc.), but rather *denominal*, the standard word meaning 'derived from a noun.' "

O.K., Jim—what's with the trend toward denominal gerunds?

"*Shirting* is a perfectly respectable word that is listed by most dictionaries— 'fabric, such as broadcloth, suitable for making shirts.' I suspect it is more common in England than in the U.S.A. It is very common in India, where I spent last summer (virtually all the instances I have seen of the word have been in signs on Indian tailor shops)."

I would not like to get in a scrap with Professor McCawley, who is capable of taking on Noam Chomsky barehanded, and I accept *shirting* as a good, short name for a certain kind of fabric. (When Margaret Fuller said, "I accept the universe," Thomas Carlyle replied, "By God! She'd better.") But I have a hunch *shirting* was used by the copywriter to evoke an elegant English image, and the word the ad should have used is *shirt*. That is the finished product, after the shirting has been tailored into a form that can be sent to the laundry for mangling and burning.

This straining for effect, says editor Rothenberg, "is one of the most obvious abuses—sorry, abusings—of the English language." Although most linguistic types would tell him to keep his shirting on, he has put his finger on a usage that has a distinctly la-di-da flavoring.

You quote the professor of linguistics: ". . . not nominative *(which is a case, contrasting with* accusative, genitive, *etc.). . . ." Later on you write about the need to use commas where they belong. I would prefer to omit the comma after* case *or write "a case that contrasts with. . . ."*

However, I really would like to correct the professor on the use of contrast *in the above context. Opposite things or ideas contrast. The various noun cases are not opposed to each other. They may be compared, or better yet, they correlate or belong to the grammatical forms of a noun's declension.*

> David Shulman
> New York, New York

Flavor *is the sensation a substance produces in the mouth and* flavoring *is the substance that produces the sensation. In cooking, flavorings contribute to flavor.*

Oregano has a strong, * *sharp flavor. Oregano is a flavoring in spaghetti sauce.*

Nevertheless, I've always seasoned my culinary creations with seasonings. According to Webster's 2nd, season *once meant "that which gives a relish; seasoning," just as* flavor *in the same dictionary, technically encompasses "flavoring."*

The "seasoning" sense of "season" is obsolete. Perhaps the "flavoring" sense of "flavor" is about to bite the dust.

> Susan Seuling
> River Edge, New Jersey

*Notice the presence of a comma between the adjectives. However, if I were listing nouns, many of which were modified by two adjectives or more, perhaps I, too, would omit the commas between adjectives to avoid cluttering my sentence with a distracting number of punctuation marks. On the other hand, it's more likely that I would omit some of the adjectives. E.g., I would pluck the "red" from "red ripe tomatoes" (Do ripe tomatoes come in other colors?), thereby both avoiding the comma controversy and toning down the copywriter's purple prose.

When you nailed the use of -ing *as "denominal gerunds" you exposed just one small case of what has become Copywriters' Disease. See this week's* Times *ads and you'll find "suit dressing," "sweater dressing," "shirt dressing," "white-tie dressing," "soft-dressing," "pantsdressing," "boot dressing" . . . argh!*

> Elizabeth J. Levy
> Montclair, New Jersey

*Hey! Why does a language maven use "in" when he means "into"? (*Vide *"get in a scrap with Professor McCawley.")*

Further, why does he use "can" when he should say "may" (as in "You can use a comma after French *if you like")?*

Tisk, tisk! (It looks better with the vowel.)

Donald W. Chilton
Huntington, New York

If not in grammar, certainly in the renouned world of advertising, flavoring *has had a nominal meaning (not a Squad Squad candidate, I think) as a substitute for* artificial.

Maple flavor is flavor derived from the direct addition of refined sap obtained from the maple tree. But maple flavoring is a synthetic substitute derived from test tubes, with no family tree at all.

So flavoring *is a correct use to designate synthetic substitutes intended to make saps of the consuming public.*

Harold R. Shippee
White Plains, New York

At last some voice has spoken out against the artificial manufacture of the gerund/ denominal "case." What about Chicago's Presbyterian St. Luke's Hospital's "Birthing Rooms," where man and wife begin their "parenting" careers? Arrrgh.*

Patrick McNamara
Glen Ellyn, Illinois

N.B.: In the Pennsylvania Dutch country, besides shirting, panting *is a perfectly respectable word. Panting is offered for sale in all the general merchandise stores around Intercourse and Paradise.*

W. J. Cosgrove
Lancaster, Pennsylvania

Junta Hunt

"What the jell is going on?" demands Randy Hecht of Washington. "Is it possible that no one in the electronic media can pronounce *junta*? Jelp!"

The pronunciation dictators at the television networks are at war over *junta*. Says CBS: "CBS uses the British pronunciation of the word—JUN-ta. It's in our pronunciation guidebook." NBC agrees: "NBC news policy is to pronounce *junta* by Anglicizing it, or Americanizing it. If you have heard any of our broadcasters use HOON-ta, it must have been a slip. JUN-ta is our policy." ABC vigorously disagrees: "It is pronounced HOON-ta. It is a Spanish word and we pronounce it as such." At Cable News Network, no policy is laid down, but I am told, "The pronunciation most of our anchors use is HOON-ta."

The word is rooted in the Latin *jungere*, to join; *junta* is the Spanish word for council; when used in North America, it means "a small group of people joined together to hold power after a coup d'état." (That meaning is often spelled *junto*.)

Both the British and Spanish pronunciations are correct, but that does not solve the problem: Which should we use? The new *Collins English Dictionary* offers a clue, holding that "JUN-ta" is British usage and "HOON-ta" is the usage in the United States.

This is strictly a personal choice, but I like to spice up my English with primary foreign words pronounced the foreign way, though I reserve the right to pronounce derivatives the English way. *Don Juan* is "Don Wan" to me, unless I'm talking about the Byron poem, in which case I'll go along with "Don JU-an." Same with *Don Quixote*; although he's "kee-HO-tay" to me, I'll pronounce the adjective "quik-SOT-ik."

So let me join the cabal that conspires to pronounce it "HOON-ta." I benignly tolerate "JUN-ta," just as I do not object to the English *Argentyne*, though I prefer the Spanish *Argenteen*. The networks split again on that one: CBS and ABC go with *teen*, NBC and CNN with *tyne*.

Be consistent: If you prefer the Anglicized *junta*, say, "*Argentyne*"; if you like *hoonta*, say, "*Argenteen*." The worst mistake of all is to mix languages: You cannot say *joonta*, and you cannot say *hunta*.

Olé! Or, as we Americans say, "ole."

You seem to have made a minor slip that you and the copy editor failed to junt *out: "That meaning is often spelled* junto." *Come, now, a meaning is surely never spelled, although it is sometimes spelled out—for people who need more explication of something than the average person. (I'd suggest something like "When used in that sense, the word is often spelled* junto.*")*

Maurice M. Tatsuoka
Professor and Chair,
Quantitative Division
Department of Educational
Psychology
University of Illinois at
Urbana-Champaign
Champaign, Illinois

Shall we preserve the spelling of a foreign name in roman letters, shall we preserve the pronunciation, or both? The Germans spell it "Quichotte" because that preserves the pronunciation for them. The French spell it "Quichotte" because that gives them a pronunciation as close to the original as our "kee-HO-tay" and also a spelling rather like their interpretation of the modern Spanish "Quijote." The Russians don't choose to preserve the spelling so they keep the pronunciation and generate other problems.

I advocate a pronunciation based on spelling; thus Don Quixote sounds like "don KWIK-sote" to go along with quixotic. And should we choose the modern Quijote, then I would say "kee-ZHO-te" or "keed-ZHO-te," except perhaps in San Jose, California.

Herbert Pomerance
Oak Ridge, Tennessee

You bagged the wrong animal in your "junta hunt." Although it may be appropriate to absorb a foreign word into one's language using one's own rules of pronunciation, a problem arises when the new pronunciation corresponds to a different word and meaning in the original language.

Thus, when the Spanish "HOON-ta" becomes the Anglicized "JUN-ta," a Spanish-speaking person hears "yunta" (pronounced "JUN-ta"). This is always used as part of the idiom yunta de bueyas, *which means "a team of oxen."*

Furthermore, in Anglo-American you might say "Argentyne" or "Argenteen" but in Spanish it is always "Ar-hen-TI-na" (noun feminine) or "Ar-hen-TI-no" (noun masculine).

So, Americanos, if you want to talk animals, let's talk sheep and if you want to say it in Spanish, let's talk about "la HOON-ta in Ar-hen-TI-na."

> Carmen Brehm, Argentina
> Andre Razzino, Italiano
> Bridgeport, Connecticut

You like to pronounce foreign words "the foreign way" and cite your pronunciation of Don Wan *as an example.*

You should be aware that your pronunciation ("Dahn Wan") is merely a more modest Anglicization than that of Byron. The foreign pronunciation is "Dohn Hwan."

Chacun à son goût *(however you pronounce it).*

> Thomas M. Haney
> Chicago, Illinois

I am disturbed by your desire to "join the cabal that conspires to pronounce it HOON-ta."

The word cabal *is derived from* Kabbalah *(sometimes spelled* Cabala*), the Jewish mystical tradition. Because traditional Judaism and—even more—traditional Christianity attempted to suppress the teachings of the Kabbalah, and because the mystical teachings of almost every faith have generally been shrouded in secrecy, these teachings were maligned as a secret, dangerous, and evil body of arcane knowledge associated with Satanic rituals. This distorted view of the Kabbalah has left its mark on the English language in the word* cabal, *which denotes any conspiratorial or subversive group. Your linking of the word* cabal *with a conspiracy— however light-hearted and humorous the context—is an example of offensive religious stereotyping, just as much as would be a reference to "jewing down" the price of an article one wished to purchase.*

As the Metropolitan Atlanta Center for Kabbalah Study pursues its work of disseminating the universal Wisdom of the ancient Kabbalistic tradition, I ask you to help remove from our path the obstacle created by the linking of Kabbalah with conspiracy.

> Rabbi William H. Feyer
> Director
> Metropolitan Atlanta Center for
>   Kabbalah Study
> Atlanta, Georgia

Congratulations on your revision of Latin! Until you spelled iungere *as* jungere, *there was no letter* J *in classical Latin.*

Lorraine Korson
Burlington, Vermont

Keister Booster

"I've had it up to my keister," said President Reagan, expressing his irritation at unauthorized disclosures of his private conversations. My telephone immediately began ringing; since the analysis here of "dipsy doodle," people come to me for the etymology of Mr. Reagan's deliciously outdated Americanisms.

Keister, pronounced "KEES-ter," has a meaning of "suitcase, satchel, hand-bag," with a frequent connotation of "burglar's toolcase"; it is probably a borrow-ing, through Yiddish, of the German *Kiste,* "chest." In 1931, *American Speech* magazine gave that definition along with another: "Keister, a satchel; also what one sits on."

Now we are coming to what the President had in mind. Researchers at the *Dictionary of American Regional English* provided me with a printout of words used to describe jocularly the portion of the anatomy that Mr. Reagan had it up to, by frequency of use. The most popular word is not fit to print in this publication, but the others are *fanny, rump, bottom, rear end, behind, rear, seat, tail, can,* and *backside.* Less frequently used are the French *derrière,* the British *bum,* the bookish *buttocks,* and the highfalutin *posterior.* The President's choice, *keister,* is far down the list, between *cheeks* and the Yiddish *tochis*; slang lexicographers are keeping their eyes on *buns,* now enjoying a vogue far from South Succotash, where it takes two to tango.

Dear Bill:

President Reagan's statement that he has "had it up to my keister" with leaks shows that he has either a metaphor gap or a very low tolerance regarding press coverage.

If keister *means the area of the body I think it does, then the water generated from leaks doesn't have to rise very high to get the President's temper going. I believe he should have said "I've had it up to my eyeballs" with leaks which, given the President's height, would have been a reasonable level at which to close off press access to the White House staff. Then again, he could have said, "Those reporters give me a pain in the keister."*

> *Jerry [Gerald M. Rafshoon]*
> *Washington, D.C.*

I usually feel only minor irritation at your inaccuracies and dumb guesses, but you really should be filled in on keister. *It is from Yiddish and referred to the display box the street merchants set up on ghetto streets. It became tripe-and-kiester (tripod and display case) which confidence men used as all could be quickly folded when a policeman appeared (cf. Mauer, Partridge).*

It received its present slang meaning from one and only one scene in a Hollywood (appropriate for Reagan) film in which a conman fell and crushed his case. He said, "I fell on my kiester." The audiences, never having been on the griff, took it to mean something less recondite.

> *Richard P. French*
> *La Jolla, California*

Many years ago an admirer of mine called me his "callipygian cutie." It's a word whose definition I never forgot.

> *Sondra Mayer*
> *Great Neck, New York*

Kemp Follower

When my colleagues at the Washington bureau of *The Times* bring a political figure in for lunch, they ask me along because they know I like to pick up snippets of the latest lingo. Recently, Republican Representative Jack Kemp, whose supply-side theories are looking much better with the economic recovery, was the guest target, and the pickings were delicious. (The economist Herbert Stein coined both *supply-sider* and *Kemp follower*.)

In discussing the Mexican debt (for which the acronym MEGO—My Eyes Glaze Over—is especially apt), the potential President and former Buffalo Bills quarterback was careful not to trap himself in a metaphor with a pejorative connotation: "I wouldn't say it was the domino theory, but economic problems in Mexico would surely have a ripple effect."

The domino theory—so deeply entrenched in the language that it has lost its capitals—is now an attack phrase on those practical souls who argue that one thing leads to another, in what historian Arthur Schlesinger Jr. has called "a popular construction, or misconstruction, of the Munich analogy."

The coiners of the domino theory were Joseph and Stewart Alsop, the great columnists. Joe recalls: "When we were kids, we used to play 'domino snakes' under our grandmother's piano. You lined up the dominos on their narrow ends in a curve around the piano leg, and when you pushed one, the whole line went down. When we were looking for an image to describe the consequences of a policy, we selected 'the domino effect.' Now, it's called 'the so-called domino theory,' or the 'discredited domino theory,' but it certainly has not been discredited by experience. On the contrary, it describes what's been happening all too accurately."

The popularizer of the phrase was President Eisenhower in 1954. About a year after the Alsops' column, he used the phrase to explain his decision to offer economic aid to the government of South Vietnam, and it became the central metaphor of our involvement there through the next two decades. That is how it picked up its negative connotation, and why Jack Kemp wisely turned to "ripple effect," from the concentric circles that move out from a pebble plunked in a pool.

When contradicted by one of his questioners, the congressman politely replied, "I don't want to be disputatious, but. . . ."

That word did not knock over my domino. *Disputatious* is a good word, and perfectly correct, but it was not the "right" word in that informal circumstance. *Argumentative* would have been less pedantic than *disputatious,* and more cerebral than *quarrelsome*; if he wanted a more academic synonym, he might have tried *contentious.* But *disputatious* is at once too long and too understandable: It tries too hard, as Ambassador Walter Annenberg discovered with "refurbishing" to describe the way he was fixing up his embassy. It's the kind of word that James Fenimore Cooper might have used, setting himself up for a Mark Twain savaging. A perfectly good word, even the correct word, is not always the right word.

After the friendly disputation, the subject of the investment pool came up. (When you drop an interest rate into the investment pool, you get a ripple effect.) Representative Kemp, noting the odd rhythm of my note-taking (I scribble furiously when nobody else is making notes, and stare at the ceiling as Big News breaks), said, "Consider the effect on savings. Savings is—" he caught himself— "'savings is' or 'savings are'?"

When eyes turned to me, I smiled mysteriously and made another note. This did not satisfy one of my colleagues, who whispered to another, "Doesn't he know? Isn't he the one who's supposed to know?" He was properly shushed.

I have long been saving up for a piece on *savings.* "I wish the word *saving* as a singular noun could have been saved," lamented Vernon Hoyt of Atlantic, Iowa. "We now read and hear *a savings* of X number of dollars, or percent. The singular, it seems to me, ought to be *saving,* as in *daylight-saving time."* Adds Louis Stone of Shearson/American Express: "Why do you continue to allow literate people, including prominent advertisers, to keep saying 'a savings,' instead of 'a saving'?"

This is an example of the Mad Dash Toward Pluralization, an intolerable escapade. This department has noted the tendency of White House writers to turn *money* into *monies,* and of revenuers to turn *revenue* into *revenues,* triumphs similar to that of an alchemist turning gold into lead. The same needless stretch is happening to *saving.*

When you find a bargain in a supermarket, or when your missile's cost overrun is smaller than expected, you have come across a *saving.* A saving is singular (and a real bargain is singularer); when Altman's department store runs an advertisement reading, "How would you like your Sealy Correct Sleep Sofa Savings?" it is in error: It should firm that mattress up to *saving.* Just as what is served to you is your serving, the portion saved by you is your saving.

If you blow your saving on cotton candy or a MIRV-y new nose cone, the saving is gone; on the other hand, if you set it aside for an acid-rainy day, the portion you saved becomes your *savings.* It goes in a savings account in a savings bank (or in a super now-wow money-market management system in a less-than-full-service institution, but that does not serve for purposes of illustration). Here comes the only point you have to take away from today's harangue: A *saving* becomes *savings* only when you decide to keep it.

Now to Congressman Kemp's question: Is *savings* singular or plural? Savings *is* or savings *are*? Usagists differ, but like the little broccoli-eater in Carl Rose's classic cartoon, I say that "savings *is*" sounds funny, and if something sounds funny I say to hell with it. (Grammarians call this "the unerring decision of the native speaker.") *Savings* is a mass singular noun, not a true plural—which is why we say "much savings" rather than "many savings"—but takes a plural verb only because "savings *are*" sounds more natural.

As I was slowly turning this over in my mind, the congressman had long since passed his brief self-searching on subject-predicate agreement and was adroitly fielding a question on growth rates. "Oh, you'll see a spike of 6 percent in '83," he observed, which shot me off in another direction: *Spike* is a hot new word in three forms.

As a verb in journalism slang, *to spike* means "to kill," from the action in paper-copy days of sticking a piece of copy on a spike to hold rather than to run in the paper. In this sense, *The Spike* was the title of a best-selling novel by Robert Moss and Arnaud De Borchgrave about Soviet disinformation, and "to spike" is a favorite usage of Reed Irvine of Accuracy in Media, who suspects that not every story written about left-wing causes gets into the press.

As a noun, *spike* now figures prominently in the lingo of economists. It has replaced *peak* in discussions of lofty upthrusts on charts. The earliest *Merriam-Webster* citation is from the November 10, 1944, issue of *Chemical Abstracts,* describing a disturbing brain wave recorded on an electroencephalogram.

As an adjective, *spiky* means "abrasive, quick to take offense, inordinately disputatious." A possible source is from "to spike a drink"; a better possibility is from "to spike someone's gun," meaning to ruin or punish him, taken from the sabotage of driving a spike into a gun barrel; the most likely source is from the image of a porcupine. Speculating on the etymology of *spiky* is surely more interesting than forcing a luncheon guest to guess at the growth rate.

I believe the use of "a savings" derives only from unthinking association with "savings bank." It's called "a savings bank" isn't it? Most people fail to realize that the plural in "savings bank" refers to the savings of its many clients, a legitimate plural, or to the many deposits of each client, equally correct.

It is setting a saving aside to join other similar actions that permits you to refer to your "savings." I believe that is what is understood by the plural form so the problem of "savings is" doesn't exist. In your "much savings" the "much" implicitly refers to money as in "He has much (money in) savings" or "He has much (money) saved."

As for those happy illiterates who say "Daylight Savings Time," perhaps they could get the message without a, to them, incomprehensible grammatical explanation if they were told, "We know how to go about saving time; we don't know how to go about savings it."

>   Alfred Skrobisch
>   Commack, New York

Why does Mr. Alsop find it necessary to say narrow end? *Surely the end is the end, and the other edge is the side.*

>   Warren W. Smith, M.D.
>   Columbus, Ohio

A spike (on a chart) differs from a peak in that it rises more abruptly, goes higher, and has a narrower base. If you were being given an EKG (electrocardiogram, Greek style) by a gorgeous nurse, who suddenly bent over to adjust something, giving you a lovely view of two beautiful peaks and a valley, the doctor might later say, "I wonder what that spike means on Safire's chart."

>   Arthur J. Morgan
>   New York, New York

P.S. Spike *is also what a football player does when he slams the ball down, point first, in the end zone, after scoring a touchdown.*

Dear Bill,
      I cannot read Representative Jack Kemp's mind, but I am sure that in the context of his conversation he meant a rise, or increase, in growth rates. His usage derives from medical jargon that is not limited to electroencephalograms. In the hospital you will hear a doctor or nurse saying, "The patient's temperature spiked to 102," or without any implication of peak, "His temperature has been spiking for an hour." I suggest this usage predates the Nov. 10, 1944 issue of Chemical Abstracts.
      I must also blow the whistle on your calling spike, *in the journalistic sense of killing a story, "a hot new word." I began spiking copy on the* Herald Tribune *in 1935, and I am sure generations of reporters were doing it before then. The spike, incidentally, is still a handy device for storing your notes, releases, game stats, wire copy, etc., in case you need to refer to them after finishing your story. In these days*

of word-processor writing, storing such valuable bits of paper is the principal use I have for my spike.

> John [Radosta]
> Sports Writer
> The New York Times
> New York, New York

Porcupines are neither spiked nor spiky; their spines (or quills or bristles) are used for self-protection and -defense when their territory is invaded or they are otherwise threatened. These spines can be painful and dangerous when embedded in the flesh of an intruder. North American porcupines' spines are particularly harmful as they are equipped with barbed ends making their removal difficult and/or dangerous.

In no way can the porcupine aim and shoot its spines from a distance; it backs into its enemy and attempts to hit it with its tail, hoping some of the very loose spines will reach a target, something like an inefficient multiple-warhead missile.

The porcupines I have known are basically inoffensive if not actually shy herbivores; they do not need the negative association with your incorrect definition of spiky. May I again suggest as I have in previous notes more gently that you learn to consult a good dictionary before you set up shop as an etymologist-would-be-philologist?

> Alexander M.H. Shea
> New York, New York

Dear Bill:

"To spike a gun" does not mean, as you said, "driving a spike into a gun barrel." Such a practice would require very large spikes and the poor spiker might walk with a distinct list. Rather, the trick was to hammer a spike into the touchhole of a captured piece, so that even if it had to be subsequently abandoned, it could not be fired until a new hole had been drilled.

Since you are an adept at spiking political big guns, as well as Fowler-ing pieces, you should never give the impression that you haven't a clou.

> David [Murray]
> New York, New York

If you reflect for a moment on the bore of eighteenth-century cannon, you will see that "driving a spike into a gun barrel" would have required a supply of thick iron posts, which soldiers didn't normally have in their pockets. No, what was spiked was the touchhole, thus ensuring that the ignition of powder in the cup-shaped depression on top of the barrel could not get through to the main charge within. The touchhole could be spiked with a common nail, and if you banged that home there was no way of getting it out—not in the field, anyway.

Robert Hughes
New York, New York

Dear Bill,
    To an economist, saving *is a verb describing the act of forgoing consumption, while* savings *is a noun describing the result of previous acts of saving. At least in class, we like to say that saving represents the flow of resources while savings is the stock. To be sure, economists often trip themselves up in making the distinction.*

Murray [L. Weidenbaum]
Director
Center for the Study of
    American Business
Washington University
St. Louis, Missouri

One of your statements I find rather ambiguous; "A saving *becomes* savings *only when you decide to keep it." And you speak about blowing your saving on cotton candy or a MIR V-y nose cone. However, in tying up these statements you imply that you have* not *saved up for the candy or the nose cone; you must have paid for them immediately. Otherwise, according to your definition, had you set aside the money "for a rainy day"—or for that matter, for any time at all, since the period is not defined—this money saved would have been* savings, *so that in effect you would be blowing your* savings. *You seem to have injected another factor, one of time-plus-intent, when you arbitrarily let the decision regarding singular or plural hang on that little phrase, ". . . when you to decide to keep it."*

Warren Sturgis
Brooklyn, New York

Dear Bill:
    Re savings: *The word is now enshrined in the national budget for FY 1982. Example: "Projected reduction of 25 percent for a savings of $2 billion." Whence this singular plural? I suspect it comes from* savings *bank (originally, bank for savings, or money saved by many persons) and then,* savings *bond. One now hears*

*on radio and television, "Daylight Savings Time," as creeping pluralism creeps on.
Other words become affected. A Hallmark ad, "A greetings card for every occasion."
In my youth "greetings" came from Atlantic City, or from the Draft Board. But,
on birthdays, one sent a greeting card.*

Dan [Daniel Schorr]
Washington, D. C.

Whoa! When you find a bargain in the supermarket or *the cost overrun is smaller
than expected, that is indeed a saving. If you decide to put it into a bank account,
it is still a saving, period. The bank account is an account for savings, or a savings
account, but if there is only one deposit made in that account, then it is still a saving,
singular, and doesn't become properly savings.*

If you deposit both *what you saved at the supermarket and what you didn't have
to spend on the cost overrun, the two deposits are then properly speaking savings.
I might as well also decide to save part of my salary; one week's deposit is a saving,
the amount in the account after any number of weekly deposits is savings.*

*This makes the simple point: a saving is not converted into savings just because
it's kept. It becomes a part of savings when it is added to other savings.*

*Unfortunately the singular-plural question isn't that easily decided because we
measure a saving in the unit of currency locally used. The saving is so many dollars,
so many pounds, so many francs, etc. Thus a saving of X number of dollars is
automatically a savings, because it is a multiple. (Only a large or a small saving can
be singular; if we say a $10,000 saving, rather than a saving of $10,000, we are really
being incorrect; we should properly say a $10,000 savings.) If we begin to count the
portion we have saved—to measure it—it is no longer a saving, but a savings.*

John Thomas Boyt
New York, New York

*Spike is a volleyball term, a one-handed forearm smash across the net, usually right
into the face of an opponent. Also, there is the Spike chess opening: 1. P-KN$_4$ which
prepares the development of the king bishop on the KN$_2$ square, and threatens to
make life difficult for Black's KN by advancing to N$_5$. This impaling maneuver
doubtless gave rise to the popular Anglo-Saxon name for the opening "The Spike,"
which is recorded in FIDE ECO Vol. A, 5, page 13 gives the recorded game
between Fric-Bogolijubov, in 1932 (also reference; IRREGULAR OPENINGS by
T. D. Harding, published by Chess Digest Magazine, July 1974). The Romans spiked
wine with a lead nail to improve the taste, if not the conditioning of the brain. Of
course, there is the German derivation (from* Spiess—*a spear, spike, spit) to mean
"a philistine, an accomplice or companion in crime, uncultured or narrow-minded,*

and to run the gauntlet." And who could forget Spike Jones? Or the Marlin Spike, which dates to men of war and tall ships.

Carol Sue Clark Hager
Bogotá, Colombia

There is such a rich residue of early muzzle-loading language in our everyday speech that it is fun to recognize the exact origins of other familiar phrases [besides spike someone's gun*].*

A flash in the pan *referred to an unsuccessful firing which did not penetrate from primer to charge. Rather than to cannon, it refers to muzzle-loading flintlocks (or wheel locks, presumably) which had a shallow depression, to be filled with fine priming powder into which the spark was directed.*

He shot his wad actually means the person forgot to put in a ball after loading powder and ramming in a "wad" or "patch" to compact it behind the projectile. It signifies total futility, unlike shot his bolt, *which is crossbow talk and means he's done his best but without effect.*

Britches, properly breeches, were so named because the baggy knickers resembled the rounded breech ends of cannon—and don't ask me for a citation on that. The term, however, also refers to the buttocks, which were thought to resemble the same parts and were indisputably the back end. Any good dictionary supports this latter usage, though it would rarely be heard today.

To cap it, as to add the final touch, probably comes from adding the percussion cap that replaced the loose-powder pan and flint. It is, of course, entirely different from the "capping" referred to in dousing oilwell fires or the "cap" designated to restrict government spending.

Hoist with (or on) his own petard refers, of course, to the premature explosion of the seventeenth-century iron bucket of powder used to blast open gates and walls. That petard *was also contemporary slang for the result of flatulence is perhaps too scatalogical [sic] a note for a family publication.*

Bomb, as a term for an unsuccessful show, deserves some digging, since dud *is a parallel term originally referring to a bomb that fails to explode.* Bomb *comes from the Greek and Latin for a loud noise and is obviously onomatopoeic, but I can't find how this show-biz meaning developed except, possibly, backward from "dud."*

A bombshell *as a surprising development has easily discernible roots in gunnery.*

Broke his pick does not spring from the double-pointed tool of that name, used to break up rock or hard dirt. It refers, rather, to a slim tool like an ice pick, used by a gunner to clean the vent of burned powder and, through the vent, pierce the powder bag. Broken off in the hole, it had the same effect as spiking.

Point-blank has an obvious current meaning but specifically refers to the spot where a projectile, fired from a level bore (with no elevation), strikes the horizontal ground. Its modern counterpart would be "ground zero," I suppose. Interestingly, however, you only hit the ground at "point-blank range." To hit any sort of target larger than a mouse, the gun would have to be "elevated" (tilted).

The use of caliber *(or* calibre*) to rate a person or his mind harks back to the measurement of the bore of a gun or the diameter of its projectile. The higher the caliber, the larger the diameter. Paradoxically a high-caliber mind is seldom encountered in a person who is a big bore. Which I sincerely hope I haven't been.*

Lewis F. Owen
Member, Society of Military
Historians
Palm Beach Gardens, Florida

Shame on you! While I don't want to join the ranks of the "earlier citations" freaks, you certainly should know you can't use a secondary source as a first citation! Chemical Abstracts, *as its name implies, is an abstracting service (one of the first, if not the first, predating computers, mind you). You might have checked to which article it referred. With a little effort one finds in volume 38 (Nov. 10, 1944), abstract 5974[2]: "Physiological studies of the effects of sulfonamide compounds on the brains of Macata mulata," by H. Jasper, W. V. Cone, P. Pudenz, and T. Bennett, in* Trans. Am. Neurol. Assoc. *69, 109–12 (1943). We're already a year earlier, without even trying.*

Furthermore, the same page, abstract 5974[6], also uses the word. (Ibid., pp. 123–5) One must therefore conclude that the word was probably in common usage amongst the neurologists at that meeting. Had I more time (I'm desperately writing my thesis at the moment), it probably would not be very difficult to find an earlier citation. I have this suspicion that the coinage might go back to the Huxley who did a lot of the pioneering work on muscle contraction.

I feel better; now I can go back to work.

Barry L. Levinson
Department of Molecular
Biophysics and Biochemistry
Yale University
New Haven, Connecticut

Dear Bill:

You credit Herb Stein with Supply-sider. *The reason you credit him, I'm sure, is there is unambiguous agreement that he coined the phrase* Supply-side fiscalism. *I am wholly responsible for that unambiguous agreement, because I broadcast Stein's contribution in 1979 when suddenly everyone was talking about "Supply-side economics" and journalists were asking me where it came from.*

Early in 1976, Stein wrote in his monthly Wall Street Journal *column about a school of economic thought, "Supply-side fiscalism," that had but two members, presumably me and Art Laffer. Stein and I had been arguing for two or three years about the incentive effects of tax policy, with he arguing that the more you tax people the harder they work. Thus the fleeting, one-sentence wisecrack by him.*

But in my self-appointed role as propagandist for the movement, I was responsible for the phrases supply-side economics *(embracing monetary as well as fiscal policy) and* supply-sider. *On the very day Stein's disparaging wisecrack appeared, I broadcast to the troops that we should wear the label with pride and march under its banner. At the time, Ben Stein sat across from me in the* Journal *editorial offices, and in my constant joustings with him I flaunted his father's mocking appellation until the phrase became entrenched among those of us who thought of ourselves as constituting the "Supply-side movement."*

> Jude [Wanniski]
> President, Polyconomics, Inc.
> Political and Economic
>   Communications
> Morristown, New Jersey

Kennedy Subjunctive

Not everybody has been paying attention. The subjunctive mood, lucidly explained here, has been ignored everywhere from Capitol Hill to Madison Avenue. Now listen up; we will not go into this again.

"If I was to make a political decision," said Senator Edward Kennedy, withdrawing from the 1984 presidential race, "it would be a different announcement today."

Wrong. (Not the decision, the mood.) When you are posing a hypothesis contrary to fact, you must use the subjunctive. That's the rule, and no horsing around is allowed. Senator Kennedy was saying that he was not making a "political" decision, but one based on family concerns; therefore (to take him at his word), making a "political decision" was a situation contrary to fact. He ought then to have said, "If I *were* to make a political decision," followed with the parallel construction, "I would be making a different announcement today."

Got that? If you have *would* in the main clause, you must use *were* (the subjunctive) in the *if* clause. If I were to let this one go by, I would be derelict in my duty as self-appointed guardian of good grammar.

And now to my friends at the Book-of-the-Month Club, an organization which has done much to spread literacy and culture into every nook and cranny of the land. In an advertisement for the seven-volume set of *The Decline and Fall of the Roman Empire,* quarter-bound in genuine leather, the headline read: "If it wasn't history, it would be the most spectacular novel ever written."

Let's hear it from Professor Michael Montgomery of the University of South Carolina: "Gibbon's work is history, of course. The statement 'if it wasn't history' is clearly contrary to fact; to be consistent with the subjunctive rule, you must use *were*. The advertisers probably thought that the use of 'was' made the ad sound more idiomatic. Nevertheless, it's wrong."

Can you ever use "If I *was*"? Of course, when you are examining a real possibility, or even a likelihood: "If I *was* speeding, your Honor, I didn't realize it." Other examples: "If I was scribbling, scribbling, scribbling, your Highness, it made possible your gracious acceptance of another damned thick book." Or, in the senator's case, "If I was thinking about stimulating a draft at the 1984 Democratic convention, I am not about to tell you that today."

How about "which" versus "that"? "And now to my friends at the Book-of-the-Month Club, an organization which has done much to spread literacy. . . ."
You're ignoring Fowler's distinction.

Joe Finder
Cambridge, Massachusetts

You refer to the subjunctive when in fact the conditional mood is being described in your comments on Senator Kennedy's statement.
According to Webster's Third International Dictionary, *the subjunctive mood expresses "something entertained in thought as contingent or possible or viewed emotionally (as with doubt, desire, will) <the subjunctive mood>. Example: I suggest that he* write *(subj.) a letter."*
The conditional, as described by Webster, is a tense ". . . introducing, containing, or implying a supposition <the conditional conjunction if>."

Monique Schoen
New York, New York

Whatever inclination I might have had to sympathize with Senator Kennedy's political aspirations was destroyed by his ungrammatical statement, "If I was making a political decision. . . ." Thanks for taking up the fight to preserve the subjunctive, and for taking a swipe at the Book-of-the-Month Club who sinned in the same way as the senator.
Now along comes Robert M. Solow in the "Letters" section of The Times, *claiming to have been misquoted. What he really wrote in 1966, he says, is: "I have to admit that Milton [Friedman] reminds me a little of what Lord Melbourne is supposed to have said about Macaulay: namely, 'I wish I was as cocksure about anything as Macaulay is about everything.' "*

Who is responsible for that "was"? Solow? Melbourne? Some editor who corrected a queer-sounding "were"?

The frequency of such errors is indicative of the imperative need to educate the illiterate to use the proper grammatical mood.

> *William Lang*
> *Southbury, Connecticut*

You said, "When you are posing a hypothesis contrary to fact. . . ." *My question is, are not all hypotheses contrary to fact? After all, if they were facts, they could not be called hypotheses. Putting it another way, a proven hypothesis is no longer a hypothesis, but a fact.*

Perhaps you meant to call theses so-called hypotheses "realistic" ones, ones that realistically had a chance of happening. In any event, is not your qualifying phrase "contrary to fact" redundant, thus unnecessary?

> *Peter Hollander*
> *New York, New York*

I have been fighting a rearguard action against a huge army of writers who mistake realize *and* recognize. *And now, chagrined, I find you among them. You write: "If I* was *speeding, your Honor, I didn't* realize *it."*

Should that not be recognize? Realize *ought to mean "bring into actuality," whereas* recognize *ought to mean "understand, apprehend, or comprehend."*

Is the distinction worth keeping? Should I run up the white flag and recognize, along with Montaigne, that he who fights usage with grammar makes a fool of himself?

> *Gary Schmidgall*
> *Philadelphia, Pennsylvania*

Prof. Montgomery seems wrong to me. Since Gibbon's work is history, *wasn't sounds correct. If Gibbon's work* were *a fairy tale . . . etc.*

> *Mary V. Riley*
> *Southbury, Connecticut*

I'm glad you've once more "lucidly explained" the subjunctive for the benefit of Ted Kennedy, Book-of-the-Month, and the rest of us. Unfortunately, you confine yourself to the present subjunctive, e.g., "If I were a bell I'd be ringing."

The authors whom I encounter in my work as a book editor usually get that right. Where they falter is in the past subjunctive. "Were" has a past-tense look to them, and that's what they sometimes erroneously use, e.g., "If Napoleon were more cognizant of weather conditions, he might have avoided invading Russia." Often, when I change the "were" to "had been," the author protests, "But I want to use the subjunctive!"

> Florence Trefethen
> Lexington, Massachusetts

Let me share with you my favorite legal use of "If I was." It's Tevye, in Fiddler on the Roof, *singing, "If I was a rich man—ta-da-ta-da—etc., etc." He sees his being rich definitely within the realm of possibility (although others may not).*

> Shirley A. Smoyak, R.N., Ph.D.
> New Brunswick, New Jersey

NOTE FROM W.S.: No, Sheldon Harnick's lyric is "If I *were* a rich man." And if I were Harnick, I would use the same construction.

What was, was. Teddy was right on using the simple past tense indicating what was possible (he could have made a different decision) as distinct from stating, "If I were king" (not possible), according to Mrs. Brattig, Erasmus Hall, circa 1948, Brooklyn, N.Y.

> Lois Lindauer
> Boston, Massachusetts

Latest Returns

Even midterm elections make their contribution to the political vocabulary. In the campaign of 1982, alliteration—though never quite reaching the *vicars of vacillation* or *nattering nabobs of negativism* stage—was used extensively. The A.F.L.-C.I.O. posed the issue as *jobs or jelly beans?* At the White House, pollster Richard Wirthlin took the old give-the-guy-a-chance argument and put a new gloss on it with *the pool of patience,* using that alliterative phrase to describe the willingness of the electorate to delay punishment for unemployment. (After the third mention of *the pool of patience* at a postelection White House briefing, a puckish pundit wondered: "Why are you so preoccupied with the hospital population?")

The same Mr. Wirthlin had a hand in the 1980 campaign's *October surprise,* the warning that the opposition had a last-minute bombshell to toss. That phrase may have been coined by Richard Allen, then a national security adviser, or by Gary Lawrence, a pollster, in a memo dated May 27, 1980. Senator Edward Kennedy gave the phrase an update by charging that the Reagan administration "is waiting to spring a November surprise—a secret postelection plan to slash Social Security and tarnish the golden years of the elderly." (Pure gold does not tarnish; silver tarnishes. You can say, "Mixed metaphors tarnish the silver oratory of our senators.")

The best use of a double meaning in a slogan was in an attack on a former astronaut, Senator Harrison Schmitt of New Mexico. The campaign forces of Democrat Jeff Bingaman, Senator-elect of New Mexico, came up with "What on earth has he done?" Republicans are squirreling this away in case Senator John Glenn, who also gained fame in space, becomes the nominee for President. (That was an example of *negative advertising*, a phrase used often this year. Would the coiner please come forward?)

The outstanding cliché of election-night coverage was *mixed bag*, usually meaning "heterogeneous collection," or, in this case, "win some, lose some." This was a British coinage, first used in 1936 by Charles Cecil Rowe Murphy, a British soldier, as the title of a collection of short stories and essays, *A Mixed Bag*. Fred Mish, editorial director at Merriam-Webster, has a 1937 British citation from Lancelot Hogbin's *Mathematics for the Million*: ". . . the abstract noun of the grammarian is a *mixed bag*." The first American use was in George May's 1943 book *Financial Accounting*, and I would give it here but I would hate to dry up my readers' pool of patience.

Regarding mixed bag: *though I accept your 1936 reference—the title of a British soldier's anthology—it would seem likely that* mixed bag *has a far older origin. Doesn't* mixed bag *refer to the hunt; i.e., a partridge, a woodchuck and so on, all shot in one day?*

> David Galef
> Scarsdale, New York

Latin Shmatin

Certain Yiddishisms have implanted themselves in American English. For example, I am a language *maven*—a word that means less than an *expert* but more expert than an *enthusiast* or an *aficionado*. I do my *shtick*, or "thing," herein.

Editors are often afflicted with the agony of deciding when a foreign word or phrase has become so familiar that it no longer requires an explanation in English. The verb *kibitz*, accent on the first syllable, needs no translation to speakers of today's English, but what about a word like *tsoris*, meaning "deep trouble"? Can this less familiar term be used, say, in a headline, which requires instant understanding?

Evidently not. The editor of the editorial page of *The Washington Post*, Meg Greenfield, recently—and with great reluctance—blue-penciled a line above an editorial written by Stephen Rosenfeld about the difficulties America was facing in a Central American nation. Though you won't see it, you guessed it: "Tsoris in Honduras."

By using the fancy transliteration tsoris, *you kind of spoiled your story of the headline that didn't appear in the* Washington Post.

In Galizianer Yiddish, the mother tongue of thousands of American grandparents, the first syllable is pronounced like the German word zu. *Then, instead of not having the nebbish "Tsoris in Honduras," we would not have had the much better "Tsuris in Honduras."*

Arthur J. Morgan
New York, New York

Leggy

Legginess, as we all know, is next to sex-godliness.

At Henri Bendel, an exciting department store in New York City where everybody is on the *qui vive*, an advertising copywriter was inspired to create this line about Zandra Rhodes, a dress designer: "This fantastically leggy little trickle of pearl-edged chiffon / $2,000. . . . Come slide into her diaphanous wonders, long and short / A Zandra is to-sigh, to-die."

The store is to be commended for its forthright use of the dollar sign, which too many other merchandisers are too shy to put in front of the number; at the same time, Henri Bendel is to be censured for its abuse of the virgule, a slashing punctuation mark that ought not to be substituted for the comma or period. Those decisions are clear; but what of *leggy* as an adjective to modify *trickle*?

Geraldine Stutz, president of Bendel, who regularly writes its distinctive ad copy, was away when this word was used. The admirable woman executive, taking full responsibility, gulps bravely and says, "It was, I'm sure, meant to mean that

the dress was cut short to show lots of leg. As used by us, it seems to describe a chiffon centipede."

Leggy originally meant "long-legged," and then came to mean "characterized by a display of leg"—shows with showgirls were called "leggy burlesques." Originally insulting—at one time, long legs were not considered sexually enticing—the adjective is now a compliment. But early in its use, botanists adopted the word to mean "long-stemmed," and Oliver Wendell Holmes in 1860 wrote of "the row of youthful and leggy trees." A century later, H. G. W. Fogg—I don't know what the initials stand for—felt bound to instruct owners of greenhouses to put boxes of seedlings close to the glass "to prevent the seedlings from becoming drawn and 'leggy.' "

Here is where I forgive the Bendel copywriter for the misplacement of the modifier. Toward the end of the ad, a "dreamy perfume bottle" is described as having "a long-stemmed stopper so you can stroke perfume way down your back." Evidently, the writer was aware of the etymology of *leggy,* and closed her copy with an evocative reprise by using *long-stemmed.* A nice touch, especially appreciated by women who throw their backs out regularly while trying to dab perfume between their shoulder blades.

That leaves us with "A Zandra is to-sigh, to-die." An origin of this nominative-infinitive construction is the German *Es ist zum lachen,* "It is to laugh"; the use of that construction, rather than "It is laughable," was common among those learning English, and the current imitation of the mistake is a leggy burlesque of the amiably effusive immigrant. "It is to die" is, similarly, an imitation of the English-learner's construction, meaning, "It's so good it could kill you"—hence, the "drop-dead dress," which is the best dress in a wardrobe. "A Zandra is to-die," forgetting the unnecessary hyphen, means that a Zandra dress has the power to kill, which is pure poetry and suitable in ad copy.

However, "a long-stemmed stopper *so* you can stroke perfume way down your back" is incorrect. When the meaning is "in order to," the phrase should be *so that.* Your poetic license just expired.

Bill—

Let me challenge your description of a "woman executive." First, I think the description is sexist. Second, although some dictionaries permit "woman" as an adjective, I think common sense would suggest otherwise. We don't ever use "man" as an adjective, so why "woman"?

> Irv [Molotsky]
> The New York Times
> New York, New York

You may forgive the Bendel's copywriter for the misplaced modifier, but how can we forgive you for the insulting "woman executive"? Isn't that just "career girl" 1980's style?

> Holly S. Kennedy
> New York, New York

NOTE FROM W.S.: *Woman* was unnecessary. To differentiate from male executives, the correct word is *female*; in this case, no modifier was needed.

Let Freedom Love

As is well known (as the Russians say), or *it's a given that* (as the Americans say), superpower adversaries have staked claims on certain English words.

Communists have latched on to *liberation* and *people's*; those words in a title almost certainly identify a radical organization or leftist bureaucracy. They also see their *irredentist* twice a year, dismissing any talk of Communist givebacks as "bourgeois irredentist claims." (Let me not seriously apply toothiness to irredentism; it is a fighting word, rooted in Italian, for "unrecovered" land; it describes the Argentine yearning for the Falklands.)

In retaliation, we have recaptured *adventurism,* a word that Communists used to use in internal criticism, meaning "excess revolutionary zeal leading to the taking of unnecessary risks"; now, the word is most often applied to *expansionism,* which we have also tied onto the Soviets.

But what of *peace-loving?* That word—still hyphenated, although peacemaking and peacekeeping are not—was seized by the Communist apparat (a Russian word we stole) as part of its propaganda line painting doves on tanks and denouncing the Western warmongers. *Peace-loving peoples* are most often assumed to be Communist entities, just as *oppressed peoples* are Communist targets. Although Western political leaders such as Daniel P. Moynihan have fulminated about the linguistic invasion of the Communist propagandists—especially the truth-on-its-head seizure of *democratic*—we have to recognize that *peace-loving* now has an ironic red tinge to it.

The counterattack undertaken by our side is spearheaded by *freedom-loving.* Perhaps this is rooted in "the free world," a nice bit of one-upmanship making the point that the Communist world is unfree. Also, *freedom fighter* is a Western noun for what the Soviets would call a guerrilla representing oppressed peoples.

It is as if some secret negotiation had taken place, in a propaganda Yalta, that resulted in an agreement that the Russians got *peace-loving* and the Americans got *freedom-loving.* Such a deal says something about priorities; "better free than alive" is a slogan sure to be born.

However, it is important to get all the syllables in our phrase. Larry Misspeakes, the White House spokesman (or is it Larry Misspokes, the White House speaksman?), told Fidel Castro to stop interfering in the "democratic free-loving countries" of Latin America. Spokesman Speakes (that's it) was in error; a *free-loving* country is not a *freedom-loving* country. On second thought, perhaps he has inadvertently launched a new propaganda campaign.

Communists have latched on to many more of our words than the examples you gave. In my forays into East Germany over many years (some of them for The Times*), I heard and read dozens of our words that had been absorbed shamelessly into their special jargon:* Revanchist, Aktivist, Monopolist, Kollektiv *and a whole row of others that hardly vary from one communist country to another and need no translation.*

This is not to say that West Germans don't steal. Taking words from us has a certain snob *appeal, a phrase that was imported by the Germans much later than* sex appeal.

West German youngsters can go to a party *to listen to a* group *and, if they are so inclined, get* high *on a* long drink *or perhaps a* gram *or two of* shit, *as hashish is known there and, I think, here.*

Politicians in West Germany, took to such words of ours as appeasement, escalation, rollback, comeback *and* no comment.

I recall a headline in a West German fashion magazine that asked: Was ist IN, Was ist OUT? *I don't remember whether the question was answered.*

> Lawrence Fellows
> Greenwich, Connecticut

Lousy Latin Lovers

It is impossible to conduct the Bloopie Awards without committing a blooper.

The stumble of 1983 occurred during the award of a Bloopie to a firm that made a mistake in Latin. I adjured one and all: "Never pluralize the genetive when a Latin lover is in the room." Judged Judge Jon O. Newman of the Second Circuit Court of Appeals: "Unless your Latin lover doesn't care to see what he's doing, he ought to use two *i*'s when he's spelling *genitive.*"

While we're on judgments, this appeal from a copywriter injured by my stern dictum on his misspelling of *judgement*: "It pains me to be accused of spelling errors," writes Lawrence Watts of J. Walter Thompson in Chicago. "These hands were trained by nuns." He cites the acceptance of *judgement*, with an *e* in the middle, as a second spelling by many dictionaries, and this crunching decision in the second edition of Fowler's *Modern English Usage*: "*Judgement* is now preferred to the once orthodox *judgment.*"

My judgment is that Fowler is not to be followed on his spelling of *judgement*. (Did I hear a thunderclap? No acknowledgment necessary.) Such a spelling probably caused President Jerry Ford to mispronounce the word "JUDG-uh-ment." Let the English write *judgment* with another *e*; the Americans, without. Think about linguistic independence on the Fourth of July.

And while we're in a Latin mood, consider this excerpt from a White House briefing by a sh!-mustn't-be-named "Senior Administration Official" (and I remember the days when a mere deputy national security adviser was considered a Junior Administration Official): "In the current circumstances and the foreseeable circumstances, the President cannot anticipate sending U.S. troops to this area. Now, I'm not trying to be cute. You know, if tomorrow there were twenty divisions of new outsiders, that would be *rebus sic stantibus.*"

No member of the assembled press corps would admit ignorance of Latin, as I am forced to do so frequently. The don't-use-my-name briefer, a cute martinet called "Bud" by all the McFarlanes, was dazzling the crowd with the Latin for what the Library of Congress swears to me means "as matters stand."

Lower the Standards

"You wanna know why people don't write so good no more?" writes Senator Daniel P. Moynihan. "It is because people who get paid to teach them how don't know how either."

The cause of the senator's ire is a complaint sent to him by an educator at the City University of New York. He had read one of the Moynihan newsletters and was troubled by the effect of its big words on some members of the electorate.

"I conducted a 'readability' analysis of your newsletter," wrote the educator, "and found that the material had a readability level of 10.8 to 11.2. This means that it would be considered readable to people who had at least a 10th-grade reading level. . . . Many voters (particularly the 'inner-city "disenfranchised" ') may receive your message, but may not comprehend it."

The conclusion, which the senator found especially irksome, was: "In order to broaden the 'target audience' of your newsletter and to make your message more accessible to more voters, I might suggest that such material be written at a lower level of readability."

In response, Senator Moynihan murmurs, "God save us." He is right; the educator uses "readable" (which most often is synonymous with "legible") to mean "understandable" or "comprehensible." Readability studies are nothing new—Rudolph Flesch was conducting them in the 1940's—but to suggest that government officials adjust their prose to the words used by high-school sophomores is an offense to the electorate and a put-down to the young.

Moreover, the educator afflicts his prose with the academician's favorite tense, the craven conditional: "I might suggest." I would suggest that the use of such an uptight tense would cause any suggestion to lose force. Finally, the well-meaning but fuzzy-meaninged educator slips into split-level bureaucratese: "A lower level of readability" means "less readable," by which the educator seems to be saying "hard to understand."

In short, he should have written, "I suggest you write more understandably." That's how to get through to a senator who might be endowed with a high level of writeability.

Meteor Message

"Learn the right of coining words," wrote poet Leigh Hunt, "in the quick mint of joy."

It's no big deal, provided the need for a word exists. *Meteorologist* is not a useful word, because it seems to mean "one who studies meteors." When I tune in a weather forecast, I am rarely warned of falling meteors; therefore, I welcome a new word like *weathercaster*. In Omaha, meteorologist Gary Wiese reviewed a forecast that had turned out wrong, and called his review an *aftercast*. That is good coinage—simple, understandable, useful. Thomas Griffith at *Time* magazine offers a portmanteau coinage to describe roundabout chatterings: *circumloquacious*. And

the hot new word in political science is *neoliberal,* whose appearance was predicted in this space after the triumph of neoconservatism.

A couple of years ago, a *New York Times* editorialist described the notion of foreign aid being a burden as *moondrift.* William Steinroeder of Oceanside, New York, wrote me—as if I were responsible—to ask: "Is this a more heavenly way of saying 'hogwash'?" The anonymous *Times* writer tells me it was a "subconscious neologism," and defines the word as "midway between twaddle and malarkey, an exiguous fantasy; inspired humbug." Perhaps associated with the philosophy of Governor Moonbeam.

Not all situations need special words. J. Arthur Greenwood of White Plains, New York, wants me to advertise for "a fit designation for the 'ex-wife-with-whom-one-is-having-an-affair,' clearly a notion as pressingly in need of a name as 'neighbor-whose-house-is-on-fire.' " Those situations are too special to warrant general nomenclature.

You seem to have missed the boat on the term meteorologist *or better yet* meteorology. *Citing the* American Heritage Dictionary, meteor *derives from the Greek* meteōros, *"high in the air." But* meteorology *derives from* meteōrologia, *"discussion of astronomical phenomena." There is an obvious difference.*

As a one-time weather forecaster in the U.S. Air Force, let me point out that a meteorologist can be both a research scientist and a weather forecaster. On the other hand, a weather forecaster need not be a Ph.D. in meteorology but a highly trained technician (as I was).

Lastly, in the Air Weather Service (at least when I served), we never used the term aftercasting. *It was always* postcasting, *akin to "Monday morning quarterbacking."*

Edwin Dallas Kennedy
College Park, Maryland

Middle Initials

If you join the Army and do not have a middle initial, the Army will give you three: "N.M.I.," standing for "No Middle Initial." You then get to know yourself as Doe, John N.M.I.

"It's important to note that nothing is missing," explains Army spokesman Gerald W. Hendley. "Most people have middle initials. 'N.M.I.' would clarify that there is no omission."

Service in the armed forces may have triggered many individual decisions to include a middle initial in names. However, many individuals remain resolutely uninitiated: "Boy, have I been waiting a long time to say this!" explodes Lisa Caccavale of New York, in response to a query here about the practice. "As a secretary who's typed many a middle initial in my day, I think they are just plain ugly."

David J. Rosenbaum, an editor in U.P.I.'s Trenton bureau, denigrates them for another reason: "I'm strongly opposed to using middle initials when it is perfectly clear who is being referred to. What difference does it make that Governor Thomas Kean's middle initial is 'H'? The rule should be: Does it inform, distinguish, entertain, or illuminate? If it doesn't, it doesn't belong—toss it." He adds that this is his personal opinion and not U.P.I. style.

One narrow question I posed was: Should newspapers include the middle initial of famous people, as in "Margaret H. Thatcher"? The overwhelming response: No. "Why? The better to distinguish her from Margaret M. Thatcher?" demands Frederic C. Marston of New York, who sees a sinister trend in secretaries of state, from plain old Cyrus Vance to "Alexander M. Haig Jr." Says Mr. Marston: "The less, the better. Just as 'U.S.' is better than 'U.S.A.,' so, too, will 'Margaret Thatcher' do."

I agree; newspaper style should eschew the M. I. in the names of the most famous, unless the middle letter is so euphonious as to make the name seem naked without it. Under that rule, the M.I. stays in Robert E. Lee and Ulysses S. Grant (whose name was originally Hiram Ulysses Grant, but the acronym struck his elders as silly) and is removed from Winston S. Churchill. Albert Einstein was too smart to have a middle initial.

The exception is in the case of criminals. "I applaud the media's use of Mark David Chapman's middle name," writes Russell Tarby of Liverpool, New York, "as an appropriate distinction from the thousands of innocent Mark Chapmans throughout the country. The same goes for John W. Hinckley Jr. On the other hand, there's no need in wasting space on the middle initials of their victims, John Lennon and Ronald Reagan."

When names are less well known, reporters should use the M.I.: "Here in the boonies of journalism," opines R. Thomas Braco of *The Oswego* (New York) *County Messenger*, "we cite middle initials to make sources easier to look up in the phone book after the reporter's original notes are no longer at hand. Use of full names is also appreciated by reporters who must cover a competitor's story." (I'll remember that: When railing about deep-background leaks from national security adviser William P. Clark, I will leave out the "P," so none of my competitors will be able to look him up.)

When identifying someone with an M.I., do not use what reporter Lance Howland of Skaneateles, New York, calls the MIUIMI, or Multiple-Individual Usually Irish Middle Initial: "A local Congressman is always referred to as 'David O'B. Martin,' which I maintain should be 'David O. Martin.' A few months ago, *Time* magazine referred to Maryland Senator 'Charles McC. Mathias.' Is it McCollum, McCarthy or McCrabtree? And do we need to know?" (So that's why Senator Mathias is known as "Mac.")

At *The Yale Daily News,* managing editor John McQuaid reports that "the use of middle initials in by-lines provides an interesting study in the levels of pretension found at various college newspapers." He claims that *The Harvard Crimson* is replete with M.I.'s, while "our one remotely aristocratic by-line, Frederic M. Biddle's, recently shrank to 'By Fred Biddle.' What does this contrast imply about Harvard and Yale?"

The broader question of initializing was also addressed (and stamped and mailed) by nonjournalistic readers: Who needs that middle name, anyway? Richard Nixon, upon becoming President, dropped "Milhous"; Ronald Reagan dropped his W. (for Wilson) when he entered the White House. Recent Democratic Presidents go the other way: F.D.R., H.S.T., J.F.K., and L.B.J. all made good use of the M.I., until Jimmy Carter did away with all formality.

That's one of the keys: formality. An M.I. lends dignity. Some people resist this: "The use of a middle initial in one's own name makes the name sound less original, less distinctive," writes Judith Kirk of Amherst, Maine. "It sounds like a formula we mutter mindlessly because it has a certain rhythm." But others recognize the sonorous or serious nature of a name with an M.I.: Ed Murrow knew what he was doing by signing off as Edward R. Murrow, and financial reporter Irving R. Levine carries more weight with the R. (Anchormen, seeking informality to the point of coziness, eschew the middle marker. Who ever heard of Daniel I. Rather? Or Roger Harrison Mudd and Thomas John Brokaw?)

Proponents of the M.I. add this note: Nobody has to know what the letter stands for. "The middle initial is one of the last vestiges of personal privacy in an overfamiliar world," says Will C. Long of Hillsborough, New Hampshire. Some women smile mysteriously, some men turn stone-faced when asked what their middle initial stands for. That's their business. I always avoided giving my schoolmates my middle name when they asked what the "L" was for, because it stands for "Lewis" and I didn't like being called "Louie"; I have since dropped the M.I., except in today's piece, where it seemed fitting.

The hottest pro-initialities are people in the records business. "As a county recording officer," writes Richard Pearson Hatfield Jr., of Elizabeth, New Jersey, "I assure you that it is in the best interest of everyone to have their name recorded as completely as possible. Anyone who thinks it is funny or cute to register official papers as John Smith instead of John Xavier Smith should be aware they will suffer the curses of their heirs." (Mr. Hatfield will suffer the curses of the Pronoun Agreement Brigade, who insist on "Those who think" with "their.")

Don't let anybody tell you, however, that your name is not "legal" without the middle initial. In law, a person's name is his given name and his surname, and not his middle name; before denouncing me on your legal pads, see the *Snook* case in New York jurisprudence. And do not be intimidated by computers: The I.R.S. will punch you into its system with your middle initial, or without if you prefer, or even with your initial initial first: R. Christopher O'Brien of Brooklyn is annoyed because the I.R.S. writes to him as Robert C. O'Brien, but that's because he first filed that way, says the I.R.S. (Initial initials are a separate subject.)

With the rise of women in the executive work force, the middle initial is giving way to the full maiden name (though a few insuffragists reject "maiden name" as sexist). Attorney Carolyn Hill of Oklahoma City observed that for many years businessmen put down businesswomen by refusing to accord them middle initials; she insisted on "Carolyn G. Hill" until recently, when she began to use her full name, Carolyn Gregg Hill, because "as much as I loved and respected my husband, my accomplishments and failures have been exclusively my own." Women with given middle names, when they marry, have a choice of middle names—their old one or their maiden name. Women sometimes solve this by adopting a hyphenated last name.

A woman who lives in Kendall Park, New Jersey, has a different reason: "I always use my middle initial, lest people who hear my name for the first time think I am barking or stuttering. Typical phone conversation: 'Hello, this is Ruth Roufberg.' 'Yes, Mrs. Berg.' Sincerely, Ruth B. Roufberg."

My initial advice is to use a middle initial, or even an initial initial (as in Q. John Public) if you are having an identity crisis. "My name is so common," writes John William Smith of Birmingham, Michigan, "that it makes little difference what I call myself." But he has the solution in the next generation: "I plan on naming my son Igor Buxtehude Smith, after two of my favorite musicians." Only if the kid becomes world famous will he drop the "B."

Dear Bill:

For as long as I have written for newspapers (more than forty years), my byline has been Walter H. Waggoner. But I have considered dropping the M.I. Covering an international food conference for The Times *in Quebec in 1944, I was read, of course, by the participating delegates. On the train back from Quebec a member of the Canadian delegation found me writing a piece at my seat. Upon being introduced to me by a mutual friend, she remarked: "You are Walter H. Waggoner? I had the impression you were a large, fleshy man." (I am a skinny man of medium height.) "Because you think my prose is fat and flabby?" I asked. "No, because Walter H. Waggoner is such a solid-sounding, rather heavy name."*

Walt [Walter H. Waggoner]
New York, New York

In addition to the people who use the initial letter of their middle name in the middle of their name (Robert X. Smith, where X. stands for Xenophon, of course), there are those who really have a middle letter. It is not an initial because it isn't the first letter of any name.

The best-known example, perhaps, is Harry S Truman. If it isn't an initial, it shouldn't have a period after it, because that would imply that it is an abbreviation, which it isn't.

> Arthur J(esse) Morgan
> New York, New York

Technically speaking, the name of the 33rd President of the United States should be written with an "S" instead of the "S." that most writers use. The man did not have a middle name as most people would assume. This is because his parents wanted to satisfy both grandfathers when naming their newborn son. The political way out was to avoid using either of the grandfathers' names but to use the "S" that was common to both of them.

> Robert J. MacDonald
> Murray Hill, New Jersey

When he began campaigning for governor of New York in the mid-'50s, W. Averell Harriman immediately dropped the "W" that had served him well in his appointive government jobs for many years.

But when he was defeated in a second-term try by Nelson Rockefeller, we political reporters (I was with U.P.I.) were almost immediately informed that "Honest Ave" wanted the "W" back and, so far as I know, he's been W. Averell Harriman ever since.

> Robert E. Mack
> New York, New York

Enjoyed your article on middle initials. It seemed to address all aspects of the issue except the one which forces me to use a middle initial when I would rather not— i.e., the necessity to differentiate oneself from a celebrity.

A few years ago, when I moved in with a friend, the building office inquired of him (when he gave them my name) whether I was the *Robert Vaughn. I always thought I was.*

Also, clerks in stores who have been looking through me do double takes when they look at my name on a credit card. One almost seemed offended as he complained, "Oh, I thought you were the 'Man from UNCLE.'"

Since I added the "O" these problems have eased a bit. My only complaint now is that an occasional "junk mail" computer addresses me as Robert O'Vaughn.

> Robert O. Vaughn
> West New York, New Jersey

At Bell Labs, "birth name" is used instead of "maiden name." Both males and females can go through more than one name; the company wants to know the original name of the person.

> Art Lieberman
> Westfield, New Jersey

Winston Churchill's use of his middle initial exactly fulfills the strictures laid down by David J. Rosenbaum. The story of how he came to use it is related in My Early Life. *After the success of his first books early in the century, he received a letter from the then established American novelist Winston Churchill pointing out the possible confusion arising from the identical names of the two authors. The younger Churchill readily agreed, and added the initial of one of his middle names as a distinguishing mark.*

The use of his middle initial was limited to his career as a writer. The English press never referred to him as Winston S. Churchill—the use of a middle initial appears to be a purely American custom.

> Angela Von Laue
> Worcester, Massachusetts

Your column about middle initials jogged my memory about an old story involving the soldier who did not have a given "name" as such, only initials. When he joined the Army, he insisted that his name was R. B. Jones. This became in Army terminology "R (only) B (only) Jones" and in subsequent correspondence, as you can imagine, he became Ronly Bonly Jones.

As a practicing newspaper writer, the middle initial can be a pain. Tabloid headline writers, in the days when there were more tabloids, had a lot to do with their use and, after all, "FDR" is a lot more recognizable than "FR." I think it almost has to depend upon the person about whom we write; if he customarily uses it, or is known by it, then I think we have to go along. The mere insertion of it, because it is there and as an arbitrary matter, makes us pretentious.

In general, I think, the use of the middle initial seems to be fading. But for many years at the Post-Dispatch, *writers were identified in bylines by full names, including middle initials. Only in the last 15 to 20 years have staff members been able to use "Bob" or "Bill" instead of "Robert" or "William," if that was the way they preferred to be addressed or recognized.*

> Joe Pollack
> St. Louis, Missouri
> St. Louis Post–Dispatch

I have a little something to say
In behalf of Lyndon, and J.F.K.
I will never regard my name as official
Unless it includes my middle initial
I know that I, for one would deplore
Having just George, but no Bernard Shaw
Where would Hubert have been, without his "H"?
(Probably a checkout clerk, in Shopwell-Daitch)
I'd challenge powers that be, and bewail the fates
If I couldn't deal with W. B. Yeats
We have one for Lenin, but not for the Tsar
None for the Franklin named Pierce, one for F. D.R.
So sound ye the tocsin, and toll the bells
Honor E.E. Cummings and H. G. Wells
And in every lake, and lac, and loch
They know C. P.E. from J. S. Bach
I could go on much longer, but I shan't
I'm into I. W. Harper and J. W. Dant
I'll merely state that a man of yesteryear fame
Sam L. Clemens changed no initial, just his name.

David M. Geiger
Fair Lawn, New Jersey

Even the military was simpler forty years ago, although it took me three months to figure out that the dog tag on the chief bosun's mate on my ship which identified him as GUY NONE DUNCAN was not an indication that his maternal ancestors were from some exotic country.

S. (!) Roy Burroughs
Belmont, Massachusetts

Your article on middle initials is a great disappointment. You completely fail to deal with the problems of those of us who are the proud possessors of more than one middle name.

Why does American usage virtually insist on the single middle name? The rest of the English-speaking world allows parents to provide a child with as many names as they wish—and, pace William Arthur Philip Louis, it's not a practice confined to royalty. I once knew a man whose parents had preserved the family motto, "agens," in his names: it helped that he was a Latin scholar (and that the motto was reasonably short). Officialdom in Britain accommodates this practice; not so in America.

Social Security amputates my second middle initial. Tailors find it difficult—I own a jacket with the first three of my initials tastefully stitched on an inside pocket, but not the initial of my last name. The I.R.S. is happy to use all the names I give them, so long as I keep sending money. But form after form leaves inadequate space for what is invariably described as "middle initial," singular.

How would officialdom have coped with Prince Alfonso of Spain (1866–1934), great grandson of King Carlos III, who had a grand total of 88 names, mostly of saints and influential relatives? And how would it have handled the German princely houses of Reuss, which since 1296 have named every male child in the family Heinrich, and, in place of a middle initial, have numbered them in chronological order of birth? What would Social Security call Prince Heinrich LXIV? "Heinrich L"?

Nicholas D.J. Lane
Pittsburgh, Pennsylvania

Dear Louie:

When you write about initials, do not overlook the plight of those, such as I, who have first names that they hate but are dragooned by functionaries, computers, and various application and registration forms into giving their first names and middle initials.

In my case, that comes out "Elbert C. Daniel, Jr." There is nothing wrong with the name Elbert: Elbert Hubbard was once as famous as William Lewis Safire, and Mount Elbert is the highest peak in the Colorado Rockies (I have no idea whom it was named for). The late Theodore M. Bernstein and I used to call each other, respectively, "Menline" and "Elbert." It was our wry little joke.

Clifton Daniel
New York, New York

Individuals should have the right to display their M.I. if one of three circumstances is faced.

First, a middle initial stands for an honored relative, in my case, my father, whom I wish to pay tribute to. I can't begin to recompense him for an education at Harvard and Columbia universities, not at an assistant professor's salary. But I can leave a middle initial in, because it stands for his first name.

Also, a M.I. should be allowed if it prevents confusion with someone else. As my career commences, I must confront being confused with a more prominent historian formerly at Harvard Business School, James P. Baughman.

Finally, a matter of appearances should permit the M.I.'s use. Some of us have long last names and short first names, or vice versa. The middle initial strikes a balance between the one and the other. Note also the letter count in parens.

> *James (5) L. Baughman (8)   James Baughman*
> *Alexander (9) M. Haig, Jr. (4)   Alexander Haig*
> *John (4) F. Kennedy (7)   John Kennedy*

(Kennedy was wise to use that middle initial because not long after his death, there was a utility infielder named John Kennedy who played for the Reds.)

Imagine, if you will, having a slightly different name: John Safireson or John MacSafiresonen. Wouldn't John X. Safireson or John X. MacSafiresonen look better on paper? Don't you think that the M.I. can therefore be justified as a balancing mechanism? A means of giving readers a breather before getting to the long last name, or a rest after reading the first?

Compare the symmetry of William (7) Safire (6) and Ronald (6) Reagan (6).

I would therefore offer the following rule. Middle initials may be used if the total number of letters in either the first or last name is greater than the other by a factor of two (2).

> *James L. Baughman*
> *Associate Professor*
> *School of Journalism and Mass*
>   *Communication*
> *University of Wisconsin*
> *Madison, Wisconsin*

. . . And Mr. Safire will suffer the curses of the Pronoun Agreement Brigade, Irony Battalion, which insists on "which" with "brigade."

> *Richard C. Firstman*
> Newsday
> *Long Island, New York*

I suspect your preference for omitting the middle initial stems from the fact that your first initial—W—has three syllables in it (every other initial has only one syllable). The action of speaking W makes the next syllable that follows it a natural stress —thus W S gives a natural stress to S whereas W L S gives a natural stress to L with the S—the most important initial—falling into subordination. If you changed your first name to the chummy "Bill" then I suspect you would be more happy with BLS than plain old BS over your column.

On second thoughts, perhaps BS would be just right on occasions.

> *Jan R. Harrington*
> *New York, New York*

Middle Women

The middle-initial problem seems especially acute in women. A composite correspondent, Henrietta Legion, complains that she was distressed, when first married to a Mr. Jones, at having to choose between middle names: Was it to be Henrietta Yolanda Jones, using her given middle name, or Henrietta Legion Jones, using her maiden name as a middle name?

The Lexicographic Irregular whose name is Legion says she rejected the thought of two middle initials—Henrietta Y. L. Jones—as confusing, and then went on to reject a middle name entirely. She thinks of a middle initial as masculine or pretentious, or both, and tends not to use one. In the case of women who become famous, there is a tendency to use the maiden name as a middle name, as if to signal to old school chums that, yes, the Sandra O'Connor they are reading about was the Sandra Day with whom they went to school, or to use the married name only in personal affairs, such as joint checking accounts.

Many women shy away from the use of a middle initial as too much an assertion of self. Betsy Wade, a *Times* colleague, analyzed a list of the Women's Media Group, an organization with a fairly descriptive title, which meets once a month in the private dining room of The Four Seasons in New York. If you are a member of that bunch, you are in, and if you can eat at the best restaurant in town, you have arrived. Of the 134 members, only seven members use full middle names and not one uses a middle initial.

Miss Dis of '83

When asked about the abusive attack from Soviet leader Yuri Andropov on President Reagan's defense strategy, Defense Secretary Caspar Weinberger replied: "Standard Soviet disinformation."

New York Senator Daniel P. Moynihan, co-chairman of the Intelligence Committee and a staunch defender of linguistic precision, writes: "Clearly a misuse of the word. Cap meant to say *misinformation*. Or *lie*. But got caught up in the etymological escalation that goes on around here.

"Another point," adds the senator, "Americans don't know what *disinformation* is because we don't do any. We don't do any because we have so little facility in languages. Including our own."

I shall have to speak sharply to the senator about sentence fragments, but let us today take up the difference between *misinformation* and *disinformation*.

In verb prefixes, *mis* means "badly, wrongly, perversely, or mistakenly," while *dis* means "reversing the action or effect of the verb that follows." Thus (I like *thus* almost as much as *hence*), *misbelieve* means "to hold wrong views" and *disbelieve* means "to not believe." In the same way, *misplace* means "to put in the wrong place," and *displace* means "to substitute for." *Mis* louses up, *dis* boots out.

Misinformation is wrong, or false, news. It is not information because it is in error, either by ignorance or design. The basic meaning of the word is "wrongness," and not the motive for being wrong.

Disinformation is false news spread with malicious intent. The word first appeared in English in *The Times* of London in 1955, taken from the Russian *dezinformatsiya,* the name of a department of the K.G.B. assigned to black propaganda. Says Arnaud De Borchgrave, author of a novel about its activities: "It is the political equivalent of the military *deception. Misinformation* becomes *disinformation* when the false report is deliberate."

Apply that definition to Secretary Weinberger's accusation. He evidently believes that Mr. Andropov is deliberately, with malice aforethought, uttering an untruth. That would be *disinformation.* The senator is in error but he is merely misinformed.

Perhaps you have missed a nuance on the meaning of disinformation. *De Borchgrave was caught on this in at least one review of* The Spike, *I believe. He used* disinformation *interchangeably with* black propaganda, *implying the Soviets were behind a variety of front organizations and personalities with a view toward deceiving and persuading gullible public opinion in Western countries.*

I am under the impression that disinformation *is a more limited, technical term with application within the world intelligence community: when one intelligence agency concocts, leaks, or otherwise plants information with the sole purpose of confusing or misleading an opposing intelligence agency or government for tactical or strategic reasons.*

Disinformation, *in this sense, has nothing to do with propaganda, which is intended for public consumption. Andropov's remarks on U.S. defense strategy, then, were hardly meant to deceive any U.S. professional; they were just standard propaganda. But those mysterious cases where the bona fides of a Soviet defector have been called into question, so that there are unending doubts—that's probably disinformation . . . done by professionals . . . so that people like yourself and your contacts in the U.S. intelligence community still don't know what's real and what's not.*

The point of all this is not inconsequential. De Borchgrave's twisting of the concept was the basis for a not-so-thinly disguised and unfair attack on the left.

Philip G. Ryan
New York, New York

While disinformation *might mean what you say it means, it doesn't seem to mean that ("false news spread with malicious intent") for the reasons you cite. If, in* verb prefixes, *"dis means 'reversing the action or effect of the verb that follows,' " then* disinform *(the verb) would mean something like "taking away information"—or is that* uninform? *If, then, the noun form carries the same meaning,* disinformation *would seem to mean "a lack of information." You don't explain how translation from verb to noun adds "malicious intent." Perhaps what Secretary Weinberger wanted was* malinformation?

But I like disinform. *It reminds me of "Forget I said that," or "The jury will disregard . . . etc.," and conjures up epistemological dimensions.*

Janet B. Hubbs
Brielle, New Jersey

Monitor

In school, I hated *monitors.* They were the smart little kids who sat in for the teachers during exams, or patrolled the halls to make sure none of us raced up the down staircase.

President Reagan, however, likes the verb. *Monitor,* from the Latin for "warn," means "keep an eye on"; it is a passive activity, a far cry from *investigate* and even farther from *prosecute.* When he called for the Department of Justice to pursue its "vigorous monitoring" of the case of the purloined, filched, pilfered, stolen, or whatever briefing paper, it sounded busy, but what did it mean?

History buffs recalled the "masterly inactivity" of James Mackintosh, that English espouser of "disciplined inaction," or the "watchful waiting" proposed by Grover Cleveland and later raised to policy levels by Woodrow Wilson. Lovers of oxymorons compared "vigorous monitoring" to Churchill's "adamant for drift."

At the Justice Department, wrote Philip Gailey of *The New York Times,* "officials said that they had not understood what Mr. Reagan meant by the use of the word *monitor* and that after considerable debate in the department's criminal division, the term *active review* was agreed on as the best description of the agency's role."

Meanwhile, at the same press conference that had considered the meaning of *stolen*, Susan Page of *Newsday*—respectful, charming, relentless—asked if the President meant that the Justice Department was conducting an investigation. "I've called it monitoring," said the President, "but that's what it amounts to." At that point—with the verb given a meaning of action it had not formerly possessed—lawyers at the Justice Department picked up the phone and called the F.B.I. The "vigorous monitoring" became "investigate"; the search was on for the "mole." The origin of that word in this context required some digging.

You refer to James Mackintosh as "that English espouser of 'disciplined inaction.' " As he was born at Aldourie on the bank of Loch Ness, I should think he would properly be considered Scots. Certainly he was so regarded by his contemporaries.

                                                          Linda E. Connors
                                                          Madison, New Jersey

My Fellow Americanians

Queries have poured in from New Yorkians, Floridenos, Illinoisies, Vermontans, and even Parisites asking, "What do we call the native of (wherever)?" How do we decide among Whereveronians, Whereverites, Whereverans, and Whereverers?

When faced with the problem of toponymic derivatives, I turn to Professor Allen Walker Read, the etymologist who tracked down the source of "O.K." (*Oll korrect*, not *Old Kinderhook*—stop writing me about this. O.K.?) In *The Connecticut Onomastic Review*, a journal perused by people that the Puritan divine Cotton Mather used to call *Connecticotians* (the first derivative form), Professor Read points to a second derivative form—*Connecticutensian*, which sounds a bit itsy-poo—used by clergymen in the eighteenth century. The *-ensian* form is not unknown in Connecticut: Students at Yale were called *Yalensians* before that gave way to the current *Yalie. Connecticutensian* was followed by *Connecticutter*, which was later cut to *Connecticuter*, with only one *t*, in the *United States Government Printing Office Style Manual.* With a display of federal arrogance, the stylists there decided: "In designating the natives of the several states, the following forms will be used . . . Connecticuter."

That strikes me as plain silly: The single *t* makes the word look as if it should

be pronounced *kyooter*, as in "Yale freshmen are cuter." Professor Read agrees: "This goes against the *Sprachgefühl* that the agent of *cut* is *cutter*, and intrudes the comparative form of the adjective *cute.*" He also points out that the heavy hand of federal government writes *Michiganite*, despite the likelihood that most citizens of that state use *Michigander, Michiganer,* and *Michiganian.* (Why can't Detroitniks make up their minds?)

While sprachgefooling around—that word is the German for an instinctive feel for a language—we can take a pot shot at the Printing Office preference for *Massachusettsan* over the earlier *Massachusettan.* The Read form, on the analogy of *Alabamian* and *Floridian*, strikes my ear as better: *Massachusettsian.* (So why not *Texian?* Because Texans are different.)

Aren't there any rules for toponymic derivatives? (Does anybody else call these "toponymic derivatives"?) "No," says Simon & Schuster's David Guralnik, who calls it "the noun designating a resident of a certain city or state." (A guralnik is a follower of *Webster's New World Dictionary.*)

For example, states whose names end in *a* usually add an *n: Iowan, Minnesotan, Montanan, Nevadan, Dakotan.* But watch out for Alabama, correctly cited above as *Alabamian*, along with *Floridian, Carolinian, and Louisianian.* Federal style is *Arizonan*, and that is what Senator Barry Goldwater calls himself, but many locals will fight for *Arizonian.*

The G.P.O. (can the Public Printer, or the Superintendent of Documents, be impeached?) calls for *Utahan*, but *The Deseret News* of Salt Lake City stands firm on *Utahn*, which looks the way the word sounds.

Nobody even tries to lay down tip-toponymic law to cities. You're a *Rich-monder* if you come from Richmond, Virginia, and a *Richmondite* if you come from Richmond, California; similarly, *Springfieldians* are also Massachusettsians, while *Springfielders* are Ohioans.

Cities with compound names offer even less rhyme or reason: A resident of Las Vegas shooting craps with a resident of Los Angeles is a *Las Vegan* fading a *Los Angeleno*. When a man from Dodge City vacations in Daytona Beach, he is a *Dodge Citian* among *Daytonans*.

You think we're the only ones without rules? When a boy from Liverpool and a girl from Cambridge run off to Barbados, a *Liverpudlian* and a *Cantabrigian* frolic among the *Bajans*. (And when you're in Guatemala, do as the *Guatemaltecos* do.)

As a Connecticut-born, and lifetime Connecticut (senior) resident, I protest both Connecti-CUTTER and Connecti-CUTER. Natives of Connecticut are "Nut-meggers"—a name well-rooted in the history of The Nutmeg State.

If this is too much history for the Washington bureaucracy to absorb—and if they do, indeed, need a suitable suffix for Connecticut—I would refer them to no less an authority than Jonathan Swift. His inhabitants of Lilliput were known as Lilliputians (one t); and he invented the country, so who should be better qualified to establish a precedent?

And if "Louisianians" would prefer to be called "Cajuns," in honor of their Acadian origins, why not? Or how about "Sooners" and "Tar-heels"? Do sportswriters hold the copyrights?

I really don't know what to say about a suggested name for the residents of the great state of Maine: "As Mainiacs go, so goes the Nation"?

Stephen M. Edson*
Riverside, Connecticut

*A former "Greenwichite" now turned "Riversidian" (not "Riversidean"?).

J. Frank Dobie, the famed Texian folklorist and writer, made a distinction between "Texian" and "Texan." A "Texian" is one whose ancestors settled what is now the state of Texas before it became a Republic in 1836 and prior to joining the Union in 1845. "Texans" are merely residents of the state.

William A. Nail
Glenview, Illinois

P.S. I am a Texian, too.

Some time ago, the question arose as to the proper designation for the inhabitants of Marcus Hook, a small town south of Philadelphia and a part of the port area. The irresistible and succinct appellation was "Marcus Hookers."
Can you top that?

> Irvin R. Glazer
> Springfield, Pennsylvania

When writers write about inhabitants of other planets, they usually follow the Latin base, as in Mercurians, Martians, Jovians, Plutonians, etc. But Venus-dwellers are always "Venusians," rather than "Venereans." Is this to avoid association with veneral disease?

> Arthur J. McReady
> Little Neck, New York

My Reception, Your Shivaree

"I'm *wore out,*" says a Southerner after a hard day. Another Southerner will nod and agree: "I'm 'bout to *give out,* too."

A Westerner would more likely use *worn out* or *weary,* and a Northerner *tuckered* or *shot,* or *done in.*

Most Americans, regardless of region, say, *"I'm pooped,"* or, *"I'm pooped out"*; runners-up to the triumphant *pooped* are *bushed, all in, exhausted.* Trailing but still showing strength in this stressful contest is *beat*; wheezing and falling by the wayside are *had it, played out, dog tired, petered out, fagged out,* and *at the end of my rope.*

Then, hours after the marathon is over, come the real stragglers, with no regional emphasis: *dead tired, fatigued, frazzled, too pooped to pop, knocked out, washed out, licked, 'bout had it, ready to drop, pegged out,* and *on my last legs.*

The purpose of this bone-tiring study (leaving readers *dragged, guffed, and whipped*) is to illustrate the healthy existence of regional differences in American speech. Diversity abounds without reference to region, as the wide variety of synonyms found everywhere proves, but certain regionalisms persist: Southerners are *wore out* and Westerners *worn out,* and neither have any sympathy for Northerners who are merely *tuckered.*

The tireless scholars at the *Dictionary of American Regional English,* who published their first volume in the fall of 1985, have passed along some preliminary findings that tell us much about ourselves.

"What do you call a noisy neighborhood celebration after a wedding," they asked a cross section of the nation, "where the married couple is expected to give a treat?"

I know the answer to that: a *reception*, where the uncles get nostalgic and the matron of honor gets maudlin and the caterers get rich. However, I am in a 15 percent minority, betraying an Eastern background. Fully half of those polled, especially in the West, respond *shivaree*, an altered form of *charivari*, based on the Greek word for "headache" (presumably a reference to the morning after). Runner-up to *shivaree*, with no regional bias, is *serenade*. In West Virginia and Ohio, that big party is a *belling*; in upper New York State and Pennsylvania, it's a *horning*, and in lower New York State and New Jersey, it's a *skimmelton*.

Sobbing matrons of honor are no strangers to me, but I have never been invited to a *skimmelton*, much less a *callathump* (New Jersey) or *propabini* (Michigan). Some of the other responses are recognizable as descriptions of any big party: *wingding, bash, blowout, jamboree, hoedown, luau, to-do, send-off*, and the ever-popular *drunken brawl*.

On several matters of food, people in New England don't know what the rest of the country is talking about. When non-Northeasterners speak of *poached eggs*, Yankees order *dropped eggs*. And when asked, "What do you call ears of corn that are just right for eating?" Yankees will say *sweet corn* while the rest of the country knows it as *roasting corn* or *corn on the cob*. (On a follow-up question, "If you don't have sweet corn, you can always eat young ———," the blank was filled overwhelmingly by *field corn*, followed by *horse corn, cow corn, yellow corn*. I flunked that one, with a helpless *corn al dente*.)

Names for old cars show both regional differences and a national lingo. The nation's preference is *jalopy*, with *tin lizzie* the second choice, but in Northern states you are likely to hear *junker* or *wreck*; in the South and midland, *rattletrap*; in the Gulf States, *T-model*; and in Texas, *hoopy*. Other terms, without regional emphasis, are *flivver, heap* (rare in the Far West), *jitney, junkheap, bucket o' bolts, crate, puddle-jumper, scrapheap, chugalong, death trap, dune buggy*, and—some people like literary allusions—*wreck of the Hesperus*.

The real trick in dialect geography is to find objects that no "national" words describe. For example, what do you call the strip of grass and trees between the sidewalk and the curb? Most people have no answer for that, but of those who do, it's *parking strip* in the Plains, Northwest, and Southwest; *parkway* in the Northeast; *curb, curbing, curb line, curb strip* in the North and North Midland; *terrace* in the North-Central States; *boulevard* in the Upper Middle West; and *tree lawn* along the Great Lakes. Then you get a sprinkling of *bern, island, sidewalk plot, right o' way, neutral plot, devil strip, street lawn*, and a grumbling *unpaved pavement*.

For this authorized leaking from *DARE*, I am indebted to Joan Hall, associate editor. As a careful lexicographer, she probably would not go along with the following radical speculation, but from a look at the printouts, I would suggest that a good, quick way of telling where a person is from is to listen to how he or she says the familiar form of "mother": *mom* or *mommy* is generally Northern; *mum* or *mummy*, Northeastern; and *mamma*, Southern. My guess is that *ma* or *maw* tends to be Western. Now you can play 'Enry 'Iggins.

What turned me on to regionalisms was a mistake I made about a Civil War battlefield: I wrote that the Battle of Shiloh is the Northern name for the Battle of Pittsburg Landing. Exactly the opposite is the truth.

But that churned up a nice pile of North-South mail. David Christmas of Setauket, New York, reports that what Northerners call *mountain laurel* is referred to as *ivy* in the South, while what Northerners call *rhododendron* is called *laurel* in the South. E. A. Hancock of Blacksburg, Virginia, writes: "People in New England speak of a small stream as a *brook* (at least in poetry); in the South, a small stream is a *creek* or *run*. In the South, teacher says to pupil: 'Stay after school this *evening*'; Middle Western folks say, 'Come in *tonight*' (for late afternoon)."

The North-South preposition war has never abated: Northerners wait *for* the clerk to put the cornmeal in a *bag*, while Southerners wait *on* the clerk to put the grits in a *sack* or a *poke*.

Though Standard English calls for *bring* to mean "here" and *take* to mean "there," this dialectical variation shows: "I was reared in the South," writes Henry Smith of Middletown, Rhode Island, "where *to bring* is to come from there to here with something and *to take* is go away from here to there with something. Here in the North, *to bring* is all-inclusive in moving that something, and *to take* is 'to steal or misappropriate.' " In that vein, "*Carry* is used to mean 'transport' in the South," advised Michael Niemann of Pontiac, Michigan, "as in 'I carried Jim over

to Atlanta in my new car,' a usage never encountered in the North to my knowledge."

Southerners think Northerners who use *anymore* to mean "these days" are
weird, and Northerners look askance at rednecks who invert -*ever*, using *everwhat*
or *everwho* to stand in for *whatever* or *whoever*. Ron Butters, editor of *American
Speech* magazine, points to the Southern and South Midland use of the "conjunc-
tive which," as in "The President was not happy with the results of the election,
which I couldn't be happier about that." Such comments set Northern pundits
scratching their heads.

In penance for my Shiloh error, and as a service to those who like to refight
the Civil War (Yank) or War Between the States (Reb), here are a few battle
names that indicate which side you're on: *Bull Run* is *Manassas* in the South,
Antietam Creek is *Sharpsburg*, *Stones River* is *Murfreesboro*, *Cedar Creek* is
Slaughter's Mountain. Observe the pattern: The North, usually invading unfamiliar territory, used bodies of water or landmarks for nomenclature; the South used
the names of the towns.

This hardly covers the subject, but I feel *cooped, dished, dragged out, at row's
end, nearly dead, out of gas, whupped,* and *shot down.*

*Your column discussing regionalisms failed to include an upper New York State
term for an old car, "winter rat." Such a term designates a car characterized by
extensive rusting from the sanded and salted roads, and makes its appearance along
with heavy winter coats in mid-October.*

> Kenneth E. Gale, M.D.
> Syracuse, New York

You mentioned the term dune buggy *for a junker. In this state, a dune buggy is a
special, jeep-like vehicle with very wide tires which is used to transport people, for
a fee, across the tops of the dunes (sand) along Lake Michigan shores on the
Sleeping Bear Dunes.*

> Frances W. Lauman
> Saginaw, Michigan

In regard to your discussion of regional variants of "sweet corn," may I offer one:
ros'nears *(ROS-nears) for "roasting ears of corn."*

> Ron Saffell
> Girard, Ohio

Where I come from (Holley, NY, just west of Rochester, which I left about 1929), there are three kinds of corn: pop corn, sweet corn, and field corn. Pop corn is good for nothing but popping, altho I have heard that it can be boiled on the cob and eaten, if it's all you have.

Sweet corn is a different thing from field corn, with a smaller ear and a sweeter kernel, and is raised only for eating and to sell to canneries for other people to eat. It comes white, like Country Gentleman, and yellow, like Golden Bantam, and in hybrids (I think Luther Hill is one of these), and each has its vociferous champions.

Field corn comes in two basic kinds, flint corn for horses and dent corn for cattle. Each of these, of course, has many varieties and hybrids. This is the corn which is ground whole for cornmeal, and which is degermed and skinned to make hominy, or samp, which in turn is cracked in the South to make grits. Grits are not cornmeal.

Some of our neighbors here in Pennsylvania don't bother with sweet corn at all, since they feel that field corn, if picked early in the milk stage, before the kernel has entered the dough stage, is just as good to boil or roast and eat from the cob. I don't know how canneries feel about this, tho.

Donald H. Rogers
Ivyland, Pennsylvania

Some further investigation is warranted concerning your claim that the North used bodies of water for nomenclature because of unfamiliarity with the territory.

To begin with, one cited example—Sharpsburg—is in the North, albeit in a border state. More to the point, however, the North had a penchant for riparian nomenclature which had nothing to do with unfamiliarity. While the South named its armies after geographic areas (for instance, Lee's Army of Northern Virginia), the North used river names, for example, the Army of the Potomac and the Army of the Cumberland.

James Moore
Detroit, Michigan

Fannie Hamilton, my Vermont Yankee grandmother, has this definition of a "Yankee"—where she first heard it, I never learned:

> *If you will ask a European what a Yankee is*
> *he will say an American; if you ask an American,*
> *he'll say a northerner; if you ask a northerner,*
> *he'll say a New Englander; if you ask a New Englander,*
> *he'll say a Vermonter, and if you ask a Vermonter*

*what a Yankee is, he will say, "Someone who
eats cheddar cheese with his apple pie."*

> Susan E. Mowery
> Key West, Florida

Your propabini *for the neighborhood wedding celebration may be a variation of the
Polish* poprawiny *(pŏ′ pră vĭ′ nē). My parents'* poprawiny *in 1941 in Bayonne, New
Jersey, is said to have lasted three days. And they could not leave on their honeymoon
until it was over!*

> Elaine Petsu
> Piscataway, New Jersey

A shivaree *is a wedding reception? The bride and groom can expect a shivaree from
friends after the formal "reception," during their first night. When my father
declared a shivaree after my wedding, it was a threat. In the movie* Oklahoma, *the
shivareers greeted the bride and groom with the clanking and clanging of pots and
pans. The mirthmakers then herded Laurie and Curly to the haystack.*

> Paul D. Browning
> Granby, Massachusetts

In Wisconsin during the 20s, the word shivaree *referred to a tumultuous greeting
given to a newlywed couple after they had retired for the night. I can remember
neighbors with dishpans (do those exist anymore?) and wooden or metal spoons
making a racket until the couple would come out and pay them. If anybody had a
bugle, that was used, too.*

> Anne B. Warzyn
> Kansas City, Missouri

You say that in lower New York State and New Jersey, the word skimmelton *is used
to mean "a noisy neighborhood celebration after a wedding." I wonder if you are
aware that Thomas Hardy, in* The Mayor of Casterbridge *(Chapter XXXVI), uses
the words* skimmity-ride *or* skimmington, *defined by a character in the book as "a
foolish thing they do in these parts when a man's wife is—well, not too particularly
his own." As described by Hardy, it involves a parade of mummery, effigies, etc.*

> John F. Crowther
> Old Lyme, Connecticut

Consider the linguistic and ritual similarities between the Shivaree and the Shava Brochah.

> Rita Lasar
> New York, New York

Your column on regional expressions is full of it. An uneducated Southerner, or anyone anywhere who is uneducated, may say "I'm wore out." A Southerner is just as apt to say "plumb tuckered."

As for the strip of grass between curb and sidewalk, there is another name for it: apron. An apron of grass is worn by the lawn on the other side of the walk. Where I live, that strip is owned by the city, but maintained by the homeowner. All lot surveys begin on the inside edge of the walk (away from the curb); where no walk exists, the survey is made as if the walk were there.

A charivari is not at all analogous to "reception." The first is given to the newlyweds to heckle them; the latter is given by the family of the bride (usually) to entertain guests.

> Ann Y. Hayden
> Watertown, New York

What do you call the strip of grass between the sidewalk and the curb or street? Why, if you live in South Florida, as I do (a displaced Great Necker), you call it a swale. "Swale your dog" is the admonition here, just as New Yorkers are asked to "curb him."

> Phoebe Starfield Gozan
> Coconut Creek, Florida

It seemed strange to me to discover that tree belt was not included in your list for the strip of grass and trees between sidewalk and curb. Having grown up in Connecticut, 72.3 miles from Broadway, I always assumed that tree belt was a rather common term for this area.

I do not recall hearing anyone use parkway, but I do know devil strip from hearing my wife use it, undoubtedly because she learned it while growing up in New York City and Greenwich, Connecticut.

> Robert F. McNerney, Jr.
> Worcester, Massachusetts

A few days ago I was reading Sinclair Lewis' Babbitt. In the first part of the third chapter I noted the use of "grass parking" to describe the part of a lawn that goes between the sidewalk and the curb.

> Sally W. Garvey
> New York, New York

Southerners, like everyone else, waited for the clerk to put grits in the sack or bag. It was the clerk who waited on the customer, i.e., served him. I never heard the word poke except in the expression pig in a poke and I remember being very puzzled, as a child, about what that could mean.

Carry did not mean just to physically transport, as to carry someone in an auto. It also meant to escort: On my first date, I carried a girl to the moving pictures (we walked together). (This is apparently a Scotticism—I have found it often in Boswell.)

You do not give the Southern name for the "strip of grass and trees between the sidewalk and curb." We called it the park (not parking strip or parkway). It was often deeper than the front yard (between house and sidewalk) and it would have been ridiculous to call it a strip.

When I was a student at Duke University in the thirties, I noticed that students at the University of North Carolina at Chapel Hill twelve miles away said "on class" whereas everywhere else (Duke included) the expression was "in class." I have not noticed any lexicographer who has pointed out this remarkable local usage—remarkable because confined to so small a place.

> Lewis White Beck
> Rochester, New York

As a native of NYC married to a Rhode Islander, and living that first year in Berkeley, California, I was annoyed by my husband's insistence that I buy something called "rare-ripes" to put in salad. These turned out to be "green onions" in California, which to a New Yorker are "scallions." Visiting Rhode Island, I noticed that they had "cleansers" to dry-clean their clothes, to the rest of the country's "cleaners."

Probably the oddest regionalism is the "coffee cabinet." This is a thick milkshake made with coffee syrup and coffee ice cream. Though my spouse insisted that a "cabinet" must be coffee, I have seen signs in Rhode Island that advertise simply "cabinets," listing different flavors.

> Dolores Du Bois
> New York, New York

I remember moving to California from New England thirty years ago, going to a stationery store and asking for "elastics," and being met with blank incomprehension. Pointing to the product, I discovered they were rubber bands. I'm not sure whether "rubber bands" hasn't taken over because our language, even in New England, has become much more standard over the years. I still know, however, New Englanders who refer to victims of "shock" for stroke. "He had a shock and died" can be misleading to the unknowing.

I always refer to my "pocketbook" (or sometimes "bag") which I'm inclined to misplace, bulging as it is, in odd corners. People return my "purse," and in department stores it's called the "handbag" department.

We lived outside Philadelphia when our children were small, so they still refer to "suckers" for lollipops. I went "coasting" as a child in Massachusetts; they went "sled-riding," and going "sliding" seems another way to refer to going down a hill on a sled.

I always wore "stockings" when Westerners wore "hose," but pantyhose seems to have triumphed.

> *Betty Darnell*
> *Burke, Virginia*

I was raised in South Carolina to call a burlap bag a croaker sack, I suppose because that's what ya use when ya go giggin'. Years later, when I tried to spell the word for the first time, I thought it must be "croquer" sack or some such. (I am a French cultural historian if that goes anyway toward explaining this misconception.) It was not, of course, in the dictionary. Only when I recalled its common use down home did I figure out how it must be spelled and that what I really meant to write was "burlap bag."

> *Bland Addison, Jr.*
> *New York, New York*

My grandmother was born in Baltimore, Maryland in 1860. She would say "spigot," not "faucet"; "bill of fare," not "menu"; "surface car," not "trolley car."

> *Muriel Hyman*
> *Great Neck, New York*

We would have composed an elegant addendum to your notes on exhaustion, but we were too used up after a weekend ski trip to manage more than this postcard. Loyal but listless readers,

Joan Zegree
August Piper, Jr.
Seattle, Washington

Negarrogative

Feel ready for a good crusade, and the nuclear freeze leaves you cold? Here comes an idea from Peter Persoff of Oakland, California: "Why not deal with the glaring lack of an acceptable negative interrogative form of 'I am'? Ain't I right in saying we need one?"

Although I have a metaphoric problem of staring angrily into the nothingness of a "glaring lack," I believe it is about time to fill the negative-interrogative gap.

You say, "I am." You ask, "Am I?" But when you ask in the negative—when you mean "Am not I?"—you never say, "Am I not?" or "Amn't I?" or even "Am not I?" Instead, you are taught to say, "Aren't I?"

But that's silly. You would never turn it around to say, "I aren't." If "I aren't" is bad grammar, then "Aren't I?" is just as bad.

What to do? In olden times, the English language treated "ain't" with respect, as a contraction of "am not," or "amn't," later confused with "a'nt," or "are not." The word's first appearance in print was in 1778, in the novel *Evelina,* by Fanny Burney: "Those you are engaged to ain't half so near related to you as we are." That was *ain't* standing in for *aren't.*

As the general use of *ain't* increased, the arbiters of correct usage began to look down their noses at the term. It became a dialect usage calling for stern correction. When the third edition of *Merriam Webster's Unabridged* came out in 1961 and failed to declare the word substandard, great mockery of the lexicographer ensued. A cartoon had a caller asking for Dr. Philip Gove, then Merriam-Webster's editorial chief, and the receptionist replying, "He ain't in."

Ain't it about time to decide when the word is correct and when it ain't correct? In both instances in that sentence, I would say that, for standard usage, the word should be frowned on (not only would I say it, I do—avoid the craven conditional). Don't substitute *ain't* for *isn't,* because *isn't* is clearly the contraction of "is not" and works naturally even in the negative interrogative. (Isn't that clear?)

In the same way, for standard prose use, eschew *ain't* and spit it out whenever some other contraction works (say "they aren't," not "they ain't"). But when it comes to the *first-person* negative interrogative, withhold your automatic reproof.

Jacques Barzun, the great usagist, is caught between eras on this: "The negative interrogative form for the declarative 'I am' is an especially hopeless situation," he says, "ever since 'ain't' became vulgar. 'Am I not?' and 'Aren't I?' are the acceptable choices." But how can "I aren't" be correct? " 'Aren't I?' is grammatically wrong," Professor Barzun sighs, "but is perfectly good usage."

Now I'm ready to take the plunge. Rather than say "Aren't I?" when I mean "Am not I?" I am prepared to reach back into the linguistic past to legitimize "Ain't I?" Put this down as coming from the Voice of Authority (which is going to lose a lot of authority in its promulgation, but what's a mandate for?): Only in the first-person-singular negative-interrogative of the verb "to be" is the contraction *ain't* acceptable in standard speech.

Ain't it the truth? (No. Like "Ain't she sweet?" that's third person and substandard, because "isn't" makes sense.) Ain't I gutsy? (You bet I am; better to sound vulgar than to adopt the grammatically wrong but acceptable "Aren't I?") O.K., mailman, back up the truck and heave out the bags.

Once we open the door to "ain't" as the first person interrogative, its use as the first-person declarative will be inevitable. For some reason, it sounds fine in the interrogative, e.g., "Ain't I the cat's pajamas?" Ditto in regionalisms and colloquialisms: "I ain't agonna listen to you any more." (This is merely an example, not a threat.) But the sound isn't one of music in more formal declarative statements such as "I am of two minds and so ain't a hawk or a dove."

Unfortunately, I do not have a constructive suggestion, only doubts about yours, but this may be just—a negarrogative column deserves a negarrogative letter.

> Stanley Budner
> New York, New York

You really should have tried to convince Mr. Persoff that "aren't I?" is indeed an acceptable negative interrogative form of "I am." If you and I and Charles Kuralt and Jacques Barzun all say "aren't I," then how can it be wrong? Inconsistent maybe. Illogical maybe. But wrong? Let me paraphrase the late Paul Roberts on the subject of usage: You and I and Charles Kuralt and Jacques Barzun don't avoid "ain't" because it's wrong; it's wrong because we avoid it.

> Martha Kolln
> Assistant Professor of English
> Pennsylvania State University
> College Park, Pennsylvania

The tough kids in my childhood neighborhood used to beat up on language as much as on other kids. But they were consistent. Ain't was a multipurpose negative and was decried by local English teachers because it ignored both person and number. Common street usage was: I ain't, you ain't, he ain't, she ain't, it ain't, we ain't, you ain't, they ain't; instead of contractions for I am not (aren't), you are not (aren't), he is not (isn't), she is not (isn't), it is not (isn't), we are not (aren't), you are not (aren't), they are not (aren't).

"Aren't I" was probably another rebellion against the upper class for only fancy people used to say "Am I not" which sounded "terribly English" in those days and therefore not acceptable in American usage. But then, maybe the English said the same thing. I don't know. At any rate, everyone has the right to say no and there are all kinds of ways to get the message across. Is it not so?

> *James Forte*
> *Arlington, Massachusetts*

There is more to the problem of "ain't" than was presented in your article. Not only do we need an acceptable negative interrogative form, but also a form to fill out the following paradigm for other usages as well.

I xxx	*we aren't*
you aren't	*you aren't*
he isn't	*they aren't*

This should contrast for emphasis, focus etc. with:

I'm not	*we're not*
you're not	*you're not*
he's not	*they're not*

I congratulate you on your sensible adoption of "ain't" for the first person only and feel it should also be applicable for any sentence where one would use "we aren't" if the subject were plural.

> *Carrie Anne Estill*
> *Assistant Editor*
> *Dictionary of American*
> *Regional English*
> *The American Dialect Society*
> *Madison, Wisconsin*

I find it absolutely mind-scattering that you'd waste as many words as you did re "ain't I?" and "aren't I?" Simply borrow from the French, you garrulous, windy old fuddy-duddy. Or, better still, the Spanish. With one word the Latins take care of a problem on which you wasted an estimated 150 words, and you still didn't come up with an urbane solution. Nota bene and to wit: "¿Tu eres loco, verdad?"

> Jack V. Priest
> Williamsburg, Virginia

Ain't I happy with your recommendation for the first-person negative-interrogative contraction? You bet I am. But I ain't satisfied with the restriction of usage to the interrogative form. I amn't happy and aren't happy, but mostly I ain't happy.

> Ray Jordan
> North Haven, Connecticut

Your article on aren't I/ain't I *ignored a third variant recognized by British writers,* an't I *(pronounced with the* a *of* father*). The* OED *recognizes* an't *as a contraction of* am not, *tho it seems to suggest a relationship with* aren't. *In any event, the form seems to have been developed among the* r*-dropping English, and may later have been misinterpreted by* r*-pronouncing* Americans as* aren't *(the two forms are apparently distinguished by the* r*-sounding Scots).*

Altho you have come out for ain't I *(a perfectly respectable upper-class British form—now, however, old-fashioned),* an't I *seems to me to pose fewer social problems at present if only because it is perfectly respectable in speech in Britain. The spelling is admittedly unfortunate since it suggests the same pronunciation as* ant. *We could pull a Bernard Shaw and write* a'n't *(he wrote* ca'n't, *if memory serves me—possibly* can"t*). A better remedy (following Simplified Spelling Society proposals) is* aan't.

The relation of am *to* aan't *is no more strained than between* will *and* won't, *and certainly much less so than between* go *and* went.

> Edgar A Gregersen
> Professor of Anthropology
> Queens College
> Flushing, New York

You might be amused by the terms the eminent linguist-anthropologist Charles Hockett proposed for r-dropping and* r*-pronouncing: "rless" and "rfull." Altho Hockett in his heyday (before the triumph of Chomsky) was the most important linguist in America (probably), these forms never caught on.*

Ain't?! Never! Why bother apologizing for a form of the verb "to be" that is repellent to the ears of those who care about the sound of the language? "Ain't" isn't needed. Neither is the usage "Aren't I."

The many ways of expressing the negative interrogative of "I am" offer a delicious assortment of feelings that would be nearly totally obscured by "ain't" or even
"amn't" (which isn't half bad or awkward once you've forced yourself to say it a few
times).

First, what is difficult about "Am I not"? It allows an assertiveness that immediately puts the listener on the defensive; a small change of inflection and you are
imploring the listener for a compassionate understanding, even sympathy. With a
little practice, "Am I not" will impart a message of incredulous disbelief that the
affirmative statement could be construed as false.

However, I have other ways of expressing the negative interrogative. Moi? has
a brevity that is too beautiful for words; it can also serve to break the tension of a
disputative confrontation. Repeat the statement, ending with an inquisitive rising
inflection, but without the verb: "You are not intelligent!" — "I, not intelligent?"

Or repeat the entire statement, verb and all, merely ending it with a rising
inflection; stress on different words changes the intent in a dramatic way.

In a diplomatic way—and analogous to the French, which also lacks a negative
interrogative—one might say "Do you mean I am not . . . ."

Not to belabor the point, but surely part of the richness of a language is in the
way it is spoken. Why belittle its power with a word that sounds more like a grunt
resulting from a gentle elbow to the midsection?

Bob Lehr
New York, New York

Your discussion of the ungrammatical expression "aren't I?" is, I think, off the point.
It's a matter not of grammar but of pronunciation, and involves the common
phenomenon that linguists refer to as an "intrusive r."

People often pronounce the word law as though it were almost homonymous
with "lore," and they turn a phrase like "the idea of it" into "the idear of it."
President Kennedy repeatedly turned Cuba into "Cuber," and I constantly hear
sherbet spoken (and even find it written on restaurant menus) as "sherbert."

Those who rightly avoid the vulgar "ain't I?" need not succumb to the grammatically wrong "aren't I?" but should instead treat the latter as an example of the
intrusive r. What they should take care to say (or write) is "a'n't I?"—a perfectly
acceptable contraction of the perfectly grammatical "am not I?"

Caldwell Titcomb
Professor of Music
Brandeis University
Waltham Massachusetts

Nine Yards to Hell

When B. T. Collins signed on as California Governor Jerry Brown's chief of staff in 1981, he gave reporters an assessment of his new boss: "Sometimes I'd like to strangle him; other times I'd follow him to hell and back. You sign on, you sign on for the whole nine yards."

The whole nine yards is one of the great etymological mysteries of our time. I get queries on it all the time: "Do you know where 'the whole nine yards' comes from?" asks Alan Chamberlain of Mohave Community College in Kingman, Arizona. "Our only information about it is that it's not supposed to be related to football, and it does not appear in any of the standard word or phrase sources."

He can say that again. "Stumps me completely," reports Stuart Flexner, boss of Random House's reference department. "I'm sorry to report that I've come up with exactly zilch," adds Sol Steinmetz of Barnhart Books. These guys are the heavy hitters of slang etymology; if they don't know, only one other source is left: Dr. Fred Cassidy, director-editor of the *Dictionary of American Regional English* (Volume I published in 1985), known to the lexicographic world as "the man from *DARE*."

"I am also thoroughly puzzled about it," replied Professor Cassidy, offering two leads churned up in his thousands of interviews: the contents of an army truck, and something to do with a bolt of cloth. Frustrated, I went on the *Larry King* show, an all-night talkfest with a nationwide audience of argumentative insomniacs, and broadcast an appeal for the origin.

"I am a seamstress," responded Mrs. Daniel Raymor of Lago Vista, Texas, "and there are times when it takes all seven or eight yards of cloth to produce a dress. Also, fabric was of a much rougher texture than we have today. Therefore, nine yards was all that was put on a bolt of cloth. If you had a fancy dress, you must have used the whole nine yards of the bolt. 'Dressed to the nines' would also apply."

Richard Carlsen of Manchester, Connecticut, caught my plea on WPOP radio and wrote: "Next time you pass by a construction site where they are using a large cement mixer—one of those trucks with a revolving cylinder on the back out of which cement pours down a chute—ask them if it's going to take 'the whole nine yards.' You see, one of those large, elephant-like conveyances will hold nine cubic yards of cement. Hence, any job that requires all the truck has will take 'the whole nine yards.'" Mr. Carlsen added: "Now all I have to do is find out where to mail this. I think they said *The New York Times.*"

And now comes a late flash from the man from *DARE*, who has unearthed a possible nautical derivation: "In a square-rigged, three-masted sailing ship of former times, each mast carried three *yards*—the rods supporting the sails. So the 'whole nine yards' would mean the sails were fully set. If this is so, the phrase is older than I thought. And the recent alleged use in yachts, saying that the surface of a spinnaker is nine square yards, if that's true, may be transferred from former sailing-vessel use."

Now we have three possibilities. The mystery is still unsolved, but a few clues are on the table. Lexicographic Irregulars are the only people who can help, since the experts are exhausted. We will persevere on this; we will not flag or fail; we will go the whole nine yards. (And don't start sending theories about *zilch*; it is from a 1930's magazine character. Stick to the subject. Bah-bah fer now.)

Concrete, certainly one of the most basic substances of civilization, has tripped up more careful writers than all of the grammar rules promulgated since Chaucer. Cement is to concrete what vermouth is to a martini—an ingredient.

No way can the nine yards of cement [sic] that Richard Carlsen refers to be placed within the context of distance. Carlsen's yards are cubic yards—volumetric. B. T. Collins's yards are linear.

Daniel J. McConville
New York, New York

If you and Mr. Carlsen ate lunch together, you could, as you watched the cement pour out of the truck at the construction site across the street, break flour together.

T. C. Rhoades
Senior Contract Manager
Turner Construction Company
Boston, Massachusetts

It is with no little trepidation that I venture to challenge the man from DARE *on the nautical origin of "the whole nine yards," but a ship carried a course, topsail, topgallant, royal, and skysail on each of its three masts. Each of these sails was carried by a yard. Under full canvas, she also carried various jibs, staysails, studding sails, and a spanker, all of which are inadequately described by "nine yards."*

What surprises me are your Western citations. I had not heard the expression before moving to New England (some thirty miles up the Connecticut River from Mr. Carlsen). I asked a coworker who frequently used the phrase about its origin. He told me that he had picked it up while working summers on construction crews building I-91 in Vermont, and that it referred to the capacity of a cement truck. When you have "the whole nine yards," you have all there is. Mr. Carlsen's confirmation makes this the prevailing opinion in the Connecticut Valley, at least.

Mrs. Raymor's suggestion that "dressed to the nines" is related is also doubtful. The OED *gives its meaning as "perfection" rather than "completeness," with the earliest citation from Burns (1787).*

> Walter Siff
> Longmeadow, Massachusetts

Doesn't the "man from DARE*" need a good lexicographer? "The rods supporting the sails"? Sounds as if he was carrying a transit. We used to call them* spars.

> William Kemble
> Bedford Hills, New York

Noisemakers

Most of the time, it's a mistake in pronunciation to mix languages. There are exceptions: You are permitted to call an "EN-voy" an "ON-voy," but you cannot call an "EN-clave" an "ON-clave." You can call an "EN-dive" an "ON-deev," but you cannot mismatch languages and call it an "EN-deev" or an "ON-dive." Got that straight?

I enjoy issuing marching orders about pronunciation. Such instruction in this space is not arbitrary, because regional differences are recognized. It is "SOUR cream" in New York and "sour CREAM" in the rest of the country, just as it is "CHOP meat" in New York and "chopped MEAT" in America.

O.K., wise guy, how about Illinois? Looks French, but hardly anybody says "Ee-lee-NWAH." So is it "Illi-NOY" or "Illi-NOISE"?

In 1936, H. L. Mencken laid down the law: "In Illinois the state name is pronounced Illinoy." In 1938, Alfred Holt agreed: "The French-English compromise is the preferred form: 'noy' rather than 'noise.'" But not every reporter went along: John Kenyon's authoritative *Pronouncing Dictionary* of 1944 noted that the form with a *z* ending was "not infrequent generally" and was "especially common in the South." In *Word Study,* the G. & C. Merriam house organ, Professor Daniel Gage gave the *z* a logic: "To pronounce the final syllable 'oy' is to leave the word neither French nor English, just as in the case of *St. Louis* the dropping of the final *s* sound leaves the word a hybrid of pronunciation."

Turn now to Dr. Allen Walker Read, the O.K. etymologist who has dug more deeply than anyone into the "noy-noise" controversy. He finds that the name is derived from the Indian *ilini,* meaning "man," which became *Illiniwek,* the final *iwek* meaning "is" in plural ending form. French explorers changed the plural to the French *ois* and applied the name to Algonquian peoples in the Middle West. Early pronunciations included the *z* sound, especially by Spaniards who spelled it "Ylinneses."

Pronunciation detectives always look for evidence of rhymes, and Dr. Read found one from 1779: "From these lank loins have sprung two boys / Shall trail it through the Islenois."

That makes a case for the *z* ending, but Thomas Jefferson, laying a plan before the Congress in 1794 to divide the old Northwest into sixteen nicely rectangular states, called one of them *Illinoia* (rhymes with paranoia). And John Hay, the poet who had been Abraham Lincoln's secretary, in 1871 rhymed "Illanoy" with "boy."

Since etymology can find substantiation for both pronunciations, what does dialect geography say about the word's position on the map of usage? *The Linguistic Atlas of the United States and Canada,* a huge effort with some sections yet unfinished, offers this evidence: A large minority still uses the *z*, and the size of the minority grows in use with the distance from the state. Thus, one-tenth of Iowans call it *Illinoise,* as do a quarter of the people of Nebraska, and over a third of Minnesotans and North Dakotans prefer the *z* ending.

The answer to "Which is correct?" Both, but as you get closer to the state, start dropping the *z* ending. Tell them that in "Duh MOYN" and "DES Plaines."

I never knew when I was growing up in the state that Illinois could be pronounced with a z ending until I read your article and am grateful that I reached maturity and then some before learning the awful truth. Imagine singing the bleacher song of the University of Illinois with a z:

   We're loyal to you, Illinois

or the official state song:

   By thy rivers gently flowing, Illinois, Illinois

the verse ending with these moving lines:

   Grant and Logan and our tears, Illinois, Illinois,
   Grant and Logan and our tears, Illinois.

Now about St. Louis: here usage seems to contradict or at least qualify the findings of the professorate, for the centennial of the Louisiana Purchase (1904) was celebrated by a world's fair, hailed in a popular song which began:

   Meet me in St. Louis, Louie,
   Meet me at the Fair.

                                        Gerald Carson
                                        Newtown, Pennsylvania

Pray do not encourage the forces of darkness by quoting the learned Prof. Gage on the "logic" to be served by pronouncing the esses in Illinois and Saint Louis. That is a gage I must pick up.

Communication, courtesy, custom, consonance and cosmopolitan empathy are better guides to pronunciation than logic is. Hybridization is the very essence of America's vigour.

If, as a form of solidarity with those under duress of war, Americans can learn to pronounce Kabul as the Afghans do (cobble), surely we can cherish the native woodnotes wild of our own country. Native is the key word. Deference is due, as Mencken and Hay knew, to the souls that call a place home.

Imagine the tiresome predictability, knowing that at a gathering of outlanders some leering male will break into a quick soft shoe and say, "Oh, you're from St. Louieee; Meet me in St. Louieee, Louieeeeeee." He will then insist that that is the "proper" pronunciation. Ah, no.

It is Saint Louis, pronounced Sāint Loo'is (and Sənt Lö'əs, if you're in a hurry), Missouri (Mi͞zër'ə not Mi͞zoor'e, as some St. Louisans pronounce it), as our larger allegiance is, in this case to the state, whose citizens pronounce it Mi͞zër'ə. (The St. Louisans, you see, are so busy keeping the ee off the Louis that it sneaks onto the Missouri.)

If each of us comprehended what home meant to every other, what wars could divide us? To pronounce the name of a place as its people do is the beginning of understanding. Those who call a place home love it best, and their love commands the respect of our tongues.

Anne Wadsworth Symington
Native Saint Louisan
Great, great granddaughter of
    John Hay
Philadelphia, Pennsylvania

First of all I would like to ask why the pronunciation of Illinois—a proper name —cannot be determined by Illinoians. I am from Joliet, Illinois (Ill-uh-NOY), which lies on the Des Plaines (Dez Planes) River. If anyone ever says Illinoiz there, they are considered incorrect. (For that matter, according to a 19th-century law, they can be fined $5 for saying Jolly-ette rather than Joe-lee-ET). And if my name, Mutz, is pronounced to rhyme with "puts" rather than "nuts" or "toots," I don't complain. But I do correct people when I can, because it is my *name. I think Illinoians, former and present, should dictate how the state is called.*

Ronald R. Mutz
New York, New York

Ain't no chopped MEAT or no CHOP meat neither here. We eat "hamburg" and follow it up with a "cremee" (pronounced KREE-mee), a soft ice cream cone. Usually we go "downstreet" (DOWN-strit)—into town, downtown, or what have you—to pick up some food, and when we return we park the car in the DOY-add. Took me a long time to discover that the pronunciation of DOY-add actually meant "dooryard," which in turn meant driveway. Of course, Vermont's never felt that it is "the rest of the country," so technically you're still right.

> Dennis Kitsz
> Roxbury, Vermont

How about envelope?

A particular abomination coming in is the use of "right field line" with the emphasis on field for right, field line—evenly accented.

> John L. Liddle
> Riverside, California

Nomicnomics

Country-music vocalists are not all Republicans. When Mac Davis performed his latest release, "The Beer Drinkin' Song," at the annual awards show of the Country Music Association, he drew a gasp from the 4,400 stompin' spectators when he sang that one of the things that would drive a man to drink was *Reaganomics.*

George Bush, campaigning for President in 1980, described candidate Reagan's supply-side theories as *voodoo economics*; two years later, Urban League president John Jacob was saying that *Reaganomics* "is giving voodoo a bad name."

The most rampant combining form used to be *-arama*; then it became *-oriented*, which gave way to *-intensive.* In the economic field, however, there is one combining form that sails on through presidencies: *-nomics.*

In the summer of 1969, I wrote a memorandum for my White House colleagues using the term *Nixonomics* to hail the ingenious replacement of the Democrats' "new economics." About that time, columnists Evans and Novak were the first to use *Nixonomics* in print. Walter Heller, a father of the "new economics," was quoted in *Time* magazine in November 1969, using *Nixonomics* disparagingly. Since that time, the term I used with such high hopes has fallen on hard times.

The key to the phrasemaking was the *n* at the end of *Nixon,* which matched the *n* at the end of *econ* and produced a word easy to say. During the Ford years, the combining form lay dormant, though there was a half-hearted effort at *Fordonomics.* In Mr. Carter's time, *Carternomics* was occasionally used, but it did not sing; *Jimmynomics* was also used to disparage the President's economic policy. Nothing really caught on after *Nixonomics* because the *n* was lacking at the end of the President's name.

Along came Reagan. Nobody can spot the coiner of *Reaganomics* because the coinage was as instantaneous as "As Maine goes, so goes Vermont." The rush of usage of *Reaganomics* seems to have overcome previous barriers and changed the way *economics* is split: what used to be *econ-omics* is now *eco-nomics,* and whatever word or name you like can be used in place of the *eco.* Hence, *Volckernomics, Trudeaunomics,* even—shades of back-formation—*Hoovernomics.*

Personally, I resist the use of any *-nomics* coinage that has no *n* at the end of the first word. Economist Henry Kaufman puts forward *Kaufmanomics,* and economist Martin Feldstein may be credited with *Feldsteinomics,* but neither *Mondalenomics* nor *Kennedynomics* comes trippingly off the tongue. (*Glennomics* is a sure thing.)

Meanwhile, another use of the combining form is coming upon us. I was buying a stereo for my car. James Meyersburg of Auto Sound Systems in Bethesda, Maryland, told me that in one high-priced model "the ergonomics are beautiful." Pressed for an explanation, he said, "The pushbuttons feel nice."

Ergonomics—based, like "economics," on the Greek word for "work"*—is the scientific study of man working in his environment. The word has been with us since 1950, and as the "interfacing" between the faces of people and the face of a machine increases, the word will become more familiar. Right now, ask anybody what *ergonomics* is, and the answer will be "The crackbrained economic schemes of President Ergo."

No Problem

"As I approached customs at Charles de Gaulle Airport in Paris," writes Howard Meyer of New York, "I was waved through by an inspector who rejected my offer to open up the baggage with the words 'No problem.' That has replaced *O.K.* as the principal Americanism."

Interesting. I have been tracking the worldwide use of *no problem* for some time. (How long is *some time?* Quite a while.) A friend traveling through Dubrovnik, Yugoslavia, last year, sighted a T-shirt with the rhyming Serbo-Croatian words

*See page 12.

nema problema. A colleague reported that a phrase growing in popularity in Russia is *nyet problema*; it is even possible that the phrase was originally Russian and was picked up and popularized by Americans.

"The phrase would not be used in the same way as it is heard in American English," says Professor Horace Lunt, head of the Slavic Languages Department at Harvard. "Here, it is 'social noise,' used along with 'You're welcome' or 'O.K.' There, the phrase would communicate a more literal 'I do not believe there is a problem with what you have said.'" Michael Strumpen-Darrie of Berlitz confirms this, adding that the narrow, literal meaning runs through the dozen leading languages.

Certainly the phrase in the United States has broadened its meaning to a general "I'm glad to help" or "You're welcome." But linguists must be wondering: Does it threaten the all-conquering *O.K.*? To what other countries has it spread in its English form?

I have asked Lexicographic Irregulars who are presently moles behind the Iron Curtain to keep an eye on this and report developments; the initial response, as might be expected, has been a resounding *No problem*!

Not Un-

Not infrequently, not illiterate television spawns not uncontroversial grammatical contretemps. When Susan Mercandetti, producer of ABC's *Nightline*, nabbed futurist Herman Kahn as a guest, the following interchange was not unworthy of notice:

Ted Koppel: "And a final quote: 'We must have a credible first-strike capability.' . . . Dr. Kahn, would you still hold to that view?"

Herman Kahn: "I think the exact term was 'not incredible,' and there's a distinct difference. You really can't achieve a capability which looks like it would be used, but you can achieve a capability which the other side cannot feel will not be used if he's too provocative. And the term 'not incredible' really carries an extraordinary amount of weight."

Koppel: "There is a potential on this program tonight for us to drown in double negatives. I wonder if you could put that into a straightforward sentence, Professor Kahn."

Kahn: "Absolutely not. . . . The attempt to put these in straightforward sentences simply confuses. Take the concept of 'not probable.' 'Not probable' is, say, less than 0.5; 'improbable' is less than 0.1. Therefore, 'not improbable' is quite different from 'probable.' It's called a litote, and it's a perfectly legitimate grammatical construction."

Herman Kahn is absolutely right, almost. Litotes (pronounced "LIGHT-uh-tease") is a Greek word that has come to mean "understatement for effect": If I say I expect to get not a few letters about the use of *hopefully* in the item below, what I mean is that I expect to get a canal barge laden with mail from purists crazed by hopefully-hatred. *Not a few* is understatement for effect; it really means *a bundle.* It is also cute, arch, and itsy-poo. I am ashamed of using *not the best image* earlier.

Dr. Kahn's mistaken use of *litote* was unthinking, which is excusable for the author of *Thinking About the Unthinkable*; the word always ends with an *s*, whether singular or plural; you cannot correctly say "litote" any more than you can properly say "kudo"—only if it has the *s* is it correct, which is better than "not incorrect."

When is the use of litotes effective? Dr. Kahn makes a good case for *not improbable*, and G. P. Gennaro of East Brunswick, New Jersey, sends in a flock of usages from a recent newspaper: "G.M. Declares Recalled Cars Not Unsafe" (that's a lawyer at work—the company really thinks the cars are fairly safe). "A not uncritical account of the new Sandinist Government" (that's legit litotes—it is not a critical account, but not uncritical either). "The departure of Mr. Begelman was not unexpected" (coy; the departure was expected).

When in doubt, eschew the double negative and accentuate the positive (there's a step in the right direction). Litotes is overused and much abused by the la-di-da crowd, but an occasional precise use is not unreasonable.

In your critique of Herman Kahn's corrected self-quote that "we must have a first-strike capability that is not incredible" rather than credible, you completely missed the beam while dealing with motes. The usage of credible here was in its secondary meaning, not that of "believable" but rather "worthy of confidence; reliable" (Heritage). For this secondary meaning, incredible does not function as an antonym! Misusage by Kahn; miss by Safire. No litotes from me.

Edgar H. Leoni
New York, New York

If you don't want to use above *and* below *to refer readers to other portions of your text, why not put* supra *and* infra *to work as we lawyers do? They mean the same as the English pair, but probably don't seem so directional in the sense of up and down.*

Besides, supra *and* infra *are just sitting there begging to be used by others than lawyers. The jobs of meaning "earlier in this text" and "later in this text" are quite suitable for these two words.*

Would that they are not shunned for their highbrow sound, or for their association with those perceived princes of obfuscation, the inventors of legalese.

> Charles H. Reach III
> New York, New York

Probably the ultimate in this category was by James Thurber with his line: "Not altogether unmeaningless."

> Richard Mullins
> Fayetteville, New York

The ultimate example of litotes is, of course, George Orwell's "A not unblack dog was chasing a not unsmall rabbit across a not ungreen field," cited in his 1946 essay on "Politics & the English Language." He suggested memorizing it as a way to cure oneself of the not un- *formation.*

> Pauline Feingold
> New York, New York

Verbal expressions of quantities mean different things to different people. When Robert Kennedy asked twenty-four physicians how they interpreted the word sometimes, *for instance, he got responses ranging from about 5 to 60 percent.*

> Michael A. Stoto
> Cambridge, Massachusetts

On Laying Low

"For a couple of decades," I wrote about the word *entitlements,* "the word lay low, like Br'er Rabbit."

"For shame, sir!" writes Frank Salvidio, who teaches English at Westfield State College in Massachusetts. "When it comes to Brer Rabbit and Brer Fox, there is only one authority: Joel Chandler Harris, and Mr. Harris tells us no fewer than nine times on a single page that it was Brer *Fox* who lay low, and *not* Brer Rabbit."

For those of you who like to throw in gratuitous phrases at the ends of sentences, here is the derivation: "Tar-Baby ain't sayin' nothin', en Brer Fox, he lay low." Note, in *Uncle Remus and His Friends,* the absence of an apostrophe as a substitute for the missing letters in "brother": We cannot prettify *Brer* by writing it as *Br'er.* I submit this correction as an aid to political figures who are searching for a new way to say: "No comment." Try "Like Tar-Baby, I ain't sayin' nothin'."

One Man's Terrorist

What's in a word? Recognition, if you're not careful. In a conference with six reporters, Ronald Reagan caught one of his own mistakes before it had a chance to become a gaffe. Asked about his plans to proceed in Middle East negotiations without the P.L.O., the President replied: "This would require, of course, the agreement of the other Arab states." Instantly, he went back a few words and corrected that to "of the Arab states." Letting "other" stand would have presumed the P.L.O. to be an Arab state; in catching his error first, he showed fast foot.

In the same meeting, as he was talking about the undue play given to the switch from *curb* to *halt* in the bishops' pastoral letter, the President talked of the time when civilians were not targets "before Hitler invented total war." He was almost right on the phraseology.

Total war—the phrase, if not the activity—was popularized in 1935 by a book, *Der Totale Krieg,* by General Erich Ludendorff, who had been a German strategist in World War I. In Ludendorff's use, *total war* did not mean "directed at civilians" or even "more ferocious war than usual"; rather, he had in mind *Wehrwirtschaft,* or "war economy," the mobilization of a nation's entire economy behind the war effort. During World War II the meaning of the phrase changed to its current "all-out war, including the targeting of civilian populations."

Mr. Reagan was especially careful when it came to labeling the group (often called the *contras,* from the Latin for "against") fighting against the Sandinist regime in Nicaragua and the group (usually called *guerrillas*) fighting against the government of El Salvador. (Note my slant in *regime* versus *government. Regime,* with its regal, imperious overtones, derogates the ruling clique; *government,* in American English, sounds permanent.)

Speaking about the anti-Sandinist *contras* in Nicaragua, Mr. Reagan objected to "enforcing restrictions on the freedom fighters as to what tactics they could use." When a reporter gulped and said, "All of a sudden now we're aiding 'freedom fighters'; I thought we were just interdicting supplies," the President pressed home the phrase: "I just used the word, I guess, *freedom fighters* because . . . the thing that brought those people together is the desire, as I said, for the same revolutionary principles that they once fought for and have been betrayed in."

What about the pro-Communist guerrillas in El Salvador? "I don't call them freedom fighters because they've got freedom [in El Salvador] and they [the guerrillas] are fighting for something else. They're fighting for a restraint on freedom."

Thus, in Reagan terminology, the *freedom fighter* is one who fights for freedom; the one who fights against freedom, by overthrowing a freely elected government, is a *guerrilla*, or when he specializes in striking terror, a *terrorist*. Logical.

The phrase *freedom fighter* was popularized in 1956, when Hungarians rose against the Communist regime imposed by the Russians, although the first citation found by Oxford lexicographers is from 1958. The United States Air Force, in 1959, called its Northrop N-156 "the Freedom Fighter," later changing its designation to the more prosaic F-5.

Freedom fighter was coined in 1942, by British poet John Lehmann, in a poem depicting a scene in a tenement in Vienna, as workers gather to commemorate a shooting in February:

> *Breathing inside were mothers, boys remembering*
> *A year ago, the shudder of the guns,*
> *There, their freedom fighters staining red the snow.*

Ouch!

Pat Caddell, the pollster, maligned a candidate while doing some research on him. Surveying potential voters about Jerry Springer, candidate for nominee as governor of Ohio, Mr. Caddell asked if voters knew that the candidate had used a bad check in paying for the services of prostitutes.

Mr. Springer, denying that the check had bounced, used the pollster's attack as the springboard for a riposte. (Too much bouncing around in that sentence.) He confessed his sins on television and added that "the next Governor would have to take some heavy risks and face some hard truths." That was because "Ohio is in a world of hurt."

The use of *heavy* to modify *risk* is standard 1960's slang—the once-weighty adjective has a second meaning of *serious*, or *worrisome*—but the *world of hurt* caught my eye.

Hurt has traveled from verb to adjective ("hurt feelings") to a present participle, as in "He's hurting." (No, that's not a gerund—a gerund is a verb form ending in *ing* that functions as a noun, like "Swimming is fun." I am passing that along because I have always confused participles and gerunds.) "He is hurt" means that the subject is injured, but "He is hurting" does not mean that a person is suffering physical pain; it refers instead to a political or financial difficulty. In 1967, Secretary of State Dean Rusk announced that "the North Vietnamese are hurting."

Now candidate Springer has taken that metaphor of emotional pain and encapsulated it in a phrase using *hurt* as a noun, object of a preposition, as "a world of hurt." That phrase, rooted in such long-standing terms as "the world of words," but popularized in a more recent scatological expression, marks a genuine advance in the slang usage of *hurt.* Mr. Springer—whose check, he insists, did not bounce —may or may not survive the Caddell zapping, but he has already made his linguistic contribution to the 1982 campaign.

Among the pollsters, who take great pride in the fairness of their questions, Mr. Caddell is—to use a recent Black English expression—"hurtin' for certain."

Out, Damned Gnat

I was trying to be helpful. In tracking the derivation of "straining at a gnat and swallowing a camel," I pointed to the King James Version of the Bible, Matthew 23:24, and wrote: "The original spokesperson, lest we forget, was Jesus of Nazareth."

"That would have been appreciated by 'Ma' Ferguson, the Texas Governor," writes the Reverend J. Carter Swaim pastor emeritus of the Church of Covenant near the United Nations in New York, "who, when Spanish was proposed as a second language for schools in the Lone Star State, replied: 'Not while I am Governor! If English was good enough for Jesus Christ, it is good enough for Texas children.' "

The original words, which may have been spoken in Aramaic or Hebrew, have come down to us from the Greek New Testament, and it was my luck to have picked up one of the classic misprints in biblical history.

"The expression 'strain *at* a gnat,' " writes David N. Freedman, director of the University of Michigan's studies in religion, "in the King James Version is an error for the correct rendering of the Greek text of the Gospel, which would be 'strain *out* a gnat.' "

That changes the metaphor. The mental picture of scribes and Pharisees turning blue in the face trying to swallow a small bug (straining *at* it) is quite different from the same bunch carefully filtering out any little critters in their drinks (straining them *out*).

The mistake in the first edition of the King James Bible was not spotted and went through subsequent printings over the centuries. The erroneous translation put a new idiom in the English language, which sage commentators use to this day, despite the possibility of a saint in Heaven trying to explain that it was not his fault that Jesus was misquoted.

Because the wrong reading was plausible, the *at* stayed in until 1881; it takes at least a century to straighten people out. "Usage alone has guaranteed the permanence of the false image," says Mr. Freedman, general editor of the Anchor Bible, "while the correct reading has made very little progress in general usage, and is likely to remain a curio of interest only to scholars."

Not so; right here and now, generations yet unborn (is that redundant?) will be set straight. The Anchor Bible rendition is: "You blind guides! Straining a fly out of your drink, and then swallowing a camel!" Sooner or later, even the scribes get it right.

In discussing Jesus' remark about straining out a gnat and swallowing a camel you missed a chance to let your readers know that Jesus was as fond of word play as you are. In the original Aramaic, which Jesus probably spoke, the word for gnat was galma *and the word for camel was* gamla.

> Martin Gardner
> Hendersonville, North Carolina

Your item put me in mind of another case in which misunderstanding of a classical phrase has become enshrined in the language.

    Hamlet (I:iv.15–16):   . . . *it is a custom*
More honoured in the breach than the observance.

This turn of phrase, of course, is often used by today's educated people. And, about ten times out of ten, they use it wrong, taking it to mean: "This is supposedly the custom, but it is more often ignored than followed."

    That is not what Prince Hamlet means at all. His visiting friend Horatio has just asked him what that booming of guns is all about.

> Hamlet: *The King doth wake tonight and takes his rouse,*
> *Keeps wassail, and the swaggering upspring reels;*
> *And as he drains his draughts of Rhenish down,*
> *The kettle-drum and trumpet thus bray out*
> *The triumph of his pledge.*
>
> Horatio: *Is it a custom?*
>
> Hamlet: *Ay marry is't,*
> *But to my mind, though I am native here,*

And to the manner born, it is a custom
More honoured in the breach than the observance.

Clearly, the much-quoted line means "It is a custom so bad that the best way to 'honor' it is to ignore it." Not a good custom which most people are too slack to observe, but a bad custom which good people are unwilling to stoop to.

Unlike the "gnat and camel" error, this one arose not from misquoting but from misunderstanding the words. But what your authority David N. Freedman says of the "gnat" case—"Usage alone has guaranteed the permanence of the false image"—is true also in the "breach" case. If you know and understand the original text, do you use it wrong and be understood? Use it right and be misunderstood, unless you bore your hearer with pedantic exegesis? Or just avoid it? My sad solution is avoidance, but I wish there were a happier one.

Wallace Irwin, Jr.
Larchmont, New York

Out of Molehills

"Hee was carefull and liberall to obtaine good Intelligence from all parts abroad," wrote Francis Bacon in his 1622 history of King Henry VII. "Hee had such Moles perpetually working and casting to undermine him."

That was the first figurative use of *mole* in connection with espionage, too remote a link to constitute a coinage. In 1650, Henry Vaughan used a mole to signify a man at work inside a hierarchy—"Perjuries were gnats and flies, It rain'd about him bloud and tears"—but it was not until the spy novels of John le Carré that the word attained popularity as "an agent placed inside a rival organization."

Two years ago, I gave credit to David Cornwell—that's le Carré's real name —for this coinage. Since then, I have heard from a clandestine member of the Lexicographic Irregulars, Edward Jay Epstein, the leading writer in the gray world of spies and moles. "In 1932 the Soviets recruited a Captain Fedossenko as a double agent and gave him the alias 'The Mole,' " Mr. Epstein informs us, writing as always in code. "You can find this episode on pages 123–124 of the book *The Conspirators* by Geoffrey Bailey, written in 1960, which long antedates *Tinker, Tailor.*"

Although C.I.A. professionals long preferred *penetration agent*, the agency has succumbed to common literary usage and now routinely refers to *mole* as a synonym for *agent in place*. Representative Donald J. Albosta, Democrat of Michigan, a House ethicist, used the term matter-of-factly in announcing his intention to follow the molehill (and, incidentally, to climb the mountain of publicity): "We don't know who the mole is, and the President did not tell us who the mole was. We have to try to find that out."

If and when he does, reporters will be burrowing under mounds of citations to find such entries as that of the nineteenth-century German philosopher Hegel: "And as the mole continues to dig, we must listen to his labor in order to discover the truth."

The wrigglings, evasions, charges, and innuendos of Washington investigations churn up words and phrases that enrich and enliven our vocabulary, and if they do not illuminate the political system, at least they light up the language. Stay alert.

Pas de Guts

When the French government threw forty-seven Soviet officials out of the country for spying, a spokesman for Mr. Mitterrand told reporters that the action demonstrated that his government had no intention of having a *ventre mou.*

Interesting problem in translation: *Ventre* means "belly," and *mou* means "soft." At first, the reports were that France was determined to show that it was not "the soft underbelly" that some suspected it might be. That was taken from a recollection of Winston Churchill's phrase about the Balkans' being "the soft underbelly of the Axis." (An *underbelly* of an animal or fish is the lower, less protected portion of the belly.)

On sober reflection, the English-writing journalists covering the story turned to an American colloquialism to render the meaning of *ventre mou:* "gutless." That is a long step from "soft belly," but far better expresses the meaning of what the French spokesman (irritated at a premature disclosure of the news to *The New York Times*) said. It is the difference between the work of a translator and an interpreter.

We shall now see whether the French, jealous of the purity of their tongue, will stick to the French phrase or adopt *gutless.* These days, it takes a Frenchman *avec beaucoup de courage* to use an English word.

I refer here to your sentence, "An underbelly *of an animal or fish is the lower, less protected portion of the belly."*

Any biologist will tell you that the general term animal *includes all classes of fishes as well as many "lower" organisms. Moreover,* Webster's New World Dictionary *defines animal as "any living organism except a plant or bacterium, typically able to move about." In short,* animal *suffices,* fish *is redundant. If you had wished to differentiate between fish and other animals which have underbellies, you might have used the more specific* tetrapods, *which includes the classes amphibia, reptilia, aves, and mammalia.*

For this minor oversight (which has unfortunately been compounded by your self-proclamation as grammatical crusader), I award you, in the name of all serious biologists, the pliant viscera (and soft underbelly as well) of a pickled herring for inadvertently pruning the phylogenetic tree.

> Drew Schembre
> Middlebury, Vermont

Describing his first meeting with Stalin in The Hinge of Fate, *Churchill says that "possession of North Africa [we] could threaten the belly of Hitler's Europe." All of southern Europe, not just the Balkans, was the "soft belly" (underbelly?) as opposed to the "hard snout" of northern France. After bogging down in the Italian campaign, I recall (but cannot locate) that someone then referred to Italy as the "tough old gut" rather than a soft belly. Churchill's major interest in a Balkans campaign was to give the Western Allies a foothold in Eastern Europe and to prevent the Russians from taking over.*

> Maurice Bach
> Elizabeth, New Jersey

I'm sure the insult was unintentional. Yes, ventre mou *can be translated rather literally as "soft underbelly" or more imaginatively as "gutless." But the two results definitely do not show "the difference between the work of a translator and an interpreter." A translator's work is written; an interpreter's is oral.*

In this case, the difference is between the work of a hack translator and that of a competent translator, since one of the basic rules of the game is to translate ideas, not words. Hence, a translator who renders ventre mou *as "gutless" or "spineless" isn't interpreting; she is simply doing her job properly.*

> Marilyn Thomson
> Member of the Société des
> traducteurs du Québec
> Westmount, Québec

In common usage, the difference between the work of a translator and an interpreter is that the translator does his in writing, while the interpreter delivers his translation orally, either consecutively or simultaneously. Your implication is that the translator renders a word-for-word translation and the interpreter translates the meaning of what is said or written. In fact, that is what they both strive for. Of the two, the translator, having more time, is more likely to hit upon a correct equivalent, but that is beside the point.

I do think you owe us translators an apology. A translator's work is different from an interpreter's, but it is certainly not inferior.

While I am at it, what does the last paragraph of your article mean? I had never seen the expression ventre mou, *but* en avoir dans le ventre *means "to have guts," and* mou *means "soft" or "weak." "Gutless" is, as you wrote, a long step from "soft belly," but it does not seem far at all from* ventre mou.

Lida Ouwehand
Río Piedras, Puerto Rico

The Phrasedick Brigade

Vast numbers of Americans have nothing better to do than pore through old books searching for previous usages of famous phrases. (To reach "vast numbers," as pollsters do, I have extrapolated from seven letters and an unsigned note slipped under my door; as newscasters say with excruciating fairness, a poll of this size reflects a potential sampling error of plus or minus 99 percent.)

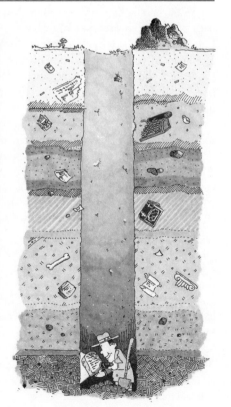

Whenever these people see the words *coined by,* they bristle at the presumption of authorship and are impelled to prove that somebody wrote it down earlier. Such literary hawkshaws are members of the Phrasedick Brigade, and do for previous usage what members of the Squad Squad do for redundancies.

Time was, lexicographers could toss out a citation and years would pass before anyone would stick an earlier citation in a bottle and float it back. Now, in the era of Instant Replay, the phrasedicks are out in force the next day.

Take *the right stuff,* the phrase meaning a combination of ambition, determination, and guts, used by Tom Wolfe as a book title a few years back. An earlier use, cited here, was by W. Somerset Maugham in 1927.

That was not good enough for John O'Shea of New York City, who happened to be perusing a short story by P. G. Wodehouse titled "The Awakening of Rollo Podmarsh," written between 1923 and 1926: "There was, she considered, the right stuff in Rollo."

Rollo's right stuff was immediately eclipsed by Michael Oliver and Robert Tannenbaum, both of New York, who independently came up with *The Right Stuff,* a political satire by Ian Hay published in 1909. Mr. Tannenbaum adds that "Ian Hay" is the pseudonym of John Hay Beith, which accounts for my oversight.

They haven't even scratched the surface. "Joseph Conrad uses *the right stuff* in this sense [motivation, skill] in his short story 'Youth,' published in 1902," points out Samuel Gorenstein of New York. He cites the passage: "But they all worked. That crew of Liverpool hard cases had in them the right stuff."

I had just about closed out this file when Barbara Kaplan of New York (the center of phrasedickism is evidently New York) came in with an 1864 entry from Anthony Trollope's *The Small House at Allington,* in which Lord DeGuest says proudly of his protégé: "I knew he was made of the right stuff."

Wait—hold that elevator! Here comes Christian Brown of the *Today* show with a letter that Herman Melville wrote to his first publisher, John Murray of London, in 1848, telling him how things were progressing with *Mardi*: "The arrangement you propose for my next book is not altogether satisfactory to me. At the least, I should want the advance doubled." That's the right stuff right there, as every author will attest, but the citation occurs in the next sentence: "It shall have the right stuff in it, to redeem its faults, tho' they were legion."*

That's the winner; further entries will not be entertained in this century. If you spot it in your family Bible, keep your discovery to yourself.

Same story with *acid rain,* that seemingly modern phrase that has been beating down on the Environmental Protection Agency; it was triumphantly tracked here to 1975. Gary Brooten of Philadelphia quickly bid 1972 with a story he wrote for *The Philadelphia Bulletin* about a United Nations conference in Stockholm: "That rain in southern Sweden is mild sulfuric acid . . . acid rains are causing calcium to seep out of forest soils. . . ."

His ace was promptly trumped by Philip Shaver, the leading phrasedick in Princeton, New Jersey, who happened to be leafing through the 14th edition of the *Encyclopaedia Britannica,* published in 1929, and found under "Smoke and Smoke Prevention" these words: "Evil Effects of Smoke—Acid rain is also directly harmful to plant life and affects adversely the soil, although soot is a valuable manure."

Close, but no funky cigar, Phil; from the Georgia Institute of Technology in Atlanta, Professor William Chameides reached for his handy copy of *Air and Rain,*

*Also see page 251.

the Beginnings of a Chemical Climatology by Robert Angus Smith, published in London in 1872, probably written in 1858: "It has often been observed that the stones and bricks of buildings . . . crumble more readily in large towns, where much coal is burnt, than elsewhere. I was led to attribute this effect to the slow, but constant, action of the acid rain."

What does this teach us, other than to save every smudge of our valuable soot to tuck around our aspidistras? First, it reminds us to write "found so far" after every "earliest use" of a phrase, which is a precaution to writers and a challenge to readers. Next, it shows that not everyone is staring at television or reading the latest newspaper; somebody, somewhere—even as you read this—is reading an acid-stained climatology text or the letters of the author of *Moby Dick* to his skinflint publisher or the adventures of Rollo Podmarsh. We should never forget that most people know something that almost everybody else doesn't know and are dying to pass it along.

Our newfound humility should extend to coinages that are obviously recent. *Squeal rule,* for example, was identified with great certainty here as having originated in an editorial in *The New York Times,* and President Reagan promptly seized on that fact to excoriate the antisqueal forces in a speech defending his policy to inform parents when children request birth-control devices from the Feds.

My citation was accurate; the phrase *squeal rule* did appear first in a February 1982 *Times* editorial. However, the idea evidently originated several days earlier in a column on the Op-Ed page by Russell Baker. Mr. Baker entitled his piece "Uncle Sam Squeals," and this may have been the genesis of half of the highly effective editorial phrase. "I wasn't trying for a coinage," reports Mr. Baker, "just straining for vernacular diction." (In a radiant review of my colleague's memoirs, *Growing Up,* in *National Review,* the critic wrote: "Within *The New York Times,* Russell Baker compares as a grammarian to the house conservative, William Safire, somewhat as Red Smith compares to Howard Cosell." Pinko rag.)

Pillow Talk

I will not be able to lay my head on my pillow tonight without passing along this urgent commercial message: In the language of pillow advertising, *squooshy* has just been superseded by *huggable.* (Sometimes that is spelled *hugable,* but the single-*g* spelling is not preferred because the word then sounds like *huge-able,* and is unsuitable in describing small cushions.)

Squooshy had a good run. An altered form of *squash,* the word means "crushable," the opposite of "springy." It was influenced by *squishy,* meaning "pliant, yielding to pressure," often expressed as *squishy-soft.* However, *squishy* had a liquid connotation—the sound of wringing a wet rag—perhaps from *squirt.* (A squishy pillow would be used only on a waterbed.)

"Du Pont has introduced a new pillow called Quallofil," reports Alan York, pillow executive of Rose York Associates, "and the words that are the biggest in the industry now are *huggable, scrunchable, squeezable, plumpable.*" That is because the synthetic pillow filler, which used to be springy, and once was valued for being *nonallergenic,* is now made in a form closer to goose down or duck down, and can claim down's huggable characteristics.

A competitor, N. Sumergrade & Sons, advertises its fill as "so downright downlike" that it will "fool your head." Howard Dickert, marketing vice president of the Perfect Pretender Pillow, explains: "The customer wants to know that a synthetic pillow is just as huggable as a down pillow, which has snob appeal."

Thus, a Du Pont ad run by B. Altman & Company promises: "You can scrunch your Quallofil pillow . . . and it's refluffable." It then derogates all previous synthetics: "Not springy like foam or 'mushy' . . . Some polyester fibers clump or mat." "Feh!" says Du Pont of the stuff it has been turning out for years, adding as an afterthought the words that had previously been the major selling proposition: "Pure, hygenic, nonallergenic." (The copywriters are evidently allergic to the clean spelling of *hygienic*; somebody sleeps on a bag of rocks tonight.)

Though Quallofil likes *refluffable,* Perfect Pretender is more comfortable with *fluffs right back.* The verb *to fluff,* formerly *to fluff up,* is probably from the Scottish *flue,* "a loose, hairy mass," rooted in the Latin *villus,* "shaggy hair," and influenced by *puff.* Its current slang meaning is "to err," as in befouling *hygienic,* of all words.

One word about pillows has always troubled me: *ticking.* What does a pillow have in common with a time bomb? Nothing; the material that encases the down, or synthetic fiber, or shaggy mass of whatever, is the ticking, from the Latin *theca,* "sheath."

Before laying me down to a conclusion, let me add this tag line: Every pillow has a *hangtag* to describe the material. A *corner label,* or *silk label* (made of rayon), is sewn on the *ear* of the pillow. The *law label* is a hangtag that frequently shouts, "Do not remove this label under penalty of law." My sister-in-law Gladys was always intimidated by these hangtags, figuring their message was directed at her and not the seller. When they fell off, she used to sew them back on, law-abidingly.

Dear Bill,

Emancipated at last! I enclose proof of the last vestiges of my bondage.

No longer do I lie awake at night expecting the knock on the door and the dread question, "Is this Der Tag?" as I cowered in my bed on my label-free mattress facing charges of ticking—tampering or pillow-pillaging!

Once the news was in print, I stripped the last labels from things bought in 1960

—and waited for repercussions. So far—so good—but if anyone calls, you tell them you have no sister-in-law named Gladys. You invented her.

Love,
Deep Down

The word scrunch *is in the dictionary as a verb. Its derivatives* scrunchable *and* scrunchability *are not yet, because we believe they are new words, less than a year old. Here's the story.*

The word scrunch *first came to our attention in a document called the Brand Gruber Report, a marketing survey about pillow buying. Most of the women surveyed used* scrunch *as a verb to describe the action used to test a pillow. One can scrunch the pillow, or scrunch one's head into the pillow.*

The advertising people were on the lookout for a good descriptive word for the new "Quallofil" pillow. Because scrunch *was used so easily and naturally by the survey group, and because everyone seemed to grasp its meaning immediately, it became apparent that* scrunch *carried a lot of ad-copy potential.*

Soon the adjective scrunchable *and the noun* scrunchability *joined the verb* scrunch, *which was dignified by* The Wall Street Journal. *The new word showed up in advertising and store promotions.*

Then Barbara Mayer of A.P. used scrunchability *in a story, presumably with the blessing of the A.P. copy desk. Headline writers across the country picked it up, and a new word was born.*

Joanne Schreiber
Consultant, Marketing
Communications Department
E. I. Du Pont de Nemours
& Co. (Inc.)
New York, New York

Plugsville

If you are reading this carefully, you are a word freak who would like to receive a book about words as a Christmas present. (You would not like to "be gifted"; that's something else.) Here is a list that can be ostentatiously tacked on large empty stockings:

Words, by Paul Dickson, a collection of outlandish terms from *nuddle* ("to rub or push with the nose") to *pyrolagnia* ("sexual arousal from watching fires"). Good section on color words: *ferruginous* ("rust-colored"); *subfusc* ("dusky"); *taupe* ("mole-colored; rhymes with rope"). Delacorte. $13.95.

1,000 Most Important Words, by Norman Schur, a vocabulary enricher for those who want to extend their expressiveness and not merely show off. *Plangent,* for example, describes anything that resounds in a mournful way. I can hardly wait to write about "the plangent tone of his concession speech . . . ." Ballantine. $3.50.

Listening to America, by Stuart Berg Flexner. Flexner is the whizbang of slang, who provided me with the citation of *dipsy doodle* from Raymond Chandler. His latest work is the cornball's cornucopia, a po' man's potpourri of colorful expressions, linking Americanisms into brief and insightful essays. In a piece on *candy,* I learned that poet Hart Crane's father invented Life Savers ("for that stormy breath"), that *fudge* meant "cheat, hoax" and became associated with candy when girls used the making of the sugar candy as an excuse, or fudge, to stay up late, and that *jelly bean* in 1915 meant "a weak or inferior person." (The White House will probably consider that etymology a dipsy doodle.) Simon & Schuster. $24.95, and worth it.

Words in Action, by Robert Greenman, a selection of useful words in their native habitat. The answer to the question: "How is it used in a sentence?" Times Books. $16.95.

A Supplement to the Oxford English Dictionary, Volume 3, O-Sez. What literate home or library can hope to call itself *au courant* without this stupendous achievement? New Zealander Robert Burchfield has done it again—produced the work that gets to the roots of our language. Even if you cannot afford the rest of the *Supplement,* get O-Sez. Be the first on your block to really know what's going on with *P* and *R* and the first half of *S.* Specialized, but fun; if you can't afford it now, wait a few decades for the paperback and harangue your local library in the meantime. Oxford University Press. $125.

You state that (according to Paul Dickson) subfusc means "dusky." Subfusc is short for the mediaeval Latin adjective subfuscotinctum (sp?) meaning "beneath the dark dyed cloth." The only use of it I know of in English is to refer to the proper dress for wearing beneath academic gowns (dyed dark, usually black). (At Oxford, subfusc for men is dark suit, white shirt and collar, and white bow tie, for women dark skirt, white blouse, black bow tie.) I can see how -fusc- might have something to do with "dusky," but I don't see where the sub- comes in.

Kenneth J. Sheridan
Balliol College
Oxford, England

You are too modest. In your recommendation of the Vol. 3 Supplement to the
OED, *you neglected to mention that you were the only American mentioned in the*
editor's preface as one of the defenders of the "faith" of "proper usage of words."
Sort of a maven of mavens.

On another subject, a few weeks ago you wrote about the "soon to be published"
DARE. *When? I've been reading articles for almost two years about the imminence*
of the publication, always in such vague terms. "Soon" is perhaps the first evasive
word a child runs into. And it means different things to each hearer: just compare
what a child or a parent thinks of when they hear "Christmas will soon be here."
Therefore, do you know when DARE *is coming out? I'd even settle for the econo-*
mist's great evasion, "1st quarter of next year." Or was your "soon to be published"
meant to cover up the fact that you don't know when either?

> *Peter K. Oppenheim*
> *San Francisco, California*

NOTE FROM W.S.: The first volume was published in the fall of 1985.

I'm writing to thank you for sending the OED Supplement, *Volume III to Plugs-*
ville. But I must point out—though I'm sure you are already aware of the typograph-
ical error—that Volume III brings us only to Scz. *We will have to wait until at least*
1984 for Sez *and beyond, sez Bob Burchfield.*

> *Eileen Tobin*
> *Publicity Manager*
> *Oxford University Press*
> *New York, New York*

NOTE FROM W.S.: Volume IV of the *O.E.D.* supplement was published in 1986,
and is a goddam treasure trove.

Thank you for mentioning the origin of the word fudge. *I have often wondered about*
the origin of the term fudge-factor *as we use it in mathematics. Now it is clear.*

A fudge-factor *is a number or a letter or quantity or entity which is introduced*
illegitimately, usually with some cleverness, into the solution of a problem so that
one may arrive at a desired result. It is a device largely used by students but is
certainly not absent from the pages of higher erudition.

> *Robert Blefko*
> *Kalamazoo, Michigan*

Political Mileage

It began when President Reagan announced he was ready to "go the extra mile" to achieve a budget compromise. Speaker of the House Thomas P. (Tip) O'Neill Jr. took the metaphor a step further by deriding the President's trip to Capitol Hill with: "He'd walk a mile for a camera." That was a play on the Camel cigarette slogan of a couple of generations ago—"I'd walk a mile for a Camel"—and surely drew a smile from pun-loving geezers, even if it whizzed past most of the population.

Dan Schorr, of Cable News Network, tells me he has seen this extra-mile usage reported as "the President said he would go the last mile." No. The "last mile" refers to a walk taken by a condemned man on his way to execution. No political mileage in that.

The "extra mile" is from the Biblical enjoinment contained in Matthew 5:41. One would expect such a religious reference from Reagan to whiz by a man like Tip O'Neill.

> Mac E. Barrick
> Shippensburg, Pennsylvania

Power of the Press

Political polemics is usually ignored, but language columns get read in high places. Much derision appeared in this space about the overuse of *cautiously optimistic*, a straddling phrase used by President Reagan and repeated by scores of timid hopefuls.

When asked his assessment of chances for the evacuation of Beirut by the P.L.O., the President replied: "I'm reasonably optimistic. Now, see, I didn't say 'cautiously.' I'm reasonably optimistic. . . ." A few days later, chief of staff James Baker appeared on *Faze the Nation* and dutifully repeated: "We're reasonably optimistic," explaining for anybody who might have missed the nuance, "That's more optimistic than 'cautiously optimistic.'"

Somebody up there is reading, which makes me pretty hopeful. Not overly hopeful; reasonably hopeful.

Pray, Why Pre?

Whenever King Hussein tosses out a hint that he might join negotiations if the Israelis were to suspend settlement of the West Bank, the answer from Jerusalem is a terse: "No preconditions."

The immediate reaction of most Americans to that response is: "Why '*pre-conditions*'? Why not just 'No conditions'? Isn't *precondition* redundant?"

No such challenge was offered in 1967, when the Israelis launched a pre-emptive strike. There is no such thing as an "emptive" strike. In Latin, *emere* is "to buy," and *praeemere* is "to buy beforehand," or to take action before another action takes place; *pre-emption* is sometimes called "doing it to others before others do it to you." Nobody accused the Israelis of being redundant in 1967.

Why, then, the concern about *precondition*? Yes, it can be redundant. It is a condition of your employment that you get paid. You set certain conditions before you enter into a marriage: who does the dishes, the family position on GATT, etc. Why, then, call them *preconditions*?

"Redundancy is not always a bad thing," replies Fred Mish, editorial director of Merriam-Webster. "Not all *conditions* are *preconditions*; for example, hard work is a necessary *condition* of success, but it is not a *precondition* because the condition is met in the process. The two words are not absolutely interchangeable. When you want to stress the *before* element of a situation, then *precondition* is better and clearer than *condition*."

Lawyers will say that *precondition* comes from *condition precedent* (rhymes with *antecedent*), which means, among other things, a condition that must be in effect before an agreement becomes effective. No, that's not the etymology; *condition*, in that sense, means "state of affairs," but in the sense we're talking about, it means "prerequisite."

Samuel Taylor Coleridge first used *precondition* in 1825; it's a good word; don't knock it. What we can knock, however, is the epidemic of ill-fixed *pre*fixes.

"I have known many couples who deny their engagement," writes Mary Pat Gassmann of Olney, Illinois, "but will admit to being *pre-engaged*. Some of these couples even go so far as to have 'pre-engagement rings.' "

Precooked? The meal is either uncooked or cooked. Buy it cooked, or half-baked, not *precooked.*

Pretested? That means it was tested before it was tested, a redundancy worthy of scorn from the Squad Squad.

Preplanned? Now we're getting silly. I've heard of *postplanning,* which happens when White House staffers say, "How do we make it look as if we planned it this way?"

Portions of this item were prerecorded.

Although not yet a member of the Squad Squad, I am writing to point out to you one other, and to me most obnoxious, use of the prefix pre-: *that is, in pretentious used-Cadillac commercials in which, to avoid the word* used, *which may be fraught with low-class connotations, the cars are described as* pre-driven. *Of course, this is not a truly redundant usage, but it certainly is in the same category as* pre-cooked.

> *Ronald Gans*
> *New York, New York*

Precedent does not rhyme with antecedent. The rhyming sounds must have different consonants before them, or one may have no consonant before it.

I am a songwriter, and take great care in these matters. "Credent" or "needn't" would have served you well.

> *Walter Marks*
> *New York, New York*

You failed to cite what I believe is the most egregious example of redundancy involving pre-: preheat, *as in "preheat the oven," often found on frozen-food packages. Presumably, it means "heat the oven to (for example) 350 degrees before you place the food in the oven," but it's still a barbarism in my book.*

> *Stephen Calvert*
> *New York, New York*

I cannot agree with your judgment concerning the word pretesting. *In statistics and econometrics the term has quite precise meaning, which differs from that of* testing.

A pretest estimator *generally is one that depends on a preliminary test of signifi-cance. It is not obvious that a more felicitous term could be coined for this concept.*

Richard E. Quandt
Professor of Economics
Princeton University
Princeton, New Jersey

Every time I hear about some well-intentioned "program for predelinquent *girls,"
I wonder glumly what can be the use of it all, since clearly they are destined for
eventual delinquency no matter what. Perhaps someone was trying to put "preven-tive" and "delinquent" together; if so, the effort certainly failed.*

Anita Monsees
Syracuse, New York

*As a devoted devotee of the Squad Squad in its campaign against tautological
tautologies, I wish to point out that said squad qualifies for acronymic legitimization
—so important in this era. That is, if the Squad will stand for it, "SQUAD" can
stand for the Society for the Quashing of Unnecessary Adjectival Deployment.*

*On a further note, perhaps the Squad Squad might appoint a subsquad to
combat the rampant nounization of verbs, verbization of nouns, and izationization
of everything else.*

Brian J. Buchanan
Brockport, New York

The word precooked *has a long and ancient usage in English. The Romans used*
precooked (precox) *to describe early ripening or maturing. Our Latin borrowing*
precocious *is derived from it. In Rome this word was also used for a seemingly early
ripening peach. The Greeks naturalized the fruit and the word. They in turn were
invaded by Mohammedans to the east who took the word and added the Arabic
article* al *in front of it. With religious fervor it spread through the Middle East and
Northern Africa to the shores of Spain. There, in Spanish, it remains as* albaricoque.
The French say abricot *and we* apricot.

*Remember the Greco-Roman Moorish precocious peach the next time you reach
for a "precooked" T.V. dinner.*

William Meraz
San Francisco, California

Pseudo Salestalk

"It's nice to have your own money to spend, isn't it?"

Sounds like an innocuous observation; in reality, those words are a sneaky salesman's way of asking a young person: "Tell me, now, if there's somebody else you have to consult before buying."

"How'd you hear about us?"

According to Steve Salerno, in an article in *Highwire,* the national student magazine published in Lowell, Massachusetts, the hidden meaning of that piece of sales language is: "Were you recommended? If so, I can probably get away with charging you more."

"Have you been looking for [the product] for very long?"

That means: "Do you have other price information I'm going to have to contend with, or are you a novice?"

The author also tells young people to keep an ear open for sales euphemisms. For example, no smooth salesman says, "Let's sign the contract"; rather, the archly offhand words are *Let's approve the agreement,* or *authorize the paperwork,* or *O.K. the forms.*

While I had *Highwire* on the wire, I inquired about the latest teen-age talk.

Are teen-agers still calling parents *rents*? No such luck, says editor Ed Miller; *toad* refers to a parent now, and "my old man" is "my old toad."

What is a current expression of approval? *"Bold rave, radical, and dual are in,"* reports Miller. Dual? "Apparently it has something to do with the desirability of a dual exhaust system on one's car," he says, "and *dual* in the sense of 'double' conveys the idea of 'twice as good.' " "All of these expressions can be used with the intensifying prefix *mega,"* the editor adds, "thus *megadual,* which is defined as 'totally awesome.' "

The verb *to rap,* meaning "to chat," has developed into *rapping trash,* probably a play on "wrapping trash." (In Washington, a garbage-collection company advertises itself: "We don't talk trash, we haul trash.") *Pseudo* means "suspect," or "fake," as in "Are those really Calvin Kleins? They look pseudo to me."

The teen-age use of drug lingo, which I think has peaked, or spiked, may have come to its logical conclusion with the simple English word *drugs*—not *snow, aitch, hash,* or even *pot*—used to exclaim approval. "For instance, your friend says, 'Let's go over to my house and listen to the new Dire Straits LP,' to which you reply, 'Drugs!' "

What words are generally eschewed by young people? *Highwire's* publisher, Vidar J. Jorgensen, says that in choosing a name for the publication, they tested *Teen News, Youth Journal,* and *Student.* "Students hated all the names we liked," he observes. "We wound up with a word for a balancing act between generations." When he announced proudly that his quarterly was now going monthly, and I responded, "Drugs! Megadual!" there was a silence; publishers are always the last to get the word.

I wonder if you have noticed the current trend toward the synthesis of the word mushrooms *into* shrooms?

In the area of words connoting strong approval, the kids say, "Tits," always accompanied by an upward thrust of the thumb. I don't know its genesis, but perhaps it is somehow related to "dual."

Oddly enough, they often revert to standard English. My own teen-ager frequently says, "Excellent," when that is precisely what he wants to convey. Evidently there is still some hope.

David Mann
Kinnelon, New Jersey

Dear Bill:

Other phrases of praise by teens are tubular, killer *(as in, "Your dad bought you a Porsche? Killer!"), and* full on. On drugs *is a phrase which signifies craziness, as in "My mom won't let me stay out all night. She thinks I'll get drunk. She's on drugs." But my favorite, a term of opprobrium for intellectuals, is* braino, *meaning someone you wouldn't want to "party" with.*

Ben [Benjamin J. Stein]
Los Angeles, California

Rain, Rain, Go Away

"The Soviet Army," wrote Zbigniew Brzezinski in *The New York Times,* "has not hesitated to engage in chemical warfare, 'acid rain,' against the Afghan freedom fighters."

No. A confusion has arisen between *acid rain* and *yellow rain* that threatens to wash away meaning.

Acid rain is rainfall that has been polluted by chemicals, usually sulfur and nitrogen oxides, which in raindrops become sulfuric and nitric acid. *The Barnhart Dictionary of New English* has the earliest citation, in a May 23, 1975, article by Boyce Rensberger of *The New York Times*: "Scandinavian and American researchers suspect that acid rains have killed fish in many lakes in both regions." Two years later, *Maclean's* magazine wrote of "acid rain, the latest environmental shocker, an ecological time bomb on a short fuse. . . ."*

Yellow rain, though it falls, or rains down, from the sky, is not a type of rain. David Guralnik of *Webster's New World Dictionary* defines it as "a form of chemical warfare where toxins are sprayed from planes or dropped as bombs in the form of a yellowish powder. The toxins, T2 and trichothecene, are fungal."

The first use in print, I think, was in a column I wrote in *The New York Times* on December 13, 1979, headlined "Yellow Rain," with the lead: "The Laotians call it 'the yellow rain.' It struck four times during the month of February 1978, killing and sickening hundreds of Hmong tribesmen near Xiangkhoang."

The information came from a source on the National Security Council staff, then headed by Zbigniew Brzezinski. The phrase appeared (in a document classified "secret" because it might reveal the method of intelligence gathering) in a summary of interviews with Hmong refugees. I used it in a lead and headline to dramatize the horror implicit in the weapon: While arms controllers could talk abstractly about "chemical warfare" and most civilized people matter-of-factly about "poison gas," the characterization of it as *yellow rain* by terrified tribesmen brought home the fear of near-primitive innocents. The phrase was made famous by a superb series of reports and editorials in *The Wall Street Journal,* which ultimately encouraged the United States government to stop treating the information as classified and to start raising the issue in the United Nations.

*See page 230.

Raising Cain

Not content with straightening out the English-speaking world on the use of language, this department is branching out into issuing ukases on biblical allusions.

After the Kahan commission report was released on the massacre in the refugee camps in Beirut, former Israeli Defense Minister Ariel Sharon was quoted as saying that the report had put "the mark of Cain" on his country; he subsequently said he refused to "bear the mark of Cain."

Most people think the mark of Cain to be a badge of dishonor, akin to the letter *A* embroidered in red on the dress of an adultress, as popularized by Nathaniel Hawthorne in *The Scarlet Letter.*

Not so, according to David Noel Freedman, of the University of Michigan and the general editor of the Anchor Bible. "Mr. Sharon and many others have misunderstood and therefore misapplied 'the mark of Cain,'" writes Professor Freedman. "Perusal of the biblical story in which it is mentioned shows clearly that the mark that was put on Cain by God was intended not as a symbol of guilt or a punitive stigma but rather as a sign of divine protection."

He cites the passage in Genesis (4:13–15) as translated, of course, in the Anchor Bible. Cain, having murdered his brother and been banished, protests to God that he is likely to be murdered himself. " 'If so,' Yahweh said to him, 'whoever kills Cain shall suffer vengeance sevenfold.' And Yahweh put a mark on Cain, lest anyone should kill him on sight." A similar protective marking is mentioned in Ezekiel 9:4–6.

Professor Freedman does not take up Cain's cause—hardly anybody does—but concludes that when Cain showed remorse, "God took pity on him and expressed His compassion by putting a protective mark on the miscreant. The *mark of Cain* therefore is not part of the punishment but a symbol of divine protection."

That struck me as putting too many angels on the head of a pin. I turned to Professor Michael Coogan, who is into the Old Testament at Harvard Divinity School. He is willing to grant the immediate protective context of the mark of Cain, but adds: "In the larger context, the mark is negative because Cain has been banished and cursed. The mark is a sign of divine protection but only in the context of punishment and disgrace."

After long and careful deliberation (biblical scholars call it "weighing Anchor"), I am now prepared to pass semantic judgement on *the mark of Cain.* (It is *mark,* by the way, not *sign,* which may be a more literal translation of the Hebrew word, or *brand,* which used to be the more frequent usage; current usage commands *mark.*)

Mr. Sharon used the phrase in its correct current meaning. The mark is something to be ashamed of, not to wear as protection. Sometimes etymology steers you wrong.

The theologians and academics cited failed to perceive (in their zeal to determine whether divine approbation or opprobrium was intended) the essence of Cain's mark. Neither was primary. The mark identified Cain, allowing him to travel safely in exile—it was in fact the first passport.

> Tony Weinberger
> Chester Depot, Vermont

The issue in the "mark of Cain" is not whether it signified God's compassion or opprobrium. God makes Cain a "ceaseless wanderer on earth" (Gen. 4:12) because, stigmatized yet protected, Cain can spread far and wide the message of God's retribution for fratricide. If Cain were quickly dispatched, God's great power—and even greater mercy in sparing the murderer's life—would not get communicated to the world and set the precedent it does.

But there is something more here. In my opinion, God also felt implicated in the crime: Abel's blood "cries out to Me from the ground" (Gen. 4:10; my italics), presumably because it was God who created a seething jealousy in Cain that led him to murder Abel. Indeed, Cain's memorable question, "Am I my brother's keeper?" (Gen. 4:9), was, I believe, meant to remind God of His complicity—others (including God) may also be keepers, and they are responsible, too.

If God Himself felt guilty, the mark that protects Cain seems to me to express God's recognition that there were extenuating circumstances, as Cain insinuated with his question. God can hardly condemn a man to death for a crime for which He is also culpable.

Steven J. Brams
New York, New York

Dear Bill:

I grudgingly give up with you on "The Mark of Cain," but I hope you will stand firm on King Canute. He did not try to roll back the ocean but brought the stupid members of his cabinet to the beach to show them that he could no more do what they wanted than he could turn the tide back. It was Mrs. Partington and her mop that attempted the feat.

Jacques [Barzun]
Charles Scribner's Sons,
Publishers
New York, New York

I was told, by a scholar, the question really was how many infinitely small angels can dance on the infinitely sharp point of a pin, an issue perhaps of moment to mediaeval scholars.

D. B. Luten
Berkeley, California

Now that we have finished with Cain, let us realize that no one, not even Thomas Aquinas, ever put any angels on the head of any pins.

Someone named D'Israeli, however, did at one time speculate as to putting spirits on the point of a very fine needle.

Bill Schorner
Pittsburgh, Pennsylvania

Red Tape

An unconscionable delay caused by bureaucratic inertia has caused me to put off informing you of the latest word on the etymology of the phrase *red tape*.

In the early nineteenth century, legal papers and official reports in Britain were bound up with a ribbon, or tape, of a dull red color. For many years, it was thought that the first metaphoric use of this item—to mean "rigid formality, bureaucratic delay"—could be found in one of Washington Irving's sketches, written in 1839 and later included in *Wolfert's Roost*: "His brain was little better than red tape and parchment." But that was straining, crediting the modern metaphor to a phrase that on its face meant merely "little better than a government document." Thomas Carlyle's use in 1840 was closer, using the phrase as a compound adjective: "Keep your red-tape clerks. . . ."

I have written that Charles Dickens was suspected of giving the phrase currency in its modern meaning, but I could never come up with a citation. Comes now Peter James of Toronto with his welcome "Search no more!" He found this apt passage in chapter 43 of Dickens's *David Copperfield*, written in 1849: "I wallow in words. Brittania, that unfortunate female, is always before me, like a trussed fowl, skewered through and through with office-pens, and bound hand-and-foot with red tape."

That certainly drove home the meaning of *red tape* as we know it today, even in Maggie Thatcher's Britain. But in the latest supplement of the *Oxford English Dictionary*, a much earlier citation from Lord Hervey's "Poetical Epistle to the Queen" has to be considered as the earliest written use: "Let Wilmington, with grave, contracted brow,/Red tape and wisdom at the Council show."

That was from 1736. The phrase seems to have been around almost as long as bureaucracies.

Registration Drive

I used to think I was a registered Republican. John Martin, who resigned as U.S. Attorney in New York, was described as "a registered Democrat." We're both wrong.

"One is a *registered voter*," writes John Westergaard of New York. "If Mr. Martin is a Democrat, he is an *enrolled Democrat*. One registers to vote. One enrolls in a party. You might check it out."

I don't want to check it out. (What I want to check out is *check it out,* which is what those Times Square characters say when they thrust into my hand an invitation to a massage parlor.) This is too delicious a put-down to subject to fierce scrutiny. How many locutions are left to hit one's friends over the head with and establish linguistic superiority? (Used to be, when somebody said, *"Des-PIC-able,"* you could say, "You mean *DES-picable,"* but go find a lexicographer to back you up on that now.)

Try it next election time. When your friend says, "I'm a registered Republican," let him have it in the slats with "I'm an enrolled Democrat." That's the American way.

Whether you are a registered voter or a registered Democrat (or Republican) depends on which state you live in. Maybe in New York you register as a voter and then enroll as a Democrat; that's what we do in Illinois. But in many states (especially in the South) you do register in the party and can only register that way. The political difference between the two systems is absolutely tremendous, and must not be obscured by using the same words to describe both systems.

> *Phyllis Schlafly*
> *Alton, Illinois*

I consider myself a "registered Democrat" because when I registered to vote, I did so as a Democrat (as opposed to an independent, Republican, Liberal, or Conservative). If I were a member of the Democratic Party, a dues-paying, card-carrying member that is, I would also be an "enrolled Democrat," appearing as such on the membership rolls of that organization. I am not; I am not a member of any party in that sense. I think there is a subtle difference here that is blurred by making the distinction you made in your column. Most voters are not actually members of any party, and are therefore not "enrolled," but simply "registered" to vote in certain primary elections.

> *Richard E. Kramer*
> *New York, New York*

Right Stuff in the Belly Pulpit

Does John Glenn have *the Right Stuff* in his head, and the *fire in the belly,* to ascend the *bully pulpit?*

Here is a report on three etymological finds that will delight all dedicated phrase detectives:

It was pointed out here that *fire in the belly*—that burning lust for office without which no candidate can be taken seriously—was traced by the *Oxford English Dictionary* to a citation in 1951. The lexicographers had a hunch the phrase was of British origin, recently imported into American political parlance.

Before writing that, I should have checked with my brother Len, the compiler of *Good Advice* and a Robert Louis Stevenson buff. He informs me that the speculation about British provenance was correct, and submits a citation some seventy years before that of the first in the *O.E.D. Supplement.*

Stevenson, in an 1882 preface to *Familiar Studies of Men and Books,* was comparing historians Thomas Carlyle and Thomas Babington Macaulay. "Carlyle, indeed, had so much more depth and knowledge of the heart," wrote Stevenson, "his portraits of mankind are felt and rendered with so much more poetic comprehension, and he, like his favorite, Ram Dass, had a fire in his belly so much more hotly burning than the patent reading-lamp by which Macaulay studied, that it seems at first sight hardly fair to bracket them together."

Gotcha! The "Ram Dass" referred to was probably the seventeenth-century Indian teacher and author of a classic work on religious duty, unless it was the sixteenth-century Sikh guru of the same name, usually spelled with one *s*. (Look, I can't spend all day on this.) The fact that Stevenson, who contributed Jekyll and Hyde to the categories of personalities, was the originator of a current political expression makes a nice footnote to history.*

One last note on this: José de Vinck of the Alleluia Press in Allendale, New Jersey, has found the same phrase with a different meaning in the Douay version of Ecclesiasticus: "Begging will be sweet in the mouth of the unwise, but in his belly there shall burn a fire." This cannot be considered the origin, because we are talking about ambition, not heartburn.

Bully pulpit is a phrase associated with the forum offered by the presidency, and is often used in conjunction with F.D.R.'s 1932 definition of the job as "pre-eminently a place of moral leadership." As every political writer knows, it was his cousin Theodore Roosevelt who first used the phrase *bully pulpit*.

But go try to find where and when he said it. Dictionary writers like me have finessed the citation by vaguely referring to "called by Teddy 'a bully pulpit,'" but we have all worried about its being apocryphal.

Comes now a note from Thomas Curtis of Clayton, Missouri, attaching a letter from Janet Weiland of *Case Western Reserve Law Review* in Cleveland. In the introductory essay to volume nine of Theodore Roosevelt's collected works, George Haven Putnam, publisher and son of G. P. Putnam, used the word *bully*— meaning "jolly, hearty, dashing"—twice in this remembrance of a conversation with T.R.: ". . . all of his political activities brought to him keen pleasure and enabled him to have (using the boyish vernacular that he never outgrew) a bully time! I remember one such reference that he made during his first Presidential term to the advantages of speaking from the White House. I had accused him (as had been done by others) of a tendency to preaching. 'Yes, Haven,' he rejoined, 'most of us enjoy preaching, and I've got such a bully pulpit!' "

On the third phrase, I had just about given up hope. *The Right Stuff*—a phrase referring to the ambition and guts necessary for success—was the title of a 1979 book by Tom Wolfe about modern pilots and astronauts, and has been borrowed in other lingos to mean everything from good marijuana to a desirable sex partner. I ran the traps around the lexical trade, even asked my brother, who assured me it wasn't Robert Louis Stevenson; nobody knew the origin. Then, lo! along came a note from Paul Crapo of Belmont, Massachusetts, with this passage from page 176 of the Penguin edition of W. Somerset Maugham's 1927 novel *Ashenden: Or, The British Agent.*

". . . they liked him because he was always ready to listen to their speeches,

---

*Stevenson also coined the phrase *footnote to history,* which is appropriately pointed out down here.

and when he praised their works they were even willing to admit that, though a philistine, he had a certain instinct for the Right Stuff."

The capitals are Maugham's, indicating an earlier usage. We'll be hearing a great deal more of that phrase if John Glenn becomes the nominee of the Democratic Party. His supporters are already calling Walter Mondale "the Wrong Stuff."

Speaking of that side of the political spectrum, here is the freshest word on the *egghead* front: "I have long been interested in the word *egghead,*" writes Arthur Schlesinger Jr., the historian at the Graduate School of the City University of New York, "—I suppose because I was one of those to whom the word was first applied."

Phrase buffs have long known that the word was popularized in Stewart Alsop's column in 1952, quoting an unnamed "young Connecticut Republican" who was later revealed to be the columnist's younger brother, John: "Sure, all the eggheads love Stevenson. But how many eggheads do you think there are?"

My liberal friend, evidently suffering from insomnia during the Reagan years, writes: "The other night I saw on television a film that had given me much enjoyment when it came out half a century ago—*Hallelujah, I'm a Bum.* Lewis Milestone directed; Al Jolson, Frank Morgan and Madge Evans were the leading players; and the screenplay was by S. N. Behrman and Ben Hecht."

Now comes Schlesinger's sighting: "To my surprise, one character in the film, an amiable left-wing agitator with a large, smooth, oval head, played by Harry Langdon, is called 'egghead.' "

The earliest citation to date remains the 1918 letter from Carl Sandburg— "*Egg heads* is the slang here for editorial writers"—but Schlesinger's sighting gives continuity to the term's early usage.

Warm thanks are due to all those in the Lexicographic Irregulars' Phrasedick Division.

Anent Ecclesiasticus, I unwisely first thought it a misnomer for Ecclesiastes, vainly searching the latter's (thankfully much shorter) tantalizing similarities. Then the Britannica made me cry "Alleluia!" There can be no "Douay version of Ecclesiasticus," since it is only found in the Douay Version, being non-canonical for Protestants and Jews. Not having a Douay Version, I found Ecclesiasticus 40:30 in a Biblia de Jerusalem I picked up in Buenos Aires a year ago.

> *Louis Marck*
> *New York, New York*

In 1908 the popular author Owen Johnson, who wrote stories cbout Yale student life, employed the term egghead *as a nickname in* The Prodigious Hickey *(Boston,*

1919 edition), p. 12: "His genius lived in the nickname of the Egg-head . . . which he had bestowed."

Later, in another book, The Varmint *(New York, 1910), p. 39, Johnson wrote, "Why, Egghead, howdy-do?"*

It is not specific that he meant to use the nickname for an intellectual, but the context may imply it.

David Shulman
New York, New York

In German Eierkopf *has always been a common word.*

In English, the original egghead was created by Lewis Carroll and John Tenniel in Alice in Wonderland:

> *. . . the egg only got larger and larger, and more and more human: when she had come within a few yards of it, she saw that it had eyes and a nose and a mouth; and when she had come close to it, she saw clearly that it was HUMPTY DUMPTY himself.*

Humpty Dumpty was, of course, the forerunner of William Safire, always discoursing on Semantics:

> *"When I use a word," Humpty Dumpty said in a rather scornful tone, "it means just what I choose it to mean—neither more nor less."*

John Maass
Philadelphia, Pennsylvania

The phrase the right stuff *is in Herman Melville's* Billy Budd, Sailor, *published post-humously in 1924 but completed before his death in 1891. The quotation can be found on page 47 of the 1981 Bantam Classic edition of* Billy Budd, Sailor and Other Stories: *"Be it parenthesized here that since the mizzentopmen, having not to handle such breadths of heavy canvas as the lower sails on the mainmast and foremast, a young man if of the right stuff not only seems best adapted to duty there, but in fact is generally selected for the captaincy of that top, and the company under him are light hands and often but striplings."*

Aron Rothstein
Hot Springs, South Dakota

Root of All Evils

"This brochure was printed with monies originating outside Government sources." So announced a missive from the President's Commission on Executive Exchange.

A few days later, President Reagan told the National Association of Manufacturers: "I am proposing that $60 million of the monies already appropriated for our worldwide military assistance programs be immediately reallocated to El Salvador."

Money is a singular noun. When you have a lot of it, you still have a singular noun. Two bits, once the price of a haircut, is money; a million dollars is *real* money.

However, an irregular plural exists for people who like to add an *s* to their words: *Monies* can be found in most dictionaries and in the vocabulary of pompous writers.

Why is it picking up steam at 1600 Pennsylvania Avenue? Hard to say; perhaps the new habit of adding an *s* to *revenue* has something to do with it. Tax revenue is the government's main source of income; perhaps to make it seem like more, the agents at the Internal Revenue Service have taken to calling it *revenues.*

Cash is ready money; *funds* are available means, including money; *currency* is the medium of exchange, usually assumed to be paper money; *specie* is coin. Such is the synonymy of money.

The plural monies *should bring you vollies of complaints to turn over to your attornies. Fowler and Partridge say* "moneys, not monies." *Bergen Evans labels* monies *obsolete. Why be led astray by mere bankers and presidential scripters and other linguistic donkies and monkies?*

> Spencer Brown
> Pleasantville, New York

At the risk of sounding like a "pompous" *writer myself, I will simply quote from three moments in Act I, Scene 3 of William Shakespeare's* The Merchant of Venice: *"Signior Antonio, many a time and oft in the Rialto you have rated me about my* moneys *and my usances." And later, "You come to me, and you say, 'Shylock, we would have* moneys.'" *And still again, "'Fair sir, you spet on me on*

Wednesday last, you spurn'd me such a day; Another time you call'd me dog, and for these courtesies I'll lend you thus much moneys'? "

Barney Rosenzweig
Los Angeles, California

Rose Were a Rose Were a Rose

"I only wish you were as perceptive about politics as you are about grammar," writes Senator Edward M. Kennedy, following a piece about the use of the subjunctive mood.

In that instructive harangue, I quoted the senator's error in using *was* instead of *were* in his withdrawal statement. "If I was to make a political decision," he had said on what soon became a great hallelujah day for Walter Mondale, "it would be a different announcement today."

It turns out that this was not the first time the senator had been taken to task for flubbing the dub on the subjunctive. In acknowledging his recent error, the senator adds: "I did want you to know that the error you cited I have made before—and I was corrected at the time by my mother."

In a letter dated January 13, 1975, Rose Kennedy had written: "Dear Teddy: . . . Please say, 'If I *were* President,' not, "If I *was* President.' The reason is the old, what used to be known in Latin as, 'condition contrary to fact.' For instance, 'If I *were* he,' 'If she *were* more capable,' etc. Love to all, G'ma."

In passing along this good advice from one of America's favorite matriarchs, the senator adds cryptically: "Maybe the next time I make an announcement, I will get it right!"

Hmm. Perhaps he means another withdrawal in 1988, that time grammatically pure. Or perhaps, next time the world turns to him for an announcement, it will hear: "If I were to reject this overwhelming appeal from the convention, I would be derelict in my duty. Therefore, my friends. . . ." Either way, critics from his mother to me will cry, "By George, he's got it!"

Sexth Sense

Words that sound the same but have different meanings are called *homophones*; words that sound similar and have similar but different meanings have been dubbed *confusibles* by Adrian Room.

The confusible that has been bugging Lenore Tobin Schattner of Pound Ridge, New York, is *sensual/sensuous*. Is there any difference, and is the difference worth trying to preserve?

Yes. Both words have to do with the senses, but have quite different meanings. *Sensual* deals with physical and sexual feelings; having your ear nibbled by a toothy Danish model is *sensual*. But that sensation, as we all know, is lewd, gross, carnal, and not to be sought by the upright and reverent. John Milton, the poet, wanted a word to denote all the senses of the body that did not carry the pejorative baggage of *sensual*, and coined the more neutral *sensuous*. (We think that's why he coined it; it could be that he just couldn't think of the word *sensual*, or he made a mistake. Happens to all of us.) Samuel Coleridge reintroduced the word a couple of centuries later, with credit to Milton, for the same reason: He needed a word to describe a person whose senses were alive to imagination and other spiritual stimulants.

The way to remember the difference is that *sensual* is close to *sexual*, while *sensuous* is close to *sensitive*. The compliment is *sensuous*; the insult is *sensual*.

Let's get down to the brass tacks of current synonymy. If you are a toothsome dish contemplating the seduction of some innocent lad, your feelings are *sensual*, if not all the way to *sexy* or *randy*; you are a *voluptuary* and maybe a *libertine*, ridden with *fleshly* desires, stuffing your face at *sybaritic* repasts, and someone should lay a guilt trip on you. On the other hand, if you delight in beauty and form, and if the pine-needly air of the forest inspires you to break out in song, you are *sensuous* and are likely to start bragging about your invincible vulnerability.

If that's not a difference worth defending, what is?

Are you mad? "Sensuous" a compliment, "sensual" an insult? Not in the lexicon of those toothy, brilliant advertising geniuses who are the backbone of America, and who will be hiring, and perhaps nibbling, this year's most promising mannequin. If she is a toothsome dish contemplating the seduction of some innocent lad, that is exactly what sells quality products, from Rolls-Royces to underarm deodorants. They couldn't care doodly squat if she delights in beauty and form, or if the pine-needly air inspires her to breakout in song. That sells no "Preparation H" in Peoria.

Pejorative? That would describe the phrases these fine men would use to describe someone not prepared to go the whole nine yards in pursuit of the American Dream. Young man, I am afraid you had best reconceptualize the order of your priorities.

Everett S. Crosby
Germantown, New York

If any of your readers take your advice and try to preserve the distinction between the "confusibles" sensual and sensuous, they will be up against some commanding purveyors of contemporary usage. In 1963 James Baldwin wrote, "The word 'sensual' is not intended to bring to mind quivering dusky maidens or priapic black studs. I am referring to something much simpler and much less fanciful. To be sensual, I think, is to respect and rejoice in the force of life, of life itself, and to be present *in all that one does, from the effort of loving to the breaking of bread" (*The Fire Next Time, Dial Press, p. 57). On the continuum from physical to spiritual senses, Baldwin would seem to be pushing dangerously close to the realm Milton and Coleridge carved out for sensuous. When you say that "the insult is sensual" you cannot be talking about the same word Baldwin is.*

Perhaps the usage of this book reviewer is closer to your meaning: ". . . a summer at the Italian lakes, in Greece or in Provence, is meant to provide even the most humdrum traveler with a heightened sensual awareness. We all intend to eat and drink deeply and to linger over the smell of olive wood. We long for those hot and languorous southern nights, dark wine, the exotic. Secretly, a sensual awakening is the dream of all of us" (Kim Chernin, San Francisco Chronicle *review, 10/24/82, p. 8). A bit less airy than Baldwin's respect for the force of life, but yet not as base as your "lewd, gross, carnal." Maybe these words remain confusibles not because writers and speakers wildly improvise, but because the realm of the purely spiritual that Coleridge and Milton wanted to characterize has become more and more encroached upon in our age by the physical. The borders of each are less distinct in our time, the distinction less worth the effort of preserving.*

Thom Hawkins, Coordinator
Writing Center
University of California
Berkeley, California

Sharing

"Christmas is sharing" goes a line in a 1966 song by Spence Maxwell and Percy Faith, and that is surely a proper poetic use of the verb *to share*—to take a part of what is mine and give it to you, and vice versa.

But are we burdening *share* with too sticky-sweet a meaning of late? Observe the noun: "Stock certificates" are now the warmer "shares"; "stock holders" have become "share holders" and even the more permanent-sounding "share owners." But it is in the verb form that *share* is creating resistance: "Take the expression 'I want to share an experience with you,' " writes Enno Hobbing of Washington. "It's just plain wrong. *Share* comes from *sceran*, to cut, and the share of a plow, which divides. You and I can 'share an experience' if we have it simultaneously or together. . . . In no way can I share a sole experience, which is an abstraction, with you. I can *tell* you *about* my experience. . . ."

It is not "just plain wrong," since the verb *share*, as in "to share in," was in active use in 1594 when Elizabethans were "sharing in the glory." Something about its current overuse borders on gushiness, however, and generates strong reactions.

"In my own vocabulary, which is a word hoard different from everyone else's, *sharing* is something that children do, or refuse to do, with their toys," Dennis Baron, associate professor of English and linguistics at the University of Illinois, tells us. "But when people use *share* to mean 'tell, recount, narrate,' as in, 'Thank you, Binky, for sharing that with us today,' I feel as if I'm being bamboozled. Nothing material—and usually, nothing spiritual—has changed hands. Somehow I always feel that the person who uses *share* this way is being insincere. Am I too cynical?"

An Australian correspondent in Washington, Peter Samuel, has the identical impression. He, too, felt the need to break off part of his feelings, as he filed them to newspapers around the world, and send that portion to me: "President Reagan said, in his opening comments at a press conference, he wanted 'to share with' us his reflections on the death of Mr. Brezhnev. Then I read that Terence Cardinal Cooke of New York, speaking in the Roman Catholic bishops' debate, wanted 'to share with' his fellow bishops his thoughts on the morality of the MX missile. To cap it all, my 'realtor' wrote me (no 'to' there) to say she wished 'to share with' me her 'marketing strategy' for my house."

Mr. Samuel then roared: "What the hell is the matter with the good, workman-like four-letter word *tell*?" He concludes: "This fad for the verb *share with* is part pomposity, part sentimental gushiness."

Partly because of its rhyme with another much-used word ("Christmas is caring . . ."), *sharing* is a word picked up from psychology and used heavily by would-be psychologists. Evidently its vogue use has been noted by a variety of noncynical Lexicographic Irregulars in the last year, and I thought I would tell, recount, and narrate their reactions to you.

Dear Bill:

   In answer to your question about the verb share, *I am happy to share with you my thoughts on the subject.*

   Sentences such as the above are increasing in frequency, though you might have noticed that they are usually uttered by public speakers (or speakers used to public speaking). Clergymen are especially fond of sharing in their sermons, as by telling their audiences that they would like to share with them a story, a joke, an experience, and even a dream. There is a hint of pompousness or condescension in this usage, as though the speaker, out of the goodness of his heart, is willing to share something belonging exclusively to him. Agony columnists like Dear Abby and Dear Meg, who talk down to their readers, usually use it in the intransitive, in sentences such as "Thanks for sharing. God bless." The usage has also a formal overtone that would make the following sentence sound inappropriate: "I'd like to share with you a gag I recently heard on the tube." In this sentence "tell" would sound better than "share with."

   I suspect that this usage developed in religious and educational circles, where the word share *has strong emotional and psychological connotations. In religion people are exhorted to share with the poor, to share their blessings, and the entire community to share in each other's joys and sorrows. The cults have taken up sharing as a major doctrine. In the Unification Church, for example, the Reverend Moon's disciples call confession "sharing" (Nathaniel Sheppard Jr. and Jo Thomas,* Cults in America, *1979). In education children are constantly urged to share and share alike; there is even a "sharing time" in primary school, which Carter Good's* Dictionary of Education *(1959) defines as "time when children discuss experiences and/or objects brought to the classroom." Note that both the Moonies and the children "share" (i.e., talk to others about) their personal experiences.*

   How old is this usage? This is hard to pin down, but the evidence from citations (and lack thereof) indicates that it developed during this century, perhaps from another modern extension of the verb, "to share (i.e., reveal, disclose, tell) secrets, confidences, intimacies," in which the verb retains the connotation of "take part in, have a share or portion in," which is of course the original sense of the verb.

   A closely parallel usage is found in the Latin word impartire, *the source of the English verb* impart. *Literally, Latin* impartire *means "to share or take part in" (from the verb* partire, *"to divide, part") but its ordinary meaning is "to give, bestow, communicate." Thus in English one can impart ("give, bestow") knowledge or an air of mystery, as well as impart ("communicate, tell, disclose") a secret or a plan of action. Can one impart an interesting experience to another? Yes, in both senses of the word (though the usage is somewhat formal). Can someone share an experience with another? Yes, but only by partaking in it, not by retelling it or by hearing it being retold. Therefore never say to someone "I'd like to share with you a marvelous experience" unless you seriously intend to have one with that particular person.*

> Sol [Steinmetz]
> Clarence L. Barnhart, Inc.
> Bronxville, New York

Bill,
 You might want to mention this cloying usage of share, *of which I occasionally find myself guilty: "Dear Mr. Letterwriter: Harvey Bigwig has* shared *your letter with me, and I am happy to be able . . ." etc., blah, blah.*
 What it means is, "My boss didn't feel like answering your letter so he stuck me with it."

> Allan [M. Siegal]
> New York, New York

I always feel subtly blackmailed when "sharing" is used. How can I refuse to cooperate with somebody "sharing" something with me? Actually, when they initiate one of these stories with an introductory command, "I want to share with you my memories of an unhappy childhood," I feel like telling them, "No, thanks. I have plenty of my own."
 You didn't mention the true perpetrator of this garbled usage. Werner Erhard of est *gave it vogue in the mid-70's. That alone earns him ten linguistic demerits.*

> Marcia Spires
> New York, New York

I want to "share" an unusual usage of share. *My nursery-aged son asked to bring something to school "for share." I assumed he would need 20 cookies for snack time. After a lot of explaining by him, I realized the activity was really "show and tell."*

> Joan Adler
> Brooklyn, New York

I find the people I know using share *instead of* tell *are not pompous but rather uncomfortable about either being in a position of authority or being called on to exercise authority, so they descend into this false kind of cozy folksiness. It's the same crowd that not long ago interfaced, talked about things being in the ballpark, and they're the ones who are now replacing "Thank you much" with "You bet."*

Sally Sherwin
New York, New York

Sherpa Run-Up

The men who choreographed the summit meetings in Versailles and Bonn early this month are called "Sherpas." The etymology is easy: Sherpas are members of a Tibetan people renowned for their skill as mountain guides. When Sir Edmund Hillary's team reached the summit of Mount Everest in 1953, Sherpa Tenzing was widely celebrated. (Many readers thought that Sherpa was his first name, but Sherpa Tenzing was the equivalent of New Zealander Edmund.)

Lexicographer Sol Steinmetz of Barnhart Books has, as usual, the first citation on file: "There was an array of experts," ran a *New York Times* account of a Khrushchev-Eisenhower meeting in 1959, "—Sherpa guides, as one British wit put it—behind the mountaineers at the summit."

The British are good at diplomatic coinages; *summit* itself was a term put into the language of high-wire statecraft by Winston Churchill. American cookie-pushers are less vivid; the hot new word at the Versailles economic summit was *differentiation,* a fairly dull moniker for treating countries behind the Iron Curtain singly rather than as a bloc. When anyone used it on me, I replied, "I'm more worried about *disintermediation.*" That shut 'em up. (It's a company's way of avoiding the mediation of banks by dealing directly with investors.)

At a briefing in the White House Roosevelt Room before the trip, a passel of pundits was treated to the inside lingo of the National Security Council when General Robert (Bud) McFarlane—a member of "Haig's Junta," on temporary duty as deputy national security adviser—made one of his rare public appearances.

"In the run-up to this Eureka speech . . .," began General McFarlane, talking about the preparations for President Reagan's address to his college in Eureka, Illinois, in May. At that point, the pundit sitting next to me jotted down a note: "Run-up?"

Assiduous research (I called Sol again) shows this, too, to be a Britishism. In cricket, a player gains momentum before bowling the ball by running up to the point of releasing it; in British politics, a period before voting is called the run-up to election. (Steinmetz has a 1958 citation on that; the members of Haig's Junta ought to hire Steinmetz to find out where they are coming from.)

General McFarlane also allowed as how some strategists "buy on to our approach." This was not in the transcript of his remarks. The odd locution may be a combination of "to buy our approach" (as in "I'll buy that!") and "to sign on to" (a variant of "sign off on").

The general's superior, national security adviser William Clark, is no stranger to Haigravations, having served as a civilian in the State Department for nearly a year. In his first public speech in his new job—a collection of banalities piled on obfuscations, laced with sycofancy footwork—he came up with a Stranglovism that might just be the euphemism of the year: The subject was military strategy, which he viewed as "a planning continuum." At the lower end of that spectrum was the training of foreign troops and the supply to them of our "support capability." And then: "At the higher end of the conflict spectrum . . . any conflict with the Soviet Union could expand to global dimensions."

Nobody is sure exactly what Mr. Clark meant in that speech—it was a lulu of obfuscation and banalities—but some of us suspect that "the higher end of the conflict spectrum" is a way of not saying "war."

Dear Bill,

Horrors! The wrong date (1959) appeared in print for the "earliest" citation for Sherpa guide.

The date I gave you over the phone was 1955, a mere two years after the Mount Everest feat. The summit meeting referred to was that of July 1955 between Eisenhower, Bulganin, Eden, and Fauré, though Khrushchev (then Communist Party boss) was part of the Russian delegation, along with Molotov and Marshal Zhukov. Khrushchev, in effect, was a Sherpa guide of the highest rank.

> Sol [Steinmetz]
> Clarence L. Barnhart, Inc.
> Bronxville, New York

That's not disintermediation*! That may be one formal definition, but on Wall Street* disintermediation *is defined as a loss of liquidity by a financial institution (a financial intermediary). The loss is due to a differential in the rate of interest in the marketplace and the rate the institution pays its depositors. When the market rate is higher, the institution loses funds or is disintermediated.*

Salomon Brothers, the investment banking firm, once ran a contest to find a better word for this phenomenon. The best Wall Street could come up with was circumfiduciation, *which is as bad as* disintermediation.

> John Kubacki
> New York, New York

> *This feeble, labored wittishism,*
> *Isn't meant to be a critishism.*
> *Are writers who use "Britishism,"*
> *Guilty of a soleshism?*
>
> Marthe Charles
> Plainview, New York

The Sidewalk Shuffle

A service occasionally performed in this space is linguistic astronomy. You know how astronomers look through telescopes at a blank space in the sky, make a few calculations, and announce with certainty that one day a star will be discovered there? In the same way, I seek to anticipate word coinages caused by vocabulary vacuums.

Take that awkward moment when a person walking toward you tries to get past you just as you are adjusting your direction to get past him. He moves to his right just as you move to your left; you both smile glumly; both of you move in the other direction simultaneously, still making passage impossible; the feinting and shifting continue until coordination takes place or a fistfight ensues. What, asked Ernest

Heyn, associate publisher of *Popular Science* magazine, is that called?

1. *The Alphonse-Gaston Routine.* Lillian Greenberg of Rockville Centre, New York, suggests this reference to "the legendary exponents of Gallic politesse, who hindered progress of any kind by refusing to precede the other ('After you, my dear Alphonse . . .')." She suggests that after the first shift, one of the Alphonse-Gaston dancers should conclude the gavotte with, "The gigue is up." On that same line, John Dolan of Randallstown, Maryland, suggests calling the routine "passongaston." Judge Jon Newman, of the United States Court of Appeals for the Second Circuit, has a different combined form: " 'Gaphonse' might be appropriate. I reject 'Alston' because he unhesitatingly managed the Dodgers for many years. But my preference is 'Gastonette,' conveying the literary allusion with a homophonic suggestion of 'minuet,' and even 'castanet,' if the foot-shufflers are wearing clattering shoes."

2. *Dance steps.* Elizabeth Thompson of New York suggests "the hesitation waltz"; Ray Gordon of the city prefers "the no-go fandango" or "the zig-zag shag"; Paul Browning of Granby, Massachusetts, likes "the circumdance" and "the shuffle": "Each mirrored step is a mutual embarrassment." He adds, considering himself a born loser: "In each circumdance between the stacks in a library, my shuffling partner holds the more erudite book." Other readers like "the pedestrian sidestep," "the pedestrian shuffle," "the sidewalk sidestep," "the stutter-step," and, on the analogy of "gridlock," E.C.K. Read of New York suggests "pedlock."

3. *French expressions.* Beaucoup entries on this angle, from "contrechance" to "double deux" to "do-sideux." The best was from Gary Muldoon of Rochester, New York: "faux pas de deux."

4. *Lurching.* The late humorist H. Allen Smith, in his book *Larks in the Popcorn,* used that word to describe the situation that he considered a pedestrian art form. Raymond Bostock of Branchville, New Jersey, recalls: "As a sport, lurching requires a fairly crowded sidewalk or a rather narrow hallway with a good scattering of people. The approach must be made with an absent-minded expression but with careful anticipation of the direction in which the victim will first lurch. The object of the game," Mr. Bostock rather fiendishly writes, "is to prolong the lurching as long as possible. Four or five lurches is very good, six is exceptional. When the victim says, 'What the hell ——?' the game is over."

Snake-Check

"This has to be snake-checked," said Secretary of State Al Haig at a meeting not long ago. Two schools of thought have emerged about the origin of this colorful term.

"It's an old military expression," writes William Huebner of Wethersfield, Connecticut. "I heard it in the jungles of New Guinea in 1943. Our platoon sergeant informed us that when we enter our sleeping bags or put on our clothes, 'Snake-check them first.' We did, and we often found any number of critters taking up residence during the cold evenings in the jungle.

"I imagine what Al Haig meant," concludes Mr. Huebner (and a dozen other ex-grunts), "was to check out a statement or position before wearing it in public to be sure no unwanted critter was contained within it."

The other school suggests that the term has to do with an implement used by people engaged in cleaning out pipes and drains. A long, flexible tool is called a snake, which it resembles; from this, the verb *to snake out* has come to mean "to retrieve from a seemingly inaccessible place." The *out* is no longer necessary: Vera Cantor of Stamford, Connecticut, passes along a bill that reads: "Snake 2d-floor hall basin and add chemical . . . $40."

"If you don't know what's in a pipe," agrees David Steinberg of Virginia Beach, Virginia, "run in a mechanical snake and root it out." Paul Milikin of Sarasota, Florida, offers a slight variation: "A snake is also a steel wire used to assist in threading electrical wires," and by metaphoric leap, the snake-checking is to make certain the wires are connected.

Which is the more likely etymology, the direct snake in the grass or the indirect snake in the drainpipe? I passed along to Secretary of State Haig the opinion of readers suggesting the search for snakes on bivouac, and received this gracious reply: "Your readers are essentially on the mark, though they must have had smaller snakes than we did on bivouac—we used to 'snake-check' our knapsacks." Secretary

Haig adds: "We found more interesting things than snakes in our socks!"

I would accept that as definitive, coming from a busy man who took the time to respond to a language query. After all, what does Al Haig know about plumbers?

Snugging at the Fed

Will the Federal Reserve Board reduce the availability of reserves in the banking system, thereby restraining the growth of the money supply, and thus either valiantly stop a resurgence of inflation or foolishly abort a recovery? (*Abort* now goes with *recovery* the way *awash* used to go with *oil.*)

New York Times financial reporter Michael Quint quoted an unnamed government securities dealer as replying: "There are those who think the Fed has snugged a notch, those who think they have snugged two notches, and those who think they have not snugged at all."

This was zipped down to me by business/financial editor John M. Lee with an electronic note: "Fed policy is arcane enough without dealers clouding it further. Maybe semanticists can shed light."

Most of us know the adjective *snug* from its early nautical sense, "trim, tight, neat, protected from bad weather," and quickly recall Benjamin Franklin's letter of 1772 to the shapely Miss Georgiana Shipley that included the doggerel: "Here Skugg lies snug as a bug in a rug."

The same nautical associations adhere like barnacles to the hoarier verb *to snug.* By battening down the hatches, furling the sails, stowing the movables, and lowering the topmast, sailors snugged their ship, making it trim and stormworthy.

The securities dealer made a nice figurative extension of the act of preparing for inflationary storms: By tightening money, the Fed snugs the economy.

Another waterlogged word popped up in a quotation recently: "I think the company has been able to get its dobber back in good shape, and I think I have as well," said a hotel executive about recovery from a tragic skyway collapse. Writes Steve Boone of Point Pleasant Beach, New Jersey: "What is a dobber? Is it a Missouri barnyardism?"

A *dobber,* sometimes called a *bobber,* is a cork or plastic float that a fisherman ties to his line to keep the bait at the desired depth and to let him know when a fish is nibbling. When your line gets fouled or some fish steals your bait, you look forward to the day when you get your dobber in good shape.

Safire's Investment Advice: When the Fed snugs, sell; when the dobber ducks underwater, buy.

So I Lied

In a piece about anachronisms, I suggested that the Yiddishism "so I lied" might have originated as the punch line of a long-forgotten joke.*

To use a disputed Yiddishism: not to worry. Somebody remembers the joke. John McCarthy writes from Singapore (funny, that doesn't sound like a Jewish source) that the old story goes this way:

> "What's green and flies backward?"
> "I dunno. What?"
> "A red herring!"
> "But a red herring isn't green."
> "It could turn green."
> "But a herring can't fly."
> "So I lied."

From these roots, great expressions grow.

You must be receiving more than one letter with the authoritative text of the red herring story, as follows:

> *"What is red, hangs on the wall, and whistles?"*
> *"Don't know."*
> *"A herring."*
> *"But it isn't red."*
> *"So, you could paint it red."*
> *"But it doesn't hang on the wall."*
> *"So, you could hang it on the wall."*
> *"But it doesn't whistle."*
> *"So, it doesn't whistle."*

I dimly recall a novel published perhaps 20 or 30 years ago, called So it Doesn't Whistle.

Adam Yarmolinsky
Washington, D.C.

You used what you call a "disputed Yiddishism," to wit: not to worry.

I decided not to worry about not to worry once I learned that in Italian the negative imperative of the familiar singular is an infinitive. Non preoccupare = not

*See page 32.

to worry. *Latin is Greek to me, and I can't remember my French well enough to call it* my *French, but I am familiar enough with Italian to be possessive about it.*

As a Southerner I used to stare stupidly at those New Yorkers who'd ask me, "Are you here long?" Twenty years in New York (Yiddishly speaking) and I'm still not entirely certain if they mean "Have you been here long?" or "Y'all gone be round awhile?" I think they mean how long have I been here, since the literal translation of "We haven't seen each other in a coon's age" is "It is a long time that we are not seeing each other," Italianally speaking.

Anyway, I'd pretty well satisfied myself that Not to worry *and* Are you here long?, *among other expressions all of which escape me now, came over from the Old Country in their native Italian and made a literal move into heenglish.*

But what do I know?

> *Honey Naylor*
> *New York, New York*

Dear Bill:

My father was in the textile business. When I was a child, he came home one night and told my mother—staggered—that a buyer had broken an agreement saying: "So I lied."

The phrase thereafter had special meaning in our family: a comment on character. It was definitely not a joke in origin; the buyer said it crossly, ending the discussion.

When your item appeared, my mother noted it—and even reminded me of the name of that buyer!

> *Tony [Anthony Lewis]*
> *Boston, Massachusetts*

Ah, Bill, what lovely complexities herrings arouse. Especially green herrings.

Here is an entry of January 8, 1950, in my Moscow Journal, *published in 1961. That means I heard the story in 1949 when "Armenian jokes" were the rage in Moscow:*

> *Then, the Armenian joke in the form of a riddle:*
> *"What is it that is long and green and is hanging in my living room —and squeaks?*
> *"You can't answer it?*
> *"The answer: a herring!*
> *"Why? But, of course. It is hanging in my living room because I hung it there. It is long because it is a herring. It is green because I painted it green. And it squeaks—well it squeaks just to make it difficult for you to guess what it is!"*

And then the Armenian joke to tell after telling half a dozen of them:

> "*Why are Armenian jokes so silly?*
> "*Of course. Because the Russians make them up!*"

> Harrison [E. Salisbury]
> Taconic, Connecticut

Squeal Rule

Rarely does one side in a controversy grab the moral high ground by the coinage of a phrase.

A generation ago, opponents of the union shop urged the passage of what they called *right-to-work laws,* building their argument into the name of the game: Who could be against the right to work? (Organized labor called the legislation *union-busting laws.*) In the same way, the *truth-in* construction was effective, from *truth-in-securities* in 1933 to *truth-in-packaging* later. More recently, issue-titling was enhanced by groups that favored legal abortion and called themselves *pro-choice,* a move that was then countered by antiabortion groups that selected the positive *pro-life.*

Now a debate revolves around (or centers on) a regulation propounded by the Department of Health and Human Services requiring those who use tax dollars to supply minors with contraceptive devices to notify the minors' parents. Supporters say the law on which the regulation is based calls for the agency to "encourage family participation," and a family cannot participate unless it knows of the teen-ager's request; opponents call the rule an intrusion into privacy likely to result in more unwanted pregnancies and more abortions.

The regulation is named "the Squeal Rule"; its label is a powerful weapon in the hands of the opponents. In 1865, a British slang dictionary defined *squeal* as "to inform, peach," and identified the term as "a North Country variation of squeak"; *squealer* in the sense of "informer" is a derogation of a person who provides information to the police.

The implication, of course, is that the one doing the squealing sounds like a pig. The sounds made by animals, applied to humans, reflect the human attitude toward the animal: Dogs can be authoritative ("he barked") or mean ("he snarled"), while lions are intimidating ("he roared"), and mice are frightened ("he squeaked"). Birds are cheerful ("he chirped"), and criminals who talk are said to be singing. In metaphor, the lowest form of animal life is not the snake ("he hissed") but the useful, delicious pig: Nobody knows the truffles he's seen. If you want to hail an informer, call him a *whistleblower,* and if you want to condemn him, call him a *squealer.*

When did "Squeal Rule" originate? "At the time the Parental Notification Rule was proposed," says Russ Mack, spokesman at H.H.S., using the official designation, "which was in February 1982. That's when I first heard it called by Planned Parenthood and other opponents 'the Squeal Rule.' "

Did Planned Parenthood coin it? "No," says Daisy Voigt, a media-relations coordinater, who in the course of coordinating media relations answers questions like these. "I'm tempted to say that I first saw it in *The New York Times.*"

A quick check at that coordinated medium shows an editorial of February 5, 1982, titled "Squealing on Teen-Agers." On February 26, in an editorial blasting "the Government's new squeal ruling," the headline was "Abortion and the Squeal Rule." Three weeks later, the editorial capitalized the phrase in the copy: "The strangest of all is the speciousness of the arguments with which the Administration suggests the Squeal Rule."

The Times's editorial page fiercely defends the anonymity of its editorials, and nobody knows which writer has written which editorial, but this department "has learned," to use television news's favorite phrase, that the coiner of *Squeal Rule* was Mary Cantwell. (Somebody squealed.)

Thanks to the coinage, the battle is being won by the antisqueal forces; the proponents of the rule are stuck with the bureaucratic *parental-notification rule.* No imagination at all can be detected; nobody has tried *full-disclosure requirement* or *truth-in-dispensing.*

This matter was brought to my attention by Irving Kristol, editor of *The Public Interest,* who heard an NBC-TV reporter say that the Squeal Rule was "already creating problems." Mr. Kristol writes: "As an illustration of such a problem, he turned his television on a 'sexually active girl of 13'—those were his exact words."

"I really think," comments the father of neoconservatism, "you ought to take this phrase, *sexually active*—which I take to be what we used to call *promiscuous*

—and do something with it. Is it possible to be promiscuous anymore? Or was Don Juan sexually active?"

Promiscuous, rooted primarily in the Latin *miscere,* "to mix," originally meant "elements mixed together without discrimination"—a sort of "Duke's mixture" in the tobacconist trade. About the turn of this century, it began meaning "sexually indiscriminate," the first citation in a 1924 letter from Cyril Connolly, the British critic and editor: "I am not promiscuous but I can't be loyal to an icicle." (The word has been used frequently since then, but never more tellingly.)

For the difference in connotation between *promiscuous* and *sexually active,* let us turn to lexicographer David Guralnik: "*Promiscuous* is a judgmental word; the idea is that the behavior is not desirable. *Sexually active* is without judgment; it is neutral. Today, if a writer wants to be critical he will use *promiscuous*; if he wants to avoid sounding judgmental he will use *sexually active.* That is why you hear *sexually active* more often than *promiscuous.*"

Writers who dwell on these words should remember that the hands-off, I'm-not-knocking-it *sexual activity* should not be confused with *sexual variety,* which it overlaps: The latter denotes promiscuity (oops! I made a judgment) of a bisexual nature, its participants called *swingers,* or if single and frequenters of singles bars, *swingles.* They don't worry about the Squeal Rule at all.

The distinction which you (and David Guralnik) have drawn between promiscuous *and* sexually active *is incomplete and misleading. Yes,* promiscuous *is judgmental, and it is so mainly because it denotes a multiplicity of partners.* Sexually active, *on the other hand, is indeed neutral, because it means merely "not sexually inactive," i.e., not celibate. A "sexually active girl of 13" is not a virgin, but she probably has only one boyfriend. Most married persons are sexually active; far fewer are promiscuous.*

> *Amy B. Unfried*
> *Bronxville, New York*

*Daisy Voigt, a media-relations coordinat*or, *not coordinat*er.
   The latter looks more like something I would have misspelled, not *William Safire.*

> *Charles B. Forster*
> *Brooklyn, New York*

Dear Bill:
   I believe that you missed an important point. The alternative to "The Squeal Rule" is "The Sneak Rule," according to which youngsters will be encouraged to

sneak important matters which affect the entire family past their parents. It is hard for me to believe that those who oppose squealing also are in favor of sneaking. Parents are often and properly held legally responsible for the consequences of the actions of their minor children. As long as such children are under the responsibility of their parents, it does seem to me that the parents have a responsibility to establish certain moral rules for the household. Should it be the business of the United States Government to promote sneakiness in minor children?

In the old days, in immigrant neighborhoods, the whole neighborhood felt responsible for all the children in it, and it was not uncommon for neighbors to challenge the conduct by children of which they knew the parents would not approve, and to do so even before the parents learned of it.

Moral life has a certain communal structure, and it does not seem wise simply to leave parents in isolation from each other, from the major institutions of our society, or from their own children.

We may and should debate all these things, but every fierce battle cry deserves a matching battle cry.

> Michael [Novak]
> American Enterprise Institute
> Washington, D.C.

I do not believe it is correct to impute to the pig the low esteem in which human squealers are held. As one who grew up on a farm, I can assure you that the pig is held in very high esteem indeed, so much so that it is a valuable target of thieves. However, pigs apparently dislike being picked up and tend to squeal immediately and continuously when they are lifted. There are few sounds on a farm louder or more piercing than a pig's squeal (hence the expression "screamed like a stuck pig"). Many a foiled pignapper found himself caught because the pig "squealed on me."

I would suggest that the term squealers when applied to humans is not because they "sound like a pig," as in your column, but because of their success in attracting attention with their alarms.

> Robert F. Bradford
> Berkeley, California

Struct Me Pink

Elizabeth Drew of *The New Yorker* noted it first: "Now everything is 'structural.' 'Structural' is a very popular and useful term. Some years ago, the concept of 'structural' unemployment—unemployment no one knew what to do about—gained general acceptance. Now, according to the Reagan Administration, the group that promised the balanced budget, there are 'structural deficits.' "

A few days later, Hodding Carter 3d took it a step further: "With the doctrine of original sin out of the running in many circles these days," he wrote in *The Wall Street Journal,* " 'structural' will do very nicely to explain why nothing can be done about this evil or that. It won't last, of course, and given the way these cycles work, we'll be back to concepts and conceptual—as in 'conceptual failure'—only too soon. All of them beat having to employ another word. You know: responsibility."

As a card-carrying member of the Conceptual Frameworkers' Union, I have long been pondering the buildup of *structural.* Its first recorded metaphoric use —meaning "built-in," in contrast to "peripheral" or "superficial" or "changeable" —was in a 1904 Harvard lecture by S. H. Butcher: "The subject matter of poetry is the universal—that which is abiding and structural in humanity."

Snatching a leaf from structural linguistics, French anthropologist Claude Lévi-Strauss paved the way for a generation of literary critics with a "scientific" reading of written works. He found a unity in sign-systems and their opposites that his followers called *structuralism* (except for those who called it *semiology*). This was followed, inevitably, by *poststructuralism,* led by the antisemantic Jacques Derrida and his chaos-embracing *deconstructionists,* whose pyrotechnical vocabulary I ought to dissect someday.

In 1961, economists took up the word; Dudley Dillard, in the *Britannica Yearbook* of that year, used the word in its "permanent" sense: "A leading question was how much of unemployment was *Keynes-ian,* arising from a deficiency of aggregate demand, and how much was structural unemployment associated with long-term shifts in economic activity between industries and regions."

That led to a field of *structuralists,* believers in fast growth, who were opposed by *monetarists,* who feared inflation. In the 1980's, the adjective *structural* was taken from unemployment and applied to the deficit; it now means "underlying," and contrasts with *cyclical* deficits. *Structural* is applied to red ink the way "uncontrollable" is applied to expenditures. Since *hard-core* has been used as a synonym for "structural unemployment," we can expect "hard-core deficit" soon.

While this was going on, academics took up *structured* as a participle to mean "disciplined," the opposite of *permissive.* Psychologists played with *structured* in the same sense for a while, replacing it recently with *supportive environment.* In the 1970's, government bureaucrats had a field day with *structure* as a present-tense verb to mean anything from "plan" to "shape" to the ever-popular "coordinate." The word sounds important—the *r*'s and the *u*'s make a *harrumphing* sound that appeals to people who feel the need for underpinnings.

This department is determined to overlook no recent example of structure in its adjectival form. Are you feeling achy and painful? Check out *structural integration,* which Joel Homer in *Jargon* describes as "a system of deep muscle manipulation . . . supposed to reduce tension and increase body awareness." It's really a rubdown that hurts, a massage for masochists; I've tried it, and I much prefer structural unemployment.

The phrase structured programming *has been extensively used in the field of computer science for over a decade. The earliest reference that I have been able to find is a 1969 memo by Edsgar W. Dijkstra ("Notes on Structured Programming," EWD 249, Technical University of Eindhoven, The Netherlands).*

Unfortunately, structured programming does not have a universally accepted definition; as with most technical terms in computer science, each author wishing to use the phrase precisely must first define their own interpretation. Typically, the phrase is used to describe a disciplined approach to writing computer software. Many researchers have proposed realizations of such disciplines, from programming methodologies to actual linguistic constructs for programming languages. All claim their creations "support" structured programming. (How's that for redundancy!)

A computer program defines a sequence of operations to be performed by a computer. More accurately, a program defines a set of possible sequences; the sequence actually executed by the computer depends upon the data input. Each sequence is called a path *through the program. An accepted tenet of computer science is that the complexity of a program is to a large degree dependent on the complexity of the program's paths. Structured programming seeks to reduce this complexity. One way in which this may be done is to limit the possible forms of paths. "Structured" programming languages such as Pascal or Ada (the DOD's new super-language—as in the B-1B super-bomber, the M-1 super-tank, the MX super-missile, etc.) provide a basic set of building-block constructs from which "structured" paths can be fabricated. A language such as FORTRAN, on the other hand, does not provide these sorts of constructs, which often makes FORTRAN programs much more complex than their Pascal or Ada counterparts.*

One final note, the term often applied to an "unstructured" program is spaghetti code, *referring to the way in which the paths of such a program twist and turn, and hopelessly intertwine.*

Alexander L. Wolf
Amherst, Massachusetts

One of the new uses of structure *and its derivatives is in "structured programming." This describes a style of computer programming which has proven particularly effective and is now being widely adopted as the standard technique. The essential feature of structured programming is that it breaks a problem down into a series of less complex problems that can be solved by procedures having simple, easily understandable structures. The technique was originally formulated by E. W. Dijkstra; an early successful realization was in the development of a large system for* The New York Times *by IBM.*

> Mary W. Gray
> Professor of Mathematics,
>   Statistics, and Computer
>   Science
> The American University
> Washington, D.C.

Psychologists use the term Structural *to describe one of the first systems, or schools, of psychology, so-called "Structuralism." In 1898, Professor E. B. Titchener of Cornell applied the term to Wundt's brand of psychology, which was concerned with discovering the structure of mind or consciousness. (Wundt is credited as the founder of modern psychology.) The term was suggested to contrast with Functionalism, which is interested in mental functions and/or utilities.*

> W. Scott Terry, Ph.D.
> Department of Psychology
> University of North Carolina
> Charlotte, North Carolina

The use of the word structural *to mean "built-in" was already prevalent in nineteenth-century philosophy. Three individuals made use of the word* structural *in their own native languages in the manner in which it is employed today. The earliest was none other than Karl Marx, then Sigmund Freud, and finally Ferdinand de Saussure. All three of these men, lecturing before 1900, introduced the concept of structuralism into philosophic thought.*

In addition, structuralism is the dominant philosophic framework from which family therapy developed, a movement that is distinctly American in its origin and evolution. Structuralism entered the field of psychology, on the American scene, via a lecture given by Ludwig von Bertallanfy in 1945. As a result of his work and that of Gregory Bateson, structuralism entered the field of social psychiatry, which then influenced the evolving field of family therapy.

While structural *has achieved popularity in current political and economic thought, I wanted to call attention to the "backwaters" out of which the word arose.*

> William J. Hiebert
> Rock Island, Illinois

Sunny Side Up

Asked about the prospects for peace in Lebanon, President Reagan told a press conference he was "optimistic." The next day, the unseen administration official whose job it is to bring the President's vocabulary into sharper focus—akin to the fellow in the circus who follows the elephants with brush and pail—told *The New York Times* that "the President should have said he was 'hopeful' rather than 'optimistic' at his news conference." (I stubbornly use the old-fashioned *press conference*; the White House, fearing that *press* does not cover the electronic media, and eager to impress the world that the conference is a presidential device

to make *news*—not an institution belonging to the scribblers—uses *news confer-ence*. That was Ron Ziegler's only permanent victory.)

Evidently the cleanup official felt that the President had gone too far by saying he was "optimistic," and that "hopeful" was a more generalized and weaker locution. In this diplolingo, you can be hopeful for anything, but you must have some reason to be optimistic. When Al Haig was carrying the nego-tiating ball between the Brits and Argies, he found refuge in the comment "I'm always hopeful." That was supposed to mean, "Don't blame me if this doesn't work out"; the word carried the diplomatic connotation of unfounded optimism.

Such usage turns the standard synonymy on its head. According to *Webster's New Dictionary of Synonyms, hopeful* "usually implies some ground, and often reasonably good grounds, for one's having hope" and "suggests confidence in which there is little or no self-deception." *Optimistic,* on the other hand, "implies a temperamental confidence that all will turn out for the best" and even "a willingness to be guided by illusions rather than by facts."

Thus, the President was right, and his official corrector was wrong. It is as if the elephant turned around, grabbed the broom with his trunk, and started clean-ing up after the cleanup man. Perhaps diplomats should take as a mnemonic Rodgers and Hammerstein's "The Cockeyed Optimist"; optimism is an upbeat way of looking at life and not a calibration of cheerfulness based upon fact. *Hopeful* is the word with the built-in foundation. Usagists will keep a cheery eye on this battle; it may be that the diplomats will win.

A third synonym may come into greater use: *sanguine,* which implies a greater measure of optimism than *confident,* and more confidence than either *hopeful* or *optimistic.* The only trouble with *sanguine* is that it is rooted in *bloody,* and that's not the best image to use in comments about peace.

A newer word, *upbeat,* was tossed in casually above. (I don't like that use of *above*; if the newspaper has chopped this column up into horizontal bits, or jumped the paragraph to another page, *above* is silly. See below.) *Upbeat* is general cheerfulness, derived from the upward stroke of a conductor's baton indicating an unaccented beat, usually at the end of a bar. (That etymology is uncertain, since a *downbeat* usually starts the music; possibly the *up* comes from the upturned corners of the lips in a smile, and the *down* from the opposite in a glum look.) *Upbeat* is informal usage, on the way from slang to standard, and means *cheerful* or even *happy,* the most exuberant forms of optimism.

A negative note: Watch out for *positive.* This is a word of meandering mean-ing, beloved of diplomatic spokesmen. When you try to jam a battery into your ministereo ("Walkman-type," say the envious competitors of Sony), you see the plus and minus signs, indicating the positive and negative electrical poles, telling you in which way to jam the battery. It could be—and this is speculative—the "plus," symbolizing positive, reinforced the connotation of "not negative"; hence, a "positive development" is a step in the right direction. However, it may range from a baby step to a possible breakthrough.

Hopefully, we can be optimistic about the increased use of *sanguine* and the standardization of *upbeat,* but it's impossible to be positive about *positive.*

Upbeat is usually used as an adjective modifying tempo, and implies a faster tempo. To "pick up the beat" means to increase the tempo (which can be measured by the frequency of downbeats). Thus a piece or section that is upbeat has had its beat picked up. Finally, the association between a faster tempo and happier music leads to the use of the term upbeat for optimistic.

> Daniel Pitt
> Durham, North Carolina

I share your dissatisfaction with the phrase the above, *but is there a substitute most writers would unhesitatingly embrace? To eliminate the factor of page make-up (as you point out, "the above" isn't always to be found at that location), we might consider such alternatives as "the foregoing" and "the aforementioned."*

> Thomas G. Morgansen
> Jackson Heights, New York

Sweet-Talk Patrol

"Made from red ripe tomatoes, natural sweeteners . . ."

What is a "natural" sweetener? We all know what unnatural sweeteners are —saccharin and aspartame and those chemicals that are usually identified as "artificial" sweeteners.

I have a sneaking suspicion that a "natural" sweetener is that stuff that nobody with a tire around his midsection wants to know about in a list of ingredients. This department, however, is not afraid to confront the word:

Fructose. That's a natural sweetener. *"Natural sweeteners,"* says Mark Gutsche, a Del Monte spokesman, "is not table sugar or sucrose. It is a corn sweetener, which is high in fructose. Fructose, unlike sucrose, is not processed and refined; it is the natural form of sugar found in fruits and vegetables; it is natural."

Among the Lexicographic Irregulars, there is a special group that calls itself the Sweet-Talk Patrol. Just as the Squad Squad specializes in redundancies, these correspondents deal with euphemisms (like "natural sweeteners" for the unfamiliar and suspicious-sounding "fructose"). Ed Cowan, my *Times* colleague, has noted the change in White House telephone listings over the years from *chauffeur* to *driver* and most recently to *vehicle operator*. Nobody wants to let on that the White House staff is transported in cars, much less limousines.

Similarly, Paul Hampden of Ridgefield, Connecticut, has noted a radio commercial for a laundry product that uses *delicate* as a noun: "add a little to the water with your *delicates*." Not long ago, these stockings, brassieres, and diaphanous panties were called *unmentionables*; before that, *undergarments*, and before that, the horrifying or ludicrous *underwear*. (Students of dialect will recall that *delicate thins* is the name of a type of pancake; it's nice to know we have a product that can rinse off the maple syrup.)

All this heavy analysis from the label on one bottle of ketchup. It's a good thing my family won't let me read the newspaper at the table.

On "natural sweeteners," you have been had. The word natural *is used in contemporary advertising to attract those who assume anything "natural" is good and anything "processed" is bad. Ingredient listers, sometimes indulged by deregulators, avoid pejoratives. Fructose is indeed a natural sugar found in fruits. So is sucrose, which in the quantities used around the world comes from sugar cane and sugar beets and is known to all as sugar. Glucose is a sugar found in fruits almost without exception. Glucose is very natural; it is the sugar found in the bloodstream. Sugars are added to fruits to make jams and jellies and by such processing to preserve them—hence "preserves."*

Are the sugars added different from the small quantities of sugars which occur in the fruits? Not in the slightest way. Does the term natural *create a difference? Only to those prepared by promises of freedom from human frailties. For statistical purposes, the small amounts of sugars in the fruit are referred to as intrinsic. The amounts added in processing are just that.*

As to corn sweeteners, fructose and glucose are monosaccharides. Sucrose is a disaccharide. Sucrose consists of two monosaccharides chemically bound. One of them is glucose and the other fructose. All of these compounds and hundreds of others all ending in ose *make up the class of chemicals called sugars. These also belong to a more general class called carbohydrates.*

Fructose is somewhat sweeter than glucose and sucrose is therefore sweeter than glucose. This disparity used to create a regulatory problem since among sugars, sweeter was judged better and, of course, costlier. There is a fascinating anthropological chapter here. Then about twenty years ago the manufacturers of corn sweeteners learned how to change (isomerize) glucose into fructose, and as a result the regulatory restraint was lifted.

Non-nutritive or artificial "unnatural" sweeteners are another matter. Saccharin and cyclamates are chemicals with no recognized food value or common food association. Aspartame is related to amino acids, the structural units of proteins, but this does not automatically classify it as a food. The Congress extended the use of saccharin in foods after the Food and Drug Administration recommended that it be prohibited under existing law. There is a story here you will appreciate.

In 1907, Dr. Harvey Wiley, a sugar chemist who was chief of the Bureau of Chemistry at the Department of Agriculture, advised President Theodore Roosevelt that a person eating canned corn sweetened with saccharin would be deceived because he would think it contained sugar when actually he would be eating "a coal tar product" of no food value "extremely injurious to health." Roosevelt is said to have replied, "Injurious to health? My doctor gives it to me every day. Anybody who says saccharin is injurious to health is an idiot."

Thus the government approved the first non-nutritive sweetener; presumably this event established the precedent for congressional authority.

S. M. Cantor
Overbrook Hills, Pennsylvania

The last section of your essay contains some errors in interpretation because of your reliance on the definition of "natural sweeteners" by Mark Gutsche, a Del Monte spokesman. It would be better to consult a nutritionist or a carbohydrate chemist on food terminology than a food company flack; it is largely the advertising business which distorts the language with respect to food.

Aspartame and saccharine are chemically synthesized "artificial" sweeteners as you correctly define them in your essay and "natural" sweeteners are those compounds, usually sugars, synthesized by living organisms. Fructose (F) is a natural sweetener and is one half of the sucrose molecule; the other half is glucose (G). Sucrose, or common table sugar, can then be represented as G-F and as such occurs "naturally" in the juices of many plants, including sugar cane and sugar beets, from which it is commercially obtained. The refining of sucrose removes coloring matter, other impurities and undesirable flavors, and gives a product of greater than 99% purity. The residues from this refining process are known as molasses and intermediates in the process are sold as various grades of "brown" sugar.

Since fructose is considerably sweeter to our taste than glucose, efforts were made to convert glucose to fructose on a large scale. These efforts were made by the Japanese, who found a bacterium that contained an enzyme that did just this. If one starts with either 100% glucose or 100% fructose in aqueous solution, the enzyme converts either pure sugar to a 50-50 mixture of the two. The bacterium is now grown on a large scale and the enzyme is commercially available and is able to convert about 50% of the glucose in corn syrup to fructose, thereby increasing the sweetness of the product.

If Mr. Gutsche can explain how this process from starch to high fructose corn syrup makes a more "natural" sweetener than either the sugar cane or the sugar beet, I'll eat my hat, yours, and *his.*

Henry W. Kircher
Professor
Department of Nutrition and
    Food Science
University of Arizona
Tucson, Arizona

Tell It to the Marine

"I thought they taught English at the Naval Academy," writes Charles Maechling Jr. of the Carnegie Endowment for International Peace in Washington. He attached a clipping quoting a letter written by General Robert Barrow, Commandant of the Marine Corps, to the Secretary of Defense, and widely disseminated by the Pentagon.

General Barrow was complaining to his civilian chief about incidents involving United States Marines serving in Lebanon. He contended that the episodes had been "timed, orchestrated and executed for obtuse Israeli political purposes," which the Israelis promptly denied.

What did the general mean by the word *obtuse?* A Marine Corps spokesman, asked this question, replied as if by the numbers: "The letter speaks for itself." But what is the key word supposed to say?

The harassed spokesman looked up the dictionary definition: "blunt, dull, insensitive." From that, he ventured a tentative interpretation: that the Israelis had taken a bold, blunt move.

That didn't add up; a "political purpose" is a phrase that demands a modifier imputing deviousness, not dullness. Besides, the only man who knew for certain what General Barrow meant was General Barrow. I went on up the line, and a higher-level spokesman, Lieutenant Colonel Walt DeForest, sent word to the general that a language columnist wanted his definition of the word *obtuse*.

Crisp as a command barked out on a drill field came the definition from General Barrow: *Obtuse* to him meant "vague, unclear, difficult to understand."

The general may be the only one to give the word that meaning. To most of the rest of the English-speaking world, *obtuse* means "blunt and insensitive," not "vague and unclear."

My purpose was not to make fun of a brave officer who evidently had been asked, for political purposes, to write a letter to the Secretary of Defense. On the contrary, my job on this page is to be helpful. What word was he reaching for that sounds like *obtuse*?

Obscure means "vague, murky, not easily perceived"; that was part of what he had in mind, since it nicely modifies "political purposes." But the general's definition included a second meaning, as he reported to me: "hard to understand," which is not precisely the meaning of *obscure*.

For that hard-to-understand shade of meaning, we can turn to *abstruse*, which is rooted in the Latin for "to thrust away" as if to hide. That means "recondite, profound, difficult to comprehend."

I think that the head of the Marine Corps inadvertently took *obscure* ("vague") and mixed it with *abstruse* ("complicated") to come up with *obtuse*. The trouble is that *obtuse* already has a meaning, which is "insensitive," and is neither "vague" nor "hard to understand." Before using an unfamiliar word to excoriate another government, the Pentagon might try looking it up. The State Department is better at this sort of thing: It may be *obfuscatory* or *obscurantist* at times, but it is rarely obtrusive when heaping obvious obloquy.

Here is a good way to avoid confusion: *Obscure* and *abstruse* are usually applied to murky or profound *things*, and *obtuse* is ordinarily applied to an unfeeling *person.* For example, Eric Conger of New York, writing about a political coinage by my *Times* colleague Mary Cantwell, asks: "How could you resist pointing out the delicious etymological aptness of the name Cantwell, whose owner we are to credit for coining the phrase *squeal rule*? Or did you, and am I obtuse?"

He is having fun with the noun *cant*, which comes from the Latin *cantus*, meaning "song," and originally described the singsong dialect of beggars and thieves; it now refers to any insider lingo or argot, and one who uses *cant* well is apt at coining political phrases. Mr. Conger, in asking if he is being *obtuse*, wonders if his antennae missed anything.

According to *A Dictionary of Soldier Talk*, the new lexicon by Elting, Cragg and Deal, the mock-cool reaction to any military blunder is to dismiss the victims profanely "if they can't take a joke." I salute our commandant and his unique modifier for "political purposes"; in years to come, militant solecists may obscure the meaning of *obtuse*.

Permit me to add my voice to many others you will hear in defense of General Robert Barrow.

"Most of the rest of the English-speaking world" takes obtuse *to mean what* Webster's NCD *gives as "1. Not pointed or acute."*

Usage has carried the word well beyond the world of angles of plane geometry. This comment, while friendly, is intended to be pointed rather than obtuse.

> Fred McClafferty
> Stamford, Connecticut

Poor General Barrow was no doubt a victim of broken and dirty typewriter keys somewhere along the line.

My nomination for the word you seek is obfusc, *which seems most appropriate for his letter.*

> Robert S. Knox
> Rochester, New York

P.S. Since obfusc *still describes things, let's invent* obfuse *for people.*

Dear Bill:

I'd like to suggest a modification in what you say about obtuse. *Your point is of course right, but the misuse of the word was not due to its application to things when it should apply only to persons. An* obtuse *remark is correct, though* remark *is not a person. The whole business is more complicated and defies settling by simple rule-of-thumb.*

First, the literal sense of the word needs to be noted in each case. An obtuse *angle, an* obtuse *tool or weapon suggests an* obtuse *mind, which may utter an* obtuse *remark; that is, the literal quality of an object becomes a figurative mental attribute, retaining in that form the limitations of its original meaning.* Obtuse *is intransitive; it can't figuratively fit "obtuse purpose" as General Barrow wanted it to. Other figurative adjectives can do this: a* solid *piece of wood, a* solid *citizen, a* solid *purpose. But the* volatile *issue we read about is nonsense.* Volatile *(able to fly) can apply only to a mind or temper. The issue should be called* explosive, *because material things can blow up and send fragments flying.*

To sum up, the meaning of the transferred epithet must be understood first in its literal sense and then it is clear which figurative uses are possible. A rigid mind *and a* rigid purpose, *but obviously not a* rigid remark.

> Jacques [Barzun]
> Charles Scribner's Sons,
>   Publishers
> New York, New York

Your editor slugged your piece "Tell It to the Marine." D'ye know a source for this other than W. T. Sherman's second letter to John Hood in the famous scholarly exchange over Cump's order to all *residents of Atlanta to get out? The general's derision was phrased: "Talk to the Marines." See his memoirs, or Edmund Wilson's wonderful appreciation of the book in* Patriotic Gore *(in the streets of Baltimore!).*

> Maurice F.X. Donohue
> Kirby, West Virginia

While you offered several plausible (and, as usual, interesting) explanations about obtuse, *you omitted one that I recall from the vernacular of my adolescence in the '60's. At that time, one who was bright (not "brilliant") might be referred to as having an "acute mind." Conversely (and based on geometric principles), if one was dull-, not sharp-, witted, he was called "obtuse."*

> Charles R. Ragan
> San Francisco, California

General Barrow, although a learned man, is not a graduate of the Naval Academy. He is, however, a fine Marine in the true tradition of the Corps.

By publishing Mr. Maechling's remarks about the teaching of English at the Naval Academy, you have done an injustice to a fine institution. Since both of you are on the Washington scene, I would expect that someone would "check the facts" before allowing such an attack to appear in print. The Academy has survived such cheap shots before. General Kelley, now nominated to be the new Commandant of the Marine Corps, is also not a Naval Academy graduate.

> William P. Shuman, Jr.
> CDR., USN (Ret)
> Lancaster, Pennsylvania

To the Editor, The New York Times:

According to William Safire, he expended considerable effort in chasing down what I meant by the word obtuse *in my letter concerning incidents involving Israeli Defense Forces and my Marines serving in Lebanon. I accept his criticism of my use of the word.*

It is regrettable that Mr. Safire did not concurrently expend a modest effort in determining the origin of my letter. In his article, he states that I "evidently had been asked, for political purposes, to write a letter to the Secretary of Defense." On this point, he is wrong, and I would be interested in what he means by the word "evidently."

My letter to the Secretary of Defense was initiated by me alone! It offends me that anyone would purport to know or speculate that I wrote my letter at the request of any of my civilian superiors. That is not the Marine way!

> *General Robert H. Barrow*
> *Commandant of the*
> *Marine Corps*
> *Washington, D.C.*

As you probably will be told by many, your reference to the way military blunders are referred to is incorrect. The phrase is not profane but obscene. The divinity is not involved. It is, of course, "Fuck them if they can't take a joke."

> *David Irish*
> *Washington, D. C.*

Terrific Honorific

Where you stand on the use of *Ms.* usually reflects where you stand on feminism.

The earliest spotting of that term was on a 1767 gravestone in Plymouth, Massachusetts ("Here lies Interrd the body of Ms. Sarah Spooner"). That early usage—perhaps by an absent-minded chiseler—was reborn in the late 1960's as a blend of *Mrs.* and *Miss.*

Ordinarily, *Ms.* would not deserve a period, since it is not the abbreviation of a longer word; however, its partial derivation from *Mrs.* is the source of its period. In Britain, when the noun or honorific is used, most users eschew the period, but a writer for *The Times* of London goes further, denouncing the entire attempt as one of the excesses of the women's movement.

"This is a rallying point for common sense," wrote Trevor Fishlock, a name I have not made up, when *The Times*'s stylebook banished the title. "It is artificial, ugly, silly, means nothing and is rotten English. It is a faddish, middle-class plaything, and far from disguising the marital status of women, as is claimed, it draws attention to it. It is a vanity."

Phyllis Schlafly, who organized the opposition to the equal rights amendment,

rejects it also: "When the women's movement made it a piece of its jargon in the late 1960's," she says, "at that point it became an irritation and offensive to people like me."

At *The New York Times,* where the honorifics *Mr., Mrs., Messrs.* are insisted upon as a sign of respect, the stylebook has not accepted the new term: "Ms. As an honorific, use it only in quoted matter, in

letters to the editor and, in news articles, in passages discussing the term itself."
(That is how we get to use a great many taboo words in this space.)*

Ms. is the name of a magazine. One of the editors, Gloria Steinem, says, "Polls
show that one-third of American women use it as an option. Its presence in the
language is an important option for women. It allows us to be identified as
individuals."

Some have leapfrogged the issue, rejecting not only *Ms.* but all the other
honorifics as well. "We never use *Miss, Mrs.,* or *Ms.,*" says Wendy Crisp, editor
of *Savvy,* an excellent magazine about women in business. "We use first and last
names, and in subsequent references use only the last name. We use *Mr.* for men
to acknowledge a gender difference."

Halfway through that last quote, I had the urge to write the words "adds Miss
Crisp." But that would be wrong, because I don't know her marital status. So would
"adds Wendy Crisp," because it is a "subsequent reference" and the repetition
of the first name seems awkward. What about "adds Crisp"? Too crisp. "Adds Ms.
Crisp"? That seems about the best way out in this case, even though she drops
the *Ms.* in her publication; she would use the *Mr.* on me.

In the past, my judgment has come down against the *Ms.* because it fuzzes
up the clear information about marital history in *Miss* and *Mrs.* To the angry
riposte that men have no such marital distinction—*Mr.* covers both married man
and bachelor—I have replied that I wish we had. Ambrose Bierce wrote that
Miss/Missis/Mister "are the three most disagreeable words in the language.
. . . If we must have them, let us be consistent and give one to the unmarried men.
I venture to suggest *Mush,* abbreviated *Mh.*" (Good idea, didn't catch on; neither
did *Ex-Mrs.,* my more recent idea to identify divorcées, because of the confusion
with Christmas.)

But, as what *Cosmopolitan* editor Helen Gurley Brown calls "nonmilitant
feminism" takes hold, we should pause to reconsider the resistance to *Ms.* Is the
function of language solely to convey information, or should it be to conceal as
well? The computer and the credit card, in conjunction with a new immigration
act, are ushering us into an age of systematic invasions of privacy; a national
identity card seems around the corner. Under this threat, can individuals not strike
back in some way to say to the Nosy Parkers of this world, "None of your business"?

Since men can preserve their privacy with *Mr.,* why can't women with *Ms.?*

I feel myself coming around. Mrs. Schlafly has a good rule: "I believe in calling
people what they like to be called. I'm willing to address Betty Friedan as Ms.
Friedan." That seems sensible enough; an honorific is meant to honor, not to
annoy.

As for me—if anybody wants to sign herself "Ms.," I'll address her as "Ms."
If she deliberately obscures her marital history by using only a first and last name,

*Friday, June 20, 1986, will be remembered as a major milestone on the road to linguistic freeedom:
On that date, *The New York Times* announced its intention to use the honorific *Ms.* in both news
articles and editorials.

I will respect her wish: "Dear Wendy Crisp," I'll write, savvily, and in subsequent reference—the toughest decision—I'll write, "adds Ms. Crisp," leaving it to stylebook-bound copy editors to change it to "adds the executive" or "she added" or "according to the source mentioned above." Not for me to assign my correspondents unwanted honorifics or to penetrate their veils: I love a Ms-tery.

I was living in Hollywood, California, when I received my first piece of mail addressed to "Ms." early in the 1960s. It was an unsolicited letter. Since that date I've been the recipient of much other similar mail—now come to be called "junk."

I resented that first "Ms." I figured if a company or organization had gone to the expense of soliciting my purchase and/or support, the least they could have done was go a few more thousand dollars in their expensive campaign and determine if that initials-only name in the phone book was Mr., Mrs., or Miss. I felt then, and still do, that it's a coward's way out. I favor—in such mail—being addressed as "Dear J. E. Davis" to the alternative "Ms." I've always used my maiden name before, during, and after marriage. Ergo: neither "Mrs." or "Miss" is appropriate in my case.

> *Jeanne Davis*
> *Westport, Connecticut*

Your commentary on the use of "Ms." ignores one of the most essential functions of that title: to refer to a married woman who has not adopted her husband's surname. I ceased to be Miss Fabricant when I married Mr. Homer; but it would hardly be accurate to call me Mrs. Fabricant, as that title describes the wife of Mr. Fabricant. Without Ms., I would be forever relegated to the ranks of the untitled!

> *Judith Fabricant*
> *Brookline, Massachusetts*

I do not consider Ms. to be a product of current feminist thought, as I can remember being addressed that way, in business mail, as early as 1961. The term may have appeared in secretarial manuals long before it gained wider usage.

Ms. makes sense to me because:

(1) As a girl, my name was Nancy Norton, to be formally addressed as Miss Nancy Norton.

(2) When I married, I became Mrs. Owen Mason.

(3) After divorce, according to etiquette, my name should be Mrs. Norton Mason (combining maiden and married names). This seems too formal, for most

purposes, and too confusing as well. To use Mrs. *Nancy Mason is improper because* Mrs. *cannot precede a feminine name; it must be attached to a male. What to do? For a woman of 40 or so, going back to* Miss *sounds spinsterish and, if she has a bunch of children, inappropriate.*

Ms. *is derived not so much from* Miss *or* Mrs. *as it is from the old original,* Mistress, *in its primary definition: "a woman having authority or ownership; the female head of a family." As such, it is just right for a growing number of women.*

> Nancy N. Mason
> Evanston, Illinois

P.S. I could address you as Master *William Safire if you were under 13 years of age. Perhaps* Miss *should have the same cutoff date, all others being* Ms. *until they choose to become* Mrs.

Whenever I read a discussion of the term Ms., *I am surprised that no one mentions its advantage for female owners of androgynous names. Granted, not many women can claim to be named after their grandfathers, as I was, but more than a few are the victims of whimsical parents who bestow male names on them.*

For reasons I have never fathomed, my parents chose to name me after my paternal grandfather, Sydney. *Once married, I discovered the difficulty of identifying myself perspicuously by mail. If I signed my name "Mrs. Sydney Pressman," unknown correspondents assumed my husband's name to be "Sydney." If I signed my name "Sydney Pressman," I was sure to receive a reply addressed to Mr. Sydney Pressman—and this at a time when being a woman might give one an edge on getting a job or publishing a research paper. Then along came* Ms. *and the relief of finally having at hand a form of address to identify me as a female. And certainly knowing that a person is a female is as important as knowing that that person is married!*

So, in the future, when you discuss Ms. *with your linguist friends, remember us unfortunate females whose parents named us Sydney, or Willie, or Quentin, or. . . .*

> Ms. Sydney Pressman
> Schenectady, New York

I'm divorced after a 25-year marriage and I have two adult children. I'm not Mrs. *any more and I feel uncomfortable with* Miss. *(I'm not Lauren Bacall.)*

Ms. *works for me and I'm delighted to have you on my side.*

> (Ms.) Joyce Mendelsohn
> Forest Hills, New York

You write, and I quote (v. tr.), "Halfway through that last quote, I had the urge to write. . . ."

For years I've insisted that my students not use quote as a noun. Eighty-five percent of the Usage Panel of The American Heritage Dictionary *considers quote as a substitute for* quotation *unacceptable in writing.*

I wish you'd start a file of this usage and do a piece on it in a future column. It's probably a losing battle to fight this particular infelicity. I find its use widespread among English professors.

Perhaps you might even be willing, upon mature consideration, to make a quote *contrite* unquote *statement about your use (i.e., misuse) of the term.*

> *Samuel N. Bogorad*
> *Professor Emeritus*
> *Department of English*
> *University of Vermont*
> *Burlington, Vermont*

NOTE FROM W.S.: *Quote* is now a noun and is an acceptable alternative to *quotation*. The 20th edition of Bartlett's, in the twenty-first century, will be known as *Bartlett's Quotes.*

Dear Bill—

In re: the use of that dreadful "Ms."—when it was first slammed down on us —by the aggressive feminists and, I suspect, the public relations account which handles the magazine MS., *I had a rubber stamp made—which I use.*

> *Mail Addressed to Me as "Ms."*
> *Will Not Be Accepted.*
> *Return to Sender.*

I resent this unauthorized (by me) use of Ms. *Even if I were not a married woman, I'd resent it—I am a married woman, not an embryonic book!*

> *Irene [Corbally Kuhn]*
> *New York, New York*

You say that the identity card seems around the corner. I would suggest that it is already here. Try to do something without showing a driver's license. It is needed almost as much as the internal passport in Communist countries.

> *Ralph Slovenko*
> *Professor of Law and Psychiatry*
> *Wayne State University*
> *Detroit, Michigan*

You might be interested to know that I received more than 200 letters in response to my piece in The Times, *about 20 from people in Britain and the rest from people in the United States. About three quarters of those were a furious attack on my observations. Half a dozen were obscene. The rest were thanks for making a stand against what their writers generally described as a tyranny. What impressed me, of course, was the reaction from the United States to a small piece in a foreign newspaper, while the reaction in my own country was relatively muted.*

Trevor Fishlock
South Asia Correspondent
The Times
New Delhi, India

P.S. I noted that you said you had not invented my name. In terms of oddity in nomenclature Fishlock and Safire, it seems to me, are in the same glass house!

Ms. is a bastardized, mongrelized, homogenizing, unpronounceable, non-descript nonsense syllable which some 5 percent of American women have had the gall to attempt to foist on the rest. Accepted by an unmarried woman, it may well indicate an ambiguity which she perhaps hopes will be considered indicative of the married state. Accepted by a married woman, it arouses doubts as to her satisfaction with that state. Women in countries with cultures similar to ours have no hang-ups about being addressed as "Madame/Mademoiselle," "Señora/Señorita," "Frau/Fraulein," and the like. They feel neither degraded nor threatened by such titles. That Webster's Eighth Collegiate Dictionary *(1973) includes* Ms. *indicates nothing more than that its editorial staff is as vulnerable to a compulsion to be with it as are others who subscribe to the delusion that any change is* ipso facto *for the better.*

In fact, having clearly signed my name as "(Miss) Belle Schiller," I expected the courtesy of being so addressed.

(Miss) Belle Schiller
New York, New York

That Icy Tingle

Tammy Wynette, the country singer, was the star performer at a White House South Lawn barbecue for friendly congressmen. She belted out her theme song, "Stand By Your Man," with her arm around the President of the United States —demonstrating how to stand by one's man.

Asked later how he felt during the entire experience, Mr. Reagan replied gallantly, "I had goosebumps."

An icy tingle crept along my skin when I saw that response in print: Could it be that the President was using a euphemism? That roughened condition of the skin caused by the erection of papillae is usually called *goose-pimples*—was *goosebumps* a way of saying the same word without the ugly *pimples*?

No. *Goosebumps* is a word traced by Mitford Mathews in his *Dictionary of Americanisms* to 1867, a variant of *gooseflesh,* probably first used in 1810 by the English poet Samuel Taylor Coleridge. The words denote in humans what is often called *horripilation* in animals—a bristling of the hairs in fear or anger—which shares a root with *horrible.* Humans experience what Johnny Mercer, in "That Old Black Magic," called "those icy fingers up and down my spine," caused by cold, fear, sexual excitement, patriotic fervor, or gustatory anticipation.

Curiously, the most frequently used word—

goosepimples—does not have an early citation. Etymology fails us on this score, but dialect geography comes through with evidence of what that deliciously creepy feeling is called throughout the United States.

"*Goosepimples* is by far the most common response, with *goosebumps* being offered about half as frequently" reports Joan Hall, associate editor of *DARE*, the *Dictionary of American Regional English,* the first volume of which was published in the fall of 1985. "*Gooseflesh* comes in a distant third." No geographic distinction shows itself, but older people tend to say *gooseflesh,* while younger people lean toward *goosebumps,* an observation that Mr. Reagan's demographic advisers will be glad to note.

Joan Hall makes *gooseflesh* a single word, and uses two words for *goosepimples* and *goosebumps*; other lexicographers differ. Here comes my decision on the one-word versus two-word controversy on gooseflesh-related matters (and issuing these *diktats* always gives me a chilly thrill): In each case, use one word. All three variants are collectives—nobody ever gets one goosebump, although a native speaker would say "*gooseflesh* is" and "*goosepimples* are."

Lexicographic Irregulars across the country are going to read this and say, "Why, that city boy is talkin' about *chicken skin.* Or *duck bumps, thrill bumps, chilly bumps, turkey bumps.* Or he's fixin' to say he's *about to sprout feathers.* Or he's got *prickles, pins and needles, French knots, eggerbumps, ash spots, white measles,* or *chill bugs.*"

As Tammy Wynette would sing, giving Mr. Reagan a tingle-inducing squeeze: Stand by your dialect, man.

My use of goosepimples *was once denounced by a European publisher as crude Americanese. When I researched the subject I found that* goosepimples *(euphemized* goosebumps) *is indeed an Americanism. Indo-European and Finno-Ugrian languages I am familiar with avoid* -pimples *and stick to* -flesh (-skin).

*According to Mencken (*Amerlang, *Suppl. I, 505)* goosepimple *is a "characteristic Americanism" not used by speakers of British English, who prefer to say* chicken-flesh.

> Leslie C. Tihany
> Fort Thomas, Kentucky

That Which Hunt

This is the last time I am going to take a crack at *that* versus *which.*

In describing the Book-of-the-Month Club as "an organization which has done much to spread literacy and culture," I spread illiteracy and solecism.

The reason I confuse *which* with *that* is that my mind is cluttered with terminology like "restrictive versus nonrestrictive clauses," and with unhelpful rules of thumb like *"which* refers to things, *that* to persons or things." To clean the slate in my personal thought processor (that's what I now call my mind), I am putting "transfer" next to that old thought and pushing my "command" button.

All gone! Fresh start.

Some clauses *define* words, the way adjectives do, and like adjectives, become intimate parts of the words they define; these defining clauses take *that.* (Remember: Defining clauses say, "Take *that!*")

Other clauses stand by themselves; if removed from the sentence, they would stand as sentences themselves. Since they are slipped in like parenthetical remarks (this is the way to slip in a parenthetical remark), we can call them *parenthetical clauses.* (Remember: Parenthetical clauses say, "Say *which?*")

Now to dazzle ourselves with illuminating examples.

Here is a defining clause: "The distinction *that we are drawing here* is worthwhile." In that sentence, *that we are drawing here* defines "distinction." The clause has no independent life; if you said to somebody, "That we are drawing here," you'd get a funny look and deserve it.

Here is a parenthetical clause: "The distinction, *which is worthwhile,* is what we are drawing here." In that sentence, *which is worthwhile,* crying out to be separated from the rest of the sentence by commas or parentheses or—which is even more dramatic—dashes, is obviously a free spirit of a thought. It is also capable of standing by itself; say, "Which is worthwhile" out loud in public a few times; few of your friends will argue.

I know a warlock grammarian who never mixes up his *thats* and *whiches*; his theory is: "If it hollers for a comma, it's a *which.*"

Thank you for your explanation of the rule concerning that *and* which, *which I've never applied correctly more than half of the time. I had a teacher in school who used to declare, "You never have a naked* which!" *He was referring, of course, to the comma business. I also remember the old pedant saying, "There is nothing inherently beautiful, gentlemen, about the naked human body." So while I could never figure out which to use,* that *or* which, *I've always known which one to clothe.*

Tracy Kidder
The Atlantic Monthly
Boston, Massachusetts

My private mnemonic device for keeping that *and* which *straight is "The house that Jack built." It is clearly unthinkable to say "The house* which *Jack built," and even less thinkable to say "This is the dog* which *worried the cat* which *killed the rat* which *ate the malt* which. . . ." *So I just think of the nursery rhyme, and that tells me which word is* which, *and that's* that.

R. E. Bell
Montreal, Quebec

This Bud's on Me

When common usage makes a change for the worse—toward fuzziness, away from precision—we can put up a fight for a while.

"I have recently noticed an increase in the use of *burgeoning debts,*" writes Andrew Chant of the Toronto-Dominion Bank, after chastising me for insisting on the spelling of *judgment* without a middle *e.* "To *burgeon* is to sprout. The growth implied in *burgeoning debts* is that of *mushrooming.*"

Jacques Barzun, in Follett's *Modern American Usage,* agrees; he puts the misuse of *burgeon* under malapropisms: "To *burgeon* means to put out buds; figuratively to come out in a small, modest, hopeful way, not to spread out, blossom and cover the earth."

Growing is a good, general term; getting specific, you can say something is *nascent,* just coming into being, or *burgeoning,* getting under way and budding nicely, or *mushrooming,* growing like hell. Don't let the words slop over each other.

My banker correspondent provides a nice distinction: "My savings account burgeons; my charge accounts mushroom."

Time Out Twice

"Our first-period English class," writes Matt Ritchie of New Haven (Indiana) Junior High, probably with Mrs. Donald Steiner, his teacher, jabbing a piece of chalk in his back, "recently ran into a controversy over whether the plural for *timeout* was *timesout* or *timeouts.* We would like you to tell us: Which is the correct plural?"

The best way to make a compound noun plural is to add the *s* to the most important part of the noun. For example, in *attorney general,* the key noun is *attorney,* and the *general* modifies it; therefore, the plural is *attorneys general.* In *lieutenant general,* the *lieutenant* modifies the key word, *general*—so the plural is *lieutenant generals.* Same thing with *courts-martial, poets laureate,* and *girlfriends* —since the *court,* the *poet,* and the *friend* are central, those words get the *s*. On that theory, Professor Ron Butters wrote in this space, while I was lying fallow, that he preferred *Eggs McMuffin,* pointing to the analogy of *eggs Benedict* and *oysters Rockefeller.*

Similarly, any mother-in-law will tell you that her motherhood is most important: That's why we have *mothers-in-law.* When we expand that to *in-laws* in general, we make plural the *law,* which dominates the *in.* The rule is fairly understandable: Pick out the key word and add the *s* to that.

What do you do when a compound noun has no word that stands out as obviously the most important? With a *forget-me-not* or a *ne'er-do-well,* tack the *s* on the end. When in doubt, most lexicographers and even most usagists would agree with Dolores Harris, an editor of Houghton Mifflin's *American Heritage Dictionary:* "On the whole, except for special cases such as *mother-in-law,* the pluralization of hyphenated words occurs at the end of the word." She said a mouthful, or two mouthfuls.

Booze blurs these distinctions. Strictly speaking, you should order *gins and tonic,* but few people do; most *teen-agers* will say, "Two rye and ginger ales," as *grown-ups* growl. I prefer "two bourbons on the rocks" because of the awkward double plural of "two bourbon on the rockses," and to show my friends that I practice good grammar even while getting sloshed.

All that suggests *timeouts.* But let us see what is happening in the real world: The National Basketball Association doesn't go along with this modern, permissivist dribbling. Says Liz Kubec, the hoopsters' flack, "The N.B.A. pluralizes *timeout* as *timesout.*" That's official.

In baseball, the question is scorned for its false premise. "Baseball does not have a *timeout,*" reports Katy Feeney, a press agent for the National League. "There is only *time,* which, according to the handbook of the National League, is the announcement by the umpire of the legal interruption of play, during which the ball is dead."

In hockey and football, however, the word from the officials is that the plural is *timeouts.* They have as little right to say which is correct as the woman jumping center for the basketballers, but common usage is on their side. That's what the fans say. As for the confused football quarterback, can you imagine him saying, "How many timesout have I remaining?" No; the usage is "How many timeouts do I have left, for God's sake?"

Go with *timeouts,* Matt. That's my judgment call. (No; it's either my *call* or my *judgment,* never my *judgment call.*)

I'm sorry to report that your judgment may have been a bit askew when you eschewed the phrase "judgment call." In baseball there is a definite distinction between a judgment call and what might be referred to as a "rules interpretation call." A game cannot be protested if an umpire is believed to have erred on a judgment call—that is, on whether or not a pitch was in the strike zone, whether or not a runner was tagged out, etc. However, if an umpire is believed to have made a mistake in interpreting the rules, a manager can submit a protest to the league office and, if the protest is upheld, the game will be replayed from the point at which it was protested.

For example, if a batted ball hits a base runner before it has passed an infielder other than the pitcher, the runner is out, the ball is dead, and the hitter is awarded first base (to stand on, not to take home with him). This situation came up in a game between the Boston Red Sox and Toronto Bluejays about three years ago:

With a Toronto runner on first base, a ball was hit between first and second. The first baseman made a futile dive for the ball, which hit the runner. The first base umpire immediately signaled that the runner was out. The Toronto manager came out to argue, and the home plate umpire (who is umpire-in-chief ex officio) joined in. The manager argued that the first base umpire had made an error in interpreting the rules—that, since the ball had gone past the first baseman, the runner could not be called out. The umpire-in-chief agreed and overruled his colleague, which he's entitled to do in a case of this sort. However, the first base umpire now explained that, in his judgment, the first baseman and the runner were on the same line between first and second base when the ball hit the runner and, therefore, the ball had not gone past the first baseman. This changed his call from a rules interpretation call to a judgment call; the umpire-in-chief did not overrule him, after all; and, although the Toronto manager announced that he would protest the decision, he didn't. (And, if he had, it would have been overruled.)

So not all calls are judgment calls—at least, not in baseball.

Ralph Hickok
author, New Encyclopedia of
Sports
New Bedford, Massachusetts

Am defending a "judgment call," as different from a "rules call"—seems right for the umpire's opinion and signal that Mookie is safe at first—he might have been out on an infield fly, or at second on a ground-rule double.

E.M.Y.
(Mrs. Richard G. Tilt)
Ridgewood, New Jersey

Tired Couples

As a grimly responsible political journalist, I telephoned a target of an intended harangue and asked politely if a story I had been given was true. He shouted, "No!" and hung up. I dutifully ran the charge and his denial, with the words ". . . but he flatly denies that."

Joseph Hixson, a former colleague at the New York *Herald Tribune,* wrote to object to the *flatly.* He recalled that a copy editor once axed that adverb out of his copy, with a gruff "He denied it, right?"

"I found myself unable to tell him how one could deny more than deny—i.e., flatly," ruminated Mr. Hixson. "A friend who's served on a news copy desk suggested that 'flatly' means 'categorically.' But I shrewdly riposted that 'categorically' might refer to a series of accusations to which an all-encompassing denial was being applied. Put it that the copy editor at the *Trib* smelled a 'very unique' and was determined to squash that. Plaintiff rests."

Sounds like a job for the Nitpickers' Patrol. Sorry, Joe: *Flatly denied* is not redundant, the way *very unique* is. The *flatly* is a legitimate intensifier, adding zip to the denial. (To say "he flat-out denied that" is a mistake, however; *flat-out* is derived from auto racing, when the accelerator pedal is pressed flat to the floor, and means "maximum effort." It should not be confused with the simple *flatly,* which means "without reservation or equivocation.")

But the query got me to thinking: Why "flatly denied"? Why not "roundly denied"? The answer—and this is what the old copy editor may have had in mind —is that "flatly" and "denied" is a tired couple, often rightly derided as "wedded words."

John Scott Fones of New York recently sent me a list of words that lean on each other, and are not often used alone. They include: *shirk / responsibility; shorn / locks; blithering / idiot; caught / red-handed; gird / loins; brazen / hussy.* No more flat denials or grimly responsibles from me, although those who nitpick have unmitigated gall.

Tyger, Tyger, Burning

When Elizabeth Dole, our new Transportation Secretary, was working in the White House a year ago, reports flew about Washington that she was West Wing window dressing, less than influential. At the time, James Baker, the chief of staff, scoffed at those reports in this way: "Elizabeth Dole has one of the toughest jobs here. She has excellent political judgment and is extremely bright."

He meant well. To many people, *bright* is a compliment when applied to a person, a synonym for "smart, clever, mentally quick." Rooted in the Old English word for "gleaming" or "white," the sparkling-clean term is often intended to please the person so described.

But as used today, *bright* has a connotation that dictionaries have not yet caught. When you are asked to say something nice about a fellow who is not *brilliant,* you call him "bright"; it is an almost-compliment that says more about what it fails to say than what it says. When applied to a child, the word is unfailingly upbeat—everyone wants to have a bright child, eager and able to learn —but when applied to an adult, *bright* carries a subtle put-down.

The meaning is "less thoughtful than *intelligent,*" "far less profound than *wise,*" and, as noted above, "less bright than *brilliant.*" *To have the smarts* is to possess an innate feel for what is the profitable thing to do, but *to be bright* is to stand there with eyes wide, tail wagging, head cocked alertly, awaiting the sunshine of a mentor's wisdom.

Bright is to an intelligent adult what *cop* is to a policeman and *pol* is to a politician. It rubs the wrong way and feints with damned praise.

You have done the fine descriptive word bright *a great disservice. It is possible that insular Washington thinks it has large quantities of brilliant people but most assuredly the voters are not quite that confident. We reserve* brilliant *for the occasional Super Nova among us. In chess tournaments brilliancy prizes are regularly withheld because even the grandmasters have been insufficiently spectacular.*

I, for one, feel that brilliant *requires demonstrable proof of extraordinary performance beyond expectations. Super Nova is a particularly apt analogy in the case of artists whose brilliance is recognized posthumously.*

Intelligent is an amorphous word covering a wide range of values—are there intelligent forms of life in outer space? What is the level of intelligence of a chimpanzee? While most of us probably use intelligent *to cover average or better than average it hardly seems to be clearly superior in many uses.*

Bright is not used as a short form of bright-eyed and bushy-tailed as you seem to indicate, but rather as the opposite of dull (-witted).

Frank E. Nothaft
New York, New York

My colleagues and I find your comments on bright *odd. In our corner of academe, at least,* bright *is still considered high praise. In reading letters of recommendation for doctoral candidates, we look for the word, and we don't find it as often as we would like.*

You cite no authority, and neither do we. Nonetheless, in an occupation in which brightness is rarely enough encountered, brilliance is indeed rare. To hear someone described this way virtually automatically leads us to question the describer as well as the described.

If, however, bright *has dimmed, this would lead us to suggest that the language has become overwhelmed by hype. If anything less than brilliance is damning by faint praise, we have lost a useful, and to us at least, still rare enough, compliment. Meanwhile, we will still couple the word with "not too" (the meaning of that is clear enough), with "enough" (our faint—very faint—praise), and with "very," the latter reserved for folk whom the more effusive might call brilliant.*

> *D. Charles Whitney*
> *Research Assistant Professor*
> *College of Communications*
> *University of Illinois*
> *Champaign, Illinois*

You're correct in calling bright *a put-down. But you missed the heart of the matter:* Bright *is what men call a brilliant woman.*

Many men will call another man brilliant *if he made it through college with a B average. But they'll call the woman who ranked second in her class of 1600 "a bright girl." If the woman wears a Phi Beta Kappa key, these same men will ask her whose it is.*

> *Marie Shear*
> *Brooklyn, New York*

Under Covert

The moment has come to penetrate the mystery surrounding the pronunciation of the most secret word in the language. Whether you are for or against covert action in Nicaragua—whether you are pro-Sandinist or contra-Contra—you have to break into the open with the way to say *covert.*

When linguists speak of "covert classes" of words, they are groping for ways

to tie words together that will bring about some insight into the structure of speech. Most linguists pronounce the word as dictionaries indicate is preferred: "CUHV-ert," with the first syllable rhyming with a hard *shove*.

For example, when Allen Walker Read recently gave a paper on "The Criteria for a Class of Jocular Words in English" at Arizona State University, he made a valiant effort to find a covert class in the lexicon of funny words. *Pixilated*, a word first spotted in 1848 to mean "eccentric," now defined as "kooky," came from the English *pixie-led*. The familiar *dingbat*, popularized on television's *All in the Family*, was first spotted by Professor Read in an 1838 reference to an alcoholic beverage. Another deliberately humorous word was *hugeacious*, coined by the Canadian author Thomas Haliburton in 1843 and since replaced by *humongous*.

The professor with *pizazz* soberly dissected Western jocularisms like *discombobulate, hornswoggle,* and *lalapalooza*; he came to the conclusion that no covert class could be found in the lingo of humorous exaggeration: "We can best enjoy the flowering of the play spirit by leaving it in its untrammeled, untidy state." (His students promptly absquatulated.)

In breaking my head over Read's "covert classes," I was struck by the fact that linguists and regular people are pronouncing the same word differently. The tribe of philologists says "CUHV-ert," while most people who buy dictionaries say "COH-vert." How come?

The first pronunciation—still preferred in most dictionaries—is the same as *cover: uh,* not *oh.* But when congressional committees vote on denying covert aid to opponents of the Sandinists in Nicaragua, all the newscasters pronounce the word as if they were in *clover.* "This is a 'spelling pronunciation,'" says Dr. Fred Cassidy of *DARE.* "No native speaker would say COH-ver for *cover,* or LOH-ver for *lover,* nor *glove* to rhyme with *stove.*"

What has brought about the hush-hush switch? (Those of you who internally pronounce words while silently reading will have trouble with *hush-hush switch.*) Karl V. Teeter, professor of linguistics at Harvard, points to *covert*'s antonym, *overt,* pronounced like *over* with a *t* added, and explains: "It is not uncommon in languages that words which occur in antonymous pairs influence each other in pronunciation, a principle named 'lexical polarization' by Yakov Malkiel." Those words at sword's point become like each other, same as fierce political enemies. "When, and only when," says Professor Teeter, "*covert* is used in the sense opposed to that of *overt,* a secondary pronunciation develops—COH-vert, in mimicry of OH-vert."

Now the secondary pronunciation has taken over. "Heard COH-vert again this morning," reports the ever-cheerful Dr. Cassidy, from somewhere out in the field. "Several speakers. Nobody pronounced it any other way." That confirms my independent research with one of the great experts of spook-speak, Richard Helms, former director of Central Intelligence. "It's always been pronounced COH-vert, as opposite in meaning to OH-vert, with us," he says, adding that this opinion about pronunciation does not constitute an admission of anything that may or may not have taken place in the past.

Up the Down Staircase

When a vivid metaphor is used against you, think twice about using a metaphor in response. Critics of an immigration bill that may pose a danger to privacy have charged that the bill leads down a "slippery slope." I have long sought the originator of that doubly alliterative phrase, to no avail; the locution is effective both in law and in political argument.

An example of the round-heeled response was provided by Wyoming Senator Alan Simpson: "There is no 'slippery slope' toward loss of liberties," argued the

Republican author of the Senate bill, and then plunged headfirst down the meta-phoric drain: "only a long staircase where each step downward must first be tolerated by the American people and their leaders."

Somehow, a long staircase downward is not a figure of speech that makes for a spirited defense. The argument calls for firmer footing. Before executing his riposte, the senator might recall American folklorist H. W. Thompson's line: "There is a slippery step at every man's door."

You wrote that "slippery slope" is doubly alliterative. Not so! Alliteration, as it is defined by all reputable lexicons, is the sequential repetition of similar sounds or letters at the beginning *of words. If you mean to include the letter* p *as the partner in the putative double alliteration, you are slovenly sloppy in putting* p*'s in a position put aside for primary letters.*

> *Robert M. Richter, M.D.*
> *Brooklyn, New York*

NOTE FROM W.S.: Merriam-Webster, a reputable producer of lexicons, says that alliteration *usually* involves initial consonants.

Use or Lose

There hasn't been a solid, imperative piece of folk wisdom offered in Washington since Bert Lance's "If it ain't broke, don't fix it."

Now we may have one. Secretary of State George P. Shultz, whose only previous metaphorical leap was to apply the nautical "Steady as you go" to eco-nomic policy, came up with a "saying" to describe the need for the P.L.O. to "exercise constructively" its authority to speak for the Palestinian people.

"We have a saying around here," Mr. Shultz told a press conference. " 'Use it or lose it.' "

Phrasedicks at the Library of Congress were able to come up with a statement of Jean de La Fontaine, a seventeenth-century French author and hedonist, fre-quently used by lawyers: "Use alone constitutes possession."

Most researchers point to a bureaucratic origin: If money is not spent by an agency in a given budget period, it must be returned to the Treasury or otherwise not expended. Thus, if a September 30 deadline faces a bureaucrat, he may say to a subordinate, "Use it or lose it."

This could be a big one. The entire Phrasedick Brigade is hereby alerted; early citations, especially in print, are sought.

Henry Ford, in a New York Times *interview on Nov. 8, 1931, said, "Money is like an arm or a leg—use it or lose it."*

> Representative Ivan Swift
> House Education and Labor
> Committee
> Washington, D.C.

You're showing your youth. When you get to be my age (66) you'll use the expression Use it or lose it *to apply to both male and female reproductive organs. Ask your doctor.*

Good luck in your old age.

> Richard M. Lederer, Jr.
> White Plains, New York

Your request for early citations of "Use it or lose it" immediately brings to mind Goethe, Faust *I, lines 682 to 685:*

> Was du ererbt von deinen Vätern hast,
> Erwirb es, um es zu besitzen.
> Was man nicht nützt, ist eine schwere Last;
> Nur was der Augenblick erschafft, das kann er nützen.

Loosely translated:

> *What you have inherited from your ancestors*
> *You must first earn in order to own it.*
> *What you don't utilize is a heavy burden;*
> *Only what the moment creates, it can use.*

According to Büchmann's Geflügelte Worte, *William A. Cooper believes it likely that the thought was borrowed from a letter dated October 25, 1518, written by Ulrich von Hutten to Willibald Pirkheimer. In the* Wolfenbütteler Ausgabe *by Burckhard of 1717, page 41, it reads:*

> Sed quidquid horum est, proprium non habemus,
> nisi nostris quibusdam meritis illud nobis conciliemus.

Goethe's translation is in Wahrheit und Dichtung, *part 4, 17, book and ending:*

> Aber, was auch deren Wert sei, ist nicht unser eigen,
> wenn wir es nicht durch Verdienste erst eigen machen.

Again freely translated:

> *Whatever its value may be, it is not our possession,*
> *unless we are making it our own through efforts.*

Fred R. Homburger
Lancaster, Pennsylvania

Son John Todd—dairy farm hand and Chinese-speaking, ancient philosopher buff
—discovered that the most important man in the history of Confucianism after its
founder is Meng Tzu, or Mencius (372–289 B.C.), who has been traditionally
regarded by the Chinese people as their Second Sage. Mencius mentioned that: "See
and you will find them, neglect and you will lose them" (Wm. T. De Bary, et al.,
Sources of Chinese Tradition, *Vol. I, Columbia University Press, 1960).*

Charles C. Todd, Jr.
Chester, Virginia

I want to complain about your characterization of La Fontaine as a hedonist with
the implication that that was all he was. I think if you had remembered La Fontaine
(despite the soft life he had) as one of the great masters of French writing and a
fabulous fabulist you would have traced the origin of "Use it or lose it."

In any case "L'usage seulement fait la possession" is the first line of Vol. IV
Fable XX of La Fontaine's Fables *("The Miser Who Lost His Treasure"). This*
is Fable 225 ("The Miser") in Perry's Aesopica, *and as translated by Lloyd Daly*
(1961) in Aesop Without Morals.

*There is a similar thought in Montaigne (*Essays *I, 42), roughly that it is*
"enjoying, not possessing, that makes us happy," which is followed by a citation
from Horace. The emphasis here, however, is on the ability to enjoy possessions
conferred by good health and self-confidence, not on "Use it or lose it" as in La
Fontaine or Aesop.

Sanford L. Segal
Rochester, New York

The Vanishing Haircut

Thirty years ago, at the bar of the old Hotel Vesuvio in Naples, I asked deported gangster Charles (Lucky) Luciano how he spent his time. The international vice overlord replied: "I get up in the mornin', I go to the barber, I go to the track and the day is shot."

That was in another era. The title of *international vice overlord* has been retired, along with *rackets kingpin*; now, the best the underworld can come up with is *fugitive financier.* And what do fugitive financiers do these days? They go to the *hair stylist* and the *race course* and the day is shot.

The word *barber* has been rubbed out, as if by some linguistic Frank Nitti. It was briefly resuscitated in the subtitle of a Broadway musical—*Sweeney Todd, the Demon Barber of Fleet Street*—but barbers have snipped the word out of their vocabulary, much as marketeers sold "salesmen," administrative assistants shredded "gal Fridays," fountain attendants jerked around "soda jerks," and funeral directors buried the "morticians" who had previously interred the "undertakers."

At the White House, a pair of unisex hairdressers (better change that to "a couple of people who cut hair for both men and women") recently departed, leaving the assignment of cutting the presidential and vice-presidential hair to Milton Pitts, who has a barbershop in a nearby hotel. During the contretemps about haircutting privileges, a reporter asked Attorney General William French Smith if he had his hair cut by a stylist or by a barber; the conservative Californian confessed: "I don't even know what the difference is between a barber and a hair stylist."

Splitting such hairs is the purpose of this column. *Barber,* from the Latin *barba,* beard, has been in the English language since 1300, but it might not last out this century. *Hairdresser,* introduced by novelist Tobias Smollett in 1771, became the name of the occupation devoted to the care of women's hair. Recently—Mr. Pitts estimates the date around 1960—*hair stylist* became the occupational title for one who attends to the hair of both men and women. Today, despite some overlap, *hairdresser* usually applies to those who care for women's hair and *hair stylist* for men's hair.

But is "stylist" pure euphemism? Mr. Pitts insists that there is a sharp difference between *barber* and *hair stylist.* "A barber is passé," he says. "A barber ordinarily cuts hair with a clippers as well as a scissors and slaps on some oily dressing afterward. That's not what I do. A hair stylist shapes the hair to the contours of the face. It started about twenty years ago with the 'razor cut,' and since then developed into a layer cut with scissors."

Evidently, barbers conspired cleverly to include more services, and thereby more expense, with the simple haircut of a generation ago. Merchandising demanded a change of vocabulary: "Ten bucks for a haircut?" Of course not; a *haircut* had to be changed to a *hair styling,* and the mix of services (washing, cutting, drying, and setting) sold as a package.

I asked Mr. Pitts if he also did chin styling. "We hardly ever get a call for a shave," he said. "If somebody loses his razor and it's too early to get to a store, maybe we'll have a call for a shave. That's a word that's gone out of the business." What about a *trim?* "That's still used occasionally, by bald men."

And what of the familiar peppermint-stick barber pole outside his door—does that have a new name? "You mean the hair-styling pole? Actually, when this thing wears out, I'll get a sign that just says 'hair styling.' No pole." (The William Marvy Company of St. Paul, Minnesota, leading manufacturer of barber poles, still refers to them in the old-fashioned way.)

Some of us, probably led by our traditionalist Attorney General, will go to the barber for a haircut, grimly ignoring accusations of indulging in occupational slurs. But the generation to come may be parted in the middle: one half sticking their heads into word processors and typing "shave and a haircut, and raise the sideburns," and the other half maneuvered into going to a hair stylist for a styling. The

latter is what my son does, and he's a member of a singing group that affects handlebar mustaches and will soon have to call itself a hair-styling-salon quartet.

You wrote that "Some of us, probably led by our traditionalist Attorney General, will go to the barber for a haircut. . . ."
    Some of us "get" a haircut or "take" a haircut.

> Irving B. Zeichner
> Trenton, New Jersey

Our managing editor, Mert Proctor, at our HQ in Germany, comments:

> *Safire column refers to a meeting with Luciano in the bar*
> *of the old Hotel Vesuvio in Naples. Give him a call and*
> *say a faithful reader and admirer wonders if he was implying*
> *by using "old" that the Vesuvio to which he refers no longer*
> *exists or is merely ancient. If he has not been there recently,*
> *the Vesuvio and its high-ceilinged bar still exist.*

> Frederick M. Shaine
> Director
> The Stars and Stripes
> New York, New York

Bill—
    Yes, I ask for a trim since I'm bald. However I also was in Naples in 1953 as a Navy pilot living in the Hotel Patria, wearing civilian clothes and doing covert aerial photography for the Navy and NATO. I knew Lucky also—since he ran all the girls in town and if any one of my enlisted men got into trouble in a local bar they were not to be turned over to the Shore Patrol since the Navy wasn't supposed to know we were there—so I worked a deal with Lucky to have the barkeeps call me. I would come and get the men—I used to go to the track with him. What were you doing in Naples at that time and how come you had to know Lucky also?

> Arthur [Glowka]
> Stamford, Connecticut

NOTE FROM W.S.: I was a corporal in the U.S. Army at the time (1953), working for the American Forces Network. Lucky was a fascinating interview, but I assumed he was retired.

"The Vanishing Haircut" was almost comprehensive in that it made no reference to tonsorial parlors, a term I have heard for years.

C. John Kuhn
Livingston, New Jersey

My husband and I had dinner tonight at a restaurant where a young lady came to our table, introduced herself as Laura, and placed a business card on our table. The business card gave the name of the restaurant and listed her name as Service Specialist. Now that is progress. Waitress to Service Specialist!

Rose Harrington
Oceanside, New Jersey

Vogue Word Watch

Some words or phrases appear like comets in the evening sky of language; they are watched by lexicographers and are used by speakers who like to be hip, with it and *au courant*—or, as they would now say, "on the *qui vive.*"

These are vogue words, and the time of their streakage helps historians define an era or locate a moment. Anyone who uses *compatible* or *disharmonious,* or tosses about *zero-based,* betrays himself as a product of the Carter years; in those days, we were describing any deception as *doing a number on.* Gone, all gone; where are the vogue words of today?

At congressional hearings, that's where the vogue words are. I dropped by a subcommittee hearing of the House Committee on Public Works and Transportation, where members were bemoaning the state of America's *infrastructure*—the bridges, tunnels, roads, dams, and canals that form a kind of circulating system for the body politic. A few years ago, all you heard was *reindustrialization;* that never made it to the top of the neoliberal agenda, but perhaps the *infra* will dig.

A word does not have to be freshly minted to be in vogue. *Infrastructure* surfaced in England soon after World War II when British Labor Minister of Defense Emanuel Shinwell used it to describe the airfields and signal communications of his military establishment; Winston Churchill rose in Commons to say, "As to this new word with which he has dignified our language, but which perhaps was imposed upon him internationally, I can only say that we must have full opportunity to consider it and to consult the dictionary."

Two months later, when the word reappeared in debate, Churchill was armed for combat: "In this debate we have had the usual jargon about 'the infrastructure of a supranational authority' . . . these words 'infra' and 'supra' have been introduced into our current political parlance by the band of intellectual highbrows who are naturally anxious to impress British labor with the fact that they learned Latin at Winchester." (Churchill meant to say *eager,* not *anxious.*) Under such a barrage of scorn, the word hunkered down, to pop up again during the Vietnam War and to flower in the early 1980's.

At the House hearing to which I went for my vogue-word fix, Senator Christopher Dodd of Connecticut was testifying: "It's hard to rally people around terms like 'infrastructure,' " he admitted, unwittingly following in the footsteps of the hapless Mr. Shinwell, "but we're talking about jobs."

Another witness, David Mahoney, the decisive chairman of Norton Simon Inc., set forth his ideas on the capital budget, a means of separating long-term investments from current expenditures, thereby making possible more businesslike planning to build and maintain the nation's you-know-what.

The subcommittee chairman, James Oberstar of Minnesota, interjected another vogue word in a question: "Isn't there a great deal of *collegiality* in the decision-making process?"

"Collegiality is important," the second-to-none Mahoney acknowledged, "but after the issue goes through all the collegiality, it gets to the somebody who has to decide."

Keep your eye on that comet: *Collegiality* should be good for at least a year in vogue, replacing *team player,* which was tainted by Watergate, and substituting for *consensus,* overused by Lyndon Johnson. It is closely associated with *colleague,* a vogue word imported from academia by Henry Kissinger and now used in place of *associate, assistant,* or *coworker* in introductions. ("Meet my colleague, Ms. Fandango.")

Over in the Senate, John East of North Carolina—our only multidirectional senator—

was using another hot word in worrying aloud about the *hemorrhaging* of the federal budget. Writes an irate Meyer Rangell of Bloomingburg, New York: "To cure the hemorrhage he wants to *cut* (or should it be *leech* or *bloodlet*) the budget . . . bloody nonsense!"

Down at Foggy Bottom, State Department types are doing *signals.* In the 60's, Governor George Wallace's slogan was "Send Them a Message," but *message* is out and *signal* is in, often in the negative form: Nothing is to be done lest it send the wrong signal.

Inadvertently, I just adverted to the latest vogue verb: *doing.* Long ago, in the early Reagan years, people were *into* this or that; whatever it was they were into, they are now *doing.* The early slang use—as in *doing time* in jail—has reappeared in vogue as *doing drugs, doing the scene, doing needlework.*

I used to be into infrastructure; now I'm doing collegiality.

GOTCHA!

You grouped "doing needlework" with "doing drugs" and "doing the scene." Hardly. Needlework is a manufacturing process (however humble); "doing" is here synonymous with "making," and is in no sense comparable to the use of the word in the latter two examples. If, however, you wish to say "needleworking," who would I be to argue?

> *Robert M. Richter, M.D.*
> *Brooklyn, New York*

I find particularly repellent that doing *is now a vogue word in scholarly circles, such as "let's* do *philosophy." I still think that* teaching, writing, thinking about *are more appropriate than* doing *in this context.*

> *Murray N. Rothbard*
> *New York, New York*

Why do Americans so often get parliamentary nomenclature wrong? You wrote that "Winston Churchill rose in Commons." If so, it sounds like a large communal eating area. The proper English usage is "the Commons." The same is true of "the Lords" and also of "the House." On the other hand, one can certainly rise in Parliament.

Why the article is used in this fashion I have no idea. Nor can I understand why Americans, who also speak of the *House and* the *Senate, but of* Congress *tout* court, *are prone to this solecism. After all, you yourself had the correct usage at hand: your reference to John East "in the Senate" on the very same page of your article.*

Theodore K. Rabb
Princeton, New Jersey

Voids in Woids

In a piece on the need for new words to cover familiar situations, I advertised for a neologism to mean "the in-laws of your children." In Yiddish, the relationship is denoted by the word *mache-tunim,* derived from the Hebrew noun plural of *mechutanim,* "related by marriage."

In passing, I derogated the supposed need for new words to cover highly specialized relationships, shrugging off the query from a reader who wanted to know what to call "an ex-wife with whom one was having an affair." However, since most of the mail came in with suggestions for that query and not mine, let me pass them along:

"A divorced couple, neither of whom has chosen another mate," writes L. Sprague de Camp of Villanova, Pennsylvania, "are quite likely to continue sporadic sexual relations, at least until one or the other sets his sights on someone else. How about *amorex*? When the affair is broken off, the amorex would become an *ex-amorex.*"

"Because I am having an affair with my ex-husband," writes an Arizona woman —how did I get involved in this?—"I have three suggestions." *Conjugate,* as a noun, is one; the others, interspersed with embarrassing and unnecessary confidences, are *paramate* and *metamour.*

Other submissions are *marry-go-round, mistrex* (limited to the female), and *expousal.* Perhaps the best is *spousetress* for the female, *spouster* for the male. Personally, I will continue to say "the ex-wife (or husband) with whom he (she) is having an affair."

Now can we get to mine? Most Lexicographic Irregulars let me down on "the relations of your married children," but Gene Fried of Peekskill, New York, and Arnold Lewin of Cortland, New York, report the word in Spanish to be *consuegros.* "In-laws" are *suegros,* and once removed—via your children—they become *consuegros.* But if we're going to use a foreign word, we might as well stick to *machetunim.*

Most suggestions included *out-laws,* but that is not conducive to good relations with the kid's new in-laws; they might respond by calling you *horse thief.*

The best idea for a name for your children's relatives was submitted by a neologenius who demands anonymity: *kinderkin*. Let's see if it flies; it's a lot more useful than *spousetress*.

As a former Spanish teacher I was explaining to an adult education class one evening the Spanish word consuegros *("co-in-laws").*

"Unfortunately," I said, "we have no word in English to describe this relationship."

"Yes, we do," a student said.

"We do?" I said. "What is it?"

"Them," she replied.

William Barbour
Brewster, Massachusetts

Dear Bill—

Spous etress *won't do: Where's the missing* s*? As for spousestress, you see where that lands you—at the marriage counselor's.*

Jacques [Barzun]
Charles Scribner's Sons,
Publishers
New York, New York

For the past decade, my wed-laws *and I have been spreading this word, coined by Robert Fitzwilliam of Wellesley, Massachusetts, my daughter-in-law's father. This conveniently applies not only to parent-in-laws but brothers, sisters, etc. of both families.*

Carol O'Daniel Beane
Woodstock, Vermont

The Spanish word suegro *for "in-law" sounds reasonably like the Yiddish* schvigger *for "mother-in-law" and* schvogger *for "brother-in-law." As in Hebrew roots, the consonants are identical (with a little license for the equivalence of* u *and* v*), and they appear in identical order. Could it be that one derives from the other?*

William H. Angoff
Princeton, New Jersey

My own proposal for a word meaning "more than friend, less than spouse" is leman, an archaic word which evidently had a similar meaning once. My friends prefer sweetie, but that word is too affected for general use. The major drawback to leman, as I see it, is its pronunciation. My dictionary gives as the one of preference the same one as for the fruit; that pronunciation nonetheless seems to sound better than LE-man.

I wish you could suggest a word for a young woman between the ages of fifteen and thirty or so. Guy does very well for young men of those ages, but not everyone can bring himself to use gal. Woman is most definitely not appropriate for young ladies less than twenty, and my mother would probably say for young ladies less than thirty. I have taken to using young lady, as you see, but that expression is inappropriate in most of the same situations sweetie is. Clearly I am seeking a word to be used in casual speech, but I suppose we need one for more formal situations also.

> Gail Schweiter
> Madison, Wisconsin

As an indication of her willingness to share her son's affection with his new mother-by-marriage, one of my aunts referred to her new relative, in German, as meine Mit-Mutter "my co-mother." Surely an expression of considerable generosity and goodwill.

> Maria Grimes
> Falls Church, Virginia

I can add two foreign words that mean the in-laws of your children (not neologisms):
In Russian the father-in-law of your child is svat to you and the mother-in-law is svat'ya.
In German they are Gegenschwieger and Gegenschwiegerin, respectively.

> Vera Efron
> West Wardsboro, Vermont

Regarding the term consuegro (a), it does not exactly mean "once removed," but rather "in-law–to–in-law," or "back-to-back" in-laws—as does the term concunado (a), which denotes the relationship between the siblings of one spouse and those of the other.

> Danielle Salti
> New Brunswick, New Jersey

Vox of Pop Sixpack

Who speaks for the average man? Out of whose mouth comes the voice of the people?

A bit of doggerel in the presidential campaign of 1920, sung by the supporters of James Cox and Franklin Roosevelt, used the Latin term *vox populi*, for "voice of the people": "Cox or Harding, Harding or Cox?/ You tell us, populi, you got the vox."

At that time, the chorus of voices that intoned "Harding and Coolidge" went under the name of *John Citizen* for highbrows, *Joe Zilch* for lowbrows. Curiously, in the naming of *Everyman*—that ordinary person who supposedly speaks for the community—there has long been a difference between the upper-class John (from the Hebrew "God is gracious") and the lower-class Joe (from the Hebrew "He shall add," a considerable comedown from the name John).

John Bull, the personification of England in Dr. John Arbuthnot's 1712 book, was the probable start of it all; in America, *Brother Jonathan,* possibly Jonathan Trumbull, a friend of George Washington, was the predecessor to *Uncle Sam.* John's diminutive was used in the Civil War: *Johnny Reb.* Somewhere along the way, a *Q* was acquired, possibly from John Quincy Adams, but in the mid-1930's *John Q. Public* emerged as the form preferred over *John Q. Citizen, John Q. Taxpayer, John Q. Voter,* or, most recently, *John Q. Consumer.* "We are all the children of John Q. Public," cried William Allen White, editor of *The Emporia*

Gazette, admonishing organized labor in 1937 to avoid setting class against class.

John Doe had something to do with the dignification of the common man. That was the name in English common law for the unknown or fictitious person in legal proceedings; *John Doe* was the first unknown party, *Richard Roe* the second, *John Stiles* the third, *Richard Miles* the fourth. (A good name for a tenants' association would be Doe, Roe, Stiles & Miles.) This legal use of John as the typical name—buttressed in the United States by the adoption of John Hancock's name as the term for any strong signature—locked in *John* as the first name of the classier spokesman for vox pop, and was popularized on specimen checks. (In 1735 a *cousin John* was the Harvard College man's term for a privy, and a *john* is still a slang term for toilet, but that does not fit my theory.)

Down among the lower classes, *Joe* was asserting himself. *Joe Bunker* was an early nickname for an American, replaced in this century by *Joe Doakes;* in World War II, *G.I. Joe* had a friend—usually nondescript—named *Joe Blow,* and a less well-known naval pal, *Joe Gish. Joe Schmo* is best portrayed by Woody Allen. In specialized usages, *Joe College* is the typical rah-rah collegian and *Joe Cool* the typical hipster.

Come now to a press conference after a Business Council meeting in Hot Springs, West Virginia. A reporter asks the chairman of the Federal Reserve Board, Paul Volcker, about a change in money-supply figures: "How do you expect Joe Sixpack should react?" Replies Mr. Volcker, evidently familiar with the version of Everyman updated to one who buys beer in packs of six bottles or cans: "I don't think Joe Sixpack should be concerned in the least. . . . I think if you give Joe Sixpack that impression you are doing him and the country a disservice."

Thus, today we have *John Q. Public* wearing respectable spectacles; *Joe Sixpack* is sitting in his undershirt looking like Archie Bunker (a descendant of Joe Bunker).

"*Joe Sixpack* is gender-identified," writes Roger Green of Albany, New York. "Are there any gender-neutral classifications, like *Leslie Middleclass, Terry Americana?*" No; in all evocations of the *little man,* it is a little *man:* The male use embraces the female. There is no *Jane Q. Public* or *Alice Sixpack,* just as there never needed to be an *Everywoman.*

In 1787, The Contrast, *by Royall Tyler, was produced at the John Street theatre in New York City. The satire, which was the second American play and the first American comedy, was meant to show the merits and faults of the young United States by juxtaposing thoroughly American characters with European characters. One of the American personages is a patriotic New England hayseed named Jonathan whose ingenuous Yankee character quickly became a cliché found in many American plays and whose name inspired the term* Brother Jonathan *as a personification of the United States.*

> Randy Weiner
> New York, New York

War Words

For the time being, it's settled: The name of the island group is the Falklands. Argentines (pronounced *teens* in the Americas, *tynes* in Britain and on two American networks) may still call it the Malvinas, but that must be used now in a sentimental or defiant sense.

I am hardly the first would-be lexicographer to write about this. In "Thoughts on the Late Transactions Respecting Falkland's Islands," published in 1771, Samuel Johnson—before whom all of us in the word dodge genuflect—mounted a vigorous defense of the British ownership, concluding with: "After all our broils, foreign and domestick, we may at last hope to remain awhile in quiet, amused with the view of our own success. We have gained political strength by the increase of our reputation; we have gained real strength by the reparation of our navy; we have shewn Europe that ten years of war have not yet exhausted us; and we have enforced our settlement on an island. . . ."

For this historical insight, I am indebted to Lexicographic Irregular Richard M. Nixon, who was perusing Will and Ariel Durant's *Rousseau and Revolution* late one night and noted this passage about Dr. Johnson: "He called patriotism 'the last refuge of scoundrels' but he defended with patriotic warmth the right of Britain to the Falkland Islands in 1771." Mr. Nixon writes: "You might find it amusing to point out that your counterpart in the eighteenth century shared your view on this issue. The more things change, the more they remain the same!"

In this short war, the word that first troubled me was *bridgehead*. "The press —and I believe London itself—is referring to the British landings on East Falkland as a 'bridgehead,' " writes Robert Ricker of Vienna, Virginia. "In my soldierly days, the term applied specifically to a landing on the other side of a river, from dirt to dirt with water in between. When landing from the high seas on an island or a continent, it was a 'beachhead.' And an airborne assault establishes an 'airhead.' "

I am unfamiliar with *airhead*—sounds vaguely akin to "empty-headed"—but the copy editors of *The New York Times* changed *bridgehead* to *beachhead* between editions, in a military analysis by Drew Middleton. The distinction is best explained by Cleve Corlett, of Arlington, Virginia (Virginians are hip to military history): "When the Allies landed in Normandy, they managed to secure a *beachhead*; when an armored column of the U.S. First Army seized, intact, the Ludendorff railroad bridge at Remagen on March 8, 1945, it succeeded in establishing a *bridgehead* on the east bank of the Rhine."

The Argentine junta (I say *hoonta*, the Brits say *junta*) recognized the importance of the war of words in choosing the verb *recuperate* in connection with their initial takeover of the islands. In current American usage, that word is mostly applied to getting well after an illness, but another meaning exists for such a recovery—to re-cover, or take back control of, territory or property.

Meanwhile, the Brits (not a term they use themselves, just as Yanks is not a term we use often about ourselves, but in neither case especially derogatory) invented a term for Argentines: *Argies*, with a soft *g*. "It was as if somewhere there is a store of rude names for every nation in the world," wrote Simon Hoggart in *Punch*, "which can be brought out and employed the moment we go to war, like petrol ration coupons."

Hoggart posits one theory that the term was used first by the departing governor, Rex Hunt, in a television interview soon after the Argentine invasion, and adds that it was universally used by Falklanders. "But these facts would not account for the manner in which it passed into the language overnight." For that, we must thank the men who make up the front pages of newspapers. In linguistic physics, the power of compression is the length of the name divided by the desperation of the headline writer.

The Argies' navy, most of which never put to sea, was intimidated by the presence of British *hunter-killer* submarines. For a moment, I thought this ferocious adjective was as unnecessary as the "battle" in "battle tank"—what do they make tanks for, other than battles?—but all ire subsided with this explanation from a Defense Department spokesman, Major Douglas Kennett: "There are two types of submarines. There are the subs for conventional warfare; these are the *hunter-killer* subs, which destroy ships. Submarines that launch ballistic missiles are not hunt-and-kill; they're *strategic* subs."

Then we come to *decimate*, a word used often in connection with the war in the Falklands and in Lebanon. My colleague Charles Mohr, standing at a news ticker in *The Times*'s Washington newsroom, saw this word appear and said, "Don't they know it means 'reduce by a tenth'? Why do they use it when they mean 'destroy'?"

Sorry, Charlie, usage is usage. True, *decimate* originated with the Roman legions, whose commanders punished mutiny by selecting every tenth man by lot and killing him. However, to limit the word's meaning to "one-tenth" would be like limiting *myriad* to its literal 10,000—time and usage have broadened the meaning of both words. *Decimate* now means "destroy a large portion of," and *myriad* means "a great number of."

Let me not plunge overboard into permissiveness: *Decimate* retains its fractional connotation. You cannot decimate half of anything. And you must not stretch its meaning beyond "a large portion." For example, a *Washington Post* editorialist wrote: ". . . to complete the decimation of the 'terrorist infrastructure' in Lebanon." The word probably intended was *annihilation* or *destruction.*

The finest distinction in war headlines was drawn by Carleton Chaney of Rydal, Pennsylvania, who complained of "the growing misuse of the verb *blame.*" Her example: "Argentines Put Blame on British for U.N. Delay." *To blame* is to accuse or to condemn for some fault; *to put the blame on* is to place the responsibility on. *Blame* is accusatory; *put the blame* is judgmental. A nice distinction, worth preserving through the coming negotiations (that's "SHE-ations," not "SEE-ations").

What was the most beautiful, most unusual word used in connection with any of the wars going on lately? My candidate appeared in, of all places, an article by Henry Kissinger. The subject was post-Lebanon diplomatic strategy in the Middle East, and the former Secretary of State wrote: "The dominant trend within our own Department of State—seeks to nudge the talks in the direction of a Palestinian entity, the inevitable chrysalis of a Palestinian state."

Chrysalis—accent on the *kris*—is a selection of great taste and suitability, far better than *embryo, formative stage, starting point,* or *basis.* A chrysalis is the pupa of an insect, when the insect is encased in a cocoon, halfway between larval and adult stages; by extension, a *chrysalis* is a sheltered state of being just before coming of age.

The etymology is of Semitic origin: The Latin *chrysallis* comes from the Greek *chrysallis,* which is taken from the Semitic *chrysos,* for "gold," as in the Hebrew *haruz,* "gold," and the Aramaic *hara,* "yellow." A golden word, its meaning poised on the edge of birth. It kills me to admit this, but after two powerful volumes of memoirs, Henry is getting the hang of writing.

Dear Bill,

One non-military but associated word was missing: waffle, *to talk vaguely or indecisively, or—to go a step further—to be evasive, equivocate, fail to take a firm position. I heard it used on radio many times concerning the Falklands war. Nobody seems to have written about it—I think because it's not in any of the dictionaries people usually consult. Obviously it has nothing to do with those checkered pancakes made in waffle-irons—unless you want to go back to remote Indo-European roots.*

Waffle, noun, verb, and waffling, adjective, are listed, however, in the 1973 Barnhart Dictionary of New English and the 1976 Merriam-Webster 6,000 Words. It is an import from Britain. There, it was just one of those numerous north-country dialect words that not even the big Oxford Dictionary listed. Then recently it gained wider currency, and now it has crossed the Atlantic and is gaining ground in the U.S., where we have our share of evasive talk or indecisive verbalizing.

The basic meaning is "to wave about; to flap, as in the wind" (Wright's English Dialect Dictionary)—it's related to such other words as waft and waver. So it easily came to mean shaky, unsteady, or as a verb, to move unsteadily, hesitate, vacillate. In north Yorkshire a man might be "a windy, waffling sort of chap, who never knows his own mind." And that sense has found its way from Britain into American usage since the 1960's. It's expressive enough, and a lot easier to say than vacillate, so I predict a lively future for it in American use.

> *Fred*
> *[F. G. Cassidy]*
> *Director-Editor, DARE*
> *Madison, Wisconsin*

I believe that you misread what you found between the square brackets in your Webster's regarding the etymology of chrysalis. Yes, chrysos, the root, is no doubt of Semitic origin. However, as you must realize, Semitic is not a language but a language group. Thus your statement "Chrysalis . . . is taken from the Semitic chrysos" is incorrect. Chrysos is the Greek rendering of a word borrowed from some Semitic tongue (I would guess Phoenician). Also, since it is traditional in etymology to give the earliest known version of a particular word, I think you (and the editors of Webster's for that matter) should have mentioned hurasu, the word for gold in Akkadian, the oldest known Semitic language (both Babylonian and Assyrian are dialects of Akkadian).

> *Jonathan Roth*
> *New York, New York*

You write, "In linguistic physics, the power of compression is the length of the name divided by the desperation of the headline writer."

You should have written "In linguistic physics, the power of compression is the length of the name multiplied by the desperation of the headline writer."

I am astonished that you should misuse the verb divide *in this way, probably by not thinking about its meaning.*

Words are my hobby. In 1930 I was pestered by reporters who asked what my hobby was. At first I could not think of an answer, but then, after cogitation, I replied that my hobby was collecting dictionaries.

Linus Pauling
Palo Alto, California

Watch What You Say

What time is it?

"Quarter past 10," say I, consulting the trusty old timepiece on my wrist, where the long hand is on the mark near the stemwinder, about a quarter of the way around from the top, and the short hand is on a marking just two short of the top, which I know from years of watch-looking represents a 10.

"Ten-fourteen," says my daughter, reading from a machine on her wrist that measures her pulse, counts her joggings, swallows space invaders, and otherwise does more than Milton can to justify God's ways to man.

The language is adapting to changes in the instruments of measurement. *Half-past* is passing and *quarter-to* is approaching what nuclear scientists call "two minutes to midnight"; they are being replaced by numerals, with the hour first, as the new watches dictate verbal responses.

The reason for the switch is that we are going digital. My old pie-faced watch, with 12 slices representing the hours and 60 fork-marks along the edge of the crust for the minutes, is an idea whose time has come and gone; some moving finger has written that we are now in the Digital Age.

"In the Mr. Coffee ad on television," writes Elizabeth Keenan of Knoxville, Tennessee, "Joe DiMaggio demonstrates a digital-clock coffee maker, and a voice afterward says: 'Also available in analog-clock models,' as the screen shows a clock-clock coffee maker. Is it possible that I have been telling time all these years by an analog clock? Analogous to what? I feel like *le bourgeois gentilhomme* when he found he had been speaking prose."

You have indeed been analogging it up, Miss Keenan. An analog (without the British *ue* ending) is a representation; a watch with hands, like a sundial, represents the hours of the day with the segments of a circle. The position of the hands on the clock is analogous to the position of the sun in the sky.

The phrase is a retronym, the term Frank Mankiewicz has coined to describe names of familiar objects or events that need a modifier to catch up to more

modern objects: *day baseball* and *natural turf* are in the same category as *analog watch.* Clockmakers occasionally would have used *analog clock* a generation ago, because *analog computers* were coming into vogue, and the old clocks, like those electrical computers, were able to represent a continuously variable quantity (the hands never stopped on the watch, the flow of information was not reported in finite numerals by the computer).

However, when *digital watches* came into being, the old watch became an *analog watch,* the way that a *guitar* was forced by the new *electric guitar* to identify itself as an *acoustic guitar.*

Digital comes from *digit,* or finger, which is what most people learn to count with; *digital* is the adjective for that which enumerates, or counts. "An *analog watch* has hands which point, and a digital watch has numbers or digits which appear as a readout," says Robert Stevens, a spokesman for the Seiko Time Corporation. At first, the numbers were mechanically flopped over, like old calendars, but that couldn't last; soon the technicians were able to get the L.E.D. readout.

Mr. Stevens adds an explanation of that unfloppable display: "There are two kinds of digital displays. One is the L.E.D., or *light-emitting diode,* the red or blue readout, which consumes a lot of electricity and has a battery life of about three months." That was O.K. for plug-in clocks and the like, but it was a heavy drag for battery-operated devices. "The other is the L.C.D., or *liquid crystal display,* the continuous black on gray readout, with a battery life of three to five years."

As a result of the wane of the analog watch, we are now living by the numbers, calling out our measurements of time in tiny, finite slices rather than representing time in a continuous flow. Because we "see" time in numbers, we hear it in numerals: It's 10-whatever, because it is now the "readout" on our wrist that is being imprinted in our mind's eye.

A word remains, however, to remind us of the heyday of watchmaking in the last century: *stemwinder,* used in the beginning of this piece. The device was invented to replace the need for a key, and it was the latest thing in watches until World War I brought along the wristwatch. A *stemwinder* was remembered as "the latest thing," and then merged into *spellbinder* to mean "a rousing political speech." That's what happens to the language in time.

Dear Bill—

I have understood the reference to a speech as "a real stemwinder" to mean one that is so boring it causes members of the audience to wind their watches to make sure they are running.

If you are correct, then the usage I have heard (referring to a dull speech) was sarcastic, and not merely sardonic.

> Monroe [H. Freedman]
> Hempstead, New York

When your watch was trying to tell you that it was "quarter past 10," its hour hand was not on a marking "just two short of the top" as you state. Rather, it was aimed at a point one-fourth of the distance on the arc between the 10th marking and the 11th marking—thus pointing to 10+¼ hours.

In fact, the hour hand on an analog timepiece is every bit as analogish as the minute hand. If accuracy is not of prime concern, you don't need a minute hand. Conversely, for greater accuracy, you can add a second hand. Actually, all three hands are equally accurate but not equally readable. The minute and second hands merely provide better optical resolution of the analog data.

Next, to prove what a nastily technical proofreader I tend to be, I now call attention to your statement that the old clocks "were able to represent a continuously variable quantity (the hands never stopped . . .)." That's true for telechron-like electric timepieces. These run silently or with merely a low hum. However, for timepieces that have a real tick-tock, it's NOT true. The tick-tock is caused by a mechanical-escapement device which stops ALL hands as often as from 5 or 6 to as many as 10 or even 20 times per second.

These stops are imperceptible when observing the hour or minute hands but can be seen as the second hand hesitatingly "inches" its way around the circle. Therefore there is not a continuous flow of data; the hands do stop. However, it can be said that there is a CONTINUAL flow of data even though the hands stop. Refer to the mnemonic sentence: "The continual beating of the waves along the continuous shore."

Perhaps timepieces of this latter class should have been, or in the future should be, properly called "pseudo-analog." That phrase, I rather suspect, will never catch on.

Robert W. Orth
New York, New York

Your discussion of the new language of digital clocks was—I must say it—most timely.

In abandoning such terms as half-past *and* quarter-to, *we lose our conception of time as round and cyclical, tangible as the face of a clock. Most distressing is the prospect of telling time with the younger generation. In a country of people with L.C.D. digital readouts strapped to their wrists, how will we explain to our children the meaning of* clockwise?

Eva L. Weiss
Jackson Heights, New York

The invention of the light-emitting diode and the liquid crystal display may help us resolve a usage controversy that aggravated some usage commentators in the earlier part of this century.

As you know, many usage commentators insisted, when they found it convenient, that language be logical. Time-telling was one area where logic was encouraged. Lexicographer Frank Vizetelly—editor of the Funk & Wagnalls Standard Dictionary—*claims, in his* Desk-Book of Errors in English *(1907), that in telling time the phrase* a quarter of seven *is incorrect. For Vizetelly, a quarter of seven is one and three-fourths, that is, "seven divided by four." He accepts only the expression* a quarter to seven *as correct.*

But in this particular controversy, logic, it seems, is in the eye of the beholder, for grammarian Josephine Turck Baker, who for many years edited the journal Correct English, *insists in 1904 that the* to *in* a quarter to seven *actually means "toward." For her, a quarter to seven is really six-fifteen, or "one quarter of an hour toward seven." Baker therefore insists on the form that Vizetelly rejects,* a quarter of. *A third variant,* a quarter till, *is rejected by both sides as illiterate, although it would seem to satisfy their insistence on logical rigor. That leaves the unfortunate user of usage guides to select between two forms whose logic is suspect. Better say* six-forty-five *and have done with it. Fortunately, nowadays everybody can get cheap digital watches, and the whole notion of a* quarter to, of, *or* till *the hour is being rendered meaningless.*

> *Dennis Baron*
> *Urbana, Illinois*

Wattle I Do?

"We don't talk about that around here."

"Sorry—that's a word we don't use."

Those are the responses you get—even on Mindanao-Deep background—from sensitive White House aides when you bring up the subject of *wattles.* On this word, in the eternal race between photocopier and papershredder, the shredder has won out; the ban on its use at the center of power goes beyond "executive privilege" to the depths of primitive taboo.

Wattles are those folds around the neck that are telltale signs of age in humans. In some lizards and swine, the hanging folds appear early; in turkeys and some other birds, fleshy lobes appear around the head at an early age and hang around for life; indeed, large and deeply wrinkled wattles may serve as an attraction to other turkeys.

Not so with people. Just as a *double chin* is usually an unwelcome sign of fatness, *wattles*—used mainly in the plural, like *wrinkles*—mean that time's winged chariot is catching up. In President Reagan's case, cartoonists have seized upon his wattles as one of his most caricaturable characteristics, and the winces the word evinces suggest it has become a matter of some sensitivity.

As a service to White House image makers, let me suggest a fresh approach to the unmentionable but quite natural folds under the presidential jaw. *Wattles,* I agree, is a word with a reptilian image and calls for a synonym that is not a euphemism. However, *dewlap* is a word with a happier connotation, referring to the skin hanging below the jaw of cows. The dairy industry contributes more to our economy than the alligator industry. *Dew*—from an Indo-European base of

"to run," as in a brook—has come to symbolize freshness and morning, befitting purveyors of "the New Beginning."

Geezers have *wattles*; handsome elderly persons sport *dewlaps*. I am running my hand suspiciously around my own neck as I write, and fear that I may soon be hearing a lot more of this word. Can't the cosmetics people do something about dewlaps? It seems that they have abandoned the field to the scarf manufacturers.

The President's men, by facing up to the developments around the Reagan neck, could soon develop a chin-up attitude that would turn wattle worry into dewlap envy.

I don't think wattle *can be equated with* dewlap. *I raise rabbits, which have dewlaps, meaning double chins. Nowhere is that pendulous lateral fold called anything but a dewlap, although in dogs and cattle, vertical skin pleats are called by either name.*

Of course, it's the withy kind of wattle that's part of wattle and daub. *However, given that Mr. Reagan is widely believed to use hair dye and makeup, someone may describe his visage thus. I prefer the nickname derived from the* Dick Tracy *character, Pruneface.*

In the end, wattle it matter?

> Miryam N. Kay
> Washington, D.C.

I have always associated dewlaps with part of the lip and jaw skin of some mammals, and wattles with the floppy upper neck skin of some birds.

Wouldn't it follow that what the folds are called should depend on which skin area is being discussed? I'll bet the Prez' choice is to not have his poor skin tone areas discussed at all. He also might be subconsciously wary of wattles' first syllable being associated with negative qualities. I'd opt for wattles *under the jaw, especially in view of the descriptive "woven work" meaning.*

Watt really worries me is that you could be revealing a speciesist—or worse, a genusist—streak. Do you really prefer to compare the Prez to a cow rather than to a turkey?

How about just jaw skin *or* neck skin *with no outside referents?*

> Jim Craig
> Allentown, Pennsylvania

P.S. Remember that to call someone a speciesist pig is to reveal one's own species-ism.

Webster's Ninth

" 'New Music' Groups Have Record Makers Dancing With Delight," reads a *Wall Street Journal* headline. One of the stars, Joe Leeway, is described as a man "whose eyebrows are shaven and whose wiry black hair is braided into 'dreadlocks.' "

There's an eye-grabbing word, seemingly melding *deadlock* with *dreadnought*, suggesting a couple of battleships that cannot defeat each other. However, the hairdressing context suggested another meaning.

I put my fresh copy of the newest production of the Merriam-Webster crowd to the test. Sure enough, *Webster's Ninth New Collegiate Dictionary* rose to the challenge, defining *dreadlocks* as "long braids of hair worn by Rastafarians."

Since I am among the handful of dictionary-readers who have difficulty distinguishing Rastafarians from Rotarians, I called Fred Mish of Merriam-Webster to get his citation. He directed me to the classic *Dictionary of Jamaican English* by F.G. Cassidy (the man from *DARE*) and R. B. Le Page, which defines *dreadlocks* as "hair uncut and plaited, as worn by most fully committed adherents of the Ras Tafari cult." Cassidy, thorough as always, provides a 1960 citation from an article published by the Institute of Social and Economic Research describing "the plaiting of long hair by men known as the 'men of dreadlocks' or simply "locks-men.' These men of dreadlocks were the Ethiopian Warriors and the self-declared Niyamen."

Lexicographer Mish also supplied a more recent use in *Cosmopolitan* magazine, which described singer Bob Marley's voice in 1976 as "like that of a sorcerer, an image made all the more fearsome by his "dreadlocks'—braids of hair, which, as one viewer put it, jut 'crazily from all parts of his head, making him look as if he had just suffered an acute electric shock.' "

Putting *Webster's Ninth* through its paces (catch that participial phrase, and now here I come as the subject), I turned to a letter from Peter Andrews of Brewster, New York: "In a recent book review . . . I tried to use the term *scut work* to refer to a dreary, unrewarding task. The copy editor refused to let it go through because she could find no dictionary confirmation of the definition."

With some exasperation, Mr. Andrews adds: "I have eleven dictionaries, including a facsimile edition of Dr. Johnson, and with increasing embarrassment I could not find a single reference that backed up my position. The principal definition is that a scut is the short tail of a deer or similar animal. But I am not alone in this. A friend of mine who writes soap operas for television has always referred to the mechanical chore of marking entrances and exists and other pieces of routine stage direction as 'scut work.' Another friend of mine is a doctor who uses the term to describe the task of cutting through bone and mopping up blood and the other messy details of surgery. Now here are three people from disparate backgrounds who independently have been using the same term for God knows how long to mean roughly the same thing, and it turns out the term does not exist.

"How can this be? It is inconceivable that each of us could have coined an identical usage out of thin air."

Scut, meaning "a contemptible person," has been around a long time—at least since 1873, when the novelist Anthony Trollope had a character denounce "that young scut," and that definition can be found in some dictionaries, including *Webster's New World.* But *scut work* is newer, first spotted by Oxford lexicographers in a 1972 issue of *Newsweek,* and its first appearance in a general dictionary is in *Webster's Ninth*: "routine and often menial labor."

"Our earliest citation for *scut work,* " reports Dr. Mish, "is a handwritten note by Philip B. Gove, editor in chief of *Webster's Third,* dated 1962: 'Scutwork— menial or clerk work that should be done by assistants or subordinates, common among medical interns, as "this internship has too much scutwork," i.e., marking bins, typing reports, cleaning up the lab, etc.' " (Dr. Gove, obviously on the ball in this case, took a lot of abuse from prescriptivists for not labeling informal usage as such in his dictionary. During the uproar, one cartoon had a receptionist at Merriam-Webster telling a visitor: "Dr. Gove ain't in.")

The first citation in print is from John Fischer's "Easy Chair" in *Harper's* in 1968: "Until World War II even senior scholars at leading universities did a good deal of what [Christopher Jencks and David Riesman] defined as scut work: teaching small groups of lower-level students. . . ."

Therefore, Mr. Andrews, do not despair when dictionaries do not immediately report on what you know to be a working phrase. Even if it is not codified by lexicographers, the phrase "exists," and if it lasts beyond the nonce, it will pop up in new editions. And do not castigate the lexicographer for being slow; Samuel Johnson defined his job as that of "a harmless drudge," and now we have a new term for the marvelously menial work.

As a freshman at the State University of Iowa about 1922–23 I heard an upperclassman ribbing another thus: "I'll get my girl and you pick up your old scut and we'll go to the dance." Scut seems to have been synonymous with whore in that time and area.

> Bil Baird
> New York, New York

When I was a boy in the late thirties, I lived adjacent to an Irish neighborhood. One of my friend's grandmother would refer to us as lazy or nasty scuts, depending upon the degree we'd irritated her. I asked her one time about the origin of the word and as near as I could make out its reference was those "dirty scuts," those Presbyterian soldiers of the Crown oppressing the poor Irish. These, I learned later, were the Scots, whose hatred of Popery made them more unpopular than regular Black & Tans.

> Arthur Harris
> Jamaica, New York

In the paragraph on scutwork, you quote from one of Dr. Gove's notes: " '. . . this internship has too much scutwork,' i.e., marking bins, . . . "
  Should not the "i.e." be "e.g."? "I.e." (that is) introduces a definition. "E.g." (for example) introduces a list of examples, which is what Dr. Gove was doing in the quotation above. At any rate, "i.e." in the context neither looks nor sounds right.

> William H. Herder
> Somerville, New Jersey

The following sentence caught my attention in John D. Macdonald's "A Deadly Shade of Gold": "Scut work at the Museum of Contemporary Crafts." You will find this on page 68 of the 1974 hardcover edition, but the story was copyrighted in 1965, three years before the "first citation in print" you gave in your column.

Robert J. Walker
Pittsburgh, Pennsylvania

The word scut, *used both as a verb and a noun, was common at Wesleyan University (Middletown, Connecticut) when I was a freshman in 1940. A student trying out for a position was said to scut the football managership, or scut the* Argus *(campus newspaper). Thus he became a scut. This did indeed involve doing the routine or menial work which those upperclassmen who were in charge had done in their days of scutting. (None of us bothered to tell Dr. Gove about this.)*

E. K. Fretwell Jr.
Charlotte, North Carolina

I was chuckling my way through Peg Bracken's The I Hate to Housekeep Book, *copyrighted 1958 by the Curtis Publishing Company and 1962 by Peg Bracken, when on page 4 I noticed that she used the word* scutwork. *Her definition is "the good old Navy term for chores that any boob can do, like cleaning up after people."*

Nell Griscom
Lexington, Massachusetts

Dear Bill:
No, no, please don't give your authority to the use of meld *to mean "combine."*
There are so many excellent words besides combine: *join, mix, graft, unite, amalgamate, incorporate, hook up, compound, hybridize, mingle, fuse, interlard, alloy, and even* weld, *which is probably the cause of the barbarous kidnapping of* meld *(= announce, in pinochle) to say something that needs no new word.*

Jacques [Barzun]
Charles Scribner's Sons,
Publishers
New York, New York

DREAD LOX
More fearsome than the Ras' hair,
It pierces me with salmon stare.

Festooned on bagel, tomato-decked,
My resolution soon is wrecked.
As slathered cream cheese billows forth,
My waist and I head for divorth.
Aroma rising from the sea
Proclaims, alas, that woe is me.
Complete with onion's fragrant loop,
I gulp the oeuvre in one fell swoop.
Thus is mortal quite undone
By DREAD LOX on a Jewish bun.

Jacques P. Penn
New York, New York

Weekend's Strong End

"I have heard three newscasters pronounce the word *weekend* as 'weak-END,'" writes Dan Woog of Westport, Connecticut. "Is this a trend? Has someone changed the rules of the game and not informed me?"

A quick check with lexicographers shows that they, too, are tracking the strong end for weekend. I called Sam Donaldson of ABC, one of the newscasters cited by Mr. Woog, who replied, "Not guilty! I say, 'WEEK-end.'"

Hmm. The British, when they go on holiday, take the week-END. An Englishman's clandestine rendezvous at week's end is called "a dirty week-END." Could be the British are coming; let's watch that word.

West Winging It

I have just returned from a background briefing of pundits in the Roosevelt Room of the White House. Under the ground rules, I must not identify the sources of these phrases, lest the authorized leaking gain too much authority, but it is important to pass along the lingo being used at the highest levels.

What should Federal Reserve policy be in the year ahead? The word, according to a former thundering herdsman whose name is often confused with the President's, is *accommodative*. The root is the Latin *commodare*, to fit, and my guess is that the word was chosen to avoid *stimulative* (Fed chairman gets jumpy at that word) and *accommodating,* which suggests what used to be called "a woman of easy virtue."

What tentative deal was made on arms control last year, which was later repudiated by both the Soviet and United States governments? According to the high State Department official whose name is an expletive to be deleted, this is referred to in arms-control circles as *the walk in the woods.*

What has been happening to the economy in the past year? Some have called it *recession,* others *depression* (when that dreaded word was used by a Carter administration official, it was changed to *banana*). The preferred Reagan administration phrase, from the lips of a wizard whose long, graying, blow-dried locks make him appear to be a modern Merlin, is *severe disinflationary correction.*

What have our arms-control negotiators been going through in the new Andropov era? The answer, which restored my faith in nonstarters, came from a salty old general with a yen for puns: *trial by Yuri.*

Who Needs Felt?

"In Secretary of State Shultz and President Reagan," wrote my colleague Anthony Lewis, "there is a felt commitment."

A few days later, Jerome Alan Cohen, the specialist in Asian matters who teaches at Harvard Law School, wrote that a Korean dissident leader was released because of "Seoul's felt need to respond to pressures from the U.S."

The use of *felt* in both instances draws on a 300-year history of the word used as a participial adjective to mean "aware through intellectual perception, rather than through physical sensation." Yet I get the feeling that this meaning of *felt* is changing.

That is because of the popularity, especially in academic circles, of *perceived.* For the past decade, almost every need has been a *perceived* need, as if the writer wanted to convey: "Look, it may not be a real need, but people think they have a need, so I'll avoid taking sides or looking like a liberal, or identifying with the subjects of my study, by writing of *perceived* needs." The rise of *perceived* came along with the notion that appearance was as much reality as reality.

Now that *perceive* is favored as the word for *seen,* especially with the connotation of *thought of,* what has been happening to *felt?* I submit that it is gaining a more emotional connotation, separating itself from *perceived* the way *feel* has been moving away from *think.* Today, a *felt need* is one that is arrived at for reasons of hunch or physical sensation, rather than intellectual analysis. The feeling behind *felt need* is a gut feeling.

That's good; whenever words split for reasons of clarity, the language benefits. Let's hope the trend continues. Meanwhile, if you want to get away from the voguish *felt* and *perceived*, you can try *recognized*, or the less seriously taken *noted*, or the more comprehensive *comprehended*, or the more discriminating *discerned*. In this context, I am writing about an *observed* need. ("I see, Holmes." "You *see*, my dear Watson, but you do not *observe*.")

Felt has gotten refabricated by the holistics, and specifically by Eugene Gendlin and his undergendlins. In an introduction to his book Focusing *(Everest House, 1978, and currently a Bantam paperback) Marilyn Ferguson writes: "We are conscious of only a fragment of what we deeply know. The central nervous system perceives and processes a great body of information that is stored outside the range of everyday awareness."*

Thus Gendlin's "felt sense," Anthony Lewis' "felt commitment," J. A. Cohen's "felt need," and my "felt duty" to write.

> *Mike Kellin*
> *Nyack, New York*

I must disagree with your endorsement of the phrase felt need. *If what the speaker/ writer is trying to express is a "need," then there should be a reason or reasons for that need, empirically provable. If what the speaker/writer is trying to express is a "feeling," then there should be some emotional or instinctive process for that feeling, logically justifiable or at least intellectually descriptive.*

But, based on student usage, a felt need *is self-justifying and self-satisfying and admits to no scrutiny. Its use darkens inquiry and queers conversation. A* felt need *confuses reason and emotion. Thus, this phrase undercuts clarity of thought.*

> *Jack Williams*
> *Shippensburg, Pennsylvania*

The solution to the correct use of observed *and* felt *is found in Oliver Wendell Holmes. Professor Cohen was quoting (perhaps unconsciously) from Holmes' famous passage in* The Common Law *(Harvard University Press, 1963), p. 5: "the life of the law has not been logic but experience. The felt necessities of the time, the prevalent moral and political theories, ..."*

> *Howard L. Meyer*
> *Buffalo, New York*

Wimpsmanship

Campaigning for governor of Illinois, former Senator Adlai Stevenson 3d charged that Governor James Thompson "is saying, 'Me tough guy,' as if to imply I'm some kind of wimp." The "wimp factor" immediately became part of the campaign's instant lore.

Meanwhile, out in California, Governor Jerry Brown—often called a *flake*—was campaigning against San Diego Mayor Pete Wilson for United States Senator. A *San Francisco Chronicle* political correspondent, Larry Liebert, describing a "negative strategy" being used by Governor Brown against Mayor Wilson, quoted an anonymous Brown aide as asking: "Why trade a flake for a wimp?"

Evidently the worst word that can be flung at a candidate this year is *wimp.* Gone are the *comsymps, radic-libs, eggheads,* and *limousine liberals* of yesteryear; vanished are the *nuts and kooks, troglodytes, Neanderthals,* and *little old ladies in tennis shoes.* This year the art of smearing is a form of wimpsmanship.

The word was introduced into politics during the presidential campaign of 1980, when a prankster at *The Boston Globe* removed a headline above an editorial about President Carter's anti-inflation plan. The original headline had read: "All Must Share the Burden," and the somewhat livelier—and possibily more accurate—substitute read: "Mush From the Wimp."

A *wimp* is one who is both as weepy as a *drip* and as listless as a *nebbish.* The noun may have been influenced by Wimpy, the sleepy-eyed lover of hamburgers in the cartoon strip "Thimble Theater," starring Popeye the Sailor, but is more likely rooted in the verb *to whimper.* (*Flaky,* while we're at it, is a 1950's adjective meaning "offbeat, eccentric," popularized by baseball in the early 1960's, in noun form: A *flake* was a colorful, slightly wacky ballplayer.)

Historians will remember the 1982 campaign for the emergence of a new political pejorative, which will peak only when a candidate, like a cornered rabbit, turns on his tormentors to announce: "I am not a wimp."

Win One for the Dipper

Not since Harry Truman rescued *snollygoster* (a mythical predatory bird) from linguistic obscurity has a President done so much for archaic Americanisms. Ronald Reagan—the pride of South Succotash—selected *bafflegab* from his bag of good-natured epithets during the 1982 congressional campaign: The word was coined in 1952 by a Chamber of Commerce lawyer, Milton Smith, to describe the verbosity and ambiguity of government regulations; *bafflegab* won out over two other entries, *burobabble* and *gabbalia*.

Soon after the election, and following the rise to power of Yuri Andropov, President Reagan was asked about Soviet-American relations and replied: "It takes two to tango." This expression was current about a generation and a half ago, when the tango and other South American dances invaded the ballrooms of North America. (*Tango* is the Argentine Spanish word for "gypsy festival," rooted in the Latin *tangere,* but let me not go off on a tangent.)

Comes now Mr. Reagan's characterization of estimates by Democratic politicians that tax cuts and defense spending would drive up the deficit as "real *dipsy doodle.* " Evidently the President was deeply impressed by the dance-hall lingo of the 1930's.

"Dipsy Doodle" was a song composed by Larry Clinton in 1937 and dealt with the reversal of words and expressions, such as "You love I and me love you." The origin of the phrase is labeled as unknown by *Merriam-Webster,* but to speculate, *dipsy* might come from *dipsomania,* now called "alcoholism," and the slang shortening to *dipso* (from the Greek *dipsa,* "thirst"). A second possibility: from the dance dip, in which the man pulls the woman toward him, then bends his knee and swoops forward as if imitating Groucho Marx's walk.

The *doodle* part is easier: In German, *Dudeltopf* means "nightcap," the sort worn by a simpleton. The *doodle* added a humorous alliterative fillip to the phrase; even today, the verb *to doodle* means "to draw idly," giving some substance to the theory of etymologists who argue that it is a variant of *dawdle. Doo* is the sound of the simpleton, as he fiddles with *doo-dads* and *doohickeys. (Doo wha'?)*

As baseball fans know, the *dipsy doodle* was taken up as the name for a sinking curve ball, or *sinker,* or *dip.* "Dutch" Reagan began his career as a baseball

announcer, and may have picked up the phrase in this phase of his career. Without delving into linguistic psychohistory, it seems likely that the President associated "a real dipsy doodle" with trickery or chicanery, as the phrase for a curve ball soon became a favorite with mystery writers: "I opened the front door, leaving the key in the lock," wrote Raymond Chandler in *High Window*. "I wasn't going to work any dipsy doodle in this place."

The White House interest in names of dances has not been exhausted. Yet to be used is the name for Mr. Reagan's postpipeline Western-alliance policy *(The Continental)*.

As a newly self-appointed member of the Squad Squad, I am pleased as punch to report that I have Caught You At It! Your column's "Tango is the Argentine Spanish word for . . ." is my evidence. Clearly you are trying to inform us that tango is a word from Spanish as spoken in Argentina. But since the language of Argentina is Spanish, all you really have to say is ". . . the Argentine word for . . ." and there you have it, all tidied up. The fact that the word is Spanish is now implicit and this makes it secondary (as it deserves) to its Argentine provenance.

All this reminds me of two of my pet peeves: Parmesan cheese, and Lawrence Welk's commercial on his show for that ". . . very fine automotive car. . . ."

> *John Czarnowski*
> *Philadelphia, Pennsylvania*

According to George Simon's The Big Bands Songbook, *Larry Clinton named his "Dipsy Doodle" after the unusual screwball thrown by Giant's pitcher Carl Hubbell. Thus, "Dutch" Reagan really believes that Democratic estimates of the deficit are not tricky, but merely wacky. In either case, the Democrats have every right to take umbrage.*

Chris Bannon
Providence, Rhode Island

Wiseguy Problem

I ran into an old friend whom I had not seen in too long. He clapped me on the shoulder and said, "I miss not seeing you!"

No, I replied, he missed *seeing* me; *not* seeing me was what he had been doing.

"I meant exactly what I said," said my friend coolly, "but until this moment I never realized why."

Word of the Year

Which word, in the opinion of people who care about language, is the most beautiful word of all?

To get the answer, I conducted a scientific survey of readers, along the lines of the mail poll run by the *Literary Digest* magazine that was able to predict a smashing victory by Alf Landon over F.D.R. in 1936.

Unlike the Miss America contest, which encumbers its entrants with requirements for talent and congeniality, the contest for Miss Word is strictly bathing suits and smiles. Meaning does not count. We look only for words that the ears of the behearer find beautiful. (Accordingly, *beautiful* received no votes; *lovely* did well.) The envelope, please (*envelope* didn't quite make it to the finals).

For the knockout word with a sibilant sound, a category preferred by a hissing 8 percent of the 186 respondents: In the *zh* subcategory, long dominated by Zsa Zsa Gabor, *mirage* is first runner-up, and *illusion* is the winner. *Azure,* the popular favorite, was thrown out by the Board of Judges (I am the Board of Judges) for being pregnant with meaning. In a sister subcategory (the sibilant sibling is the simple *s*), *sunset* and *russet* were frequently mentioned; *crystalline* scored higher, topped by *celestial,* but the winner was *quintessence.* Despite its heavy semantic handicap, *syphilis* ran very well. In the *sh* subcat, nothing could stop *ravish.*

For the most winsome word using the ever-popular *w,* the traditional favorites,

whisper and *twilight*, were outstripped by *wonderland, windward, dawning* and
waterfall. Perhaps because of the oil glut, *awash* made a splash. (*Glut* is a leader
in the Miss Ugly Word stakes, but that's another story.) First runner-up is the wry
caraway, and the winner is the with-it *wherewithal*.

Now, with tension building, we come to the humming sound that moves so
many language-lovers: the marvelous murmur of *m*. *Madrigal* dances along with
meander, which *mesmerizes* many men and maids (all right, cut it out). The
winner is the simple *moon*.

The sound of *v* has its advocates: *Gravel* has a wide appeal, as does *suave*,
deliberately mispronounced "Swayve" by ironic teen-agers. *Evanescent* is still
around (whatever became of San Clemente's mists?) and is runner-up to *lovely*, its
popularity influenced by the combination of *v* with a pair of attractive *l*'s.

In the *f* category we find the old favorite, *daffodil*, overtaken by *taffeta*, with
effervescent runner-up to the surprise winner, *dolphin*.

A special entry has nothing to do with individual sounds, but delights in rhythm
or alliteration: *Bumblebee* is the most familiar example, but *orangoutang, onomatopoeia, serendipity,* and *pussy willow* are winning friends. *Anemone* is the close
runner-up to noisy *tintinnabulation*.

Now we come to the sound that seems to come most trippingly off the tongue:
the lubricious, lulling, lovable sound of *l*. Most respondents included at least
three *l*-words in their lists of ten: from *lilacs, lullaby,* and *laurel* to *lavender,
lanolin,* and *soliloquy*. *Cellar door*, a Groucho Marx favorite, ranked high, as
did Monty Python's *hollow* (that's a "woody" word, in contrast to a "tinny" word
like *snicker*).

Are you ready, America? Here come the words that combine the full bosom

of the *m* sound (*mammary, maternal*) with the long-limbed, lanky, luscious legs of the *l* sound. Even the minor words in this category soar high above the winners in many of the others: *llama* and *lemonade,* for example, and *salamander* and *pell mell.* Third runner-up in this superstar category is . . . *marmalade.* Second runner-up is . . . *marshmallow.*

I'll burst into tears if *melancholy* loses. Those tears in her eyes—she's lost! The winner . . . here she comes . . . the queen of this year's dictionaries . . . as smooth and sweet a honey as ever to win the crown . . . chosen by the Lexicographic Irregulars with the unanimous approval of the Board of Judges to reign as Miss Word for the rest of the year . . . *Mellifluous!*

> *Words alone,*
> *Without their meaning,*
> *Can be ugly—*
> *Raucous unctuous*
> *Awkward gawky*
> *Execrable*
> *Nausea phlegm—*
> *Or beautiful—*
> *Remembering*
> *Mellow murmurs*
> *Meandering streams*
> *Shimmering seashore*
> *Sandcastle dreams*
> *Spanish* la paloma—
> *Why do I balk*
> *At melanoma?*
>
> *Patricia Whiting Esposito*
> *Summit, New Jersey*

Your article contains two of my three favorite words. Poe's tintinnabulation *and* mellifluous.

What happened to the third? Susurration. *The susurration of the breeze through the leaves of the trees.*

How about some words on arcane sentences? My favorite (composed by Laurence Urdang, publisher of Verbatim*):*

> *Not a succedaneum for satisfying the nympholepsy of nullifidians, it is hoped that the haecceity of this enchiridion of arcane and recondite sesquipedalian items will appeal to*

*the oniomania of an eximious Gemeinschaft whose legerity
and sophrosyne, whose Sprachgefuhl and orexis will find
more than fugacious fulfillment among its felicific pages.*

> Albert Wolfe
> Hamden, Connecticut

*Your column reminded me of the old story of the four persons discussing the
comparative beauty of their respective languages—English, Spanish, French, and
German.*

*The American said, "No language is as wonderful as ours. Take almost any word
—say* Butterfly. *It just rolls off one's tongue."*

The Spaniard continued, "It is nice, but just say Mariposa. *It has a lilt, and
conjures up an immediate mental picture of this creature."*

*The Frenchman added, "Yes, they are both lovely but they cannot compare to
our word* Papillon—*smooth as honey—a dream of a word."*

*To which the German friend bridled and remarked, "Und was ist los mit
Schmetterling?"*

> Stanley Grayson
> New York, New York

X Marks the Verb

"The federal bureaucracy has invented a new verb," says Charles DeLaFuente of
Kew Gardens, New York, who had just sent in his 1040 income-tax return to the
Internal Revenue Service. He attached an addressed envelope that he had received
from the I.R.S.; in the upper left-hand corner, where the return address of the
taxpayer belongs, is the heavy black outline of a box. Next to the box are the words
"X box if refund."

"Never mind the unanswered question, 'If refund what?' " the irate taxpayer
observed. "We all know they mean to x the box if you have a refund coming.
Maybe the ink they saved on those instructions will pay for the next round of tax
cuts."

Mr. DeLaFuente—his name means "of the fountain"—is blowing his geyser
for the wrong reason. The verb *to x* is not new. In 1849, Edgar Allan Poe wrote
in one of his tales: " 'I shell have to x this ere paragrab,' said he to himself, as he
read it over." In 1935, Jonas Bayer carried that crossing-out metaphor into the
mechanical age in *Startling Detective* magazine: "An imported hatchet man with

a .45-caliber typewriter can x out the dangerous canary." *Merriam-Webster*'s first citation in the one-letter verb's literal sense is from Henry Cassidy's 1943 book *Moscow Dateline*: "I x'd out the word 'west' in the third question, changing it to 'east.'"

Heretofore, the meaning of the transitive verb *to x* had been "to cross out, delete, obliterate." Since an *x* is a cross, that might have inspired Poe to substitute the letter for the word. Today, however, a new meaning has been added by the I.R.S.: "to mark a space in a box with an *x.*"

No eyebrows should be raised when anyone—even a bureaucrat—uses an old word creatively, or even makes up one of his own, when a linguistic void exists. If there is no word for an action, a vacuum exists, and neologicians abhor a vacuum: A new word will appear.

However, in this case, a simple and widely understood verb exists: to check. If you want somebody to put a mark in a box, it is easy enough to say: "Check here." But that supposes (not to say "presupposes") that you want the victim, or taxpayer, to put a *check* mark in the space. Evidently, in this situation, the I.R.S. wanted not a *check* mark but an *x* mark. Therefore, on the analogy of "Check box if you are asking for a refund," the I.R.S. said, "*X* box if refund" (with the words "you are asking for a" silently understood).

The solution leads to a new mystery: What's the matter with checking a box, in the accustomed manner, with the verb *to check* meaning "to place a check mark in the box"? What does an *x* mark have that a mere *check* mark does not have?

It has *x* appeal. "The wording for the return-address section of the tax return," explains Rod Young, I.R.S. spokesperson, "was requested by our Returns Processing division. The trend is toward shorter, more-to-the-point directions."

No harm in that; but why not "check box if refund"? What created the need for the new meaning of the *x* verb?

"Originally, the wording requested was 'Check box if refund,' " admitted the man from I.R.S., "but the post office does some initial sorting. They told us it would be easier for their machines to read an *x* than a check mark. The post office requested that the wording be changed to *x* to facilitate presorting."

I *x*'d that out with the post office, which prefers to call itself the Postal Service, perhaps because it wants to give the impression of serving rather than officiating. "That just doesn't make sense," responds Jeanne O'Neill, a postal spokesperson. "The I.R.S. envelope is not being machine-read; it's being done manually. We're doing this manual sortation at the request of the I.R.S., and they're reimbursing us for the cost of this added task."

If we are to believe the I.R.S., and not the Postal Service, what we have here is an example of the arrogance of automation. To accommodate a mechanical presorter (not the sorter, the *presorter*—the sort of sorting it does is *pre*sorting, which must be sorted out from the common, everyday sort of sorting), millions of envelopes were sent to taxpayers with the new meaning of the verb *to x*. And we all went along like sheep.

If we are to believe the Postal Service, the I.R.S. is bent on perpetuating some giant joke on taxpayers.

Next year, if the I.R.S. comes at me with its linguistic contortions ostensibly designed to cater to some electronic evil eye, I will put a question mark in the space provided. That's called "tellin' 'em nuthin'," or very little, which is what outer envelopes are supposed to do. That's the presort I am. This year, "*X* box if refund"; next year, "Sealed With A Kiss"? If they return it unopened, I will forward it to Occupant, White House, in the hope that he will check it out.

You raised the interesting question of why the government printed on our tax return envelope, "X box if refund."

The folks who are responsible for how our forms and envelopes look and work are merely following this forms design principle: Ballot boxes should always be marked with an "X" instead of a check mark because

1. *There is no check mark on a typewriter. An "X" is a typical character on most machines.*
2. *If handwritten, the check mark may extend beyond the borders of a box and create a chance for error in reading the completed entry.*
3. *Although handwritten "X's" may be large, the cross point of an "X" will fall into the box and prevent any doubt as to the intended meaning.*
4. *When many carbon copies of a form set are made, an "X" gives better legibility to the underlying copies.*

All of the above may not be applicable in this one case. Many times we in the general public are not aware of how professional forms analysts and designers make forms easier to fill out and use. Don't blame them for some of the dumb questions we are asked to fill out as they are the designers and not the authors of the forms.

Edwin B. Allen
Philadelphia, Pennsylvania

There is apparently another definition of the verb X not mentioned in your article. It appears in the participial form in the traffic warning signs which read

PED

XING

What started that one?

Arthur Tufts
East Norwich, New York

Memory or an aide tricked you on Edgar Allan Poe. In "X-ing a Paragrab," Poe did not mean to cross out the paragraph. The story, which must have been a pot-boiler, had to do with rival editors who got into competition on writing a paragraph with the greatest number of "O's."

A printer's devil from the rival paper apparently stole all the "O's" out of the type case, and the compositor had to resort to what (Poe says) was a recognized expedient: if a letter was missing, you used an "X" in its place. So this "paragrab" had to be "Xd."

George Kelley
The Youngstown Indicator
Youngstown, Ohio

You should have read Poe's "X-ing a Paragrab" before you came to the conclusion that "Heretofore, the meaning of the transitive verb to x *had been 'to cross out, delete, obliterate.' " The paragraph in Poe's story was* not *deleted. All the o's in it were replaced by x's. Both you and Dr. Gove are off by almost a century.*

Richard Priest
New York, New York

What sort of word is sortation? *The postal spokesperson is quoted: "We're doing this manual sortation at the request of the I.R.S. . . . . " I have sorted through the forms of sort in several dictionaries and have found nothing of the sort.*

O. B. Moore, Jr.
Atlanta, Georgia

ACKNOWLEDGMENTS

Acknowledge starts with the Latin prefix *ac-*, meaning "to," and this book owes a debt to all those pointing the way "to knowledge."

Language-lovers should feel gratified by the growing list of resources in the land of lexicography: John Algeo, Clarence Barnhart, Robert Barnhart, Jacques Barzun, Robert Burchfield, Ronald Butters, Frederic Cassidy, Willard Espy, Stuart Berg Flexner, David Guralnik, Frederick Mish, Mary Gray Porter, Allen Walker Read, I. Willis Russell, Norman Schur, Anne Soukhanov, Sol Steinmetz, Karl Teeter, and Laurence Urdang.

At *The New York Times,* offer thanks to the colleagues in charge of the column's quality control: Phyllis Shapiro and Sherwin Smith at the *Magazine,* and their editing successors Lynn Karpen and Jay Miller, as well as Steve Pickering and Mary Drohan at the Op-Ed page. In Washington, I rely on my assistant, Ann Elise Rubin, my researcher, Jeff McQuain (whose own useful work, *A Handlist to English,* is coming out this year), and Chief Librarian Sunday Fellows. At Times Books, I'm grateful to Sarah Trotta, Beth Pearson, Nancy Inglis, Charlotte Gross, Dianne Clark, and Patricia Abdale (who keep the third *e* out of *acknowledgments*).

Finally, a word to the wiseguys: my gratitude-in-certitude to those Lexicographic Irregulars who man the Squad Squad, the Gotcha! Gang, and the Nitpickers' League (some of whose members consider the verb *man* sexist). In the bizarre bazaar that is the language's marketplace of ideas, their persnickety opinions and galling corrections shove me along the path to knowledge.

Index